An Interpretive Guide to the
GOVERNMENT IN THE SUNSHINE ACT
Second Edition

Richard K. Berg, Stephen H. Klitzman, Gary J. Edles

SECTION OF ADMINISTRATIVE LAW AND REGULATORY PRACTICE

Cover design by ABA Publishing

The materials contained herein represent the opinions and views of the authors and should not be construed to be the views or opinions of the federal agencies or schools by which such persons are employed, nor of the American Bar Association or the Section of Administrative Law and Regulatory Practice, unless adopted pursuant to the bylaws of the Association.

Nothing contained in this book is to be considered as the rendering of legal advice for specific cases, and readers are responsible for obtaining such advice from their own legal counsel. This book and any forms and agreements herein are intended for educational and informational purposes only.

© 2005 American Bar Association. All rights reserved. No part of this publication may be reproduced, stored in a retrieval system, or transmitted in any form or by any means, electronic, mechanical, photocopying, recording, or otherwise, without the prior written permission of the publisher. For permission contact the ABA Copyrights & Contracts Department, copyright@abanet.org or via fax at (312) 988-6030.

08 07 06 05 04   5 4 3 2 1

Cataloging-in-Publication data is on file with the Library of Congress

An Interpretive Guide to the Government in the Sunshine Act, 2d Ed. / Richard K. Berg, Stephen H. Klitzman, Gary J. Edles
   1-59031-584-7

Discounts are available for books ordered in bulk. Special consideration is given to state bars, CLE programs, and other bar-related organizations. Inquire at Book Publishing, ABA Publishing, American Bar Association, 321 North Clark Street, Chicago, Illinois 60610.

www.ababooks.org

CONTENTS

ABOUT THE AUTHORS	ix
CHAIR'S FOREWORD, SECOND EDITION	xi
ORIGINAL CHAIRMAN'S FOREWORD	xiii
PREFACE TO THE SECOND EDITION	xv
ORIGINAL PREFACE	xxi
LEGISLATIVE HISTORY HIGHLIGHTS AND CITATIONS	xxv
Legislative History	xxv
Senate	xxv
House	xxvi
Conference Committee and Enactment	xxvii
Elimination of Annual Sunshine Act Report to Congress	xxvii
Citations	xxviii
OVERVIEW AND SUMMARY	xxxi

Chapter 1
SECTION 552b(a): DEFINITIONS	1
"Agency"	1
"Subdivision"	4
"Meeting"	7
Legislative History	10
The 1978 Sunshine Guide	14
FCC v. ITT World Communications	17
American Bar Association Recommendation	22
NRDC v. Nuclear Regulatory Commission	23
Summary	25
Subsection (d) and (e) Deliberations	25
Electronic Communications	26
"Member"	28

Chapter 2
SECTION 552b(b): CONDUCT OF BUSINESS, PRESUMPTION OF OPENNESS, AND PUBLIC OBSERVATION	29
"Joint Conduct or Disposition" of Agency Business and the Use of "Notation Procedure"	30

Presumption of Openness and "Public Observation"	39
Department of Justice 2002 Memorandum to the Federal Reserve Board	41
Federal Reserve Practices	45
Other Agency Public Observation Procedures	46
Right to Record, Photograph, or Televise Open Meetings	48
"Public Observation" in Post–September 11 Washington, D.C.	49
"Virtual" Meetings, Teleconferencing, and Public Observation	53
Public Participation	55
Public Understanding	58
Access to Staff Memoranda and the Meaningfulness of "Public Observation"	61

Chapter 3
SECTION 552b(c): GROUNDS FOR CLOSING MEETINGS — 65

Overview	65
Exemptions (1) and (2)—National Defense and Foreign Policy; Internal Personnel Rules and Practices	72
Exemption (3)—Statutory Exemption	74
Exemptions (4), (5), (6)—Proprietary Information; Accusation of Crime or Formal Censure; Invasion of Privacy	76
Exemption (7)—Investigatory Records	81
Exemption (8)—Financial Institution Reports	82
Exemptions (9)(A), (B)—Financial Speculation and Stability; Frustration of Proposed Agency Action	83
Exemption (10)—Issuance of Subpoena, Participation in Civil Action or Proceeding, Formal Agency Adjudication	88

Chapter 4
SECTION 552b(d): PROCEDURES FOR CLOSING MEETINGS — 97

Required Majority Vote on Closing and Information "Proposed to be Withheld Under Subsection (c)"	98
Voting to Close by Notation Procedure	98
Meaning of "Portion or Portions" of a Meeting	99
"Series of Meetings" Procedure	100
Recorded Vote and No Proxies	100
Requests to Close Meetings	101
Requests to Close on Other Grounds	103
Procedures Under Subsection (d)(2)	103
Requests to Open Meetings	105
Public Availability of Vote, "Full Written Explanation" of Closing, and List of All Attendees	106
Availability of Vote	107
"Full Written Explanation" of Closing	107

Contents v

    List of All Expected Attendees   108
  Expedited Closing Procedure   111
    Computing the "Majority"   115
    Documentary Justification   117

Chapter 5
SECTION 552b(e): PROCEDURES FOR ANNOUNCING MEETINGS   119
  Contents and Timing of Advance Notice   120
    Withholding Notice Information   123
    Providing Shorter Notice   124
    Providing No or Limited Notice   130
  Changing the Time, Place, Subject Matter, or Decision to Open
      or Close   133
    Changing the Time or Place   133
    Cancellation   133
    Changing the Subject Matter or Decision to Open or Close;
      Addition, Deletion or Carry-Over of Agenda Items   134
  Contents and Submission of Notice to *Federal Register*   138
    Use of "Reasonable Means" to Circulate Public Announcements   140

Chapter 6
SECTION 552b(f): GENERAL COUNSEL CERTIFICATION; PREPARATION AND PUBLIC AVAILABILITY OF TRANSCRIPTS, RECORDINGS, AND MINUTES OF CLOSED MEETINGS   143
  General Counsel Certification   144
    Effect of Refusal to Certify   144
    Delegation   147
    Timing   149
    Certification and the Public Interest Determination   150
    Contents of the Certification   150
  Retention of Certification, Presiding Officer's Statement   150
  Maintenance of Transcript, Recording or Minutes   152
  Description of Minutes   152
  Public Access to and Agency Provision and Retention of Transcripts,
      Recordings, or Minutes   153
    Obligation of Agency to Make Meeting Record "Promptly
      Available"   153
    Standard for Deletion; Extent of Agency's Duty to Edit the Record 157
    Procedural Requirements and Delegation   161
    Subsequent Review of Transcript Material   163
    Administrative Appeal Procedures   167
    Fees for Furnishing Copies   168
    Maintenance and Use of Verbatim Copies of Transcripts,
      Recordings, or Minutes   171

Chapter 7
SECTION 552b(g): JUDICIAL REVIEW OF AGENCY RULES   173

Chapter 8
SECTION 552b(h): JUDICIAL REVIEW OF PARTICULAR
   AGENCY ACTIONS   179
   Independent Enforcement Suits; Jurisdiction and Remedies 181
      Suits to Obtain Access to Transcripts   184
      "Reverse Sunshine" Cases   185
   Judicial Review Proceedings   186
      Relief Under 5 U.S.C. § 552b(h)(2)   188
      Use of the Transcript for Judicial Review   192

Chapter 9
SECTION 552b(i): ASSESSMENT OF COSTS   199
   "Reverse Sunshine" Cases   201

Chapter 10
SECTION 552b(k): RELATIONSHIP TO FREEDOM OF
   INFORMATION ACT   203
   Confidentiality of Internal Memoranda   204
   Applicability of FOIA Procedures to Requests for Access to
      Transcripts   206
   Records Disposal   209

Chapter 11
SUNSHINE ACT PERCEPTIONS, PROBLEMS, AND PROPOSALS   211
   General Considerations   211
   Need for Congressional Review   219
   The Dilemma of Openness vs. Collegiality   219
      Lack of Collegiality   219
      Definition of "Meeting"   226
   Fees and Fee Waivers   228
   Annual Reporting Requirement   230

SELECTED BIBLIOGRAPHY   233

APPENDICES   239
Appendix A: *The Government in the Sunshine Act Pub. L. No. 94-409, 90 Stat. 1241 (94th Cong., 2d Sess., S.5, Sept. 13, 1976 as amended)* 241

Appendix B: *Letter-Questionnaire to Sunshine Act Agencies from the Authors, July, 2001* 255

Appendix C: *Government in the Sunshine Act: Agency Meeting Regulations in the* Code of Federal Regulations 259

Contents vii

Appendix D: *Definition of "Meeting" in the Government in the Sunshine Act: A Chronological Chart* 264

Appendix E: *Department of Justice Letter to Covered Agencies, April 19, 1977* 266

Appendix F: *American Bar Association, Report and Recommendation on the Government in the Sunshine Act, February 1987* 269

Appendix G: *Administrative Conference of the United States Report and Recommendation 84-3 Improvements in the Administration of the Government in the Sunshine Act 49 FR 29937 (1984)* 283

Appendix H: *Letter from Steven M.H. Wallman, Commissioner, Securities and Exchange Commission, to Thomasina Rogers, Chairperson, Administrative Conference of the United States, February 17, 1995* 286

Appendix I: *Administrative Conference of the United States, Report and Recommendation by the Special Committee to Review the Government in the Sunshine Act, as reprinted at 49 Admin. L. Rev. 421 (Spring 1997)* 299

Appendix J: *Memorandum for J. Virgil Mattingly, Jr., General Counsel for the Board of Governors of the Federal Reserve System Re: Permissibility of Federal Reserve Board Efforts to Control Access to Buildings and Open Meetings, from M. Edward Whelan III, Principal Deputy Assistant Attorney General, July 9, 2002* 308

Appendix K: *Letter from J. Virgil Mattingly, Jr., General Counsel for the Board of Governors of the Federal Reserve System, to Paul Colborn, Esq., Special Counsel, Department of Justice, Office of Legal Counsel, April 10, 2002* 316

Appendix L: *Federal Reserve Board, "A Guide to the Meetings of the Board of Governors of the Federal Reserve System," 2004* 321

Appendix M: *Sample Agency Meeting Notices* 329

Appendix N: *Sample Agency General Counsel Certification Forms* 340

Appendix O: *Letter from Michael K. Powell, Chairman, and Michael J. Copps, Commissioner, Federal Communications Commission, to the Honorable Ted Stevens, Chairman, Senate Committee on Commerce, Science and Transportation, February 2, 2005* 344

TABLE OF CASES 347

INDEX 355

ABOUT THE AUTHORS

Richard K. Berg (B.A., Harvard University; L.L.B., Yale University) served in the Office of Legal Counsel, Department of Justice, the Equal Employment Opportunity Commission, and was Executive Secretary and General Counsel of the Administrative Conference of the United States (ACUS) before entering private law practice. He is now retired.

Stephen H. Klitzman (B.A., University of Pennsylvania; M.A., Stanford University; J.D., Georgetown University) is a senior attorney in the Office of General Counsel, Federal Communications Commission, an agency subject to the Government in the Sunshine Act. From 1987 to 2002, he was Associate Director of the FCC's Office of Legislative Affairs. Since 1985, he has also been an adjunct professor of communications law at the Institute for Communications Law Studies, Columbus School of Law, the Catholic University of America, in Washington, D.C.

Messrs. Berg and Klitzman served at the ACUS when Congress enacted the original Sunshine Act in 1976. The statute required agencies to consult with ACUS when enacting their individual Sunshine Act rules. The two were co-authors of the original *Interpretive Guide to the Government in the Sunshine Act,* published in 1978 (*1978 Guide*).

Gary J. Edles (B.A., Queens College, City University of New York; J.D., New York University; L.L.M., S.J.D., George Washington University) served at multimember agencies in both the pre-Sunshine Act and post-Sunshine Act eras. These agencies included the Civil Aeronautics Board, the Interstate Commerce Commission, and the Nuclear Regulatory Commission. Like Mr. Berg, he is a former general counsel of the Administrative Conference. He is currently a fellow in administrative law and adjunct professor at American University, Washington College of Law, and a visiting professor at the University of Hull Law School in England. He is the co-author of both a textbook for practicing lawyers dealing with the federal regulatory process and an article on the theory and operation of multimember agencies.

CHAIR'S FOREWORD, SECOND EDITION

The Section of Administrative Law and Regulatory Practice is pleased to publish this second edition of *An Interpretive Guide to the Government in the Sunshine Act*.

When the Administrative Conference of the United States (ACUS) ceased operations in 1995, the Section took steps to continue updating and publishing some of the important books and source material previously published by ACUS. In 1998, for example, the Section published a third edition of a *Guide to Federal Agency Rulemaking*; in 2000, it published a third edition of the *Federal Administrative Procedure Sourcebook*; and in 2001, the Section issued the *Federal Administrative Dispute Resolution Deskbook*, a logical outgrowth of ACUS's *Federal Administrative Procedure Sourcebook*.

This second edition of the *Sunshine Guide* is a unique addition to these administrative law materials. Coming 27 years after publication of the first edition in June 1978, this new work is a broad-based study of the Sunshine Act as a whole since it took effect on March 12, 1977. The Act had required that agencies consult with ACUS before enacting their original Sunshine Act rules. So this second edition builds on the ACUS consultative activity undertaken just after President Ford signed the Sunshine Act into law on September 13, 1976. This edition also incorporates the entire body of Sunshine Act case law, little of which had been decided at the time ACUS published the first edition. This second edition examines as well the academic literature on the federal open meetings law, and, perhaps most important, considers and evaluates the practical impact of agency implementation of the Sunshine Act over the past nearly 30 years.

The Section is delighted it was able to recruit Messrs. Berg, Klitzman, and Edles to undertake the daunting task of preparing this second edition of the *Interpretive Guide*. Two of the authors, Richard K. Berg and Stephen H. Klitzman, co-authored the *1978 Guide*. The courts, agencies, the public, and commentators have come to rely on the original edition as the definitive study of the Government in the Sunshine Act—what Columbia Law School Professor Peter L. Strauss describes as "the leading commentary on the Act and its history."[1] We are therefore very pleased to have retained Messrs. Berg and Klitzman's expertise regarding the early history of the Sunshine Act and their institutional memories and experience with both its initial and ongoing implementation.

We are also pleased that the third author of this second edition, Gary J. Edles, has been able to offer to this new publication his own unique perspectives as both an academic and a career government lawyer with both prior and post-Sunshine Act experience.

The Section anticipates that this thoroughly revised *An Interpretive Guide to the Government in the Sunshine Act, Second Edition*, will receive the same critical approval and will be as equally invaluable as the first edition. We are proud to add this volume to the growing list of books published by our Section. As with the others, I am confident that not only our members, but all those who practice before the federal Sunshine agencies will find this book a valuable addition to their libraries.

> Randolph J. May
> Chair
> Section of Administrative Law and
>   Regulatory Practice
> American Bar Association
> August 2005

---

1. *See* ADMINISTRATIVE JUSTICE IN THE UNITED STATES, 2d ed., at 285 n.48 (Carolina Academic Press 2002).

ORIGINAL CHAIRMAN'S FOREWORD

A significant function of the staff of the Office of the Chairman of the Administrative Conference of the United States is to furnish advice and assistance on problems of administrative procedure to the agencies and to the Congress. The Administrative Conference Act specifically contemplates a role for the Conference in advising the agencies and arranging for the interchange of information among them on matters of administrative procedure.[1] Because of the Conference's perspective over the broad range of agency and administrative programs, the consultative capacity of its staff is a unique resource—one that the Congress increasingly has recognized and relied upon.

In several recent instances, Congress has specifically directed the Conference to perform advisory and consultative services for the agencies. A notable example is the Government in the Sunshine Act, Public Law 94-409. Signed into law on September 13, 1976, the Act requires the collegial agencies of the federal government to open meetings of agency members to public observation, except where the subject matter of the meeting falls within one of 10 specified categories of exemption. Subsection (g) of the Act provided a six-month period between its enactment and its effective date to permit the affected agencies to prepare implementing regulations, and it assigned to the Office of the Chairman the duty of consulting with the agencies on the preparation of those regulations.

Pursuant to this mandate, Executive Secretary Richard K. Berg and staff attorney Stephen Klitzman held a series of meetings with representatives of affected agencies, circulated drafts and other materials supplied by the agencies, offered oral and written comments on proposed regulations, endeavored to answer questions from agency representatives, and generally served as an effective clearinghouse for Sunshine Act information in the process of preparing the regulations.

---

1. *See* S U.S.C. §§ 574(2), 575(c)(14).

Building upon that consultative activity, Messrs. Berg and Klitzman have written this *Interpretive Guide to the Government in the Sunshine Act*. The Guide brings together in concise form materials drawn from the consultative effort, as well as from the published legislative history, from proposed and final agency regulations, and from other relevant sources. In their work on the Guide the authors have had full editorial freedom, and it should be emphasized that the views expressed in the Guide are those of the authors and do not represent official positions of the Administrative Conference.

The Guide should be helpful to the agencies and useful to the Congress, the courts, and members of the interested public. I would hope that the Conference can continue to play a role as experience develops under the Act and the implementing regulations.

                        Robert A. Anthony
                        Chairman
                        Administrative Conference of the
                            United States
                        March 1978

PREFACE TO THE SECOND EDITION

President Gerald Ford signed the Government in the Sunshine Act into law on September 13, 1976. It was the last in a quartet of "open government" statutes that included the Freedom of Information Act in 1966, the Federal Advisory Committee Act in 1972, and the Privacy Act in 1974. The Act is based on the policy that "the public is entitled to the fullest practicable information regarding the decisionmaking processes of the Federal Government." Pub. L. No. 94409, 90 Stat. 1241, § 2. The purpose of the Act is "to provide the public with such information, while protecting the rights of individuals and the ability of the government to carry out its responsibilities." *Id.* The statute is codified at 5 U.S.C § 552b. *See also* Appendix A for a copy of the law, as amended.

Subsection (g) of the Act provided for the issuance of agency rules to implement the statute. Agencies subject to the Act had a statutory responsibility to consult with the former Administrative Conference of the United States (ACUS) before issuance of their regulations. Building on its consultative role, and contemporaneously with initial implementation of the statute, ACUS in 1978 published a book on the Sunshine Act, *An Interpretive Guide to the Government in the Sunshine Act*. That book analyzed the statutory provisions and brought together in a concise fashion the materials drawn from the consultative process and from agency proposed and final regulations. Since its issuance in 1978, several court decisions, including the Supreme Court's only Sunshine Act opinion, *FCC v. ITT World Communications*, 466 U.S. 463, 471 (1984), have cited to, or relied on, the *1978 Guide*.[1] Many of the more than 60 federal agencies covered by the Sunshine Act or voluntarily complying with its provisions have also relied on the *1978 Guide* for statutory interpretation and administrative procedural guidance.

---

1. *See* Table of Cases, *infra*.

Between 1978 and its abolition by Congress in 1995, ACUS served as a clearinghouse for information about the Sunshine Act. Even agencies created after 1978 consulted with ACUS when drafting their Sunshine Act rules, although they were under no legal obligation to do so. Since the demise of ACUS, no other government agency has taken over these Sunshine Act responsibilities. Therefore, we believed that there was a genuine need for a reasonably concise and reliable source of current information about the Act.

As a current tool, the obvious deficiency of the *1978 Guide* is that it has not been revised in nearly 30 years. Because the *1978 Guide* appeared as agencies were issuing their initial regulations, it fails to reflect any case law interpreting the Act, agency experience under the statute, or problems that have arisen with the Act's implementation. We hope that this edition fills that void and will remain current for a considerable period of time.

We have set out to reexamine the Sunshine Act thoroughly in light of its history. We have analyzed court decisions[2] issued since 1977 that have interpreted or mentioned the Act, and we have carefully reviewed the legal literature over the past 28 years.[3] We have also examined other sources that address Sunshine Act issues, such as the 1984 ACUS recommendation, *Improvements in the Administration of the Government in the Sunshine Act, Recommendation 84-3 of the Administrative Conference of the United States,* 49 Fed. Reg. 29,937 (1984), and its underlying consultant report; a 1986 critique of the ACUS Report by the Congressional Research Service; the proposals advanced by the American Bar Association in 1987; the 1989 Report of the Senate Governmental Affairs Committee; numerous presentations to the ACUS Special Committee to Review the Government in the Sunshine Act and its report and recommendations in 1995; congressional testimony on June 13, 1996, before the House Subcommittee on Government Management, Information and Technology, the last congressional committee to receive testimony about implementation of the Sunshine Act; and the annual reports filed by Sunshine agencies between 1999 and 2004 with the Senate Committee on Governmental Affairs.[4]

---

2. *Id.*
3. *See* Selected Bibliography, *infra.*
4. *See, e.g.,* Appendices F-I, *infra.*

In addition, we sent a letter/questionnaire to the 67 Sunshine agencies soliciting their views on how they have implemented the statute and what problems they have encountered. *See* Appendix B, *infra*. These agencies fall into three categories. Most, including the traditional independent regulatory agencies, such as the Federal Communications Commission and the Securities and Exchange Commission, have a majority of members appointed by the President and confirmed by the Senate and satisfy the Sunshine Act definition of "agency" in 5 U.S.C. § 552b(a)(1). Others, like the Neighborhood Reinvestment Corporation and the Rural Telephone Bank, which do not qualify under section 552b(a)(1), are nevertheless required by their enabling statutes to adhere to the requirements of the Sunshine Act. Some, like the Civil Rights Commission and the Foreign Service Labor Relations Board, simply follow Sunshine Act procedures voluntarily. We reviewed their responses to determine (i) what changes agencies have made to their Sunshine regulations since their original promulgation; (ii) what procedures agencies actually employ; (iii) what problems the agencies have experienced or perceived in their implementation of the Act; and (iv) how they have responded to such problems. These agency responses informed our analysis of how the statute is administered in practice and assisted in the preparation of our recommendations in Chapter 11, as well as the list of Sunshine Act agencies and their Sunshine regulations included as Appendix C.

As an editorial matter, we decided to retain the format of the *1978 Guide*, which contained 10 chapters based on the 10 subsections of the statute, plus appendices, a bibliography, and the list of Sunshine Act agencies with a citation to their regulations in the *Code of Federal Regulations*. We have revised and expanded all these materials. We have also added an eleventh chapter to assess the impact of the Sunshine Act, pose some issues for further study, and make a few recommendations. We also use the same abbreviations for the various legislative documents that were used in the *1978 Guide*. Citations to the *Code of Federal Regulations* are current through 2004. Finally, we have added a table of cases and a text index to facilitate both easier use of the Guide and further legal research.

We wish to thank the numerous individuals who have either reviewed portions of this second edition in draft form and offered constructive comment, or offered other editorial assistance. They include: Marilyn R. Abbott, secretary, United States International Trade Commission (USITC); Paul R. Bardos, assistant general counsel, USITC; Ron Battocchi, general counsel, National Transportation Safety Board; Robert Brock, associate general counsel, Federal Emergency Management Agency; Stephen Burns, deputy general counsel, Nuclear Regulatory Commission; William F. Caton, deputy secretary, Federal Communications Commission; Thomas Eisenger, former archivist, Senate Committee on Governmental Affairs; Professor William Funk, Lewis & Clark Law School; Roger Garcia, former analyst in American National Government, Congressional Research Service; Andrew Glickman, senior special counsel, Securities and Exchange Commission; Eric Glitzenstein, Meyer & Glitzenstein; Frank Herch, former director of the library, Federal Communications Commission; Maryanne Kane, chief of staff, Federal Trade Commission; Joel Kaufman, associate general counsel, Federal Communications Commission; Professor Jeffrey Lubbers, Washington College of Law, American University; Joy Medley, congressional liaison specialist, Federal Communications Commission; Meredith Mitchell, principal associate general counsel, Securities and Exchange Commission; Professor James O'Reilly, University of Cincinnati School of Law, and former chairman, Publications Committee, ABA Section of Administrative Law and Regulatory Practice; Michael O'Rourke, counsel, Federal Reserve Board, Office of General Counsel; Matthew Powell, assistant general counsel, National Science Foundation; Harold Relyea, specialist in American National Government, Congressional Research Service; Sonja Rifken, attorney-adviser, Office of General Counsel, Federal Communications Commission; Trip Rothschild, assistant general counsel, Nuclear Regulatory Commission; Professor Anna Shavers, University of Nebraska School of Law and chair, Publications Committee, ABA Section of Administrative Law and Regulatory Practice; Barbara Suhre, former supervisor, Scheduling Unit, Office of the *Federal Register*; Susan Steiman, former associate general counsel, Federal Communications Commission; Thomas Susman, Ropes & Gray; Professor Robert Vaughn, Washington College of Law, American University; and Michael White, general counsel, *Federal Register*. We have revised the text in response to their comments but they bear no responsibility for our errors.

Preface to the Second Edition

We also express our gratitude to the numerous lawyers and other staff members at the 67 Sunshine Act agencies who were kind enough to answer questions or respond to our letter/questionnaire. We were very pleased to have received replies from nearly all the agencies we contacted, many with quite detailed responses. We very much appreciate such excellent cooperation, without which this book would have been far less comprehensive and informative.

We further want to thank the American Bar Association, Section of Administrative Law and Regulatory Practice, and especially Randolph J. May, former chairman of the Section and former chairman of the Section's Publications Committee, for recognizing the need for a comprehensive reexamination of the Sunshine Act that has led to publication of this second edition of the *Interpretive Guide*. We further want to acknowledge our ABA editor, Rick Paszkiet, for his excellent editorial assistance and guidance, as well as Leanne Pfautz, Kim Knight, and Nicole Emard, of the administrative staff of the ABA's Washington, D.C., office, for their cooperation and good cheer throughout this project. We also thank for their highly professional work Kim Schmidt, computer training specialist, Federal Communications Commission; Edit/Pro typesetting; and Yvette Brown, Patrick Petit, and Steve Young, reference librarians, the Columbus School of Law, Catholic University of America.

Finally, we thank our spouses and families for their patience, support, and encouragement throughout the more than four years we worked to produce this publication.

We intend this second edition of the *Interpretive Guide*, like its predecessor, to be an objective compilation of legal authority and administrative practice. We hope it will be of valuable assistance to the agencies, the courts, private-sector attorneys, the public, and the media. Although we have sought information from Sunshine Act agencies, the Guide does not reflect the official views of the agencies that provided us with information. In a handful of situations, the final version of the text reflects a consensus compromise among the authors in areas where our opinions initially differed. Indeed, despite nearly 30 years of history, we recognize that there still remain uncharted areas and room for differences of opinion regarding several aspects of statutory interpretation or implementation. Nonetheless, this second edition of the Guide reflects our best collaborative effort to reach agreement on disputed Sunshine Act issues. In the end, however, the views expressed in this Guide are entirely the personal responsibility of the authors, who are fully accountable for any errors or omissions, which we encourage readers to bring to our attention for possible future reference and revision.

> Richard K. Berg, Arlington, Virginia
> Stephen H. Klitzman, Bethesda, Maryland
> Gary J. Edles, Washington, D.C.
> October 2005

ORIGINAL PREFACE

This *Interpretive Guide to the Government in the Sunshine Act* is an attempt to present a comprehensive, though not exhaustive, examination of the principal questions that have arisen or appear likely to arise under the open meeting provisions of the Act. It has developed out of the consultations that this office carried on from October 1976 until March 1977, pursuant to the mandate of the Act, with the agencies issuing open-meeting regulations. Our consultative activities included conducting a series of informal meetings attended by representatives of a majority of the covered agencies, circulating draft agency regulations and other materials provided by participating agencies, responding to telephone inquiries, commenting on proposed regulations, and, generally, serving as a clearinghouse for advice and information on the Act. We concluded from our experience consulting with the agencies that it would be helpful to put into some coherent and lasting form the substance of the research, thought, and exchange of ideas that took place in this process. As we were writing, our conception of the project grew, and we decided to include materials drawn from the published legislative history, as well as from the proposed and final agency regulations. The result is a compendium of material drawn from various sources, but all relevant, we believe, to the resolution of the legal and practical problems posed by the Act.

This Guide does not purport to be official or definitive. On many questions there is room for difference of opinion, and we have, in general, set forth our own views, supported by such reasoning and cited authority as seemed to us persuasive. We have also drawn heavily on and cited the agencies' own regulations and explanatory statements, which are, under established principles, entitled to respect as the "contemporaneous construction of a statute by the men [and women] charged with the responsibility of setting its machinery in motion," *Norwegian Nitrogen Products Co. v. United States*, 288 U.S. 294, 315 (1933). Finally, we have occasionally attempted to point to examples of what we consider to be the "better" agency practices in dealing with particular procedural problems. The Guide covers only the open-meeting provisions of the Government in the Sunshine Act, specifically, section 552b of Title 5, U.S. Code, as added by section 3 of the Act. No attention is given to section 4, which deals with ex parte communications in formal agency proceedings, or to the conforming amendments in section 5. Furthermore, within section 552b our discussion is limited to subsections (a) through (i) and (k), the remaining subsections being largely self-explanatory. The organization of the Guide follows the structure of the statute, a copy of which appears at Appendix A. Each chapter of the Guide is headed by a subsection of section 552b and relates that subsection to both its relevant legislative history and sample agency regulations implementing it. We have also set forth a Table of Contents in sufficient detail to function as an index. The Guide was distributed in a tentative version early in May 1977, and comments were sought from the affected agencies and other interested persons and groups. We are sincerely grateful for the many constructive comments, criticisms, and suggestions we received. We have made a number of revisions in the text in response to these comments. In this rapidly developing area of the law, however, it has not been possible to update the Guide to reflect subsequent agency experience under the Sunshine Act or subsequent changes in agency regulations, and, with some exceptions, this Guide describes the regulations and practices in effect as of May 1, 1977.

The Guide is intended primarily to reflect the consultative work on the Act carried out by this office and to serve as an informal guide to the agencies, as they continue to adjust their procedures and practices to comply with the open-meeting requirements of the statute. We hope it will be helpful to the agencies, as well as to the judiciary, to Congress, and to members of the public. Since the Guide does discuss different agency approaches to the procedural obligations imposed by the Act, it should be of some use in any analysis and subsequent amendment of the current requirements. Finally, we wish to make some acknowledgments. We are grateful for the assistance and cooperation we have received from the agencies and their Sunshine Act representatives, the "Sunshine Boys and Girls." Without their queries, comments, and collective thinking, this Guide would not have been possible. We also wish to thank Sharon Ressler for her creative work on the design and production of the book, Joseph Azar for his valuable help on the cover, Laura Sheppeard for her excellent editorial assistance, and the secretarial staff of this office, particularly Loretta Williams, Margaret Jackson, and Betty Palmer.

> Richard K. Berg
> Executive Secretary
> Stephen H. Klitzman
> Staff Attorney
> November 1977

LEGISLATIVE HISTORY HIGHLIGHTS AND CITATIONS

Legislative History

For a definitive compilation of legislative history documents on the Government in the Sunshine Act, *see* the Joint Committee Print issued in 1976 by the Senate and House Committees on Government Operations, *Government in the Sunshine Act - S.5 (Public Law 94-409) - Source Book: Legislative History, Texts, and Other Documents,* 94th Cong., 2d Sess. (Comm. Print 1976) (hereafter *Source Book*). *See also* 1976 U.S. Code, *Cong. & Admin. News* 2183, et seq.

Senate

The legislation that was to become the Government in the Sunshine Act, *see* Appendix A, was first introduced in the 92nd Congress on August 4, 1972, by Senator Lawton Chiles of Florida as S.3881. 118 Cong. Rec. 26,902-19. No action was taken on the bill, and Senator Chiles reintroduced the bill in the 93rd Congress on January 9, 1973 as S.260. 119 Cong. Rec. 646-51.

The bill was referred to the Subcommittee on Reorganization, Research and International Organizations of the Senate Government Operations Committee, where it underwent several revisions. In 1974 the Subcommittee held three days of hearings on Committee Print No. 3, Hearings on S.260 before the Subcommittee on Reorganization, Research and International Organizations of the Senate Committee on Government Operations, 93rd Cong., 2d Sess., May 21 and 22, October 15, 1974.

Subsequent to the October 1974 hearing, the Subcommittee prepared Committee Print No. 4 of S.260, which was introduced by Senator Chiles on January 15, 1975, in the 94th Congress as S.5. 121 Cong. Rec. 241-46.

On July 31, 1975, without further hearings, the Committee on Government Operations reported S.5 with amendments. S. Rep. No. 94-354, 94th Cong., 1st Sess. (1975). As reported, the bill consisted of two titles: Title I, meetings of congressional committees, and Title II, agency meetings and ex parte communications.

Title I was referred to the Senate Committee on Rules and Administration, which, on September 18, 1975, reported out S.5 and recommended that Title I be deleted from the bill. S. Rep. No. 94-381, 94th Cong., 1st Sess. (1975).

On November 5, 1975, Title I was deleted on the floor of the Senate. 121 Cong. Rec. 35,218. On November 6, 1975 S.5 as amended was considered and passed without significant further amendment by a vote of 94-0. 121 Cong. Rec. 35,321-36.

House

A bill identical to Title II of S.5, as reported by the Senate Committee on Government Operations, was introduced in the House of Representatives by Representative Dante Fascell of Florida on September 26, 1975, as H.R.9868. 121 Cong. Rec. H9211 (daily ed).

On October 22, 1975, Representative Bella Abzug of New York introduced H.R.10315, an amended version of Title II of S.5. 121 Cong. Rec. H10,242 (daily ed).

The House versions were referred sequentially to the Committees on Government Operations and the Judiciary.

On November 6 and 12, 1975, the House Government Operations Subcommittee on Government Information and Individual Rights held hearings on H.R.10315 and H.R.9868. Hearings on H.R.10315 and H.R.9868 before a Subcommittee of the House Committee on Government Operations, 94th Cong., 1st Sess. (1975).

On February 3, 1976, a clean bill was introduced in the House by Representatives Abzug, Fascell, and others as H.R.11656. 122 Cong. Rec. H670 (daily ed.).

On March 8, 1976, the House Committee on Government Operations reported H.R.11,656, H. Rep. No. 94-880, pt. I, 94th Cong., 2d Sess. (1976).

On March 24-25, 1976, the House Judiciary Subcommittee on Administrative Law and Governmental Relations held hearings on H.R.11656. Hearings on H.R.11656 before the Subcommittee on Administrative Law and Governmental Relations of the House Committee on the Judiciary, 94th Cong., 2d Sess. (1976).

On April 8, 1976, the House Judiciary Committee reported H.R.11656 with amendments. H. Rep. No. 94-880, pt. II, 94th Cong., 2d Sess. (1976).

On July 28, 1976, the House considered and passed H.R.11656, with floor amendments, and then took up S.5 and amended it to substitute the text of the House bill. S.5 was then passed by a vote of 390-5 and sent to a Senate-House Conference. 122 Cong. Rec. H7863-7902 (daily ed).

Conference Committee and Enactment

On August 26 and 27, 1976, the report of the Conference Committee was filed respectively in the House and Senate. H. Rep. No. 94-1441; S. Rep. No. 94-1178, 94th Cong., 2d Sess. (1976).

On August 31, 1976, the report was adopted by voice vote in the Senate. 122 Cong. Rec. S15,043-45 (daily ed.), and by a vote of 384-0 in the House. 122 Cong. Rec. H9258- 62 (daily ed.).

On September 13, 1976, President Ford signed the bill into law, effective March 12, 1977. Pub. L. No. 94-409, 90 Stat. 1241, 12 *Weekly Compilation of Presidential Documents* 1333 (September 20, 1976).

Elimination of Annual Sunshine Act Report to Congress

On May 11, 1995, Senator John McCain introduced S.790, the Reports Elimination and Sunset Act of 1995, to provide for the modification or elimination of federal reporting requirements, including reports to Congress required under the Government in the Sunshine Act. 141 Cong. Rec. S6513 (daily ed.)

On July 17, 1995, the Senate adopted the Hatch Amendment No. 1788 to eliminate reports with an annual or semi-annual reporting basis four years after enactment, and passed S.790. 141 Cong. Rec. S10,166-75 (daily ed.).

On November 8, 1995, the House Committee on Governmental Reform and Oversight issued H. Rep. No. 104-327. 141 Cong. Rec. H11,938 (daily ed.).

On November 14, 1995, the House passed the bill with amendments. 141 Cong. Rec. H12,232 (daily ed.).

On December 6, 1995, the Senate concurred in the House amendments, and passed the bill with a further amendment. 141 Cong. Rec. S11,6114 (daily ed.).

On December 7, 1995, the House agreed to the Senate amendments and passed the amended version of S.790. As passed, section 3002 modified the reporting requirement of 552b(j) and section 3003 provided for the termination, effective May 15, 2000, of those provisions of law that required the submittal to Congress of reports listed in House Document No. 103-7, including annual Sunshine Act reports to Congress listed on page 151 of House Document 103-7. 141 Cong. Rec. H 14,206 (daily ed.).

On December 21, 1995, President Clinton signed the bill into law. Pub. L. No. 104-66, §§ 3002, 3003, 109 Stat. 707, 31 *Weekly Compilation of Presidential Documents* 2221 (December 18, 1995).

Citations

The Sunshine Act as enacted relied heavily on the Senate version, as amended on the House Floor. Thus, this Guide also relies heavily on the Senate Report as well as on other major components of the legislative history. Repeated citations are abbreviated as follows:

Item Reports and Hearings	Abbreviation
H. Rep. No. 94-1441; S. Rep. No. 94-1178, 94th Cong., 2d Sess. (1976) (Conference Report)	Conf. Rep.
S. Rep. No. 94-354, 94th Cong., 1st Sess. (1975)	S. Rep.
H. Rep. No. 94-880 (Part 1), (Government Operations Comm.), 104th Cong., 2d Sess. (1976)	H. Rep. I
H. Rep. No. 94-880 (Part 2), (Judiciary Comm.), 94th Cong., 2d Sess. (1976)	H. Rep. II
Hearings on H.R.10315 and H.R. 9868 before a Subcommittee of the House Committee on Government Operations, 94th Cong., 1st Sess. (1975)	House Government Operations Hearings

Hearings on H.R.11656 before the
Subcommittee on Administrative
Law and Governmental Relations
of the House Committee on the
Judiciary, 94th Cong., 2d Sess.,   House Judiciary
ser. 38 (1976)   Committee Hearings

Hearing on Government in the Sunshine Act Implementation before the
Subcommittee on Administrative
Law and Governmental Relations of
the House Committee on the Judiciary, 95th Cong., 1st Sess., ser. 8   House Judiciary
(1977)   Oversight Hearing

Congressional Record

Vol. 121 (1975): Nov. 5, 6, considered and
passed Senate. Vol. 122 (1976): July 28,
considered and passed House. Amended
in lieu of H.R.11656. Aug. 31, House
and Senate agreed to Conference Report.   Cong. Rec.

Regulations

Agency regulations are generally cited first   C.F.R.
to the *Code of Federal Regulations*,
then to the *Federal Register*. When the
reference is only to an agency's explanatory
statement, the Guide cites only the
Federal Register page.   Fed. Reg.

OVERVIEW AND SUMMARY

The Government in the Sunshine Act is based on the policy that "the public is entitled to the fullest practicable information regarding the decisionmaking processes of the Federal Government." Pub. L. No. 94-409, § 2. The purpose of the Act is "to provide the public with such information while protecting the rights of individuals and the ability of the Government to carry out its responsibilities." *Id.*

Section 3 of the Act amends Title 5 of the United States Code, adding a new section 552b, titled "Open Meetings." This new section is codified as 5 U.S.C. § 552b and is divided into 13 subsections, (a) through (m).

Subsection (a) defines the basic terms "agency," "meeting," and "member." Subsection (b) declares a presumption in favor of open meetings, noting that "except as provided in subsection (c), every portion of every meeting of an agency shall be open to public observation." Subsection (c) allows an agency to close a meeting or portion of a meeting or to withhold information about a meeting or portion if the agency determines that the meeting or portion, if opened, or the information, if released, would be likely to disclose exempted information protected from disclosure under one or more of the 10 exemptions of subsection (c). These exemptions, however, are permissive, not mandatory, S. Rep., 20, and the agency may still open or release information about an otherwise exempted meeting or portion. Indeed, subsection (c) also provides that agency meetings shall be open "where the agency finds that the public interest [so] requires."

Subsections (d), (e), and (f) prescribe the procedures agencies must follow in closing meetings, announcing and changing meetings, and withholding and/or releasing substantive information regarding such meetings. Under subsection (d)(1), agencies may decide to close meetings or withhold information about meetings only by recorded majority vote of the entire membership of the agency. A separate recorded vote must be taken each time the agency proposes to close or withhold information about a meeting, except that a single vote is allowed when a series of meetings held within a 30-day period concerns "the same particular matters."

Subsection(d)(2) allows a "person whose interests may be directly affected by a portion of a meeting" to request a closure based on exemptions (5), (6), or (7). The agency need vote on the request only "upon the request of any one of its members." Subsection (d)(3) requires that within one day of any vote to close or to withhold information about a meeting taken under subsections (d)(1) or (d)(2), the agency must "make publicly available" a written copy of the vote of each member. If the vote is to close or to withhold information, the agency must also make available "a full written explanation" of the closing and a list of all expected attendees and their affiliations. Subsection (d)(4) allows an agency, a majority of whose meetings may be closed under exemptions (4), (8), (9)(A) or (10), to close its meetings by expedited procedures and to dispense with some of the procedural requirements of subsections (d)(1), (d)(3), and (e).

Subsection (e)(1) requires that the agency publicly announce, at least one week prior to the meeting, its time, place, and subject matter, whether it is to be open or closed, and the name and telephone number of an agency contact person to provide additional information. The subsection also permits the agency to provide less than seven days' notice of a meeting, provided a majority of the membership determines by recorded vote "that agency business requires" less notice and the agency makes the requisite public announcement "at the earliest practicable time." Subsection (e)(2) allows the agency to change the time, place, subject matter, or open or closed status of a meeting following public announcement, provided it announces the changes "at the earliest practicable time" and, in the case of a change in subject matter or open or closed status, a majority recorded vote is cast. Subsection (e)(3) provides that public announcement required under subsections (e)(1) and (e)(2) must also be submitted for publication in the *Federal Register*. Furthermore, agencies are to use "reasonable means" "to assure that the public is fully informed of public announcements," including posting notices on bulletin boards, publishing them in special interest journals, and distributing them to a mailing list. Conf. Rep., 19.

Subsection (f)(1) requires that for every meeting closed under one or more of the exemptions of subsection (c), the General Counsel or chief legal officer of the agency must certify that the meeting may properly be closed. The agency must retain a copy of the certification and a statement from the presiding officer of the meeting stating the time and place of the meeting and listing the persons actually present. The agency must also maintain a complete verbatim transcript or electronic recording of all closed meetings, except that it may instead maintain detailed minutes of any meeting closed under exemptions (8), (9)(A), or (10). Subsection (f)(2) requires the agency to make "promptly available" for public inspection and copying a copy of the transcript, recording, or minutes, except for information exempted and withheld pursuant to subsection (c). The agency is also required under subsection (f)(2) to maintain for at least two years a complete verbatim copy of the transcript, recording, or minutes.

Subsection (g) required the agencies to promulgate regulations implementing subsections (b)-(f) of the Act by March 12, 1977, in consultation with the Office of the Chairman, Administrative Conference of the United States, and after 30 days' notice and opportunity for public comment. The subsection also allows "any person" to bring a proceeding in the U.S. District Court for the District of Columbia to require the promulgation of regulations within the requisite period and a proceeding in the United States Court of Appeals for the District of Columbia to set aside agency regulations not in accord with the requirements of subsections (b)-(f).

Subsection (h)(1) confers jurisdiction on the U.S. District Court to enforce the requirements of subsections (b)-(f) by declaratory judgment, injunctive relief, or other appropriate relief, including enjoining future violations or releasing nonexempted portions of the transcript, recording, or minutes of the improperly closed meeting. Any person may bring an action to enforce these requirements prior to or within 60 days after such meeting is announced. The agency must answer the complaint within 30 days after service and must sustain the burden of proof. Subsection (h)(2) empowers any federal court otherwise authorized to review agency action to examine agency violations of the Sunshine Act and to afford appropriate relief, including the invalidation of a substantive action, if the Sunshine violation is of a particularly serious nature. Conf. Rep., 22. No court having jurisdiction solely on the basis of subsection (h)(1), however, can invalidate agency action taken at a meeting at which a violation of the Sunshine Act occurred, no matter how serious the violation. *Id.* at 22-23.

Subsection (i) allows for the award of "reasonable attorneys fees and other litigation costs" to any party who "substantially prevails" in any action brought pursuant to subsections (g) or (h). Such costs may be assessed against the plaintiff only if the court determines that the suit was brought "primarily for frivolous or dilatory purposes."

Subsection (j) required each agency to make annual reports to Congress concerning compliance with the open meeting requirements of section 3. This provision was amended in 1995 and annual reports are no longer mandatory effective May 15, 2000.

Subsection (k) provides that nothing in the Sunshine Act "expands or limits the present rights of any person under" 5 U.S.C. § 552, the Freedom of Information Act (FOIA), except that the Sunshine Act rather than FOIA exemptions govern in the case of any FOIA request to inspect or copy the transcript, recording, or minutes of a closed meeting.

Subsection (l) provides that nothing in section 3 authorizes the withholding of information from Congress, nor the closing of a meeting required to be open pursuant to another statute.

Finally, subsection (m) declares that nothing in section 3 of the Sunshine Act authorizes the withholding of information otherwise available to an individual under 5 U.S.C. § 552a of the Privacy Act.

Section 4 adds to the Administrative Procedure Act a new provision dealing with ex parte communications in formal hearings. Although one will occasionally see this provision referred to with a Sunshine Act designation, *see, e.g., Electric Power Supply Ass'n v. FERC*, 391 F.3d 1255 (D.C. Cir. 2004), this amendment relates to the formal hearing provisions of the APA and has nothing to do with open meetings. *See* 5 U.S.C. § 557(d). Section 5 makes certain conforming amendments to the Federal Advisory Committee Act, Postal Service legislation, and the Freedom of Information Act, including narrowing Exemption 3 of the FOIA. *See* 5 U.S.C. § 552(b)(3). Section 6 provides an effective date for the original statute of 180 days after date of enactment, *i.e.*, March 12, 1977.

Chapter 1

SECTION 552b(a)
DEFINITIONS

"AGENCY"	1
"SUBDIVISION"	4
"MEETING"	7
Legislative History	10
The 1978 Sunshine Guide	14
FCC v. ITT World Communications	17
American Bar Association Recommendation	22
NRDC v. Nuclear Regulatory Commission	23
Summary	25
Subsection (d) and (e) Deliberations	25
ELECTRONIC COMMUNICATIONS	26
"MEMBER"	28

(1) the term "agency" means any agency, as defined in section 552(e) of this title, headed by a collegial body composed of two or more individual members, a majority of whom are appointed to such position by the President with the advice and consent of the Senate, and any subdivision thereof authorized to act on behalf of the agency;

"AGENCY"

The definition of "agency" is the one used in the 1974 amendments to the Freedom of Information Act (FOIA), except that it is limited to those entities that are headed by a collegial body of two or more members, a majority of whom are appointed to such positions by the President with the advice and consent of the Senate. So the case law and other authorities under the FOIA will control. *See Energy Research Foundation v. Defense Nuclear Facilities Safety Board,* 917 F.2d 581 (D.C. Cir. 1990) (hereafter *Energy Research); Soucie v. David,* 448 F.2d 1087, 1073-75 (D.C. Cir. 1971) (hereafter *Soucie).* The Senate and House Committee Reports contain lists of agencies that appeared to the respective committees to be covered, but both reports specified that it was the statutory definition and not the lists that would govern. S. Rep., 15-18; H. Rep. II, 13-14.[1]

Congress has on occasion extended the Sunshine Act to governmental bodies that do not meet the statutory definition, for example, the Neighborhood Reinvestment Corporation. *See* 42 U.S.C. § 8103(i). Certain other agencies not subject to the Act also voluntarily comply with its provisions, for example, the Federal Open Market Committee and the U.S. Commission on Civil Rights.[2] In at least one instance, Congress has directed a regional agency, the Pacific Northwest Electric Power and Conservation Planning Council, established pursuant to federal statute, to comply with the Sunshine Act "to the extent appropriate." *See* 16 U.S.C. § 839b(a)(4).

The only noteworthy dispute involving the definition of "agency" has been over whether certain entities whose functions are primarily or exclusively advisory are agencies. In *Pacific Legal Foundation v. Council on Environmental Quality* (hereafter *Pacific Legal Foundation*), 636 F.2d 1259 (D.C. Cir. 1980), the CEQ's functions included advising the President on environmental policy and overseeing and coordinating federal programs relating to environmental quality. CEQ conceded that it was an agency subject to the Sunshine Act, but it sought to place its function of advising the President outside the Act's coverage. CEQ contended that it did not function as an agency

---

1. For a list of 67 federal agencies that have open meeting regulations, or voluntarily open their meetings to the public, *see* Appendix C, *infra*. This is an increase of 17 agencies from the 50 agencies listed in Appendix B of the *1978 Guide*.
2. *See* policy statement of the Federal Open Market Committee, 12 C.F.R. § 281.2 ("... despite the conclusion ... that the Sunshine Act does not apply to the FOMC, the FOMC has determined that its procedures and timing of public discourse already are conducted in accordance with the spirit of the Sunshine Act"); and regulations of the U.S. Commission on Civil Rights, 45 C.F.R. § 702.50 et seq., 67 Fed. Reg. 70,482, 70,487 (Oct. 22, 2002). A majority of the members of the Open Market Committee serve *ex officio* by reason of their appointment as members of the Federal Reserve Board, and consequently the Committee is not within the scope of the Act's definition of "agency"; *see* text at note 6, *infra*. The members of the Commission on Civil Rights are appointed by the President, the President pro tempore of the Senate, and the Speaker of the House of Representatives; however, none are advice-and-consent appointees. *See* 42 U.S.C. § 1975.

in advising the President and that, consequently, formulating such advice was not "official agency business." The court disagreed and held that once an organizational unit meets the FOIA/Sunshine Act definition of an agency, its status as such does not vary with the nature of the function it performs. The court concluded that the Sunshine Act covered the CEQ's advisory function, although it held out the possibility that meetings to consider such advice might be eligible for closure.[3]

Five years later the court reached a different conclusion with respect to the Council of Economic Advisers (CEA) in *Rushforth v. Council of Economic Advisers,* 762 F.2d 1038 (D.C. Cir. 1985) (hereafter *Rushforth*). The court found that CEA's functions were exclusively to advise and assist the President and did not include the program coordination and oversight responsibilities possessed by the Council on Environmental Quality. Therefore, the court concluded that the CEA was not an agency under either the Freedom of Information Act (FOIA) or the Sunshine Act. The court added that even if CEA were an agency under the FOIA, it would not be covered by the Sunshine Act because it does not operate as a collegial body, inasmuch as administration of the Council is centralized in the chairman.[4]

Finally, in *Energy Research, supra,* the court held that the Defense Nuclear Facilities Safety Board, whose functions are to evaluate Department of Energy standards for defense nuclear facilities, to investigate practices affecting safety at such facilities, and to make

---

3. Although the Council on Environmental Quality (CEQ) was established by the National Environmental Policy Act, 42 U.S.C. § 4342, as a three-member agency, appropriations legislation since fiscal year 1998 has reduced CEQ to a single member, and consequently it no longer qualifies as a Sunshine agency. Letter from Dinah Bear, General Counsel of CEQ, to Stephen Klitzman (July 25, 2001).
4. 762 F.2d at 1044. *Cf.* Nichols v. Reno, 931 F. Supp. 748, 753 (D. Colo. 1996), *aff'd* 124 F.3d 1376 (10th Cir. 1997) (Sunshine Act is not applicable to the Department of Justice, whose authority is vested in the Attorney General), Public Citizen v. Barshefsky, 939 F. Supp. 31, 35 n.6 (D.D.C. 1996) (Sunshine Act does not apply to the U.S. Trade Representative headed by a "single individual"), and Parravano v. Babbitt, 837 F. Supp. 1034, 1048 (N.D. Cal. 1993) (Sunshine Act does not apply to the Departments of Interior or Commerce headed by single persons).

recommendations to the Department of Energy, was an agency under the Sunshine Act. The court rejected the Board's argument that because its statute evidenced a congressional intention that meetings to make recommendations to the Department of Energy should be closed, the Board should not be considered an agency. The court concluded that the Board's investigative and evaluative responsibilities were sufficient to make it an "agency" under the *Soucie* and *Pacific Legal Foundation* opinions, and it indicated further that the principle of *Rushforth* would be limited to entities whose "sole function" was providing advice to the President.[5]

An agency whose members serve *ex officio* by virtue of their appointment with advice and consent to another position is not covered by the Sunshine Act. In *Symons v. Chrysler Loan Guarantee Board*, 670 F.2d 238 (D.C. Cir. 1981), the court held that the Board, whose membership consisted of the Secretary of the Treasury, the Chairman of the Board of Governors of the Federal Reserve System, and the Comptroller General (the Secretaries of Labor and Transportation were non-voting members), was not a Sunshine agency because the members were not appointed "to such position by the President with the advice and consent of the Senate." The court relied on the statutory language and legislative history, and on a ruling by the Department of Justice shortly after enactment of the statute.[6]

"SUBDIVISION"

The open meeting requirements apply not only to meetings of the full collegial body but also to meetings of "any subdivision thereof

---

5. 917 F.2d at 584.
6. 670 F.2d at 242-43, n.7, *citing* letter of Oct. 27, 1976, from Deputy Assistant Attorney General Leon Ulman, Office of Legal Counsel, to Harold Kessler, Acting Executive Director, Federal Labor Relations Council, concluding that the Council, which consisted of the Chairman of the Civil Service Commission, the Secretary of Labor, and the Director of the Office of Management and Budget, all serving *ex officio*, was not an agency for purposes of the Sunshine Act. *See also* letter of Dec. 28, 1976, from Deputy Assistant Attorney General Mary G. Lawton to Henry Rose, General Counsel, Pension Benefit Guaranty Corporation (PBGC), concluding that the Board of Directors of the PBGC, consisting of the Secretaries of Commerce, Labor and Treasury, all serving *ex officio*, also was not a Sunshine Act agency.

authorized to act on behalf of the agency." Legislative history indicates that "authorized to act on behalf of the agency" should be interpreted broadly and not in the relatively narrow sense of taking agency action as defined in the Administrative Procedure Act, 5 U.S.C. § 551(13). Thus, the report of the House Government Operations Committee states that "panels or boards authorized to submit recommendations, preliminary decisions, or the like to the full commission, or to conduct hearings on behalf of the agency" are included within the meaning of subdivision. H. Rep. I, 7. On the other hand, where a committee of members has been directed to draw up and submit an informal recommendation to the full collegial body, which recommendation is then open to full consideration by the body, it is hard to regard such an assignment as an authorization to act on behalf of the agency in any meaningful sense. At a minimum, a subdivision must have a specified membership and fixed responsibilities; an informal working group authorized to report back to the body is not a subdivision.[7]

Furthermore, the subdivision must be considering matters within its formally delegated authority. In *Federal Communications Commission v. ITT World Communications,* 466 U.S. 463 (1984), three members of the FCC's Telecommunications Committee attended an international conference at which FCC policy was discussed. The three members constituted a quorum of the Telecommunications Committee, but not of the full Commission (at that time a seven-member body). Citing the *1978 Guide,* the Supreme Court, in its only Sunshine Act opinion to date, held that the discussions in which the members participated did not constitute a meeting subject to the Act because, *inter alia,* the discussions related to decisions already reached by the full Commission and not to the disposition of applications for common carrier certifications, the only matters within the subdivision's formally delegated authority.[8]

---

7. *Id.* A subdivision must have a specified membership in order to permit a determination as to the presence of a quorum. A gathering of less than a quorum of the full body does not become a subdivision merely because it is preparing a recommendation for the full body.
8. 466 U.S. at 472-73. *See* discussion of *ITT World Communications* case, *infra* at pp. 17-22.

It should be noted that "subdivision thereof" refers back to "collegial body," not to "agency." Subdivisions made up entirely of employees other than members of the collegial body are not covered by the Act, even though they may be authorized to act on behalf of the agency.[9] The basis for excluding subdivisions made up of agency employees is well stated in the Senate Report:

> The agency heads are high public officials, having been selected and confirmed through a process very different from that used for staff members. Their deliberative process can be appropriately exposed to public scrutiny in order to give citizens an awareness of the process and rationale of decisionmaking.

S. Rep., 17.

Where a collegial subdivision is made up in part of agency members and in part of staff, the answer is unclear. Where agency members make up a majority of the members of the subdivision, the subdivision would appear to be a subdivision of the collegial body. Where staff make up a majority of the subdivision, assuming that the relationship among the members of the subdivision is truly collegial, we doubt that the Act applies.

---

9. In *Hunt v. Nuclear Regulatory Comm'n*, 611 F.2d 332 (10th Cir. 1979), *cert. denied*, 445 U.S. 906 (1980), the court held that the Sunshine Act does not apply to meetings of Atomic Safety and Licensing Boards, whose members are appointed by the Nuclear Regulatory Commission to adjudicate cases under the Atomic Energy Act. The court based its conclusion on its reading of the Act, as well as the relevant agency regulations and the comments in the *1978 Guide* on the meaning of "subdivision." *See also* Rockford Newspapers, Inc. v. Nuclear Regulatory Comm'n, No. 83C 20074; 83 C 3625, 1984 U.S. Dist. LEXIS 19244 (N.D. Ill. Feb. 22, 1984; and Central & Southern Motor Freight Tariff Assoc., Inc. v. Interstate Commerce Comm'n, No. 83-2618, 1983 U.S. Dist. LEXIS 10845 (D.D.C. Dec. 12, 1983).

"MEETING"

(2) the term "meeting" means the deliberations of at least the number of individual agency members required to take action on behalf of the agency where such deliberations determine or result in the joint conduct or disposition of official agency business, but does not include deliberations required or permitted by subsection (d) or (e);

Defining the scope of the term "meeting" is one of the most troublesome problems in interpreting and applying the Sunshine Act. The definition was revised frequently in the course of the legislative process, sometimes for obscure reasons, and the legislative history is not completely consistent.[10] The definition of "meeting" consists of a number of distinct elements. First, the "meeting" must be of at least the number of agency members required to take action on behalf of the agency—that is, enough to constitute a quorum. S. Rep., 19. A gathering of less than a quorum does not ever constitute a "meeting" under the Act. S. Rep., 2-3. The size of a quorum is ordinarily established by the agency's statute or by regulation. *See FTC v. Flotill Products*, 389 U.S. 179, 181-82 (1967) (hereafter *Flotill Products*).[11] Where the stat-

---

10. *See* Appendix D, *infra,* for a chronological chart of the definition of "meeting" as it evolved through the legislative history of the Sunshine Act.
11. Nothing in the Act or its legislative history suggests that an agency may not adopt its own rules for determining a quorum in particular circumstances. For example, there is no explicit quorum requirement in the organic legislation for the Securities and Exchange Commission, but the agency is authorized to "make such rules and regulations as may be necessary or appropriate to implement the provisions of this chapter," 15 U.S.C. § 78w(a)(1). In 1995 the Commission adopted a regulation providing that three of the five statutory members constitute a quorum unless the number of members in office is fewer than three, in which case the quorum consists of the number of members actually in office. The regulation further provides that if, on any matter of business, the number of members in office minus the number of members who are disqualified to consider the matter is two, then those two members constitute a quorum for purposes of that specific matter. The D.C. Circuit upheld the validity of the Commission's quorum rule in *Falcon Trading Group, Ltd. v. SEC,* 102 F.3d 579, 582 (D.C. Cir.

(continued on next page)

ute and the regulations are silent, a majority of the membership constitutes a quorum. *Flotill Products* at 183; *Ho Chang Tsao v. INS,* 538 F.2d 667, 669 (5th Cir. 1976). Where a subdivision is involved, a quorum of the subdivision is necessary to constitute a meeting. Where a collegial body, whether agency or subdivision, consists in part of advice-and-consent appointees and in part of members otherwise selected, all members would be treated alike for purposes of determining the presence of a quorum (unless the rules applicable to the body itself made some distinction among members in defining a quorum).[12]

Second, the requisite number of members must be in a position to exchange views. They must at least be potentially involved in the discussion. The use of the word "joint" is intended to exclude instances

---

(continued from previous page)
1996), and at least one agency, the Chemical Safety and Hazard Investigation Board, has followed the SEC's example. *See* 68 Fed. Reg. 65,403 (2003), 40 C.F.R. § 1600.5.

When the Federal Trade Commission, ordinarily a five-member agency, was reduced to three members by unfilled vacancies, it adopted a resolution stating that "when the Commission is comprised of three members, two of those members can act for the Commission, one member not participating, so long as all members are aware of the proposed action and are afforded an opportunity to participate." *See* 41 Fed. Reg. 25,036. Could it be argued that under such a rule, where two members meet without notice to the third, no quorum is present and consequently there is no "meeting?" We do not believe so. The statutory reference is not to a "quorum," but to "the number of . . . members required to take action on behalf of the agency." This means the number necessary to constitute a quorum at a properly called meeting. Whether the same number of members is authorized to act at the particular gathering in question is not determinative. For a general discussion of quorum and voting requirements, *see* Marshall J. Breger & Gary J. Edles, *Established by Practice: The Theory and Operation of Independent Federal Agencies,* 52 ADMIN. L. REV. 1111, 1182-87 (2000). *See also* Railroad Yardmasters of America v. Harris, 721 F. 2d 1332 (D.C. Cir. 1983). (A single member of a three-member National Mediation Board may act for Board pursuant to a validly issued delegation order that is narrowly tailored to prevent temporary occurrence of two vacancies from completely disabling the Board.)

12. When the Federal Election Commission had non-voting members, its regulation, former 11 C.F.R. § 2.2(d), counted only voting members to determine the presence of a quorum. *See* p. 28, *infra*.

where one or more agency members give a speech concerning agency business, and other members are in the audience. S. Rep., 18. On the other hand, a physical presence is not required. A conference telephone call or possibly a series of two-party calls would qualify as a meeting if the other requirements are met. Conf. Rep., 11; H. Rep. I, 8.

Third, the meeting must consist of "deliberations [which] determine or result in the joint conduct or disposition of official agency business." This is a complicated, somewhat ambiguous concept, and much attention was devoted in the legislative process to attempting to define when conversations among agency members rise to the level of a "meeting." At one end of the spectrum it is clear that not every reference to agency business turns a gathering of members into a meeting. The Senate Report pointed out:

> To be a meeting the discussion must be of some substance. Brief references to agency business where the commission members do not give serious attention to the matter do not constitute a meeting. A chance encounter where passing reference is made to agency business, such as setting a time or place for the agency heads to meet, would not be a meeting. A luncheon attended by a majority of the Commissioners would not be a meeting subject to the bill simply because one Commissioner made a brief, casual remark about an agency matter which did not elicit substantial further comment. The words "deliberation" and "conduct" were carefully chosen to indicate that some degree of formality is required before a gathering is considered a meeting for purposes of this section.

S. Rep., 18.

It is likewise clear that the term "meeting" includes more than the session at which the collegial body formally disposes of a matter. Congress was specific in its desire to rule out any possibility that open meetings might be merely a forum for ratifying decisions previously arrived at in closed sessions:

> The definition of meetings includes the conduct, as well as the disposition, of official agency matters. It is not sufficient for the purposes of open government to merely have the public witness

final agency votes. The meetings opened by section 201(a) are not intended to be merely reruns staged for the public after agency members have discussed the issue in private and predetermined their views. The whole decisionmaking process, not merely its results, must be exposed to public scrutiny.

S. Rep., 18.

Thus, at a minimum, "meeting" includes any gathering of the requisite number of members where a serious exchange of views achieves a consensus on a matter of official agency business.

But what of the intermediate points on the spectrum? Briefings to the members by staff or outsiders, which are accompanied by limited exchanges among the members? Discussions among the members that are serious but tentative and exploratory, not calculated or intended to lead to an immediate commitment by the agency to any course of action? Discussions that attempt to reach but do not achieve a consensus? Given the great variety of possible fact situations, articulating a practical test of a "meeting" to apply in this twilight zone has been a challenge for Congress, the agencies, and the courts.

Legislative History

The problem of defining the threshold for a "meeting" was a matter of continuing concern during Congress's consideration of the Sunshine legislation. In discussing the peculiar problems of agencies in which two members constitute a quorum, the Senate Report said:

It is not the intent of the bill to prevent any two agency members, regardless of agency size, from engaging in informal background discussions which clarify issues and expose varying views. . . . When two members constitute a quorum, however, *the agency must be careful not to cross over the line and engage in discussions which effectively predetermine official actions.* Members of such agencies must use their judgment in these situations, again with the awareness that this bill carries a presumption of openness. Their discussions should remain informal and preliminary to avoid the open meeting requirement.

S. Rep., 19 (emphasis added).

This passage is the most serious effort in the legislative history to mark out a line of distinction between those casual and informal discussions of agency business that do not qualify as "meetings" and those more "formal" gatherings that do.[13] While the reference is to the situation in which two members constitute a quorum, the passage necessarily has broader application, since there is nothing in the statute that supports a special definition of "meeting" for agencies where two members make up a quorum.[14] The quoted passage indicates that the controlling distinction is between discussions that "effectively predetermine official actions" and those that do not. It would follow that briefings and exploratory or tentative discussions would not fall within the definition of "meeting." On the other hand, the report of the House Government Operations Committee, in discussing its definition of "meeting," which

---

13. It is clear that some such distinction was intended. "The words 'deliberation' and 'conduct' were carefully chosen to indicate that some degree of formality is required before a gathering is considered a meeting for purposes of this section." S. REP., 18. "Formality," however, seems an unfortunate choice of word, since it is clear that it is the content of the discussion rather than the outward form that determines whether there is a meeting.

14. For the specific concerns of such small agencies where two members always make up a quorum, *see* Letter to Thomasina V. Rogers, Chair, Administrative Conference of the United States, from Marsha Martin, Chairman, Farm Credit Administration, Sept. 8, 1995. In her letter, Chairman Martin noted that:

> the Sunshine Act ... is extremely burdensome in an organization such as FCA which has just three full-time Board members. ... Because the Sunshine Act effectively prohibits any two Board members from discussing any issue which is before the Board, most of the substantive discussion takes place between executive assistants and agency staff who are not subject to the Act's restrictions. Board leadership and control is weakened considerably, since communication between Board members is secondhand. My personal experience is that staff members many times make significant policy decisions in facilitating Board actions. In addition, lack of one-on-one communication between Board members creates suspicions, misunderstandings, and needless disruptions in the decisionmaking process. ...

was almost identical to that in the Senate bill, said, "[t]he conduct of agency business is intended to include not just the formal decisionmaking or voting, but all discussion relating to the business of the agency." H. Rep. I, 8. To the extent the committee reports disagree over the interpretation of "meeting," the Senate Report should be viewed as the more authoritative because the Conference Report stated that the Senate's definition of meeting *as explained in the Senate Report* (emphasis added) was the basis for the final language. Conf. Rep., 11.

Both reports, quoted above, refer to substantially the same language of the definition, "deliberations where such deliberations *concern* the joint conduct or disposition of [official] agency business" (emphasis added).[15] This language was changed to its present form in the Senate-House Conference. Conf. Rep., 11. Although the purpose of the change was not explained in the report, it can only be interpreted as intending some limiting and narrowing effect.[16] That effect seems, most plausibly, to be to exclude from the definition, or to emphasize the previous exclu-

---

15. The definition of "meeting" in S. 5, as reported by the Senate Government Operations Committee and as passed by the Senate, was as follows:

    [A] meeting means the deliberations of at least the number of individual agency members required to take action on behalf of the agency where such deliberations concern the joint conduct or disposition of official agency business.

    The definition in the bill reported by the House Government Operations Committee was identical except that the word "official" was omitted.

16. The change was to substitute for "concern," "determine or result in." A test based on whether deliberations "determine or result in . . . disposition of official agency business" is very close to that suggested in the Senate report, whether the discussions "effectively predetermine official actions." Rep. Fascell, a member of the Conference Committee, explained the change as follows:

    On the issue of the definition of a "meeting," the conference report accepts the Senate wording except that deliberations would have to "determine or result in" the joint conduct or disposition of agency business, rather than merely "concern" such activities. This language is intended to permit casual discussions between agency members that might invoke the bill's requirements under the less formal "concern" standard. 122 Cong. Rec. H9260 (daily ed. Aug. 31, 1976); Source Book, p. 818.

(continued on next page)

sion of, those deliberations that "concern" agency business, yet are so general and tentative as not to "determine or result in" the adoption of firm positions regarding future agency action by the participating members. In this category might be placed briefings to and even exploratory talks among agency members.[17] Such treatment is consistent with the suggestion in the Senate Report that the test is whether the discussion "predetermine[s] official action," and obviously it has much to recommend it in terms of the practical problems of the day-to-day operations of an agency.[18]

(continued from previous page)
The phrase "deliberations [which] determine or result in the joint conduct . . . of official agency business" is puzzling and essentially circular because the meeting itself is joint conduct of agency business. Evidently, "result in" is being used in the sense of "amount to" and is intended to underline the Conference's rejection of the "purpose" test adopted in the House. *See* text at note 22, *infra*. But to say that the test of a meeting is what occurs does not tell much about what must occur in order to constitute a meeting.

17. *See, e.g.,* regulations of the Federal Deposit Insurance Corporation, 12 C.F.R. § 311.2(b), the National Transportation Safety Board, 49 C.F.R. § 804.3(c), and the Occupational Safety and Health Review Commission, 29 C.F.R. § 2203.2(d). *See also* p. 23 note 40, *infra*.

18. The practical need for exempting casual and tentative discussions was well set forth in the House hearings by Prof. Jerre Williams, testifying on behalf of the American Bar Association:

> Obviously, one of the critical facets of this legislation, and what we have been talking about today, is the definition of meeting.
>
> The ABA takes the position that there is a need for balance here. There is a need for exempting from the legislation chance encounters and informational and exploratory discussions as long as they do not predetermine agency action.
>
> The informal and casual work session is included. Outlandish suggestions come out of those sessions. Hopefully, humorous suggestions come out of those sessions, but once in a while the brainstorming matters will lead to a new and creative and important idea.
>
> The ABA takes the position that the open meetings requirement does not apply until the brainstorming gets to the point that ideas need to be adequately evaluated as a viable alternative which ought to be seriously considered.

See House Government Operations Hearings, 102. *See also* House Judiciary Oversight Hearing, 5-6.

The 1978 Sunshine Guide

On the basis of the legislative history cited above, the *1978 Guide* concluded that the definition of meeting does not cover "tentative" or "exploratory" discussions, and it sought to devise an operational distinction between such discussions and those discussions that are so immediately related to the process of determining agency action as to fall on the other side of the line. The test suggested in the Senate Report is whether the discussion "predetermines" official action. Certainly, where deliberation focused on a fairly specific proposal before the agency achieves a consensus among the participants on the agency's proper course of action, such a deliberation determines the disposition of the business within the meaning of the definition, notwithstanding that no formal action is taken and that the members are free to change their minds.[19] Where a consensus is not achieved because of the members' differing views, a harder case is presented. Because no agreement has been reached, it might be said that the discussion has not predetermined official action. Yet the process by which the members reach their individual conclusions through exchange of views with their colleagues appears to be within the drafters' contemplation of "joint conduct" of agency business.[20]

Accordingly, the *1978 Guide* concluded that the proper test is the nature of the discussion and not whether it achieves a specific extent of agreement. A discussion sufficiently focused on discrete proposals or issues as to cause or be likely to cause the individual participating members to form reasonably firm positions regarding matters pending or likely to arise before the agency is a meeting,

---

19. We do not suggest that the agency's decision need relate to an "agency action," as that term is used in the Administrative Procedure Act, 5 U.S.C. § 551(13). The agency's decision-making must relate to "official agency business," which may or may not be "agency action." *Cf.* Nat'l Ornamental and El. Light Xmas Assn. v. CPSC, 526 F.2d 1368, 1372-73 (2d Cir. 1975).
20. "The definition of meetings includes the conduct, as well as the disposition, of official agency matters. . . . The [open] meetings . . . are not intended to be merely reruns staged for the public after agency members have discussed the issue in private and predetermined their views." S. Rep., at 18.

while a discussion that is merely informational or exploratory is not.[21]

The conclusion of the *1978 Guide* on this point represented a revision of the position taken in the first draft version of the *1978 Guide* that the test of a meeting was whether a consensus was actually achieved. On reconsideration in the light of agency and public comments, the authors concluded that the tentative version relied on a somewhat mechanical application of the "predetermine official action" test. While the test is relevant and probably decisive, the *1978 Guide* concluded that it refers to the nature of the discussion, rather than the actual result. In other words, the question is whether the discussion is decision-oriented or whether the members are merely familiarizing themselves with the subject, exchanging preliminary observations, canvassing possibilities, or brainstorming.

A number of factors may be relevant in assessing the nature of the discussion, for example, its length, the circumstances in which it was initiated, whether all the members were present or had an opportunity to attend. It is helpful to bear in mind that the purpose of the Sunshine Act is to open to the public those collegial exchanges that are a part of the decision-making process, in the interest of enhancing public awareness of that process and the accountability of the agency members. S. Rep., 17-18. A discussion that significantly furthers the decisional process by narrowing issues, discarding alternatives, etc., should be treated as a meeting even though it does not and is not expected to achieve a complete resolution. On the other hand, those exchanges of views that are not of a nature to foreclose or narrow discussion at subsequent collegial gatherings might be treated as outside the definition without loss to the values the Sunshine Act seeks to achieve.

Whether given deliberations will achieve a consensus or even lead individual members to make up their minds is, of course, a question that may not be possible to answer in advance. Obviously, the more specific the subject under consideration and the more immediate its relationship to prospective agency actions, the more difficult it will be to keep the discussion tentative and informal. The difficulties of defining "meeting" in terms of what actually happens rather than the pur-

---

21. *But see Department of Justice Letter to Covered Agencies,* April 19, 1977, Appendix E, which espoused a broader interpretation of "meeting." *Cf.* pp.43-44, *infra,* for discussion of present status of 1977 DOJ letter.

pose in calling it were much discussed in the House of Representatives, and at one point a "purpose" test was adopted.[22] However, the language in the final version seems to make the test what actually happened. In effect, this forces the agency to try to meet both tests. It must treat as a meeting prospectively every gathering that is either intended to or likely to result in the members reaching firm decisions. Conversely, if a gathering has not been treated as a meeting because of the tentative and informal nature of the anticipated discussion, the agency members have a duty under subsection (b) to see that the discussion remains tentative and informal. This line of distinction is not only a fine one, but one that assumes a certain predictability about the course of such informal discussions. To administer it consistently with the spirit and even the letter of the Act requires vigilance on the part of officials who preside and restraint on the part of those who participate, to the end that discussions do not move into an area properly reserved for meetings. Indeed, it is no doubt frequently desirable to conduct briefings and exploratory discussions under the procedures required for meetings so as to avoid the somewhat artificial restraints that the distinction appears to require.

Still another element in the definition of "meeting," and one that is difficult to separate from the question of what degree of formality is necessary to constitute "deliberations" or "joint conduct," is the concept of "official agency business." The legislative history is unhelpful.[23] The bill passed by the House used the term "agency business," but there is no indication in the Conference Report that the decision to accept the Senate's phraseology reflected a judgment that "official agency business" is a narrower term. Whether "official agency business" is interpreted narrowly, as fairly well-defined pending or anticipated matters, or broadly, as any subject matter relevant to the work of the agency, will, obviously, affect the treatment to be accorded briefings and general or exploratory discussions. An argument in favor of the more narrow definition is that the phrase "joint conduct or disposition" at the least implies a matter that is before the agency or in some way susceptible of disposition by the agency.

---

22. *See* 122 CONG. REC. H7889-90 (daily ed. July 28, 1976); SOURCE BOOK, pp. 665-70.
23. *See* S. REP., at 18-19.

Where a function has been vested in the agency chairman or in an individual member, as by a delegation from the agency, or in a statute or reorganization plan, a gathering at which the chairman or member seeks the informal advice of his colleagues on the carrying out of that function would not be a meeting.[24]

FCC v. ITT World Communications

The definition of "meeting" was squarely at issue in *FCC v. ITT World Communications, Inc. (ITT World).*[25] The case involved the participation by three members of the Federal Communications Commission in a series of conferences with their foreign counterparts, in a so-called "consultative process," to exchange information on regulatory policies. The three commissioners did not constitute a quorum of the then seven-member Commission, but they did constitute a quorum of the Telecommunications Committee, a subdivision of the Commission. Plaintiff ITT challenged the members' participation in these conferences, which were closed to the public, as violative of the Sunshine Act.

At the conferences the members of the Telecommunications Committee explained the pro-competitive licensing policy of the Commission and encouraged cooperation from their foreign counterparts. The Commission itself characterized the conferences as "informal talks" designed "to improve foreign understanding of the bases for and the nature of our pro-competition policies. . . ." The Commission maintained that the conferences were not meetings because (1) no quorum of the full Commission was present and there had been no delegation to the Committee to act on behalf of the Commission at the conferences, and (2) the informal exchanges were not deliberations or the joint conduct or disposition of official agency business.

The Court of Appeals for the District of Columbia Circuit disagreed and held that the conferences were meetings under the Sunshine Act. On the quorum issue, the court held that since the members attended the conferences in their official capacities and were authorized to do

---

24. *See* regulation of the Securities and Exchange Commission, 17 C.F.R. §§ 200.43, 200.401(a).
25. 466 U.S. 463, 104 S. Ct. 1936 (1984), *reversing* ITT World Communications, Inc. v. Fed. Communications Comm'n, 699 F.2d 1219 (D.C. Cir. 1983).

what in fact they did, they were acting on behalf of the Commission within the meaning of section 552b(a)(1). As to whether the members' actions met the definition of meetings, the court agreed this was a more difficult question. While the court was willing to concede that the Act did not reach "informal background discussions" among agency members, it discerned in the legislative history a presumption that exchanges between the agency and outside parties should be open. "If we did not apply the narrowest of interpretations to [informal background discussions], it would readily swallow up the requirement of open 'hearings' and 'meetings with the public.'"[26] The court also rejected the distinction, urged by the Commission, between predecisional activities and postdecisional activities intended to interpret and implement the agency's decisions.

On review, the Supreme Court unanimously reversed the Court of Appeals decision. It ruled that the members' participation in the Consultative Process did not constitute a "meeting" as defined by section 552b(a)(2), nor was it a "meeting of the agency" under section 552b(b). The Court's reasoning warrants close analysis.

First, the Court read the legislative history to demonstrate an intent that the Act not reach informal background discussions that clarify issues and expose varying views. Construing the Act to reach such discussions would prevent them and would "impair normal agency operations without achieving significant public benefit."[27] Therefore, the Act must be read to apply only where a quorum of members conducts or disposes of official agency business. The members attending the "consultative process" conferences were a quorum of the Telecommunications Committee, but the delegation to that Committee was only to pass upon certain common carrier applications. This delegation, in the Court's view, defined the Committee's official business.[28]

---

26. 699 F.2d at 1244.
27. 466 U.S. at 470.
28. "[The Sunshine Act] applies only where a subdivision of the agency deliberates upon matters that are within that subdivision's formally delegated authority to take official action for the agency." 466 U.S. at 472. Thus, the Court held that these consultative process "sessions were not 'meetings' within the meaning of the Sunshine Act," since the "Telecommunications Committee at the Consultative Process sessions did not consider or act upon applications
(continued on next page)

The discussions in which the members participated were not discussions that "effectively predetermine[d] official actions" of the Committee. On this point the Supreme Court cited with approval the test set forth in the *1978 Guide*.[29] The conferences merely provided the members background information and permitted them to exchange views with their foreign counterparts respecting implementation of decisions reached by the Commission. Such discussions are not reached by the Sunshine Act.

Finally, the Court offered an additional and apparently independent ground for its holding:

> The Consultative Process was not convened by the FCC, and its procedures were not subject to the FCC's unilateral control. The sessions of the Consultative Process therefore are not meetings "of an agency" within the meaning of § 552b(b). The Act prescribes procedures for the agency to follow when it holds meetings and particularly when it chooses to close a meeting.... These provisions presuppose that the Act applies only to meetings that the agency has the power to conduct according to these procedures. And application of the Act to meetings not under agency control would restrict the types of meetings that agency members could attend. It is apparent that Congress, in enacting requirements for the agency's conduct of its own meetings, did not contemplate as well such a broad substantive restraint upon agency processes. 466 U.S. at 473-74.

(continued from previous page)
for common carrier certification—its only formally delegated authority...." *Id.* at 473. *But see* a commentary on this case which has noted that "the Court's narrow, hypertechnical interpretation of the scope of the Act and of the scope of the meetings in [the] ITT [case] almost certainly was influenced by its belief that foreign agencies would be reluctant to engage in coordinated policymaking with U.S. agencies if all meetings for such purposes were required to be open to the public." *See* RICHARD J. PIERCE, JR., 1 ADMINISTRATIVE LAW TREATISE, 4th ed., 295 (Aspen Law & Business, 2002) (hereafter PIERCE).

29. Such discussions must be "sufficiently focused on discrete proposals or issues as to cause or be likely to cause the individual participating members to form reasonably firm positions regarding matters pending or likely to arise before the agency." 466 U.S. at 471, *citing* the *1978 Guide* at 9.

The suggestion that the Telecommunications Committee's lack of unilateral control over the Consultative Process made the Sunshine Act inapplicable had been summarily rejected by the Court of Appeals.[30] Nevertheless, the Supreme Court appears to be saying here that even if all the other elements of a "meeting" are present, the fact that the agency does not convene the meeting and lacks the power to conduct it in accordance with the Sunshine Act takes the case out of the Act. On this point the Court may have spoken too broadly. Admittedly, its reading of section 552b(b) comports with the ordinary understanding of the phrase "meeting of an agency." But the definition of "meeting" was probably the single most controverted issue in the drafting of the Sunshine Act,[31] and it seems most unlikely that Congress, after settling on a verbal formulation for coverage, intended to further qualify the term "meeting" by the words "of an agency" in section 552b(b).[32] Furthermore, there is no indication in the legislative history that agency control of the forum is a prerequisite for a covered meeting.[33] Of course, the Act should not be construed to impose impossible requirements. But even if the agency members are not in a position to comply with the procedures of the Act governing the conduct of a meeting, they may be in a position to decline to "jointly conduct or dispose of agency business," and if so, the first sentence of section 552b(b) arguably requires that they do so.[34]

---

30. "An agency cannot avoid [the open meeting] requirement through the facile expedient of having an outside party hold the discussion, for the Sunshine Act's policy that hearings and meetings with the public be open could otherwise be ignored with impunity." 699 F.2d at 1242.
31. *See* p. 7, *supra*.
32. The terms "meeting" and "meeting of an agency" are necessarily coextensive; the Act has no application to meetings other than those of an agency.
33. "Discussions held in the boardroom or the Chairman's office are not the only gatherings covered. Conference telephone calls and meetings outside the agency are equally subject to the bill if they discuss agency business and otherwise meet the requirements of this subsection." S. Rep., at 18-19.
34. The Court's holding that subsection 552b(b) does not reach a meeting that is not a "meeting of an agency" has implications for the permissibility of other procedures for exchanges among agency members that arguably do not rise to the level of a meeting. *See* text at notes 46-51, *infra*.

In sum, the Supreme Court in *ITT World,* out of sensitivity to the need to preserve agencies' authority to participate in international forums and other meetings outside the agencies' control, appears to have attempted to carve out an exception to the Act to deal with such situations *ex necessitate.* The limits of such an exception are not spelled out in the opinion, but other situations that might call for similar treatment include testimony by agency members at congressional hearings and field trips to agency-run installations.

It may be that the Court's opinion should be understood as merely providing a gloss on the concept of "joint conduct or disposition,"[35] saying, in effect, that members are not acting jointly simply because they are discussing agency business in the same forum, and that where that forum is one which the agency does not control, the members are presumably acting as individuals.[36] At any rate, the Court's expressed concern that the Act not be interpreted to restrict the types of meetings that agency members can attend evidences a desire on the part of the Court to apply a "rule of reason" to interpretation of the coverage of the Act.

Indeed, the contrast between the interpretive approaches taken by the Court of Appeals and the Supreme Court could not have been sharper. The Court of Appeals had inferred from a brief reference in the legislative history a presumption that all exchanges between agency members and outsiders should be open to the public, even though the discussions would not have met the statutory threshold if held wholly within the agency. The Supreme Court, on the other hand, took as its point of departure Congress's manifest intent to exclude "informal background discussions," and then detailed in a footnote how Congress had sought

---

35. *But see* NRDC v. Nuclear Regulatory Commission, 216 F.3d 1180, 1188-89 (D.C. Cir. 2000) (hereafter *NRDC*), where the court characterized this portion of the Supreme Court opinion as "a second truly independent ground for the Court's decision."
36. We have previously alluded to the passage in the legislative history, "The use of the word 'joint' is intended to exclude instances where one or more agency member gives a formal speech concerning agency business, and other members of the commission are in the audience." S. REP., at 18. *See also* text at pp. 8-9, *supra.* Unfortunately, like most of the examples in the legislative history, it does not reach the harder case where the number of members sufficient to constitute a quorum participate in the discussion.

"precisely to define the limited scope of the statute's requirements."[37] The Court also recognized the practical difficulties in extending the Sunshine requirements to informal exchanges with the public and to meetings that the agency does not itself sponsor or control. In short, the Supreme Court gave at least as much interpretive weight to Congress's efforts to exclude as to Congress's intention to include and it implicitly rejected any presumption of openness to govern doubtful cases.

American Bar Association Recommendation[38]

As a consequence of the *ITT World* decision, the Nuclear Regulatory Commission (NRC) in 1985 amended the definition of "meeting" in its regulations on an interim basis to incorporate the test set forth in the Court's opinion.[39] The NRC's action set off a round of criticism and debate.

In response to *ITT World,* the NRC's action, and other developments relating to the Sunshine Act, the Administrative Law Section of the American Bar Association formed a committee to review Sunshine issues. The committee presented a report that reviewed in some detail the Supreme Court decision and attempted to provide a gloss on the statutory definition in the light of the Court's opinion. On the basis of this report, as forwarded by the Section, the House of Delegates of the ABA, in February 1987, approved the following recommendation:

> *Be it Resolved*, That the American Bar Association offers the following guidelines to Federal agencies and courts with respect to the interpretation of the term "meeting" as used in the Government in the Sunshine Act:
>
> 1. So long as discussions are not sufficiently focused on discrete proposals or issues as to cause or be likely to cause the individual participating [agency] members to form reasonably firm positions regarding matters pending or likely to

---

37. 466 U.S. 470, n.7.
38. *See* Appendix F for the complete ABA Report and Recommendation.
39. *See* p. 23, *infra.* "In what turned out to be a serious tactical error on NRC's part, the rule was made immediately effective . . . [A]ny agency which is tempted to engage in rulemaking should make it a point never to deprive the public of its opportunity for prior comment." *See* Letter from Peter Crane, attorney, Nuclear Regulatory Commission, to Gary Edles, general counsel, Administrative Conference of the United States, pp. 4, 11 (Feb. 6, 1995).

arise before the agency, the definition of "meeting" does not include: (a) spontaneous casual discussions among agency members of a subject of common interest; (b) briefings of agency members by staff or outsiders; a key element would be that the agency members be primarily receptors of information or views and only incidentally exchange views with one another; (c) general discussions of subjects which are relevant to an agency's responsibilities but which do not pose specific problems for agency resolution; and (d) exploratory discussions, so long as they are preliminary in nature, there are no pending proposals for agency action, and the merits of any proposed agency action would be open to full consideration at a later time.
2. If agencies intend to hold discussions described in subsections (b), (c), and (d), appropriate mechanisms, such as monitoring by general counsel or other agency representatives, should be undertaken to ensure that such discussions do not proceed to the point of becoming "meetings." In addition, agencies should memorialize such discussions through notes, minutes or recordings as assurance to the public of compliance with the Act.

NRDC v. Nuclear Regulatory Commission

Despite the ABA resolution and making the rule immediately effective, the Nuclear Regulatory Commission delayed fully implementing its "interim rule" incorporating the Supreme Court's definition, meanwhile continuing to apply a more restrictive interpretation of the statutory definition. Finally, in 1999 the Commission, after a further round of notice and comment, issued a final rule reaffirming the definition in the interim rule:[40]

---

40. *See* NRC rulemaking notices, 64 Fed. Reg. 24,936-42 (May 10, 1999), 64 Fed. Reg. 39,393-96 (July 22, 1999). The May 10 notice includes a detailed chronology of the events from the issuance of the 1985 interim rule, including the congressional response, to the reissuance in 1999. The congressional response included a bill to require the NRC "to adhere to certain procedures in the conduct of its meetings," *i.e.*, to include preliminary discussions and staff briefings in its definition of "meeting." *See* H.R. 2743, the Atomic Energy Accountability Act, 99th Cong., 1st Sess. *See also* a hearing held on the
(continued on next page)

> Meeting means the deliberations of at least a quorum of Commissioners where such deliberations determine or result in the joint conduct or disposition of official Commission business, that is, where discussions are sufficiently focused on discrete proposals or issues as to cause or to be likely to cause the individual participating members to form reasonably firm positions regarding matters pending or likely to arise before the agency.

10 C.F.R. § 9.101(c).

The effect of this language is to exclude from Sunshine Act coverage any staff briefings of agency members, or any preliminary or exploratory discussions among agency members, so long as such briefings or discussions are not "focused on discrete proposals or issues as to cause or to be likely to cause" the agency members to "form reasonably firm positions regarding matters pending or likely to arise before the agency."

The Natural Resources Defense Council and other public interest groups challenged this NRC rule unsuccessfully in the Court of Appeals for the D.C. Circuit. *See NRDC, supra* note 35. Petitioners argued that the NRC's definition was fundamentally inconsistent with the statute and legislative history, and the court acknowledged some sympathy for their position.[41] However, the court concluded that inasmuch as the definition was specifically endorsed and applied by the Supreme Court in the *ITT World* case, it was bound to uphold it, and the court rejected NRDC's efforts to limit the Supreme Court decision to the peculiar facts of the *ITT World* case.[42]

> *(continued from previous page)*
> bill by the House Committee on Energy and Commerce, Subcommittee on Energy Conservation and Power, "Nuclear Regulatory Commission Sunshine Act Regulations," 99th Cong., 1st Sess., May 21, 1985, Serial No. 9939.

41. "In short, were we authorized to decide the validity of the Commission's definition of 'meeting' *de novo*, NRDC's arguments would give us some pause." *NRDC*, 216 F.3d at 1185.
42. "Although *ITT* may be factually distinguished from the instant case . . . , we are not free to turn every factual distinction into a reason for ignoring the Supreme Court's considered guidance." *Id.* at 1188.

Summary

The question of the meaning of "meeting" continues to be a source of controversy, but the Supreme Court's statement of the rule in *ITT World* remains the most authoritative exposition, and despite its unofficial status the ABA's resolution is a useful additional gloss. While problems of application will remain, we should recall, as the Administrative Law Section report pointed out, "[A] meeting first of all consists of 'deliberations,' and 'deliberation' is defined as the act of weighing and examining reasons for and against a choice or measure; a discussion and consideration by a number of persons of the reasons for and against a measure. (Webster's Third International. Dictionary.) It is the element of the participants trying to reach a decision (whether or not they do so) which distinguishes deliberations from more 'casual' or 'informal' discussions."[43]

Subsection (d) and (e) Deliberations

Excluded from the definition of "meeting" are deliberations under subsections (d) and (e) to determine whether to close a meeting, to withhold information from a meeting notice, to call a meeting on short notice, or to change the time, place, or subject matter of a meeting. The purpose of this exclusion is to avoid an endless chain of meetings to close meetings.[44] Agency deliberations under subsection (f), however, regarding the withholding of portions of the transcript of a closed meeting, are not exempt from the definition of "meeting." If an agency decides not to delegate the withholding decision, its gathering to discuss the matter would come within the definition.[45]

---

43. *See* Appendix F, *infra.*
44. In an unusual case, *Washington Ass'n for Television & Children v. FCC,* 665 F.2d 1264 (D.C. Cir. 1981), the court determined that the FCC's regulation defining "meeting" was impermissibly broad in failing to exclude meetings excluded from the statutory definition as required or permitted by subsection (e). In response to this decision, the FCC adopted changes in 1983 to its definition of "meeting" to exclude meetings whose only order of business is to decide whether to call a future meeting on shorter notice than seven days. *See* 93 F.C.C. 2d 565 (1983).
45. *See also* pp. 161-62, *infra.*

ELECTRONIC COMMUNICATIONS

The revolution in electronic communication, and, in particular, the development of e-mail, has occurred subsequent to the enactment of the Sunshine Act, and could not have been anticipated by the drafters of the Act. The availability of near-instant communication by e-mail raises the question whether such an exchange of communications among a quorum of agency members constitutes a "meeting" within the meaning of the Sunshine Act.[46]

In our view, the mere exchange of e-mails, even among a quorum, would not, in itself, constitute a meeting. Despite the ease and swiftness of transmission, an e-mail is a written communication, and in the agency context more akin to an inter- or intra-office memorandum than to a face-to-face exchange of views. The use of e-mail may facilitate such exchanges outside of the forum of a meeting, but the same may be said of other devices, such as one-on-one discussions, communicating through staff assistants, or notation procedure.[47] However, if we add the element of a "real-time" exchange of views via e-mail, the case becomes harder.

As technology enhances the possibilities for agency members in remote locations to engage in simultaneous or near-simultaneous exchanges of views through electronic means, it seems clear that the definition of "meeting" cannot reasonably be limited to face-to-face encounters in the same room. Indeed, physical presence in a single location has never been the prerequisite for a covered meeting; the drafters of the Sunshine Act specifically contemplated that conference

---

46. There is no question that a conference telephone call qualifies as a meeting. *See* pp. 9, 20 note 33, *supra*, as well as many agency regulations, *e.g.,* Equal Employment Opportunity Commission, 29 C.F.R. § 1612.2(b); Federal Communications Commission, 47 C.F.R. § 0.601(b); and the Federal Deposit Insurance Corporation, 12 C.F.R. § 311.2(b).

47. *Cf.* Republic Airlines v. Civil Aeronautics Board, 756 F.2d 1304, 1319 (8th Cir. 1985) (Circulation by staff of draft agency opinion to agency members and discussion between staff and individual agency members does not violate the Sunshine Act.) Nor would discussion among two agency members when a quorum of the agency is three.

telephone calls would be covered.[48] Most significant would seem to be the temporal element. It must be recalled that a key element of a "meeting" is *joint conduct*—that is, the members are acting together. Are the communications in question made to, or among, a quorum of members more or less simultaneously, and are the members in a position to respond promptly? In other words, is the exchange reasonably "interactive"? If so, and if the subject matter of the exchange otherwise meets the statutory test, we believe such an exchange would constitute a "meeting of the agency."[49]

If such electronic exchanges of communications are not meetings within the statutory definition, nevertheless, there remains the question whether under any circumstances such exchanges might run afoul of the prohibition in section 552b(b) against joint conduct or disposi-

---

48. *See* note 46, *supra*. "The test is what the discussion involves, not where or how it is conducted." S. REP., at 19. It also might be suggested that as writings, these e-mail communications would be subject to the Freedom of Information Act, and that consequently there would be no need to bring them under the Sunshine Act. But as deliberative materials such writings would probably be exempt from disclosure under Exemption 5 of the FOIA.
49. There is a growing body of decisional law dealing with electronic communications under state open meeting laws. The great variation in statutory provisions, as well as in administrative and judicial interpretation, make these state materials of limited value in interpreting the federal Sunshine Act. One article observes that e-mail transmissions are generally treated the same as written documents. *See* Stephen Schaeffer, *Sunshine in Cyberspace? Electronic Deliberation and the Reach of Open Meeting Laws*, 48 ST. LOUIS L. J. 755, 770 (2004). However, there appears to be a strong consensus among the administrative and judicial authorities that, at the least, simultaneous electronic exchanges among a quorum of members either constitute a meeting or are a forbidden means of evading open meeting laws. *See, e.g.*, Claxton Enterprises v Evans County Comm'rs, 249 Ga. App. 870, 875-76, 549 S.E.2d 830, 835 (2001); Del Papa v. Bd. of Regents, 114 Nev. 388, 399-400, 956 P.2d 770, 778 (1998). *See also* Jessica M. Natale, *Exploring Virtual Legal Presence: The Present and the Promise*, 1 J. HIGH TECH. L. 157, 158 (2002) ("The nuances of virtual presence in relation to open-meeting laws' presence requirements [are] causing politicians and the public at large to reevaluate what it means to be present, whether a board member is present by telephoning in votes or teleconferencing or whether a meeting truly is accessible and open to the public if it is conducted online.").

tion of agency business "other than in accordance with this section." In the second ground of its *ITT World* decision the Supreme Court held, or at least strongly implied, that if there was no "agency meeting," that was the end of the inquiry. The Court seemed to rule out any possibility that subsection (b) might restrict forms of joint conduct that fell short of the meeting threshold.[50]

At present the problem seems more theoretical than real. Responding to our survey,[51] the overwhelming majority of agencies reported that the Sunshine Act has had no impact on their members' use of e-mail, although responses from a number of agencies indicated that the Act has had some inhibiting effect. No agency reported, however, any practice of exchanges of views by e-mail among agency members on pending business. Nevertheless, given the manifest advantages of conducting business electronically, it seems inevitable that the problem for the agencies will not be whether a given form of communication constitutes a meeting, but how best to conduct the exchange of communications in compliance with the Sunshine Act.

"MEMBER"

(3) the term "member" means an individual who belongs to a collegial body heading an agency.

The definition of "member" appears self-explanatory, at least with respect to the great majority of agencies. The Federal Election Commission formerly defined the term to include its two *ex officio* non-voting commissioners, the Secretary of the Senate and the Clerk of the House. (These two positions were abolished after they were declared unconstitutional.)[52] However, for purposes of determining the presence of the number of members required to constitute a meeting, the FEC counted only voting members.[53]

---

50. *See* p. 30 note 1, *infra.*
51. *See* Appendix B, *infra.*
52. FEC v. NRA Political Victory Fund, 6 F.3d 821 (D.C. Cir. 1993), *cert. dismissed*, 513 U.S. 88 (1994).
53. 11 C.F.R. § 2.2(d).

Chapter 2

SECTION 552b(b)
CONDUCT OF BUSINESS, PRESUMPTION OF OPENNESS, AND PUBLIC OBSERVATION

"JOINT CONDUCT OR DISPOSITION" OF AGENCY BUSINESS AND THE USE OF "NOTATION PROCEDURE"	30
PRESUMPTION OF OPENNESS AND "PUBLIC OBSERVATION"	39
DEPARTMENT OF JUSTICE 2002 MEMORANDUM TO THE FEDERAL RESERVE BOARD	41
FEDERAL RESERVE PRACTICES	45
OTHER AGENCY PUBLIC OBSERVATION PROCEDURES	46
RIGHT TO RECORD, PHOTOGRAPH, OR TELEVISE OPEN MEETINGS	48
"PUBLIC OBSERVATION" IN POST–SEPTEMBER 11 WASHINGTON, D.C.	49
"VIRTUAL" MEETINGS, TELECONFERENCING, AND PUBLIC OBSERVATION	53
PUBLIC PARTICIPATION	55
PUBLIC UNDERSTANDING	58
ACCESS TO STAFF MEMORANDA AND THE MEANINGFULNESS OF "PUBLIC OBSERVATION"	61

(b) Members shall not jointly conduct or dispose of agency business other than in accordance with this section. Except as provided in subsection (c), every portion of every meeting of an agency shall be open to public observation.

"JOINT CONDUCT OR DISPOSITION" OF AGENCY BUSINESS AND THE USE OF "NOTATION PROCEDURE"

The Department of Justice proposed the prohibition against conducting or disposing of agency business other than in accordance with the Sunshine Act to complement the Department's recommendation that a meeting be defined in terms of its purpose, rather than in terms of what actually occurred.[1] Although the Senate-House Conference

---

1. House Judiciary Hearings, 56. The background of the first sentence of subsection (b) suggests that it was aimed at efforts to evade compliance with the open meetings requirement. The language added by the House Judiciary Committee and adopted in the House bill was: "Members . . . shall not jointly conduct or dispose of agency business without complying with subsections (b) through (g)." The Committee Report (H. REP. 94-880, Part 2, p. 3) stated with respect to this provision, "The new language added as new subparagraph (b)(1) of section 552b would bar the conduct or disposition of agency business other than as provided in subsections (b) through (g) of new section 552b. . . . This provision will bar any effort of the number of members necessary for agency action to deliberate, discuss, conduct, or dispose of agency business other than in an open meeting as provided in new section 552b, or in a closed portion authorized by the exceptions in that section." In explaining this provision on the floor, Congressman Flowers, chairman of the Judiciary Subcommittee that authored it, stated: "The committee also recommended an amendment to subsection (b) to add language providing that agency members cannot jointly conduct or dispose of agency business other than as provided in new section 552b. The amended subsection would not preclude agencies from disposing of noncontroversial matters by written circulations." SOURCE BOOK, 616. Note that this is also the language cited by the court in the *Communications Systems* case discussed *infra* at pp. 31-32.

    Had the first sentence remained in this form in the final bill, it would have presented a serious obstacle to the Supreme Court's second ground for decision in the *ITT World* case, 466 U.S. 463 (1984), because it could be read to prohibit the joint conduct of agency business in forums other than agency meetings. *See* p. 20, *supra*. However, in the Conference Report on the Sunshine Act the provision was put into its present form, ostensibly in order to make more clear that it did not prevent notation voting. "The conference substitute provides that members shall not jointly conduct or dispose of agency business in a meeting other than in accordance with new section

(continued on next page)

Committee on the legislation dropped the purpose test, adopted by the House, the ultimate law retained the prohibition.

The Conference Report makes clear that the prohibition does not prevent agency members from disposing of business by circulation of papers instead of in meetings, and voting on the circulated papers—"notation procedure," Conf. Rep., 11. Relying on this legislative history in one of the earliest cases brought under the Sunshine Act, the court upheld the use of notation procedure. *See Communications Systems, Inc. v. Federal Communications Commission*, 595 F.2d 797, 800-01 (D.C. Cir. 1978) (hereafter *Communications Systems*).

The issue in this case was whether or not the FCC violated the Sunshine Act when it disposed of a reconsideration petition in a broadcast case by the written circulation of an agenda item—a notation procedure—rather than at an agency meeting. The court noted that "because of the scarcity of decisions involving the recently enacted" Sunshine Act, it would consider in some detail the claim by Communications Systems that the FCC violated the Act when it disposed of the reconsideration petition without holding a meeting.[2]

Affirming the FCC's action, the court cited as the "critical" statutory provision 5 U.S.C. § 552(b)(b): "Members shall not *jointly* conduct or dispose of agency business other than in accordance with this section. . . ." The court said it found "this language to be ambiguous, since the *joint* conduct or disposition of agency business could refer to face-to-face communications or conduct that resulted from more remote communications such as circulating written memoranda or voting sheets."[3]

To resolve the statutory ambiguity, the court turned to the legislative history of the "critical language," "joint conduct or disposition."[4]

(continued from previous page)
552b. This prohibition does not prevent agency members from considering individually business that is circulated to them sequentially in writing." *Quaere* whether the Conference Report's language change turned this provision into a meaningless redundancy. The Supreme Court's opinion in the *ITT World* case seems to conclude that it did. *See also* text accompanying note 50, *supra* pp. 27-28.
2. *Communications Systems*, *supra*, 595 F.2d at 798.
3. *Id.* at 799.
4. *Id.* at 801.

Quoting former Congressman Walter Flowers (D-Ala.), who offered the original language, the court noted that the "amended subsection would not preclude agencies from disposing of noncontroversial matters by written circulation."[5] The court also cited the Conference Committee Report, which states that the general prohibition against members jointly conducting or disposing of agency business other than in a meeting "does not prevent agency members from considering individually business that is circulated to them sequentially in writing."[6]

The court concluded that:

> [it] thus clearly appears from the legislative history that Congress intended to permit agency members to act on agency business that is circulated to them sequentially in writing. The FCC was therefore not in violation of the Sunshine Act . . . when it used its notation procedure to dispose of Communications Systems' petition.
>
> This interpretation of the Sunshine Act is consistent with Congress's desire to open up the federal decision-making process "while protecting . . . the ability of the government to carry out its responsibilities." Notation voting enables government agencies to expedite consideration of less controversial cases without formal meetings and following the other strictures of the Act. If all agency actions required meetings, then the entire administrative process would be slowed perhaps to a standstill. Certainly, requiring an agency to meet and discuss every trivial item on its agenda would delay consideration of the more serious issues that require joint face-to-face deliberation. Clearly, Congress did not intend such a result. We accordingly affirm the action of the Commission.[7]

Since this 1978 decision, the courts have repeatedly upheld federal agencies against challenges to their use of notation procedure instead of open meetings to "jointly conduct or dispose of agency business." *See, e.g., Pacific Legal Foundation v. Council on Environ-*

---

5. *Id., citing* 122 CONG. REC. H 7871.
6. *Id., citing* Conf. Rep. (H. REP. No. 94-1441; S. REP. No. 94-1178), 94th Cong., 2d Sess. 11 (1976) (hereafter Conf. Rep.).
7. *Communications Systems, supra* note 2 at 800-01 (citation omitted).

mental Quality, 636 F.2d 1259, 1266 (D.C. Cir. 1980) (hereafter *Pacific Legal Foundation*); *National Ass'n of Broadcasters v. Copyright Royalty Tribunal*, 675 F.2d 367, 385 (D.C. Cir. 1982); *Railroad Comm'n of Texas v. United States*, 765 F.2d 221, 230-31 (D.C. Cir. 1985); *Amrep Corp. v. Federal Trade Comm'n*, 768 F.2d 1171, 1178 (10th Cir. 1985), cert. denied, 475 U.S. 1034 (1986); *Republic Airlines v. Civil Aeronautics Board*, 756 F.2d 1304, 1319 (8th Cir. 1985); and *Elkem Metals Co. et al. v. United States*, 126 F. Supp. 2d 5672, 5675 (C.I.T. 2000).

At the same time, the widespread agency use of notation procedure has been widely cited as one of the major unintended consequences or "costs" of the Sunshine Act.[8] A leading study of the Act,

---

8. *See, e.g.*, Kathy Bradley, *Do You Feel the Sunshine? Government in the Sunshine Act: Its Objective Goals and Effect on the FCC and You*, 49 FED. COMM. L. J. 473 (Feb. 1997) (hereafter Bradley) (discussing how the GISA "has not come without significant costs," for example, "a decrease in collegial decisionmaking, staff level decisions, and increased notational voting, outweigh[ing] the benefits of the Act in fostering public understanding." *See also* James T. O'Reilly & Gracia M. Berg, *Stealth Caused by Sunshine: How Sunshine Act Interpretation Results in Less Information for the Public About the Decision-Making Process of the International Trade Commission*, 36 HARV. INT'L L. J. 425, 430 n.22 (Spring 1995) ("The Commissioners in fact do note 'vote' at the public session. The legally operative vote occurs by 'Action Jacket,' a form of written sequential voting. While this type of voting is permitted, it does not provide any information to the public.") (citations omitted); Jennifer A. Bensch, *Government in the Sunshine Act–Seventeen Years Later: Has Government Let the Sun Shine In?*, 61 GEO. WASH. L. REV. 1475, 1484 n.59 (June 1993) (hereafter Bensch) (Quotes a former Chairman of the Council of the Section of Administrative Law of the American Bar Association that the Sunshine Act "may well have diminished the collegial character of agency decision-making, created a reluctance of agency members even to discuss certain important agency matters, and shifted the decision-making process to one-on-one discussions between members, exchanging views at the staff level, and . . . by written memoranda." William E. Murane, *Chairman's Message*, 37 ADMIN. L. REV. at v (1985)). For contrary views in defense of the Sunshine Act against these concerns, see S. REP. 101-54, 101st Cong., 1st Sess., *Government in the Sunshine Act: History and Recent Issues—A Report of the Committee on Governmental Affairs, United States Senate, November 1989* (hereafter 1989 S. REP.); and (former Senator) Lawton Chiles, *The Sunshine Act Does Too Work*, Op. Ed., WASHINGTON POST, Aug. 4, 1983, at A21 (hereafter Chiles).

for example, done in 1984 for the former Administrative Conference of the United States (ACUS) by Professors David Welborn, William Lyons, and Larry Thomas, found that since enactment of the Government in Sunshine Act in 1977, there had been "a shift in patterns of decision-making behavior, at least in a number of agencies, away from collegial processes toward segmented, individualized processes in which, in the words of one commissioner," members are "isolated" from one another. One reason is a decline in the importance of meetings as "decisional vehicles" and instead "an increase in notation voting" "perceived by more than half (54 percent) of agency respondents" to a questionnaire sent out by the authors.[9] Professor Welborn and his colleagues attributed some of the increase in notation procedure to an agency desire "to dispose of minor items previously handled in meetings in order to avoid the red tape involved in including them on a meeting agenda."[10] But they also attributed a substantial part of the increase to "an aversion to public discussion of certain topics."[11] Similarly, some agencies responding to a 1986 survey of agency Sunshine Act practices by the Congressional Research Service acknowledged that they used notation voting for other than routine issues.[12] It should

---

9. See David M. Welborn, William Lyons & Larry Thomas, *Implementation and Effects of the Federal Government in the Sunshine Act*, Background Report for Recommendation 84-3, *Improvements in the Administration of the Government in the Sunshine Act*, in 1984 RECOMMENDATIONS AND REPORTS OF THE ADMINISTRATIVE CONFERENCE OF THE UNITED STATES 199, 236 (hereafter Welborn Report). *See also* Appendix G, *infra,* and JACOB A. STEIN, GLENN A. MITCHELL, & BASIL J. MEZINES, ADMINISTRATIVE LAW, Vol. 2 (Matthew Bender & Co., 1994). This treatise reprints both the Welborn Report at App. 7D-1-87 and the *1978 Guide* at App. 7G-1-149.
10. *Id.*
11. *Id.*
12. *See* Rogelio Garcia, *Government in the Sunshine: Public Access to Meetings Held Under the Government in the Sunshine Act, 1979-1984*, CONGRESSIONAL RESEARCH SERVICE REPORT, May 7, 1986, at 13 (hereafter CRS Report). For example, the National Mediation Board reported that it used notation procedure for a "substantial portion of agency business" "in lieu of a more formalized and time-consuming joint deliberative process"; the National Transportation Safety Board used the procedure "for all issues except major accident reports and special studies"; while the Nuclear Regulatory

(continued on next page)

be noted, however, that some agencies used notation voting for non-routine matters even before enactment of the Sunshine Act.[13]

In a February 1995 letter on Sunshine Act reform to the Chairperson of the ACUS, Thomasina Rogers, then SEC Commissioner Steven M.H. Wallman, joined by 11 other then current or former agency members, as well as the general counsel of the AFL-CIO, and a senior litigator with Public Citizen, Inc., noted that:

> [I]n order to avoid the notice and other procedural requirements of the Act, agencies are now more likely to vote on agency agenda matters by "notation" or "seriatim" rather than in open meetings. While the use of notational voting may nevertheless be more appropriate than a vote at an open meeting in certain instances, this method of conducting agency business is not effective in achieving the Act's goal of enhancing the public's understanding of agency decision making, and precludes the benefits that obtain from agency member collective deliberation.[14]

(continued from previous page)
Commission reported it used the procedure for matters that "normally do not have far-reaching implications," including "issues that by law require formal vote in open meeting but that are not sufficiently complex matters requiring discussion." *Id.* at 13-14. Note, however, that none of the cases cited above upheld the use of notation procedure for non-routine, significant matters.

13. One of the earliest commentaries on the Sunshine Act that was published the month the Act became effective in March 1977 also expressed concern about the Act increasing "the already common practice of many agencies to conduct business on paper—by commissioners initialing memos—rather than meeting together to decide" issues. See Thomas Fitzhugh, *Agencies Brace for Litigation Under New Sunshine Act*, N.Y. L. J. Mar. 1, 1977, at 1, cited by Stephen H. Klitzman, *Government in the Sunshine Act—Nuts, Bolts, and Tacks: A Summary of Statutory Provisions, Judicial Interpretations, and Pending Issues*, 38 FED. B. J. 114, 126 (Fall 1979).

14. *See* Appendix H, *infra*, *Letter from Steven M.H. Wallman, Commissioner, Securities and Exchange Commission, to Thomasina Rogers, Chairperson, Administrative Conference of the United States*, Feb. 17, 1995, p. 6 (hereafter Wallman Letter). Other agency officials signing the letter included the Chairman and four other Commissioners of the Federal Communications Commission, the Chairman and another Commissioner of the SEC, Commissioners

(continued on next page)

In an August 2001 letter to the authors, the then Associate Director, Records & Information Management, U.S. Merit Systems Protection Board, noted that:

> [t]he Sunshine Act has greatly increased the use of notational voting at the Board and has resulted in a decrease in the number of meetings held by the Board members over the years. When the Board came into being in 1979 regular Board meetings were held to consider the adjudication of cases. However, after a time these regular meetings became impractical due at least in part to the requirements of the Sunshine Act.[15]

Whether or not it is true that the increased use of notation voting "is yet another sign that the collegial process has broken down to a great extent under the Act,"[16] it is undoubtedly true that with a solid foundation in the legislative history of the statute, repeated affirmances by the courts, and its highly practical use for the conduct of routine agency business, notational voting procedure will continue to be widely used by Sunshine-affected agencies.[17]

(continued from previous page)
from the Commodity Futures Trading Commission and the Federal Trade Commission, and former Commissioners from the SEC, as well as the General Counsel of the AFL-CIO and a senior litigator from Public Citizen. Among other points, these officials and private-sector lawyers recommended to a special ACUS committee reviewing the Government in the Sunshine Act that agencies be given more flexibility to close meetings in exchange for reducing or eliminating reliance on notation voting. *See* Appendix H, *infra*.

15. Letter from Michael H. Hoxie, former associate director, Records & Information Management, U.S. Merit Systems Protection Board, to Stephen Klitzman, Aug. 8, 2001, p. 2. *See also* 64 COMP. GEN. 728, 736 (1985) (United States Comptroller General expressed concern about the use of notation procedure by the former Interstate Commerce Commission: "While the Government in the Sunshine Act does not bar use of notation voting and meetings should not be required for routine or trivial agency actions, we are concerned that only a small number of meetings have been held to consider cases that the ICC identifies as 'significant.'").
16. *See* Bradley, *supra* note 8, at 482.
17. *See, e.g.,* e-mail from Janis A. Kaye, senior attorney-adviser, Federal Housing Finance Board (FHFB), to Stephen Klitzman, Aug. 9, 2001, noting that in

(continued on next page)

Section 552b(b):
Conduct of Business, Presumption of Openness, and Public Observation

Nonetheless, we continue to believe, as we noted in the *1978 Guide*, that to comply with the spirit of the Sunshine Act, agencies should refrain from excessive reliance on notation procedure,[18] espe-

---

(continued from previous page)
June 1995 the FHFB adopted notational voting for "routine procedural or administrative matters." Res. No. 95-06 (June 29, 1995); and letter from Steven A. Bartholow, general counsel, Railroad Retirement Board, to Stephen Klitzman, July 20, 2001, reporting that the only modification the Board has made to its original Sunshine Act regulations is "to authorize the use of sequential circulation and notational voting to conduct agency business . . . to provide a workable and expeditious method of handling some of the more routine business of the agency. . . ."

18. In a footnote at the end of its decision, the court in *Communications Systems, supra* p.31 note 2, 595 F.2d at 801 n.8, in upholding notation procedure, cited the guidance of the Guide about avoiding "excessive reliance on notation procedure." However, the court stated it "need not address this issue because nothing in the record indicates that this case deserved any greater FCC consideration than it received." *Id.* At least one court, however, has suggested there are limits to the use of notation procedure. *See* Trans World Airlines v. National Mediation Board, 1982 WL 2077 (D.D.C. 1982) (". . . an agency may not use its power to develop internal decisional or advisory systems to avoid the need for meetings and thus to subvert the open meeting requirement," though adding that "the Sunshine Act does not require an agency to take actions like those the Board took in this case only through meetings"). Citing *Communications Systems, supra* note 2, in comparison with *Pacific Legal Foundation, supra* p. 32, 636 F.2d at 1266, the court went on to state:

> The Sunshine Act requires access to Board meetings which occur, and no court should countenance changes in Board practice to hold piecemeal meetings which, but for the Act, would have been conducted at one sitting. But the Act does not require the Board to convene to transact business which is routinely conducted on staff initiative with board advice. Unlike the agency defendant in *Pacific Legal Foundation*, the Board has not attempted to avoid the statute by a restrictive regulatory definition of "meetings." And, as in *Communications Systems,* the court could not find a violation of the Act in the facts of this case without seriously jeopardizing agency self-management.

1982 WL 2077, at 5 (D.D.C. 1982). Moreover, the authors do not know of any case in which a court has actually attempted to second-guess an agency on the use of notation procedure, and such a result seems highly unlikely.

cially where, as the Welborn and CRS studies documented, it is used to dispose of more than routine, substantive agency business.[19]

Encouraged by congressional oversight demands,[20] or on their own initiative, a number of agencies have already adopted various procedural protections to ensure that notation procedure is not used to dispose of non-routine items that should be addressed in a meeting. For example, a number of agencies provide that any member can request that an item circulated for consideration by notation procedure be placed on the agenda of an agency meeting and decided instead by joint deliberation.[21] A number of agencies using notation voting procedures

---

19. *See* Welborn Report, *supra* note 9; CRS Report, *supra* note 12.
20. *See, e.g., Supplemental Information Requested by Congressional Subcommittees to be Included in Agency Annual Reports*, Appendix III to 1989 S. REP., *supra* note 8, at 56. This "supplemental information" included among 22 items a description of each agency's notation procedure and discussion of the "public availability of records involved in reaching decisions by notation procedure (record of notational vote, circulated written materials that provide the basis of the vote, and any other methods employed to explain reasoning of decisions reached through notational voting"). But note that the Sunshine Act annual reports are no longer required. *See* pp. 230-31, *infra.*
21. *See, e.g.,* regulations of the Federal Trade Commission, 16 C.F.R. § 4.14(a), the Securities and Exchange Commission, 17 C.F.R. § 200.42(b), and the U.S. Parole Commission, 28 C.F.R. § 16.201(b), all of which allow any member to direct that an item circulated for consideration and voting by notation procedure be placed instead on the agenda of any agency meeting for joint deliberation. *See also* CRS Report, *supra* note 12, which states that eight agencies reported having such a procedure, and the 1994 Sunshine Act Annual Report of the National Transportation Safety Board, which notes that whenever a member has a question about a circulated item of Board business, the member can request "it be calendared for a Board meeting so that all Members may have the benefit of his or her views." Letter from Jim Hall, Chairman, National Transportation Safety Board, to Honorable Albert Gore, Jr., President of the Senate, to accompany NTSB Sunshine Act Annual Report for calendar year 1994.

Note, however, that the ability to move a notation item to a meeting agenda would be no procedural protection if all the members of an agency conspired to circumvent the Sunshine Act by handling even non-routine matters by notation procedure. To date, the authors are unaware of any such occurrence, but it nonetheless remains a possibility that agency Offices of General Counsel should seek to prevent.

also make available to the public information about the vote and the issue, including minutes, resolutions, and even circulated written material prepared by the staff, unless it is exempt under the Freedom of Information Act.[22]

PRESUMPTION OF OPENNESS AND "PUBLIC OBSERVATION"

The second sentence of subsection (b) is intended to establish a presumption of openness. It states that "except as provided in subsection (c) [the exemptions subsection], every portion of every meeting shall be open to public observation." 5 U.S.C. § 552b(b).[23] Neither the Act nor the legislative history, however, defines "public observation."[24]

When it was enacted in March 1976, the Sunshine Act clearly contemplated open, live meetings with agency members and the public in the same room. Nobody in 1976 was thinking of diverting the public

---

22. See CRS Report, *supra* note 12. *See, e.g.*, regulation of the Federal Trade Commission, 16 C.F.R. § 4.9(b)(1)(ii), which requires votes by commissioners to be placed on the public record "in all matters of public record, including matters of public record decided by notational voting."
23. S. Rep., 19; H. Rep. I, at 12-13; H. Rep. II, at 12. *See also* "declaration of policy" in section 2 of the Government in the Sunshine Act. For case discussion of this presumption of openness, *see* Pan American World Airways, Inc. v. Civil Aeronautics Board, 684 F.2d 31, 35 (D.C. Cir. 1982) ("Section 552b(b) establishes a broad presumption that meetings *shall be open*, not a mere requirement that the Board accede to requests that it open its meeting. Section 552b(h)(1), moreover, dictates that when and if judicial review takes place *the agency* has the burden of sustaining its action to close a meeting. Congress has demanded that agencies open their decisionmaking processes to public scrutiny; no further demand is necessary" (emphases added). *See also* Public Citizen v. National Economic Comm'n, 703 F. Supp. 113, 125 (D.D.C. 1989), *citing* Common Cause v. NRC, 674 F.2d 921, 928 (D.C. Cir. 1982).
24. A few agencies define the term. *See, e.g.*, regulations of the Federal Deposit Insurance Corporation, 12 C.F.R. § 311.2(d), and the Board of Governors, Federal Reserve System, 12 C.F.R. § 261b.2(f). Other agencies provide guidelines for public observers, *see, e.g.*, a notice of the Federal Trade Commission, 42 Fed. Reg. 13,357; or set forth more detailed rules of conduct for public observers, *see, e.g.*, regulations of the National Commission on Libraries and Information Science, 45 C.F.R. § 1703.302, the U.S. Postal Service, 39 C.F.R. § 232.6, and the Legal Services Corporation, 45 C.F.R. § 1622.2.

into a separate room from agency commissioners, requiring the public to get pre-meeting security clearances, meetings at locations "remote" from agency headquarters, or even holding "virtual" meetings entirely by telephone or teleconferencing.[25]

In contrast, the Senate Report on the Act described the substance of the open meeting requirement as follows:

> When a meeting must be open, the agency should make arrangements for a room large enough to accommodate a reasonable number of persons interested in attending. Holding a meeting in a small room, thereby denying access to most of the public, would violate this section and be contrary to its clear intent.
>
> Nothing in subsection [(b)] requires an agency to permit the public to actively participate in the meeting. Other statutes and agency regulations and policies continue to govern such participation. Section [552b] only gives the public the right to attend meetings, to listen and to observe.

S. Rep., 19.

Similarly, the Conference Report on the Act noted that "the phrase 'open to public observation,' while not affording the public any additional right to participate in a meeting, is intended to guarantee that ample space, sufficient visibility, and adequate acoustics will be provided."[26]

The *1978 Guide* noted that "while agencies may not defeat the open meeting requirement by holding meetings in facilities which are remote or inadequate for public observation, neither are they required to guarantee adequate accommodation for everyone who wishes to attend."[27] The *1978 Guide* further noted that:

> To the extent that openness has a therapeutic purpose, that purpose can be adequately served if *some* members of the public are present, particularly if they include representatives of the news media. Although it is doubtful that agencies can

---

25. In post-9/11 Washington, D.C., however, these procedures are all, or are fast becoming, realities. *See* pp. 49-55, *infra*.
26. *See* Conf. Rep., *supra* note 6, at 11.
27. *See 1978 Guide*, at 14.

require notice in advance as a condition for attendance, it seems reasonable for agencies to request such notice in order to be better able to gauge the need for public accommodations, and, where seating is limited, to seat first those who have given notice of their intention to attend[28] (emphasis in original).

DEPARTMENT OF JUSTICE 2002 MEMORANDUM TO THE FEDERAL RESERVE BOARD

Consistent with this 1978 guidance but exceeding it is a 2002 memorandum on "public observation" the Office of Legal Counsel, Department of Justice, sent to the General Counsel for the Board of Governors of the Federal Reserve System[29] [hereafter Justice Memo]. In April 2002, the General Counsel asked two questions in a letter to the Department of Justice: Consistent with the Sunshine Act, first, could the Board "place all members of the public who wish to observe an open meeting of the Board in a room that is physically separate from the meeting room, where they can observe and listen to the meeting by closed-circuit television?" Second, could the Board "screen all members of the public seeking entrance to a Board building to observe an open meeting of the Board, by obtaining personal information and conducting a security check, and refuse admission to those who either refuse to give the information or fail the security check?"[30]

The Office of Legal Counsel in its response concluded that "it would be permissible under both the Sunshine Act and the Privacy Act for the Board to engage in these actions."[31] With regard to placing the

---

28. *Id. See, e.g.,* regulations of the Commodity Credit Corporation, 7 C.F.R. § 1409.6(g), and the U.S. Foreign Claims Settlement Commission, 45 C.F.R. § 504.21.
29. *See* Appendix J, *infra,* for *Memorandum for J. Virgil Mattingly, Jr., General Counsel for the Board of Governors of the Federal Reserve System Re: Permissibility of Federal Reserve Board Efforts to Control Access to Buildings and Open Meetings,* from M. Edward Whelan III, Principal Deputy Assistant Attorney General, July 9, 2002.
30. *Id. See also* Appendix K, *infra,* for *Letter from J. Virgil Mattingly, Jr., General Counsel for the Board of Governors of the Federal Reserve System,* to Paul Colborn, Esq., Special Counsel, Department of Justice, Office of Legal Counsel, April 10, 2002.
31. *See* note 29, *supra.*

public in a separate room from the agency members, the Justice Memo concludes that "[p]lacing members of the public in a large enough separate room with adequate closed-circuit television capability would satisfy" the "open to public observation" requirement of the Act. The Memo noted that:

> Since the public is not authorized to participate in the meeting, there is nothing inherent in the concept of "open to public observation" that would obligate [an agency] to place members of the public in the same room as the [agency members]. As long as the public can adequately see, hear, and understand what takes place in the meeting, the requirement will have been met because the meeting would be "open to public observation."[32]

The Justice Memo also lends support to another meeting access procedure most Sunshine agencies are not currently using—requiring members of the public to satisfy a security check as a condition to attend an agency meeting. For example, the Memo concludes that it would be permissible under both the Sunshine and Privacy Acts for an agency to "screen all members of the public seeking entrance to [an agency] to observe an open meeting, by obtaining personal information and conducting a security check and refus[ing] admission to those who either refuse to give the information or fail the security check."[33]

The Justice Memo notes that whether an agency may deny an individual access to its building to observe an open meeting "turns on whether the Sunshine Act provides each member of the public with a right to observe an open meeting of a covered agency."[34] Interpreting the key

---

32. *Id.* at 2-3.
33. *Id.* at 1. The White House, Department of the Treasury, and the Pentagon currently have such clearance procedures to control access to their buildings. But with the exception of the Federal Reserve Board, and perhaps a few others, the bulk of the independent regulatory agencies with whom the authors have spoken do not now use such clearance procedures. However, most Sunshine agencies in these more security-conscious times do require individuals who want to attend open agency meetings to obtain a Visitor's Pass after providing appropriate identification, to go through metal detectors and x-ray machines, and in some cases to be escorted into the agency's Meeting Room. *See* p. 46, *infra*.
34. Justice Memo, at 3.

statutory language of "open to public observation," the Memo does not believe that the Act grants "a right to individuals to attend agency meetings, but rather is articulated in more general language obligating an agency to provide the public as a whole with the opportunity to observe meetings. . . . The requirement is satisfied if members of the general public have the opportunity to attend the meeting. The language does not constitute a requirement that *all* members of the public, or any particular individuals, who wish to observe a meeting be allowed to do so. . . . [A]lthough the public as a whole is entitled to observe [open agency] meetings, particular individuals can be turned away. . . . 'Open to public observation' is [therefore only] a requirement that the meeting be open to the public at large . . . " (emphasis in original).

Echoing the interpretive guidance in the *1978 Guide* noted above, the Justice Memo also cites legislative history of the Act to support its interpretation of "open to public observation." "That history," it notes, "does not reveal any congressional intent to create a right for every individual to attend" open agency meetings. Moreover, the Memo notes that "Congress used the phrase 'open to public observation' to address logistical concerns: it wanted *adequate* space to accommodate meeting observers. The legislative history indicates that an agency is not required under the Act to guarantee that every person who seeks to attend a meeting may do so, so long as accommodation for a reasonable number of people is provided." *See* S. REP. No. 94-354, at 19 ("When a meeting must be open, the agency should make arrangements for a room large enough to accommodate a *reasonable* number of persons interested in attending. Holding a meeting in a small room, thereby denying access to most of the public, would violate this section and be contrary to its clear intent.") (emphasis added).[35]

The July 2002 Justice Memo also disputes sharply a portion of a 1977 letter the head of the Civil Division in the Justice Department in the Carter Administration sent to all Sunshine agencies shortly after enactment of the Sunshine Act in 1976.[36] The 1977 letter stated in part

---

35. *Id.* at 4.
36. *See* Appendix E, *infra, Department of Justice Letter to Covered Agencies*, April 19, 1977. The letter was sent by Barbara Babcock, Assistant Attorney General, Civil Division. It raised three issues with the Sunshine agencies: the definition of "meeting," the definition of "public observation," and opening meetings "to the fullest extent practicable."

that "*[o]f course,* any person may attend a meeting without indicating his identity and/or the person, if any, whom he represents and no requirement of prior notification of intent to observe a meeting may be required"[37] (emphasis added). However, the 2002 Justice Memo notes that the Department now finds "nothing in the text of the Sunshine Act that precludes imposing such requirements."[38] Nor does the Department now "see anything in the legislative history that suggests such an effect."[39]

To the contrary, the 2002 Memo argues that "the open meeting requirement of the Sunshine Act does not provide all individuals with the right to observe a covered agency's meetings, but rather only imposes on the agency the obligation to hold open meetings—that is, meetings open to the public at large." The Memo therefore concludes that "it would be permissible under the Sunshine Act for [agencies] to require that individuals seeking to observe [open] meetings must provide personal information and satisfy a security check."[40]

The Justice Memo goes on to note that "[n]othing in the Sunshine Act . . . provides any particular member of the public with a right to observe an agency meeting. All the Act does is require the agency to open its deliberative meetings to public observation. The denial of access to an individual who fails to provide a social security number or pass the security check may prevent that particular person from observing the meeting, but it does not foreclose the public observation of the meeting by other members of the public who provide their social security numbers and pass the security check."[41]

Therefore, the Justice Memo concludes that "[agencies] may, consistent with [their] obligations under the Sunshine Act, place observers of an open meeting of the [agency] in a separate room to watch the meeting on closed-circuit television." The Memo further concludes "that it is permissible under both the Sunshine Act and the Privacy Act for [agencies] or [the Board] to require disclosure of personal information and satisfaction of a security check as a condition of entering

---

37. *Id.*
38. Justice Memo, at 4 n.4.
39. *Id.*
40. *Id.* at 5.
41. *Id.*

[an agency's] building for access to the separate room to observe the open meeting."[42]

FEDERAL RESERVE PRACTICES

Notwithstanding the Justice Memo, the Board of Governors of the Federal Reserve System has decided not to place the public in a separate room from the members of the Board of Governors.[43] However, in August 2002 the Board did adopt new procedures for persons wishing to attend an open Board meeting. These new procedures include: providing name, social security number or passport number, and date of birth, and going through a security check using information provided before admittance to the Board building; pre-registering either using a link provided in the meeting announcement notice or by leaving the information on a special voice mail, or providing this information directly to security, but having to wait until the security check is complete before they will be admitted to the building; entering through "Security Control" on the 20th Street entrance [of the Board]; searching attendees' bags and packages; passing through a security scanner; being escorted from Security Control to the Boardroom; wearing a special badge provided by security at all times; and attendees being escorted out of the building.[44] In contrast, prior to these more complicated access procedures, attendees at Federal Reserve Board meetings "could arrive at the C Street entrance, provide a picture ID and security would issue them a badge and send them to the Boardroom

---

42. *Id.* at 6.
43. Telephone interview of Michael O'Rourke, Counsel, Legal Division (hereafter *O'Rourke Interview*), Federal Reserve Board of Governors, by Stephen Klitzman, July 7, 2004. However, the Board has adopted new procedures for the "seating of [the] public in [the] Board room: the public will now only be allowed in the rows of chairs between the two back doors of the Board room. They will no longer be able to sit up around the lower side of the Board table. [The] public will no longer be given a copy of the Board table seating chart. The Board members will be identified only by the nameplates on the Board table. At all open Board meetings, there will be additional security personnel in attendance." *Id. See also* Appendix L, *A Guide to the Meetings of the Board of Governors of the Federal Reserve System* (2004).
44. See *O'Rourke Interview, supra* note 43.

unescorted."[45] The language on the Federal Reserve Board Sunshine notice announcing an open meeting has also been changed to reflect the new, more detailed access procedures.[46]

OTHER AGENCY PUBLIC OBSERVATION PROCEDURES

The public observation procedures of other Sunshine agencies are less stringent than the procedures approved by the Justice Memo. For example, a number of agencies only require individuals who want to attend open agency meetings to obtain a Visitors Pass after providing appropriate identification, to go through metal detectors and x-ray machines, and in some cases, to be escorted into the agency's meeting room.[47]

These agencies also provide the public an opportunity to observe an open meeting on closed-circuit TV in an agency "overflow" room, but only if the main meeting room is full. "We don't turn any people away from our meetings," said Ron Battocchi, general counsel, National Transportation Safety Board.[48] Like the Federal Reserve Board, none of the agencies the authors contacted go as far as the Justice Memo sanctions for security reasons by placing *all* members of the public in a room separate from the meeting room to observe the meeting on a closed-circuit TV.

David Dickey, former assistant general counsel, FERC, said "We do not broadcast our open meetings into a separate room just to avoid possible disruptions by the public." James Morris, senior counsel, Farm Credit Administration, said he thought to place all of the public in a separate room apart from the main meeting room as approved by the Justice Memo, although technically permissible under the Sunshine Act and its legislative history, might undermine the spirit and the "fundamental policy of the Act" to open agency deliberations to "public

---

45. *Id.*
46. *Id.*
47. *See* telephone interviews by Stephen Klitzman, May 23, 2003, of David Dickey, former assistant general counsel, Federal Energy Regulatory Commission; James Morris, senior counsel, Farm Credit Administration; Chris White, deputy general counsel, Federal Trade Commission; Trip Rothschild, assistant general counsel, Nuclear Regulatory Commission; and Ron Battocchi, general counsel, National Transportation Safety Board.
48. *Id.*

observation" and to offer the public "reasonable accommodations" to observe such open deliberations. Such complete physical separation of public and members might also damage the agency's public relations image and reality. Morris added that viewing open agency meetings solely on closed-circuit TV should be permissible only if the public receives a complete audio and video transmission of the meeting as it is happening and is able to see, hear, and understand each agency member individually as well as interacting with one another.[49]

Nor do the agencies we contacted, other than the Federal Reserve Board, go as far as the Justice Memo would allow and require each individual who wants to attend an open meeting to submit his or her Social Security number and to pass a security check.[50]

With regard to handling actual disruption in a meeting room, these agencies agreed it would be consistent with the Sunshine Act to use regular agency security guards as well as special, additional Federal Protective Service guards, if necessary, to remove disruptive members of the public from the meeting room and agency buildings and even temporarily to adjourn open meetings until such disruptive persons are so removed.[51]

Finally, none of the agencies the authors contacted believe it would be consistent with the letter and the spirit of the Sunshine Act for an agency to divert all the public, or only certain persons, to a separate viewing room solely on the basis of their personal status as "non-frequent visitors," "non-industry," or "non-attorney," or on the basis of their support or opposition to any pending, controversial item of agency business, such as the media ownership deregulation decided by the Federal Communications Commission at its open meeting on June 2, 2003.[52]

---

49. *Id.*
50. *Id.*
51. *Id.*
52. *Id. See 2002 Biennial Regulatory Review, Report and Order and Notice of Proposed Rule Making*, 18 F.C.C. Rcd. 13,620 (2003), *aff'd in part and remanded in part;* Prometheus Radio Project, et al. v. FCC, 373 F.3d 372 (3d Cir. 2004). *See also* discussion of We the People, Inc. of the United States v. Nuclear Regulatory Comm'n, 746 F. Supp. 213 (D.D.C. 1990) at p. 55, *infra* (hereafter *We the People, Inc.*). (An agency cannot make distinctions in terms of access to, or participation in, an agency meeting on the basis of the party's position on an issue.)

RIGHT TO RECORD, PHOTOGRAPH, OR TELEVISE OPEN MEETINGS

The Sunshine Act does not specifically confer any right to record, photograph, or televise an open meeting. As the *1978 Guide* noted, "It remains an open question whether the right to do so in a manner which does not disrupt or interfere with the meeting is a concomitant of the right of observation."[53]

As a result, one question on which the agencies remain divided, though less so than in 1978, is whether to permit the public or press to photograph, televise or tape record meetings. The Federal Communications Commission will permit use of tape recorders and cameras (no flashbulbs);[54] the Equal Employment Opportunity Commission will permit still photographs (no flashbulbs) at the beginning of the meeting and use of portable sound recorders during the meeting;[55] the U.S. Postal Service,[56] the Postal Rate Commission,[57] and the Federal Deposit Insurance Corporation[58] will permit use of tape recorders and cameras if they are not disruptive. The Board of Governors, Federal Reserve System,[59] the U.S. Parole Commission,[60] and the Nuclear Regulatory Commission[61] are among the agencies that require permission in advance for use of recorders or cameras.[62] The Federal Energy Regulatory Commission[63] authorizes recording and photogra-

---

53. *1978 Guide*, at 15.
54. 42 Fed. Reg. 12,865 (FCC).
55. 29 C.F.R. § 1612.3(d) (EEOC).
56. 39 C.F.R. § 7.2(c) (USPS).
57. 39 C.F.R. § 3001.43(a)(2) (PRC).
58. 12 C.F.R. § 303.11 (FDIC).
59. 12 C.F.R. § 261b.2(f) (Fed. Reserve).
60. 28 C.F.R. § 16.202(b) (Parole Commission).
61. 10 C.F.R. § 9.103 (NRC).
62. "In recent years, as a result of improvements in recording technology and increased familiarity with the presence of photographers at meetings, the Secretary [of the SEC] has routinely waived the advance notice and approval requirements for all types of photography or recordings" of SEC meetings. Memorandum from Richard A. Levine and C. Hunter Jones to Phillip D. Parker, Jan. 3, 1995 (hereafter Levine-Jones Memo).
63. 18 C.F.R. § 375.203(b)(2) (FERC).

phy of its meetings under specific procedural requirements, while the Overseas Private Investment Corporation[64] notes that the public "may not participate or record any of the discussions by means of electronic or other devices or cameras."

"PUBLIC OBSERVATION" IN POST–SEPTEMBER 11 WASHINGTON, D.C.

In the aftermath of the terrorist attacks of September 11, 2001, Sunshine agencies have had to consider how the security requirements of the "war on terrorism," including the Department of Homeland Security's system of color-coded threat levels—green for "low risk," blue for "guarded risk," yellow for "elevated risk," orange for "high risk," and red for "severe risk"—can be reconciled with their obligations under the Sunshine Act.[65] They have also begun to reconsider the implementation of the Act and its impact on their daily operations. Enhanced pre-meeting security checks and moving the public to separate meeting observation rooms, as discussed above, are only two of the alternative procedures Sunshine Act agencies have been considering to handle public observation of agency meetings during periods of elevated security concerns. Other special procedures include meetings of agency members at "remote locations," pursuant to an agency "Continuity of Operations Plan," or "COOP," vesting all emergency authority in an agency chairman, thus exempting the agency from the collegial authority and requirements of the Sunshine Act during the life of the emergency, and totally "virtual" meetings of Sunshine Act

---

64. 22 C.F.R. § 708.2 (OPIC). However, OPIC in recent years allows the public to record the open portions of each of the approximately four meetings a year of the OPIC members. Telephone interview by Stephen Klitzman of Connie M. Downs, corporate secretary, OPIC, July 16, 2004. Under state law, "conditions to attendance are dimly viewed, as are restrictions on photography, recording, or broadcasting" open meetings. At the same time, "disorderly conduct by attendees is not tolerated." James H. Cawley, *Sunshine Law Overexposure and the Demise of Independent Agency Collegiality*, 1 WIDENER J. PUB. L. 43, at 58-59 (1992) (hereafter Cawley).
65. *But see* John Mintz, *DHS Considers Alternatives to Color-Coded Warnings*, WASHINGTON POST, May 10, 2005, at A-6 (Department of Homeland Security may change the color-coded threat advisory system to one based on letters or numbers).

agencies conducted entirely by telephone and/or teleconferencing technology.

For example, in 1999 the Federal Energy Regulatory Commission (FERC) re-promulgated a special set of rules to govern FERC during a national "emergency condition," defined as "the time of an armed attack upon the United States, or its territories or possessions." Among the provisions, the rules provide for removal of FERC headquarters "to any location in the United States for the duration of the emergency conditions," delegations of FERC authority to specified members or other agency personnel, and continuation of "existing Commission requirements," presumably including Sunshine Act compliance, "except to the extent modified in accordance with authority exercised under this subpart."[66]

The Nuclear Regulatory Commission (NRC) has a congressionally approved reorganization plan that vests all authority of the agency during a national emergency in the chairman of the NRC and thus takes the agency outside the scope of the Sunshine Act, at least for the duration of the national emergency.[67]

Several Sunshine Act agencies in recent years have developed Continuity of Operations Plans (hereafter COOP) to govern their operations during an emergency while the agency is unable to operate at its headquarters. These plans typically require agency members and key staff to relocate to often remote locations from agency headquarters. Agencies have thus been thinking about how they could have open Sunshine Act meetings under such emergency circumstances with commissioners at a remote location for an extended period of time or able to communicate only by telephone. They have realized

---

66. *See* 18 C.F.R. §§ 376.201-202, -204-205, -208, et seq. (FERC).
67. *See* 5 U.S.C. app. 1, *Reorganization Plan No. 1 of 1990* (NRC). Section 3 of the Plan transfers to the NRC Chairman "all the functions vested in the Commission pertaining to an emergency concerning a particular facility or materials licensed or registered by the Commission, including the functions of declaring, responding, issuing orders, determining specific policies, advising the civil authorities and the public, directing and coordinating actions relative to such emergency incident." Thus, in this type of emergency, the Sunshine Act would not apply, as the NRC would be governed by a single administrator, its chairman, and not by the collegial membership covered by the Sunshine Act.

Section 552b(b): 51
Conduct of Business, Presumption of Openness, and Public Observation

that much official agency business still can be handled if the agency members act by notation or circulation procedures, or the staff acts on delegated authority. But they are also envisioning circumstances in which the members would need to meet at alternate remote locations to decide official agency business beyond staff authority. This would include not only national defense security issues that could be closed to public observation under Sunshine Act Exemption (1), but also much of the routine, unclassified work that all Sunshine Act agencies undertake. Thus, agencies are beginning to realize that they most likely will be unable to invite the public to any meetings members may have at remote locations, even assuming the agency could have meetings on less than seven days' notice.[68]

---

68. A "Continuity of Operations Plan" is "a plan that defines an agency's strategy for performing essential functions at an alternate site after an emergency that affects the habitability of the headquarters building." Agencies under their COOP plans are expected "to restore essential functions at an alternate site within 12 hours of COOP implementation and for up to 30 days." "Primary COOP Elements" include a description of "essential functions that must be performed to prevent agency operations from being adversely affected," "predesignated personnel who will be responsible for ensuring essential functions are carried out successfully," "equipment pre-positioned at the alternate site for essential personnel to perform their essential functions," a "line of succession" to ensure "decision-making is uninterrupted during an emergency," and a "delegation of authority" that "permits a designated successor to exercise selected authorities during an emergency or disruptive situation that the designated successor does not typically exercise on a daily basis." *See* FEDERAL COMMUNICATIONS COMMISSION, CONTINUITY OF OPERATIONS PLAN OVERVIEW, Feb. 4, 2004. *See also* Federal Emergency Management Agency, *Federal Preparedness Circular, FPC 65,* June 15, 2004. This 50-page document "provides guidance to Federal Executive Branch departments and agencies for use in developing contingency plans and programs for continuity of operations." Neither COOP document, however, contains any reference to, or discussion of, compliance with the Sunshine Act. Apparently, such compliance under "emergency" conditions "will be up to each agency to determine." Telephone interview of Robert Brock, associate general counsel for general law, Federal Emergency Management Agency, by Stephen Klitzman, Jan. 11, 2005. *See also* Stephen Barr, *Federal Diary: Agencies Seen to Improve Their Emergency Planning, Report Says,* WASHINGTON POST, at B02, April 28, 2005. (Also cites, however, study by the Government Accountability

(continued on next page)

As a practical matter, there may be a narrow set of acute circumstances where an agency simply may be unable to comply with all or part of the Sunshine Act, such as communications breakdowns, weather emergencies, terrorist attacks, or other national emergencies. In such acute circumstances, we believe the Sunshine Act agencies should do their best to comply with the open meeting law. Agencies could postpone nonessential meetings. If they are required to hold their meetings, at a minimum, they should memorialize the meetings as best they can with a tape or minutes, and if there is ever litigation, defend themselves on the ground that the agency did the best it could under the emergency circumstances. Sunshine Act agencies may only find some relief in the fact that a litigant's remedy under the Act is really more in equity than law—under the statute, the court can only order the agency to comply with the Act, but it cannot invalidate the agency's underlying action or award money damages, except under the most egregious circumstances.[69] Moreover, courts are likely to be sympathetic to an agency's emergency situation in a possible legal challenge.

Indeed, the Supreme Court's one and only Sunshine Act case, *FCC v. ITT World*, discussed at length above, may be helpful with regard to agency meetings in emergency circumstances. Thus, the alternate holding in this case basically constitutes the defense of "impossibility"— that is, the Sunshine Act is not intended to prevent an agency from conducting its statutory mission where circumstances make open meetings literally impossible. For example, in the *ITT World* case, foreign governments, not the FCC, called a meeting, to which the FCC sent a delegation to act as its representative. The meeting was entirely under the auspices of the foreign governments, and there was no way the foreign governments would conduct the meeting in public or feel bound

---

(continued from previous page)
Office, the congressional watchdog agency, *Agency Plans Have Improved, but Better Oversight Could Assist Agencies in Preparing for Emergencies*, GAO-05-619T (April 28, 2005). GAO study found that most agency COOP plans "exhibit inconsistencies in the identification of essential functions and significant lack of compliance with" the guidance of FEMA. *Id.* This 16-page GAO report does not mention agency implementation of the Sunshine Act as an "essential function" during a national emergency.)

69. *See* pp.188-91, *infra*.

to do so by the American open meeting law. So the Sunshine Act's procedural requirements were inapplicable.

On the other hand, emergency meetings with at least a quorum of the agency members present, either at a remote location or possibly calling in via a conference telephone call, or participating in a complete teleconferencing of the meeting, would still appear to be "meetings" of the agency. Nonetheless, we believe Sunshine agencies may still find support in *FCC v. ITT World* insofar as it suggests that genuine impossibility may be a defense to less than perfect compliance with the Sunshine Act.

Moreover, assuming the nation is facing a truly dire national emergency, such as a nuclear or terrorist attack, it seems highly implausible that an agency would be expected to comply under these circumstances with the strict letter of the Sunshine Act. After all, as Justice Goldberg stated in *Kennedy v. Mendoza-Martinez*, 372 U.S. 144, 160 (1963), ". . . the Constitution . . . is not a suicide pact." Nor, for that matter, should the Sunshine Act be one.

"VIRTUAL" MEETINGS, TELECONFERENCING, AND PUBLIC OBSERVATION

Is it appropriate under the Sunshine Act to use a telephone call-in procedure for the public to listen in to open agency meetings held entirely by teleconferencing? An example would be using a call-in number through which members of the public could listen in to an agency meeting held at a remote location entirely by teleconferencing after they register first to obtain an access code. At present, some agency rules define a "meeting" to include members participating by a "conference telephone call" in an otherwise open public meeting.[70] In such

---

70. *See, e.g.,* the Federal Communications Commission's rule at 47 C.F.R. § 0.601(b). *See also* recent amendment by the Federal Open Market Committee of its rules of procedure, 12 § C.F.R. 272.3(a), to permit members who cannot be present at a meeting in person to participate by "electronic means, such as by videoconference . . . [or[telephone conference arrangements." According to the accompanying *Federal Register* notice, "[t]he amendment should facilitate the ability of the Committee to act if unusual circumstances, such as a national emergency, prevent the Committee or any of its members from assembling in Washington, D.C." *See* 70 Fed. Reg. 7839 (Feb. 16, 2005). *See also* p. 26 note 46, *supra*.

circumstances the public's right to "observe" under the Sunshine Act is not compromised because one of the members is not physically present in the meeting room.

By extension, if an agency meeting is "virtual" in its entirety—that is, one held entirely by teleconferencing—a virtual link to the meeting for public "observers" by a similar telephone call-in[71] procedure would appear to be appropriate, provided the public can actually hear and understand the deliberations and determine who is speaking. As the Justice Memo noted, "[s]ince the public is not authorized to participate in the meeting, there is nothing inherent in the concept of 'open to public observation' that would obligate the [agency] to place members of the public in the same room as the [agency members]. *As long as the public can adequately see, hear, and understand what takes place in the meeting, the requirement will have been met because the meeting would be 'open to public observation'*[72] (emphasis added)." Obviously, the public would not have an opportunity to "see"

---

71. A model for public observation in the age of "virtual" meetings may be drawn from the way corporate press conferences are now handled on the Internet. In 2000, the Securities and Exchange Commission adopted a rule that provided, in effect, that when corporations released financial data or other information that might affect the stock price, they had to make it available essentially to all investors simultaneously. *See* 17 C.F.R. § 243.100, et seq., 65 Fed. Reg. 51,716, 738 (Aug. 24, 2000). To deal with the problem of how to communicate with the analyst community without playing favorites, corporations commonly schedule conference calls to coincide with the public announcement of quarterly results, where corporate officials discuss the quarterly report, company prospects, etc. Any investor with Internet access can plug into the conference call. Furthermore, the audio may be available on the "net" for some period. The SEC's rule does not require that investors be allowed to ask questions, but, of course, that is not necessary or permissible under the Sunshine Act. The public simply has to be able to "observe," and we see no reason why that cannot be by "audio observation." It may be that some agencies are doing this already. It's probably fairly easy to arrange, and for the interested public Internet access is a great deal easier and cheaper than attending a meeting in person. The give-and-take of an agency meeting might present more problems for this medium than what is in essence a press conference with analysts, but it still seems eminently doable.
72. Justice Memo, at 2-3.

a meeting held entirely by telephone, but with the appropriate telephone hookup and/or call-in procedure, the public clearly would have the opportunity to "hear and understand" the agency's deliberations, provided the agency members took steps to properly identify themselves when speaking. Moreover, although the public would not have an opportunity to see a meeting held by telephone, neither would the members themselves, unless it was a video conference call. The public, however, can hardly claim a greater right of observation than the members themselves. The problem here becomes more complicated where a meeting consists of the kind of electronic exchanges discussed at the end of Chapter 1.[73] We think the answer to this dilemma is simply that the public's right to observe is measured by what, in fact, takes place. If the open meeting is telephonic, the public has a right to listen to the discussion; if the meeting is an exchange of e-mails, the public has a right to read them.

Although such a telephone hookup would not provide as complete an opportunity for "public observation" as would the closed-circuit TV procedure in a separate room approved by the Justice Memo, such a telephone connection would be all that could reasonably be expected from the Commission whose members were meeting solely by telephone conference call. This is further supported by section 2 of the Sunshine Act, which provides that "it is the purpose of this Act to provide the public with [the "fullest *practicable* information regarding the decisionmaking processes of the Federal Government"] *while protecting . . . the ability of the Government to carry out its responsibilities*" (emphasis added).

PUBLIC PARTICIPATION

While the public may attend open agency meetings, and in many cases may have the right to record or photograph them, the Sunshine Act does not authorize the public to participate in an agency meeting. The court so held in *We the People, Inc., supra* p. 47 note 52, 746 F. Supp. 213, 217. In this 1990 case, a nonprofit organization, We the People, which monitored the operation of nuclear power plants and their licensing by the Nuclear Regulatory Commission, sued the NRC. The group alleged that the NRC had violated the group's First Amend-

---

73. *See* pp. 26-28, *supra*.

ment rights by banning at open NRC meetings the display of its political posters, bumper stickers, and T-shirts, all of which said "Stop Chernobyl Here."[74]

On cross-motions for summary judgment, the court held that the display of "Stop Chernobyl Here" posters, bumper stickers, and T-shirts was protected speech under the First Amendment, that the NRC public meeting was still a "nonpublic forum," and therefore the prohibition on display of visually disruptive posters or signs at public NRC meetings was a reasonable restriction of protected speech. However, the court also held that the NRC's conduct with respect to We the People was "viewpoint-based" rather than "viewpoint neutral" because the NRC simply did not like the group's specific message. Thus, the court found the NRC's conduct in barring We the People from its otherwise open meetings was unconstitutional under the First Amendment, and it granted We the People's motion for summary judgment.[75]

With regard to the Sunshine Act, the court noted that the statute "required only that Federal agency meetings 'be open to public *observation.'*" 5 U.S.C. § 552b(b) (emphasis added). "Simply put, public discourse was not a goal. The NRC has construed the Act accordingly, and has not opened its meeting room to public debate."[76]

Notwithstanding the *We the People* decision and the 2002 Justice Memo, however, some agencies have gone beyond the "public observation" provision of the law as interpreted by the courts to allow some form of public participation in agency meetings. For example, in 1983

---

74. 746 F. Supp. 213, 214-15 (D.D.C. 1990).
75. *Id.* at 217 (D.D.C. 1990).
76. *Id.* The court cited the NRC's Sunshine Act regulation 10 C.F.R. § 9.103 (1989) (Although meetings shall be open "for public observation," "[n]o additional right to participate . . . is granted. . . .") *Cf.* United States v. Rankin, 616 F.2d 1168, 1170 (10th Cir. 1980) ("Government in the Sunshine Act did not apply to adjudicatory hearing before panel of the Atomic Safety and Licensing Board, but, in any event, 'good faith belief' of defendant spectators that Act prohibited panel of Board from holding in camera hearing and that panel was not performing 'official duties' when defendants chained themselves to courtroom door, delaying in camera proceedings, was not defense to charge of impeding and disrupting government employees in the performance of their official duty, in violation of regulation, term 'official duties' not having any such restricted meaning.").

Section 552b(b): 57
Conduct of Business, Presumption of Openness, and Public Observation

the Consumer Product Safety Commission amended its Sunshine regulations to provide that "attendance by the public shall usually be limited to observation and shall not include participation except where, by majority vote, the Commission determines that data or views from certain members of the public will be permitted."[77] The reason for this change was that "on certain occasions, the Commission finds it desirable for particular members of the public to provide data or perspectives, rather than relying altogether on discussions by the Commissioners and on presentations by Commission staff members."[78] Similarly, a majority of the Board of Governors of the United States Postal Service can approve participation by an individual in any portion of any meeting of the Board.[79]

Some form of public participation was also endorsed in the 1995 letter from then SEC Commissioner Steven M.H. Wallman on Sunshine reform to the Administrative Conference. Supported by 11 other agency members, both current and former, Wallman wrote that "any alternatives to the current structure of the Act must ensure that the public receives at least as much information regarding agency decisionmaking as that currently afforded under the Act." The Wallman letter then recommended various proposals, including "granting the public the right to make oral statements or presentations in connection with agency decisionmaking as opposed to the current right of the public under the Act merely to observe agency action."[80]

To ensure that disabled persons "can enjoy full access to and participation in" open meetings of the Securities and Exchange Commis-

---

77. 48 Fed. Reg. 36,566 (Aug. 12, 1983).
78. Letter from Michael S. Solender, general counsel, Consumer Product Safety Commission, to Stephen Klitzman, July 24, 2001.
79. *See* Letter from Mary S. Elcano, senior vice president and general counsel, United States Postal Service, to Richard K. Berg, Jan. 26, 1995.
80. Wallman Letter, *supra* pp. 35-36, note 14. Wallman recommended increased public participation but "in exchange for greater agency discretion to allow private deliberations among their members." *Id. See also* Appendix H, *infra*. On the other hand, it can also be argued that the ground rules and the opportunities for public participation have to be laid out and made clear in advance out of fairness to the various contending interests. Otherwise, only the best-represented parties would be able to attend the decision-making meeting to get in their "last licks" on an agency policy matter.

sion, the SEC in 1990 amended its Sunshine rules "to provide that members of the public who plan to attend open meetings and who require auxiliary aids, such as a sign language interpreter, should contact the Commission's Selective Placement Coordinator, who will take all reasonable steps to accommodate the request in advance of the meeting date."[81]

PUBLIC UNDERSTANDING

The Congress intended the Sunshine Act "to enable the public to better understand the decisions rendered by the Government, and better acquaint the public with the process by which agency decisions are reached." Such understanding, Congress contemplated, would complement the agency records made available under the Freedom of Information Act.[82] Yet, public understanding of open meeting deliberations can often be problematic. Here, for example, is a candid description of such deliberations by a former commissioner on the Securities and Exchange Commission, Bevis Longstreth:

> The Act's ineffectiveness is well illustrated by one "shortcoming" often mentioned by the media. At open meetings, discussion proceeds on the basis of intra-agency memoranda used by the staff to prepare the members. Frequent reference is made to various points of law or fact contained in these memoranda. The memoranda themselves are not given to the public. Nor are they required to be given. An important exemption under the Freedom of Information Act—exemption 5—protects pre-decisional material that, if disclosed, might have the effect of impairing the decision-making process.
>
> On this point, one can observe a direct conflict in purpose between the FOIA exemption, which preserves the privacy of pre-decisional written materials, and the Sunshine Act, which compels disclosure of pre-decisional oral discussion. This dichotomy distorts the decision-making process because of the restraining effect that the public's presence has on the oral discussion. And, of course, since the public does not have the

---

81. *See* Levine-Jones Memo, *supra* note 62, citing Securities Act Release No. 6856 (Mar. 13, 1990), 55 Fed. Reg. 10,234 (Mar. 20, 1990).
82. *See* S. Rep. at 1, 5.

written materials, it is, at best, difficult and, often, impossible for the public to follow the discussion in a meaningful way.[83]

A similar concern was stated in the 1984 Welborn Report to ACUS.[84] Among its major findings, the Welborn Report found that agencies had implemented the Sunshine Act without ensuring sufficient public understanding of open agency meetings, including adequate public access to explanatory materials and documents.[85] The recommendation ACUS ultimately adopted, in part, therefore "strongly encouraged" Sunshine agencies to make "open meetings more useful through comprehensible discussion of agenda items and provision of background material and documentation pertaining to the issues under consideration."[86]

Heeding this recommendation, a number of agencies have taken steps to assist members of the public to better understand and to follow the course of their meetings. For example, the Federal Reserve Board has taken various "steps to provide meaningful public observation of open meetings." As explained in its 1993 Annual Report to Congress, the "Fed" ensures that:

> Members of the public who attend the Board's open meetings receive copies of the staff documents that are prepared in connection with each agenda item to be considered, to the extent that the documents are subject to release under the Freedom of Information Act. They also receive a descriptive agenda that summarizes the issues to be considered at each open meeting
> . . . .

After each meeting, a representative of the Public Affairs Office is available to answer specific questions about the proceedings. Those unable to attend open meetings may hear a recording of the discus-

---

83. Bevis Longstreth, *A Little Shade Please—The Government in the Sunshine Act Isn't Working,* WASHINGTON POST, July 25, 1983, at A13, *reprinted* as an Appendix to both the 1989 S. REP., *supra* note 8, and to the article by Cawley, *supra* note 64. For a rebuttal to Longstreth, *see* Chiles, *supra* note 8.
84. *See* Welborn Report, *supra* note 9, and Appendix G, *infra.*
85. *Id.*
86. *Id.*

sion in the Board's Freedom of Information Office, and they may purchase a copy of the recording for $6 per cassette tape. The staff documents and *A Guide to Meetings of the Board of Governors of the Federal Reserve System* also are available on the Board's public Web site.[87]

Similarly, the Federal Trade Commission often makes available before open meetings summaries of matters on the agenda in order to facilitate understanding of the discussion.[88] At open meetings of the Securities and Exchange Commission, the SEC "makes available to the public short summaries of the matter(s) to be considered by the Commission. This material informs members of the general public as to the nature of the action under consideration by the Commission and assists them in following the discussion that ensues. These summaries also provide the names of members of the staff who may be contacted for further information on the matter(s) considered."[89]

The National Transportation Safety Board has taken several steps "to provide meaningful observation of open meetings" and to "aid in the public's understanding of subjects discussed at open meetings." These steps include:

> . . . [a] statement of the item to be discussed by the presiding officer prior to consideration of each topic; efforts by the Chairman to provide the public with a clear picture of key issues being discussed rather than allowing the meeting to focus on printed documents being considered by the Board members, copies of which are not available to the public; reading the entire sentence or paragraph under consideration instead of mere references by page and line; liberal use of visual aids such as a blackboard, photographs, charts, and diagrams; Members and staff answering questions during recesses and after meetings; issuance of a press release following the meeting of any major item of public interest on which the Board

---

87. *See* www.federalreserve.gov/boarddocs/meetings, and Appendix L, *infra*.
88. *See* 16 C.F.R. § 4.15(b)(3).
89. *See* Levine-Jones Memo, *supra* note 62.

has acted; and making immediately public copies of documents adopted by the Board.[90]

At the Consumer Product Safety Commission (CPSC), the agency "generally waives FOIA for staff briefing materials, except legal memos."[91] The CPSC, however, has also expressed concern about whether or not discussing even a portion of a restricted memo in an open meeting might waive the confidentiality of the entire memo.[92]

The CPSC also notes that if a commissioner asks about an OGC memo during an open meeting, the CPSC General Counsel usually "points out the openness of the meeting and offers to discuss the memo privately which usually cuts off the public discussion."[93]

ACCESS TO STAFF MEMORANDA AND THE MEANINGFULNESS OF "PUBLIC OBSERVATION"

As the above examples illustrate, access to inter- or intra-agency memoranda, such as staff recommendations, considered at open meetings, remains a controversial Sunshine Act question. The issue was

---

90. See Annual Report of the National Transportation Safety Board on "Implementation of the Government in the Sunshine Act," 1993, p. 2. See also Letter from Annette B. Kuz, counsel, Mississippi River Commission, to Stephen Klitzman, July 12, 2001: "Staff papers, reports and background information . . . are available to the public at each meeting. Detailed staff briefings are also provided at public meetings. Finally, reports made at the meetings by the staff and statements made by the public are filed with the minutes of each meeting in the agency library and are available to the public upon request." For a highly skeptical view of these attempts to enhance public understanding of agency open meetings, see Thomas H. Tucker, *Sunshine—The Dubious New God*, 32 ADMIN. L. REV. 537, 543 (1980) ("Providing detailed briefing sheets as is currently proposed will help . . . at a certain cost in manpower and time, but still the average meeting will be barely competitive in terms of sheer public interest with watching the grass grow."). See also pp. 203-09, *infra*, for discussion of the relationship of the Sunshine Act to the Freedom of Information Act.
91. E-mail dated Jan. 29, 2003, from Alan Shakin, former assistant general counsel, CPSC, to Stephen Klitzman.
92. *Id.*
93. *Id.*

raised in the very first case brought under the Sunshine Act, *Consumers Union of the United States v. Board of Governors of the Federal Reserve System*.[94] In this 1977-1978 case, Consumers Union sought to compel the Federal Reserve Board of Governors to make available a document to be discussed in an open meeting. Consumers Union argued that without the document, it would be difficult to understand what was being discussed at the meeting, and that therefore the discussion was not meaningfully open to public observation as required by 5 U.S.C. § 552b(b). The Board of Governors denied that its discussion of the document in question would be incomprehensible.

The case was dismissed on agreement of both parties. On January 18, 1978, the Federal Reserve Board clarified its policy governing release of documents discussed at open meetings.[95] Under the clarified procedures, any person requesting access to a Board document to be discussed at an open meeting had to file a written request with the Board's Freedom of Information Office at least two working days prior to the meeting. The Board would then give such a request "priority treatment" and would make the document available by the time of the meeting, "unless there is insufficient opportunity to process the request or a determination is made to invoke an applicable exemption from disclosure."[96] The Board's present policy is to release most of the staff memoranda considered at open meetings, providing them at the meeting and through its Freedom of Information office and agency Web site.[97]

Parties may continue to seek access to staff or background memoranda or other papers discussed at open meetings, particularly when meaningful public observation of an open agency meeting is diminished by oblique references to page or footnote numbers in unavailable documents.

---

94. D.D.C. Civ. No. 77-1800, Jan. 24, 1978, dismissed on agreement of both parties (hereafter *Consumers Union*). *See also* discussion of this case at p. 204 note 4, *infra*.
95. *See* 43 Fed. Reg. 2444.
96. *Id.*
97. *See* Appendix L, *infra*, for the Federal Reserve Board's *A Guide to the Meetings of the Board of Governors of the Federal Reserve System*, and p. 204 note 4, *infra*.

Section 552b(b):
Conduct of Business, Presumption of Openness, and Public Observation

As we note elsewhere, there is an unavoidable tension between FOIA exemption 5, which recognizes a legitimate government interest in protecting the agency deliberative process as such, and the Sunshine Act, which aims at maximum exposure of that process, at least on the collegial agency level.[98] This FOIA-GISA conflict is exacerbated by the fact that staff documents are arguably exempted from disclosure under FOIA exemption 5 for inter- or intra-agency memoranda, 5 U.S.C. § 552b(5), while the Sunshine Act explicitly states that nothing in the open meeting provisions "expands or limits the present rights of any person under" FOIA. 5 U.S.C. § 552b(k). As a result, many agencies have taken the position that internal agency memoranda, though discussed at open meetings, need not be released, or that release is governed entirely by FOIA. However, an agency is required to announce a Sunshine meeting only seven days in advance— and since the processing of a FOIA request takes at least 10 days, requiring the public to use FOIA procedures can basically negate document availability under the Sunshine Act, certainly in time for a particular open meeting.

However this conflict is resolved, it would appear that the spirit, if not the letter, of the Sunshine Act is violated unless agencies take affirmative steps to ensure meaningful and comprehensible public observation of open agency meetings. Such steps would include making available to the public staff documents releasable under the FOIA, or at least written summaries of such documents or agenda items before or at the time of the meeting, and making staff members available to answer questions after the open meeting.[99]

---

98. *See 1978 Guide* at 98. A public interest litigator has noted that "with the extraordinary [judicial] expansion of [FOIA] exemption 5, that tension is more apparent than ever and cries out for the development of a basic set of principles regarding public access to government deliberations." *See* Letter from Eric R. Glitzenstein to Jeffrey Lubbers, ACUS Special Committee to Review the Government in the Sunshine Act, p. 2 (Sept. 12, 1995) (on file with the authors). Glitzenstein called for a "tradeoff in which more meetings could be closed to public access in exchange for which there would be general expansion in the public's right of access to documents, i.e., by placing new legislative limits on the invocation of the deliberative process component of exemption five." *Id.*

99. *See* pp. 59-61, *supra,* for discussion of these actions already being taken by some Sunshine agencies.

Chapter 3

SECTION 552b(c)
GROUNDS FOR CLOSING MEETINGS

OVERVIEW 65
EXEMPTIONS (1) AND (2)—NATIONAL DEFENSE AND
 FOREIGN POLICY; INTERNAL PERSONNEL RULES
 AND PRACTICES 72
EXEMPTION (3)—STATUTORY EXEMPTION 74
EXEMPTIONS (4), (5), (6)—PROPRIETARY INFORMATION;
 ACCUSATION OF CRIME OR FORMAL CENSURE;
 INVASION OF PRIVACY 76
EXEMPTION (7)—INVESTIGATORY RECORDS 81
EXEMPTION (8)—FINANCIAL INSTITUTION REPORTS 82
EXEMPTIONS (9)(A), (B)—FINANCIAL SPECULATION
 AND STABILITY; FRUSTRATION OF PROPOSED
 AGENCY ACTION 83
EXEMPTION (10)—ISSUANCE OF SUBPOENA,
 PARTICIPATION IN CIVIL ACTION OR PROCEEDING,
 FORMAL AGENCY ADJUDICATION 88

(c) Except in a case where the agency finds that the public interest requires otherwise, the second sentence of subsection (b) shall apply to any portion of an agency meeting, and the requirements of subsections (d) and (e) shall not apply to any information pertaining to such meeting required by this section to be disclosed to the public, where the agency properly determines that such portion or portions of its meeting or the disclosure of such information is likely to—

OVERVIEW

Subsection (c) sets forth 10 grounds or groups of grounds for which meetings may be closed and information regarding such meetings withheld from the public. Six of the exemptions, numbers 1, 2, 3, 4, 6, and

8, are identical to or substantially the same as those in the Freedom of Information Act, 5 U.S.C. § 552(b) (FOIA).[1] There are hundreds of cases as well as a rich literature dealing with these exemptions under the FOIA.[2] In addition, in 1976 Congress amended the Federal Advisory Committee Act (FACA) so that the grounds for closing meetings under FACA are those found in the Sunshine Act.[3] The case law and other

---

1. For example, Sunshine Act Exemption (6) covers "information of a personal nature where disclosure would constitute a clearly unwarranted invasion of personal privacy" while the FOIA covers "personnel and medical files and similar files" whose disclosure would have the same effect.
2. A discussion of court decisions construing the Freedom of Information Act is beyond the scope of this Guide. However, there are numerous sources of information about the FOIA. The Department of Justice biennially publishes its FREEDOM OF INFORMATION ACT GUIDE AND PRIVACY ACT OVERVIEW (May 2004 Edition), which is now *available at* www.usdoj.gov/oip/oip.html, and an extensive Freedom of Information Act case list, most recently revised in May 2002, *available at* www.usdoj.gov/04foia/cl-tofc.html. The Council of the Section of Administrative Law and Regulatory Practice on April 29, 2001, approved a report on the FOIA, as well as the Sunshine Act, as part of its Black Letter APA Project. *See* Section of Administrative Law and Regulatory Practice, American Bar Association, *A Blackletter Statement of Federal Administrative Law*, 54 ADMIN. L. REV. 1, 60-75 (2002), and 2004 edition at 59-75 (hereafter *Blackletter Statement*). Well-known treatises include JAMES O'REILLY, FREEDOM OF INFORMATION DISCLOSURE 3d ed. (West 2000) (supplemented periodically); ROBERT BOUCHARD & JUSTIN FRANKLIN, GUIDE TO THE FREEDOM OF INFORMATION AND PRIVACY ACTS 2d ed. (West 2001) (supplemented periodically); BURT A. BRAVERMAN & FRANCIS J. CHETWYND, INFORMATION LAW, FREEDOM OF INFORMATION, PRIVACY, OPEN MEETINGS, OTHER ACCESS LAWS (Practising Law Institute 1985) (supplemented periodically); LITIGATION UNDER THE FEDERAL OPEN GOVERNMENT LAWS 22d ed. (Harry Hammitt ed., American Civil Liberties Union Foundation 2004); and PATRICK BIRKINSHAW, FREEDOM OF INFORMATION: THE LAW, THE PRACTICE AND THE IDEAL 3d ed. (Butterworths 2001) (emphasizing English law).
3. FACA was originally enacted in 1972 and thus predates the Government in the Sunshine Act. Before enactment of the Sunshine Act, meetings under FACA could be closed if they concerned matters covered by the exemptions in the Freedom of Information Act. *See* Pub. L. No. 92-463, 86 Stat. 770, 775 (1972); Nader v. Dunlop, 370 F. Supp. 177 (D.D.C. 1973). Despite the same exemptions now, however, FACA and the Sunshine Act are mutually exclusive—an organization or entity can be an agency under the Sunshine Act or an advisory committee under FACA, but it cannot be both.

authorities under the FOIA or FACA (post-1976) interpreting these exemptions are often relevant, if not controlling. *See generally Jordan v. U.S. Department of Justice*, 591 F.2d 753, 770-72 (D.C. Cir. 1978) (en banc), noting the relationship among the principal openness statutes.[4]

There is no Sunshine Act exemption that parallels the FOIA's Exemption (5) for intra-agency or inter-agency memoranda or letters. In contrast with the FOIA, which protects an agency's predecisional or deliberative processes, the Sunshine Act is specifically designed to open those processes to public observation.[5] There is also no Sunshine Act exemption that parallels the FOIA's ninth exemption, which covers geological information. Moreover, Congress in 1986 amended FOIA Exemption (7) involving investigatory records compiled for law enforcement purposes but did not change the comparable Sunshine Act exemption.[6] Three Sunshine Act exemptions—number (5), deal-

---

4. *See also* Public Citizen Health Research Corp. v. FDA, 185 F.3d 898, 904 (D.C. Cir. 1999) (noting congressional intent in enacting Exemption (4) of the Sunshine Act, which is identical to FOIA Exemption (4) (hereafter *Public Citizen Health*). *Cf.* Common Cause v. NRC, 674 F.2d 921, 929 n.19 (D.C. Cir. 1982) (hereafter *Common Cause)* (court declines to decide whether the exemptions in the two acts "are identical in all circumstances" but concludes that Congress adopted the Supreme Court's construction of FOIA Exemption (2) when enacting the Sunshine Act); Berliner Zisser Walter & Gallegos v. SEC, 962 F. Supp. 1348, 1352 (D. Colo. 1997) (hereafter *Berliner Zisser*); Feshbach v. SEC, 5 F. Supp. 2d 774, 781 (N.D. Cal. 1997) (reliance on legislative history of the Sunshine Act to construe FOIA Exemption (8) because the two statutes are in pari materia, *i.e.,* should be considered together because they have the same purpose). *See generally* Stephen H. Klitzman, *Government in the Sunshine Act—Nuts, Bolts, and Tacks: A Summary of Statutory Provisions, Judicial Interpretations, and Pending Issues*, 38 FED. B. J. 114, 118 (1979).
5. Public Citizen v. National Economic Comm'n, 703 F. Supp. 113, 117 (D.D.C. 1989) (hereafter *Public Citizen*) (FACA case holding that Exemption (9)(B) of the Sunshine Act does not include a deliberative process privilege as does Exemption (5) of FOIA). *See also* chapter 10 for a discussion of the confidentiality of internal memoranda that are the subject of meetings subject to the Sunshine Act and the discussion of the Subsequent Review of Transcript Material in chapter 6, pp. 163-66, *infra.*
6. *See* Freedom of Information Reform Act of 1986, Subtitle N of Pub. L. No. 99-570, 100 Stat. 3207-48 (1986).

ing with accusations of crime or some censurable matter; number (9), dealing with potential frustration of proposed agency action; and number (10), dealing with litigation and adjudication matters—have no corresponding exemptions in the FOIA.

Even if the subject of a meeting falls within one of the enumerated exemptions, the meeting should be open "where the agency finds that the public interest [so] requires."[7] Analytically, the agency's public interest determination is separate from the determination whether a meeting or portion of a meeting is within an exemption, and the agency must satisfy itself on both questions before deciding to close a meeting. *See Philadelphia Newspapers, Inc. v. Nuclear Regulatory Commission*, 727 F.2d 1195, 1203 n.6 (D.C. Cir. 1984) (hereafter *Philadelphia Newspapers*).[8] As a practical matter, however, the decision regarding the applicability of many of the exemptions implicitly involves a public interest determination regarding the likelihood of certain kinds of injury to be apprehended from disclosure. *See, e.g.*, Exemption (6) (invasion of privacy), Exemption (7) (investigatory records), and Exemption (9) (frustration of agency action). In these cases the two questions tend to merge into one. Furthermore, in the cases of Exemptions (1) (national defense) and (3) (matters required by statute to be withheld) it is not always clear that the agency is free to disclose the materials to be discussed, whatever its own view of the public interest.[9] In the cases of Exemptions (2), (4), (5), (8), and (10), the determination that the exemption is applicable by no means concludes the public interest question. However, to the extent that the public interest determination is separately addressed, it is committed to the agency's "unreviewable discretion."[10]

---

7. 5 U.S.C. § 552b(c).
8. *See also* regulations of the Securities and Exchange Commission, 17 C.F.R. § 200.402(c), and the Federal Deposit Insurance Corporation, 12 C.F.R. § 311.5(b)(1).
9. For example, the Federal Election Commission has concluded that the public interest cannot be used to open meetings regarding enforcement matters because such meetings are required by statute to be closed pursuant to Exemption (3). *See* 50 Fed. Reg. 39,968, 39,972 (Oct. 1, 1985) (Commission may not waive a statutory requirement of confidentiality), now codified at 11 C.F.R. § 2.4(a).
10. *See* Clark-Cowlitz Joint Operating Agency v. Fed. Energy Regulatory Comm'n, 798 F.2d 499, 504 n.5 (D.C. Cir. 1986) (en banc) (hereafter *Clark-Cowlitz*).

Section 552b(c): Grounds for Closing Meetings

The agency procedure for closing meetings is prescribed in subsections (d) and (f). It is important to note that the agencies are not required to close meetings that fall within the exemptions. The Senate Report observes that "[c]losing a meeting on these grounds is permissive, not mandatory. The agency should not automatically close a meeting because it falls within an exception."[11] In a 1980 decision, the D.C. Circuit described the openness requirement as "sweeping, unqualified, and mandatory"[12] and the courts have often pointed out that the exemptions must be narrowly construed.[13] Nevertheless, in its en banc *Clark-Cowlitz* decision issued in 1986, the D.C. Circuit appeared to strike more of a balance between openness and administrative efficiency by acknowledging the importance of exemptions legitimately invoked by an agency in the conduct of the government's business.[14]

---

11. S. REP., at 20. *See also* Natural Res. Def. Council, Inc. v. NRC, 216 F.3d 1180, 1184 (D.C. Cir. 2000) (noting the principle that "[t]he Act's presumption of openness requires that all doubts be resolved against closure") (hereafter *NRDC*).
12. Pacific Legal Foundation v. Council on Environmental Quality, 636 F.2d 1259, 1265 (D.C. Cir. 1980).
13. *See, e.g.,* Pan American World Airways v. CAB, 684 F.2d 31, 35 (D.C. Cir. 1982) (meetings must be open unless specific portions fall within one or more of 10 narrowly defined exemptions); Wilkinson v. Legal Services Corp., 865 F. Supp. 891, 895 (D.D.C. 1994), *rev'd on other grounds*, 80 F.3d 595 (D.C. Cir.), *cert. denied,* 519 U.S. 927 (1996) (exemptions are to be narrowly interpreted). *See also Common Cause, supra* note 4 at 932, and *Philadelphia Newspapers, supra* p. 68, 727 F.2d at 1200.
14. *Clark-Cowlitz, supra* n.10 at 501 (citing to the Senate Report, the court noted that the exemptions "serve to 'protect the ability of the Government to carry out its responsibilities ....'") Judge J. Skelly Wright, author of the *Common Cause* decision, "in dissent, protested—correctly—that the court's decision [in *Clark-Cowlitz*] was at odds with the narrow view of exemptions taken by the *Common Cause* court." *See* Letter from Peter Crane, attorney, Nuclear Regulatory Commission, to Gary Edles, general counsel, Administrative Conference of the United States, p. 9 (Feb. 6, 1995). *Cf. NRDC, supra* n.11 at 1186 (observing, in the context of deciding what constitutes a "meeting," that the Supreme Court read the statute's legislative history as a balance between the interest in openness and administrative concerns).

It is clear that agencies have not been inhibited from using the exemptions to close meetings. A 1986 report by the Congressional Research Service (CRS Report) covering 59 agencies for the years 1979-1984 indicated that 40 percent of agency meetings were open, 43 percent were closed, and 17 percent were partially closed.[15] A 1984 study prepared for the Administrative Conference of the United States limited to 12 agencies during the somewhat overlapping period 1977-1981 supported the data in the CRS Report but noted variation in these percentages among agencies. Generally speaking, agencies involved in advisory or planning activities were more likely to hold open meetings than agencies that perform other functions.[16] But the pattern is clearly not inviolate.[17] The CRS Report indicated

---

15. *See* CRS Report, p. 34 note 12, *supra*. This report also documented a 31% decline in all agency meetings held between 1980 and 1984. *Id.*
16. Welborn Report, p. 34 note 9, at 223-24, *supra*. The Mississippi River Commission has never held a closed meeting, *see* Letter of Annette B. Kuz to Stephen Klitzman (July 12, 2001), and the Council on Environmental Quality held over 95 percent of its meetings in the open. Welborn Report, at 253. In contrast, the Export-Import Bank of the United States held 511 meetings, of which only three were open. *Id.* The Federal Trade Commission in calendar year 2000 closed all of its meetings. FEDERAL TRADE COMMISSION ANNUAL REPORT, GOVERNMENT IN THE SUNSHINE ACT, CALENDAR YEAR 2000. Its General Counsel has explained that the FTC is a law enforcement agency and most frequently uses Exemptions (7)(A) and (10) relating to law enforcement investigations or adjudicatory or judicial proceedings. *See* Prepared Statement of the Federal Trade Commission presented by Stephen Calkins, General Counsel, before the Special Committee to Review the Government in the Sunshine Act, Administrative Conference of the United States, pp. 2-3 (Sept. 12, 1995) (on file with the authors).
17. The Nuclear Regulatory Commission in 2000 closed only 25 percent of its meetings. *See* U.S. NUCLEAR REGULATORY COMMISSION, ANNUAL REPORT OF THE ADMINISTRATION OF THE GOVERNMENT IN THE SUNSHINE ACT FOR CALENDAR YEAR 2000. The Federal Election Commission, which administers and enforces the statutes governing the financing of federal elections, in 2000 held 31 of its 35 meetings in public despite an express provision in the Federal Election Campaign Act that prohibits publicity with respect to actions taken by the Commission in connection with its pursuit of possible violations of the statute. *See* FEDERAL ELECTION COMMISSION, IMPLEMENTATION OF THE GOVERNMENT IN THE SUNSHINE ACT, CALENDAR YEAR 2000.

that agencies most frequently relied on Exemptions (10) (court litigation or formal agency proceedings), (9) (the frustration of government action through premature disclosure), and (7) (law enforcement) when closing meetings.[18] Exemption (9) accords special authority to close meetings to those agencies that regulate commodities and other financial matters, and the Commodity Credit Corporation, for example, closes a majority of its meetings.[19] The exemptions least often employed were Exemptions (1) (classified information) and (3) (matters specifically exempted by statute).[20]

Because the statute permits agencies to close only the "portion or portions" of their meetings that fall within the exemptions, agencies must ordinarily segregate exempt discussions and open the remaining portions of their meetings.[21] Exemptions are worded in terms of categories of information to be disclosed at a meeting. So some agencies segregate information and schedule certain meetings that are limited entirely to material that justifies closure. An agency determination made in advance of the meeting must of necessity be an estimate of what is likely to transpire. One court has described this as a "foreseeability standard"—that is, "the agency must show that it was more likely than not that exempt matters would be discussed at

---

18. 1989 S. Rep No. 101-54, *supra*, p. 33 note 8, at 66.
19. *See* 7 C.F.R. § 1409.5.
20. 1989 S. Rep. at 66-67. For example, the Securities and Exchange Commission invoked Exemption (3) 101 times in 2004. In contrast, the SEC, in closing 58 meetings and opening 20 meetings, all with multiple agenda items, in 2004, invoked Exemption (5) 581 times, Exemption (7) 686 times, Exemption (9) 308 times, and Exemption (10) 790 times. *See* Annual Report of the Securities and Exchange Commission on the Government in the Sunshine Act for Calendar Year 2004, Exhibit B.
21. *Philadelphia Newspapers*, *supra* p. 68 at 1201-02. *See also Standards for Closing a Meeting of the Select Commission on Immigration and Refugee Policy*, 43 Op. Att'y Gen. 290 (1980) (in the context of FACA, acknowledging that advisory committee must structure its agenda so that classified and other exempt information is discussed separately from non-exempt items).

the closed portion or portions of the meeting."[22] In the event of a challenge, the burden is on the agency to demonstrate that an exemption is applicable.[23]

EXEMPTIONS (1) AND (2)—NATIONAL DEFENSE AND FOREIGN POLICY; INTERNAL PERSONNEL RULES AND PRACTICES

(1) disclose matters that are (A) specifically authorized under criteria established by an Executive order to be kept secret in the interests of national defense or foreign policy and (B) in fact properly classified pursuant to such Executive order;
(2) relate solely to the internal personnel rules and practices of an agency;

Exemption (1) is identical to the first exemption in the Freedom of Information Act, 5 U.S.C. § 552(b).

In like fashion, Exemption (2) is identical to the second exemption in the Freedom of Information Act. The language of the House Sunshine Act bill was taken in preference to the language in the Senate bill that was limited to matters that "relate solely to the agency's own internal personnel rules and practices." Accordingly, Exemption (2) would be available for the discussion of a personnel matter involving another agency. The legislative history indicates that the purpose

---

22. *Common Cause, supra* note 4 at 929 n.19 (D.C. Cir. 1982), *citing* Conf. Rep., at 15. The Conference Report noted that this means "that it is more likely than not that the event or result in question will occur. . . ." Conf. Rep., at 10, 20. *See also* regulations of the Securities and Exchange Commission, 17 C.F.R. § 200.401(f). Of course, the agency will seldom be able to separate entirely its calculation of the likelihood of the result from its perception of the gravity of the harm. "The test is different for a retrospective determination of whether the transcript of a closed meeting should be released" where the matters actually discussed must be evaluated. "The agency and reviewing court must base their decision on the discussions that actually did occur. If there was in fact no discussion of any exempt material, the entire transcript must be released; if exempt material was discussed, then the specific exempt portions may be deleted." *Common Cause,* at 929 n.19. *See also* pp. 157-58, 163, *infra.*
23. *Id.* at 929.

of Sunshine Exemption (2) is "to protect the privacy of staff members and to cover the handling of strictly internal matters," H. Rep. I, 9; *see also* S. Rep., 21. With respect to protection of privacy, the exemption overlaps Exemption (6), although the privacy interest in discussion of personnel matters may very well go beyond preventing disclosure of information of a personal nature and include the interests of participants in the meeting in being able to comment freely on the qualifications of members of the staff. In other words, the intent of Sunshine Exemption (2) seems to be to preserve, in the area of personnel and internal administration, the values served by the fifth exemption of the FOIA.

The *1978 Guide* noted it might be argued that the public always has an interest in matters that are sufficiently important to require the attention of a quorum of Presidential appointees, and in most respects the administrative burdens of closing a meeting are greater than those involved in holding an open meeting. The Conference Report noted with approval the Supreme Court's interpretation in *Department of Air Force v. Rose*, 425 U.S. 352 (1976) (hereafter *Rose*), of the second Freedom of Information Act exemption. The Supreme Court in *Rose* held that Exemption (2) did not authorize the Air Force Academy to withhold summaries of Honor Board hearings dealing with alleged violations of the Honor Code for cadets, from which names were deleted, if a guilty verdict had been approved. The Court distinguished between "minor or trivial matters" that may be covered by the exemption and "those more substantial matters which might be the subject of legitimate public interest." *See Rose, supra*, 425 U.S. at 365. The Court found that, given the importance of military discipline to the effectiveness of the armed forces and their relations with civilian authorities, the Honor Board summaries contained matters subject to a "genuine and significant public interest."[24] The Court observed:

> [A]t least where the situation is not one where disclosure may risk circumvention of agency regulation, Exemption 2 is not applicable to matters subject to such a genuine and signifi-

---

24. 425 U.S. 369.

cant public interest. . . . Rather, the general thrust of the exemption is simply to relieve agencies of the burden of assembling and maintaining for public inspection matter in which the public could not reasonably be expected to have an interest.[25]

On this rationale, therefore, the scope of Exemption (2) appears to be fairly narrow.

Other judicial decisions have also endorsed a narrow reading of Exemption (2). In its *Common Cause* decision,[26] the D.C. Circuit applied the *Rose* distinction to conclude that meetings to determine an agency's budget allocations that discussed personnel cutbacks, evaluations of the prior performance of a Commission's offices and programs, and possible administrative cost savings through adoption of new internal management techniques, although "inevitably imping[ing] on personnel matters," did not satisfy the requirements of Exemption (2). "The public can reasonably be expected to have an interest in matters of such importance," the court noted, so they "do not relate solely to 'internal personnel rules and procedures.'"[27] A district court later found that the discussion of the employment status of a high-ranking agency official was not a "minor or trivial" matter so as to bring it within Exemption (2). *Wilkinson v. Legal Services Corp.*, 865 F. Supp. 891 (D.D.C. 1994), *rev'd on other grounds*, 80 F.3d 535 (D.C. Cir. 1996), *cert. denied*, 519 U.S. 927 (1996) (hereafter *Wilkinson*).

EXEMPTION (3)—STATUTORY EXEMPTION

(3) disclose matters specially exempted from disclosure by statute (other than section 552 of this title), provided that such statute (A) requires that the matters be withheld from the public in such a manner as to leave no discretion on the issue, or (B) establishes particular criteria for withholding or refers to particular types of matters to be withheld;

---

25. *Id.* at 369-70. *See also* Conf. Rep., at 15.
26. *Common Cause, supra* note 4 at 937, *citing Rose*.
27. *Common Cause,* at 937-38.

Section 552b(c): Grounds for Closing Meetings 75

This exemption parallels the third exemption in the Freedom of Information Act, 5 U.S.C. § 552(b)(3).[28] While FOIA protects from disclosure segregable portions of documents covered by a qualifying FOIA Exemption (3) statute, Exemption (3) of the Sunshine Act exempts from the open meeting requirement of subsection 552b(b) any discussion of matters covered by a qualifying statute. The Conference Report says that this exemption:

> applies only to statutes that either (a) require that the information be withheld from the public in such a manner as to leave no discretion on the issue, or (b) establish particular criteria for withholding or refer to particular types of information to be withheld. The conferees intend this language to overrule the decision of the Supreme Court in *F.A.A. v. Robertson*, 422 U.S. 255 (1975), which dealt with section 1104 of the Federal Aviation Act of 1958 (49 U.S.C. § 1504). Another example of a statute whose terms do not bring it within this exemption is section 1106 of the Social Security Act (42 U.S.C. § 1306).[29]

There are other illustrations. For example, sections 2286d(a) and (g)(3) of Title 42 of the U.S. Code satisfy the requirements of Exemption (3)(A) because they require that the recommendations of the Defense Nuclear Facilities Safety Board be made public only after they are transmitted to the Secretary of Energy or the President.[30] Similarly, section 12 of Title 7 of the U.S. Code, which prohibits the Commodity Futures Trading Commission from publishing information gathered in the course of an investigation "which would separately disclose the

---

28. *See* Essential Information, Inc. v. U.S. Information Agency, 134 F.3d 1165, 1171-72 (D.C. Cir. 1988) (Tatel, J., dissenting) (referring to FOIA and Sunshine Act Exemptions (3) as "analogous"). Note, however, that FOIA Exemption (3) was also narrowed by Section 5(b) of the Sunshine Act. *See* p. xxxiv, *supra*.
29. Conf. Rep., at 14. In the *Robertson* case, the Court upheld the FAA's discretionary decision to withhold information.
30. *See* Natural Res. Def. Council, Inc. et al. v. Def. Nuclear Facilities Safety Bd., 969 F.2d 1248 (D.C. Cir. 1992), *reh'g denied,* 969 F.2d 1248, 1255 (1992), *cert. denied,* 508 U.S. 906 (1993).

business transactions of any person and trade secrets or names of customers," satisfies the requirements of Exemption (3)(B).[31]

EXEMPTIONS (4), (5), (6)—PROPRIETARY INFORMATION; ACCUSATION OF CRIME OR FORMAL CENSURE; INVASION OF PRIVACY

(4) disclose trade secrets and commercial or financial information obtained from a person and privileged or confidential;
(5) involve accusing any person of a crime, or formally censuring any person;
(6) disclose information of a personal nature where disclosure would constitute a clearly unwarranted invasion of personal privacy.

Exemption (4) is identical to the business and commercial exemption of the Freedom of Information Act, 5 U.S.C. § 552(b)(4), and was adopted with recognition of contemporaneous judicial interpretations of that exemption.[32] Because the language of Exemption (4) remains the same as that contained in the FOIA, the numerous court interpretations of FOIA Exemption (4) that follow enactment of the Sunshine Act should also be analytically relevant. *See, e.g.,* the D.C. Circuit's influential FOIA decision in *Critical Mass Energy Project v. NRC,* 875 F.2d 871 (D.C. Cir. 1992) (en banc), where the court, in deciding what information is "confidential," distinguished between information that is submitted to the agency voluntarily and that which is required to be submitted.

---

31. *See* Hunt v. CFTC, 484 F. Supp. 47, 49 (D.D.C. 1993). *See also* S. REP., at 26-27, and a detailed discussion of the Federal Trade Commission's "frequent use of Exemption (3)" to close many of its meetings pursuant to the FTC Act, 15 U.S.C. §§ 46(f), 57(b)-2(b), (f), and the Clayton Act, 15 U.S.C. § 18a(h) in its 2002 Annual Report to Congress on its compliance with the Sunshine Act, the last such report the FTC has filed. *See* ANNUAL REPORT OF THE FEDERAL TRADE COMMISSION ON THE GOVERNMENT IN THE SUNSHINE ACT FOR 2002, at p. 6.
32. H. REP. I, at 10; Conf. Rep., at 15. *See also Public Citizen Health, supra* p. 67 note 4 (when enacting Sunshine Act Exemption (4), Congress acquiesced in the judicial construction of FOIA Exemption (4)), and the regulations of the Securities and Exchange Commission, 17 C.F.R. § 200.402(a)(4).

Exemption (5), which has no counterpart in the FOIA, is described in the Senate Report as follows:

> This paragraph covers meetings which accuse an individual or corporation of a crime, or formally censure such person. The term "formally censuring any person" includes formal reprimands. An agency may discuss a company's alleged crimes, such as the submission of fraudulent documents, and consider whether to refer the case to the Department of Justice for prosecution. An agency regulating financial or security matters may wish to censure a firm for failing to live up to its professional responsibilities, or an agency may consider whether to formally censure an attorney for his conduct in an agency proceeding. Opening to the public agency discussions of such matters could irreparably harm the person's reputation. If the agency decides not to accuse the person of a crime, or not to censure him, the harm done to the person's reputation by the open meeting could be very unfair.
>
> This paragraph insures that where serious charges of this nature are formally discussed by the agency, the agency has the latitude to close the meeting, even if the discussion does not come within the precise terms of paragraph [(7)], governing investigatory files, or any other part of subsection [(c)]. The provision should not be interpreted as grounds for closing every meeting placing a company in a bad light. To be applicable, the meeting must consider formal agency action accusing a person of a crime or formally censuring a person.

S. Rep., 22.

There is some doubt as to whether issuance of a cease-and-desist order would constitute a "formal censure" within the meaning of Exemption (5). The rules of the Securities and Exchange Commission implementing Exemption (5) broadly cover the institution, continuation or conclusion of any formal or informal investigation or inquiry involving violations of the federal securities law that would seem to include issuance of such orders.[33] In any event, Exemption (10), which

---

33. 17 C.F.R. § 200.402(a) (5).

deals with the agency's participation in a civil action or a formal adjudication, would likely cover discussion of the issuance of a cease-and-desist order.[34]

Exemption (6) is similar to the sixth exemption of the Freedom of Information Act. The Sunshine Act allows an agency to close a meeting where it is discussing "information of a personal nature," while the Freedom of Information Act, 5 U.S.C. § 552(b)(6), allows the withholding of "personnel and medical files and similar files." However, the Supreme Court has concluded that FOIA Exemption (6) is to be interpreted broadly to include all information that can be identified as applying to a particular individual.[35] The same threshold test would seem to be applicable when applying the Sunshine Act.

Once the threshold is met, application of Exemption (6) requires a balancing of the interest in privacy against the public interest in disclosure. *See, e.g., O'Kane v. U.S. Customs Service*, 169 F.3d 1308 (11th Cir. 1999). This case indicates that a balancing test is used to determine whether an individual has a protectible privacy interest and, if so, whether it outweighs the public's corresponding "right to know," and that the Electronic FOIA Amendments of 1996 did not invalidate the private/public interest balancing test. Examples cited in the Senate Report of situations in which it might be appropriate to invoke Exemption (6) to close a meeting include a discussion of an individual's drinking habits or health, assessing an individual's professional competence in connection with review of his grant application, or reviewing an individual's finances to determine his eligibility for financial aid. S. Rep., 21. Both the Senate and House Reports suggest that whether this exemption should be invoked may

---

34. The availability of Exemption (10) does not resolve the issue entirely. A person whose interests may be affected by a portion of a meeting may request that the agency close the meeting, but only pursuant to Exemptions (5), (6) or (7).
35. U.S. Dep't of State v. Washington Post Co., 456 U.S. 595, 602 (1982) ("similar files" language not limited to files containing intimate details or highly personal information). *See also* New York Times Co. v. NASA, 920 F.2d 1002, 1004 (D.C. Cir. 1990) (en banc) (information must apply to "particular individuals").

depend on the official status and rank of the individual, in that the personal privacy interest of a high government official may be narrower than that of a lower-level employee or of a private citizen. S. Rep., 21-22; H. Rep. I, 11. The D.C. Circuit's *Common Cause* decision supports that approach.[36] The court noted that an agency may not use Exemption (6) "to shield itself from political controversy involving the agency and its employees about which the public should be informed."[37] The court also noted that Exemption (6) provides greater protection for private individuals, such as applicants for federal grants or officials of regulated companies, than for government officials with executive responsibilities.[38] Moreover, both congressional committee reports state—the Senate Report somewhat more emphatically—that the exemption would not be available where the individual involved prefers an open meeting.[39]

The Supreme Court's 1989 decision in *U.S. Department of Justice v. Reporters Committee for Freedom of the Press* is considered to be a landmark discussion of numerous issues addressing the balance between an individual's right to privacy and the public's right to

---

36. *See Common Cause, supra* note 4 at 938, citing Senate and House Reports (Exemption (6) does not "shelter substandard performance by government executives" discussed during budget deliberations.).
37. *Id.,* citing S. REP., at 21-22. *Cf. Wilkinson, supra* p. 74, 865 F. Supp. at 894 n.2. (Exemption (6) does not apply to discussions concerning renewal of employment contract of a "high-level employee" such as an agency's Inspector General.)
38. *Common Cause, supra* note 4 at 938. In the context of the analogous exemption to the Federal Advisory Committee Act, the Office of Legal Counsel, Department of Justice, has suggested that protecting reputation among colleagues, professional background, or performance of an applicant for financial assistance would constitute legitimate privacy interests. *Applicability of the Federal Advisory Committee Act to the National Endowment for the Humanities*, 4 Op. O.L.C. (Vol. B) 743 (1980).
39. *See* further discussion on pp. 105-06, *infra.* However, inasmuch as one purpose to be served by the exemption seems to be to permit candid exploration of an individual's qualifications or characteristics, *quaere* whether the individual's preference for an open meeting should always be dispositive. *See, e.g.,* Wu v. Nat'l Endowment for Humanities, 460 F. 2d 1030 (5th Cir. 1972), *cert. denied*, 410 U.S. 926 (1973).

disclosure in the context of FOIA.[40] Some aspects of the Court's decision are plainly applicable in the Sunshine Act context. For example, the Court made clear that a privacy interest can exist in personal information even if that information has been made available to the public elsewhere.[41] Moreover, the Court determined that certain types of information may categorically satisfy the private interest aspect of the balancing test without regard to individual circumstances.[42]

A central aspect of the Court's decision affecting the balancing process itself was its adoption of a limited definition of the public interest in disclosure. Such interest is restricted to the "core purpose" of the FOIA—"to open agency action to the light of public scrutiny"[43] or "contribute . . . significantly to public understanding *of the operations or activities of the government.*"[44] "Official information that sheds light on an agency's performance of its statutory duties falls squarely within . . . [the] statutory purpose."[45] The precise effect of this aspect of the *Reporters Committee* decision (and its progeny) on the balancing test under the Sunshine Act is unclear. In a 1994 FOIA case, Justice Ginsburg reflected the popularly held view that the Court's narrow definition of the "public interest" articulated in *Reporters Committee* "changed the FOIA calculus that underlies . . . [earlier] prodisclosure decisions."[46] Under the reasoning of the *Reporters Committee* case,

---

40. U.S. Dep't of Justice v. Reporters Comm. for Freedom of the Press, 489 U.S. 749 (1989) (hereafter *Reporters Committee*). The Court's decision in *Reporters Committee* was technically limited to FOIA Exemption 7(C) rather than Exemption (6). See 489 U.S. at 762 n.12. However, the Court later made clear that the two exemptions differ only in the "magnitude of the public interest that is required," not in the identification of the relevant public interest. *See* U.S. Dep't of Def. v. Fed. Labor Relations Auth., 510 U.S. 487, 496-97 n.6 (1994) (hereafter *Defense Dept.*).
41. *Reporters Committee, supra* note 40 at 762-69.
42. *Id.* at 780.
43. *Id.* at 772.
44. *Id.* at 775 (emphasis in original).
45. *Id.* at 771.
46. *See Defense Dept., supra* note 40 at 505 (Ginsburg, J., concurring). The "Blackletter" APA project of the ABA Section of Administrative Law and Regulatory Practice suggested that Congress may have overturned the "core purpose" standard when it enacted the 1996 Electronic FOIA Amendments. *See Blackletter Statement, supra* note 2, 54 ADMIN. L. REV. at 67. However, the

(continued on next page)

for example, there is typically no public interest in disclosure in which one individual is seeking information about another because the requester does not intend to discover anything about the conduct of the agency that holds the record.[47] However, allowing the public to observe the decisional process of multimember agencies—that is, to let the public know what the agency is doing when its members come together for deliberation or decision—has always been central to the Sunshine Act purpose of opening agency action to the light of public scrutiny and enhancing public understanding of agency activities or operations. So the public interest element of the balancing test enunciated by the Court in *Reporters Committee* will almost always be implicated in a Sunshine Act context.

EXEMPTION (7)—INVESTIGATORY RECORDS

(7) disclose investigatory records compiled for law enforcement purposes, or information which if written would be contained in such records, but only to the extent that the production of such records or information would (A) interfere with enforcement proceedings, (B) deprive a person of a right to a fair trial or an impartial adjudication, (C) constitute an unwarranted invasion of personal privacy, (D) disclose the identity of a confidential source and, in the case of a record compiled by a criminal law enforcement authority in the course of a criminal investigation, or by an agency conducting a lawful national security intelligence investigation, confidential information furnished only by the confidential source, (E) disclose investigative techniques and procedures, or (F) endanger the life or physical safety of law enforcement personnel;

Exemption (7) as originally enacted was substantially identical to the seventh exemption of the Freedom of Information Act.[48] So some of

---

(continued from previous page)
11th Circuit has noted that the Electronic FOIA Amendments of 1996 did not invalidate the private/public interest balancing test. O'Kane v. U.S. Customs Service, 169 F.3d 1308 (11th Cir. 1999).

47. *Reporters Committee, supra* note 40 at 773.
48. *See* S. Rep., at 22. The Sunshine Act Exemption (7) reflected the 1974 amendments to FOIA Exemption (7). Pub. L. No. 93-502, 88 Stat. 1561, 1563 (1974).

the case law under the FOIA is pertinent. However, Congress significantly amended FOIA Exemption (7) in 1986[49] to broaden the protection for law enforcement records. Congress expanded FOIA Exemption (7) to cover "information" as well as records; explicitly provided that the term "confidential source" includes state, local, and foreign agencies and private institutions that furnish information on a confidential basis; removed the requirement that records or information be "investigatory" in character; and, perhaps most important, substituted the phrase "could reasonably be expected to" for "would" as the standard for the risk of harm with respect to FOIA subparagraphs (A), (C), (D), and (F). It also added three limited circumstances (called "exclusions") affecting Exemption 7(A) materials where the agency, when responding to an FOIA request, may treat records simply as if they did not exist.[50] These amendments clearly ease a federal law enforcement agency's burden when invoking or applying FOIA Exemption (7).[51] However, these amendments have not been incorporated into the Sunshine Act. It remains to be seen whether the courts will seek to bend Sunshine Act Exemption (7) to accommodate the concerns behind the amended FOIA Exemption (7). *See more generally* chapter 10.

EXEMPTION (8)—FINANCIAL INSTITUTION REPORTS

(8) disclose information contained in or related to examination, operating, or condition reports prepared by, on behalf of, or for the use of an agency responsible for the regulation or supervision of financial institutions;

The Senate Report says:

This paragraph applies to meetings which disclose information contained in or relating to examination, operating, or condition reports on financial institutions. These reports are prepared by or for the use of such banking agencies as the Federal Reserve Board, Federal Deposit Insurance Corporation, and the Federal

---

49. Pub. L. No. 99-570, 100 Stat. 3207-48 (1986).
50. 5 U.S.C. § 552(c). For example, there may be situations in which the subject of a criminal investigation is unaware of it and disclosure of the investigation itself would interfere with enforcement proceedings.
51. *See, e.g., Reporters Committee, supra* note 40 at 756 n.9.

Home Loan Bank Board. This provision is identical to Exemption (b)(8) of the Freedom of Information Act and should be interpreted in the same way.

S. Rep., 25.

It should be noted, however, that in its explanation of Exemption (9)(A), the same report stated:

> The term "financial institutions" is intended to include banks, savings and loan associations, credit unions, brokers and dealers in securities or commodities, exchanges dealing in securities or commodities, such as the New York Stock Exchange, investment companies, investment advisers, self-regulatory organizations subject to 15 U.S.C. § 78s, and institutional managers as defined in 15 U.S.C. § 78m(f).

S. Rep., 24.

The term has the same meaning in Exemption (8), and the courts have construed Sunshine Exemptions (8) and 9(A) consistently with each other as well as with FOIA Exemption (8).[52]

EXEMPTIONS (9)(A), (B)—FINANCIAL SPECULATION AND STABILITY; FRUSTRATION OF PROPOSED AGENCY ACTION

(9) disclose information the premature disclosure of which would—
(A) in the case of an agency which regulates currencies, securities, commodities, or financial institutions, be likely to (i) lead to significant financial speculation in currencies, securities, or commodities, or (ii) significantly endanger the stability of any financial institution; or

---

52. *See Berliner Zisser, supra* p. 67 note 4 at 1352-53 (brokers and dealers of securities or commodities and self-regulatory organizations come within the Exemption (8) definition of "financial institution"); Mermelstein v. SEC, 629 F. Supp. 672 (D.D.C. 1988) (stock exchanges come within the Exemption (8) definition of "financial institution"). The Securities and Exchange Commission has likewise construed the two exemptions consistently. 17 C.F.R. § 200.401(g).

(B) in the case of any agency, be likely to significantly frustrate implementation of a proposed agency action, except that subparagraph (B) shall not apply in any instance where the agency has already disclosed to the public the content or nature of its proposed action, or where the agency is required by law to make such disclosure on its own initiative prior to taking final agency action on such proposal;

Exemption (9), which has no counterpart in the FOIA, consists of two parts. Subparagraph (A) is available only to agencies that regulate currencies, securities, commodities, or financial institutions and would permit such agencies to close meetings in order to protect information the disclosure of which would lead to financial speculation or would "significantly endanger the stability of any financial institution."[53] Among the agencies to which Exemption (9)(A) is available are the Federal Reserve Board, the Securities and Exchange Commission, and the Federal Deposit Insurance Corporation. S. Rep., 24.[54] It is extensively used.[55]

Subparagraph (B) is potentially available to any agency and raises difficult issues of application.[56] There are potential disadvantages to any collegial body in opening meetings and thereby airing the pros and cons of various proposed actions and the strengths and weaknesses of alternative positions. The candor of participants may be curtailed. Preliminary observations may be offered that may later change.

---

53. We read "in the case of an agency," etc., as referring to the agency holding the meeting, H. REP. I, at 12. Other agencies that have occasion to discuss information otherwise within Exemption (9)(A) might be able to close the meeting on other grounds, but could not invoke (9)(A).
54. The Commodity Credit Corporation has concluded that its programs relating to price supports for agricultural commodities and interest rates for commodity loans come within the terms of Exemption (9)(A). *See* 7 C.F.R. § 1409.5.
55. For example, in 2001, the Federal Reserve Board closed 63 of its 68 meetings. The Board invoked Exemption (9)(A) in 55 cases. *See* BOARD OF GOVERNORS OF THE FEDERAL RESERVE SYSTEM, ANNUAL REPORT TO CONGRESS ON THE GOVERNMENT IN THE SUNSHINE ACT FOR 2001 (March 2002).
56. One court has noted that the exemption is "difficult to interpret and, perhaps, more perplexing to apply." *Wilkinson, supra* p. 74 at 895.

Even public knowledge that an agency is not unanimous in support of a particular policy might possibly be regarded by some as a source of weakness in the agency's ultimate decision. However, these possibilities for frustration of agency action are inherent in the open meeting principle and, at least absent special circumstances, are not grounds for invoking Exemption (9)(B). See, e.g., *Public Citizen, supra* note 5 at 113 (applying Exemption (9)(B) in the context of FACA, court rejects the arguments that potential compromise in candid expression of views by senior government officials or the possibility that the public may draw improper inferences that may inhibit ultimate consensus is sufficient to justify an across-the-board closure of all meetings).

Exemption (9)(B) must be read in a manner consistent with the overall Sunshine Act objective of openness.[57] The D.C. Circuit has observed that Exemption (9)(B) "protects agency discussions of material whose premature disclosure could affect the decisions or actions of third parties acting in a nongovernmental capacity, thus causing a significant adverse effect upon the government's financial or regulatory interests."[58] Exemption (9)(B) would be satisfied if premature disclosure of an agency's action could lead to "financial gain at government expense" or "circumvention of agency regulation."[59]

The prototypical situation to which the exemption is addressed seems to be the regulatory action that must be imposed without notice in order to prevent forestalling action by the regulated community. *See Attorney General's Manual on the Administrative Procedure Act,* at 31 (1947). Such an example, cited at S. Rep., 24, is an embargo on shipment of

---

57. The court in *Common Cause, supra* note 4 at 932-33, noted that "for two reasons, the precept of narrow construction applies with particular force to this exemption [9(B)]. . . . First . . . Congress decided not to provide any exemption for predecisional deliberations because it wished the process of decision as well as the results to be open to public view. . . . Yet, the agencies may attempt to seize upon the language of Exemption 9(B) to avoid the perceived discomfort and inconvenience that are," quoting the *1978 Guide,* at 24, "inherent in the open meeting principle. . . ." "Second, an overly broad construction of Exemption 9(B), which applies to all agencies subject to the Act, would allow agencies to 'circumvent the spirit of openness which underlies this legislation,'" quoting S. REP., at 20.
58. *Common Cause, supra* note 4 at 936.
59. *Id.* at 934 n.40.

certain goods, which, if announced in advance, would lead to export of the goods before the embargo took effect.

There is, however, legislative history supporting the application of Exemption (9)(B) to somewhat different circumstances. The House and Senate Reports cite certain examples of situations appropriate for invoking (9)(B). The courts have looked to these examples to establish the contours of the exemption.[60] First, an agency might engage in a "discussion of the strategy an agency will follow in collective bargaining with its employees. Public disclosure might make it impossible to reach an agreement." S. Rep., 24. See also H. Rep. I, 12. The thrust of the exemption here appears to be to protect agency discussions that are aimed at developing a negotiating position as opposed to resolving a matter by unilateral action. The purpose presumably is to enable the agency to avoid divulging its fallback positions in advance of negotiation.[61] Second, an agency may be contemplating a purchase of real estate. Conf. Rep., 15. Here, too, it is not the development of the agency position so much as its intended effect that is frustrated by disclosure. Third, an agency might close a meeting to consider an embargo on foreign shipments of certain goods. This can be characterized as a situation in which the agency's action takes place, but its intended effects are frustrated by the prior notice to the affected parties.[62]

A question has been raised as to whether an agency would be able to assert Exemption (9)(B) to protect a proposed action of another agency. Although the situation may not have been in the contemplation of the drafters, the text of the Act seems to permit it, and nothing in the policy underlying (9)(B) requires a different result. The agency closing the meeting would, of course, have to make its own determi-

---

60. *See, e.g., Common Cause, supra* note 4 at 933; *Wilkinson, supra* p. 74.
61. *See, e.g.,* regulation of the U.S. Postal Service, 39 C.F.R. § 7.3(i).
62. The Office of Management and Budget had suggested that a meeting to discuss the agency's budget proposal prior to the transmittal by the President to Congress of the budget of which it is a part may be eligible for closure under Exemption (9)(B) on the ground that "the premature disclosure of budgetary information may 'be likely to significantly frustrate implementation of a proposed agency action.'" OMB Circular No. A-IC, § 7 (revised Nov. 12, 1976). That conclusion, however, was squarely rejected by the D.C. Circuit in its *Common Cause* decision.

nation as to the likelihood of harm from opening the meeting and as to the public interest in an open meeting.

Exemption (9)(B) is not available where the agency has already disclosed to the public the content or nature of its proposed action or where it is required to do so before taking final action on the proposal. As stated in the Senate Report, "Since [(9)(B)] only applies when an agency feels it must act in secret, it would be contrary to the intent of this provision for an agency to rely on it when the public is already aware of the actions being considered, or where the Administrative Procedure Act or other statute requires the agency to publicly announce its proposal before taking final action." S. Rep., 25. This exception throws additional light on the basic purpose of Exemption (9)(B), that ordinarily it is not the agency's deliberation itself so much as the efficacy of the determination that the exemption is designed to protect.

The Conference Report noted, with respect to Exemption (9)(B), that disclosure of information regarding the proposed action by a source other than the agency, as by an unauthorized "leak," would not make the exemption unavailable. Conf. Rep., 15. However, any selective public availability of information, or agency concerns over confirming the accuracy of the information, would certainly bear on an agency's determination under section 552b(c) that the public interest requires an open meeting.

Finally, it should be noted that neither Exemption (9)(A) nor (9)(B) may be invoked unless "significant" adverse effects are anticipated from disclosure. As with all exemptions, the Act establishes a "foreseeability standard."[63] Determining what is significant involves a balancing of the public interests in disclosure and in nondisclosure. *See* S. Rep., 25.[64] Of course, the standard of "significance" is not absolute, but relative to the importance of the matter involved.

---

63. *Common Cause, supra* note 4 at 929.
64. The terms "significant" and "significantly" were substituted for "serious" and "seriously" on the Senate floor. *See* 121 Cong. Rec. 53,330 (1975). According to one court, "[U]se of the word 'significantly' [in Exemption 9(B) is] intended to limit closings to instances where disclosure at the time in question would have a considerable adverse effect." *Public Citizen, supra* note 5, at 125.

EXEMPTION (10)—ISSUANCE OF SUBPOENA, PARTICIPATION IN CIVIL ACTION OR PROCEEDING, FORMAL AGENCY ADJUDICATION

(10) specifically concern the agency's issuance of a subpena [sic], or the agency's participation in a civil action or proceeding, an action in a foreign court or international tribunal, or an arbitration, or the initiation, conduct, or disposition by the agency of a particular case of formal agency adjudication pursuant to the procedures in section 554 of this title or otherwise involving a determination on the record after opportunity for a hearing.

Exemption (10) has no counterpart in the FOIA. The Senate Report explains the considerations behind Exemption (10) as follows:

> The committee felt that it would be inappropriate for several reasons to require agencies to open meetings discussing specific cases of adjudication. Public disclosure of an agency's legal strategy in a case before the agency or in the courts could make it impossible to litigate successfully the action. Public discussions of the guilt or innocence of a particular individual in agency adjudication could unfairly injure a person's reputation, or make it impossible for him to receive a fair or impartial hearing. Adjudications of the type covered by this paragraph must already be decided solely on the information in the record. Unlike other cases, the entire record on which the agency must make its decision in adjudication is open to inspection by any member of the public. . . . Finally, many aspects of the adjudicative process, such as the trial before an administrative law judge or appellate arguments before the commission, are generally open now to the public.
>
> To fall within the provisions of this paragraph the discussion must concern a particular case of adjudication. If the agency discusses a particular series of cases, each of which meets the requirements of this paragraph, the meeting may also be closed. The paragraph would not apply when an agency discusses its adjudication policies in general, such as

the policy that should be adopted towards all those that may violate a particular law.

S. Rep., 26.

The first phrase regarding agency adjudication expressly covers proceedings conducted pursuant to section 554 of the APA.[65] Whether a proceeding need be conducted pursuant to section 554 depends on the language of the statute conferring the hearing right, which is typically the agency's organic or enabling statute. This issue can, at times, be controversial.[66] What is even less clear is the precise meaning of the second phrase, "or otherwise involving a determination on the record after opportunity for a hearing."[67] Given the use of the

---

65. *See generally* SECTION OF ADMINISTRATIVE LAW AND REGULATORY PRACTICE, A GUIDE TO FEDERAL AGENCY ADJUDICATION 29-30 (Asimow ed., 2003). *See, e.g.*, Amrep Corp. v. FTC, 768 F.2d 1171 (10th Cir. 1985) (unfair and deceptive practice proceeding initially heard by an administrative law judge and affirmed by the agency).

66. *See, e.g.,* United States v. Fla. East Coast Ry., 410 U.S. 224, 234 (1973) (concluding that, in the context of rulemaking, the term "after hearing" in the former Interstate Commerce Commission statute was not equivalent to "on the record after opportunity for an agency hearing" when determining whether the statute required an APA hearing); Friends of the Earth v. Reilly, 966 F.2d 690, 693 (D.C. Cir. 1992) ("what counts is whether the statute indicates that Congress intended to require full agency adherence to all section 554 procedural components"); Railroad Comm'n of Texas v. United States, 765 F.2d 221, 228 (D.C. Cir. 1985) (the statutory requirement of a full hearing before the Interstate Commerce Commission may deny a state the authority to regulate intrastate rail traffic, but that is not the same as a hearing "on the record" subject to sections 554, 556, and 557 of the APA).

67. For example, the General Counsel of the International Trade Commission took the position that antidumping and countervailing duty proceedings are investigative rather than adjudicatory and do not constitute determinations "on the record after opportunity for a hearing." *See* Administrative Conference Recommendation 91-10, *Administrative Procedures Used in Antidumping and Countervailing Duty Cases*, 56 Fed. Reg. 67,139, 67,145 (Dec. 30, 1991). That conclusion has been criticized. *See, e.g.,* James T. O'Reilly & Gracia M. Berg, *Stealth Caused by Sunshine: How Sunshine Act Interpretation Results in Less Information for the Public About the Decision-Making Process of the International Trade Commission*, 36 HARV. INT'L L. J. 425 (Spring 1995).

disjunctive term "or," the latter phrase must embrace at least some proceedings not governed by section 554 of the APA.[68] Syntactically, the phrase appears to be qualified by "particular case of formal adjudication." However, there is a suggestion in the Senate Report that the term "adjudication" was not intended to exclude formal rulemaking. *See* S. Rep., 26, which cites as an example of a situation in which the agency should choose to open a meeting, notwithstanding the availability of Exemption (10), "a formal rulemaking proceeding where general agency policy, rather than the facts of a particular case, are determinative." The House Judiciary Committee Report likewise assumes that Exemption (10) includes all formal agency proceedings, whether adjudication or rulemaking. H. Rep. II, 9. Noting the legislative history, the *1978 Guide* suggested that despite the use of the term "adjudication," the exemption was not intended to exclude formal rulemaking.[69] The courts have since endorsed this interpretation.[70]

The Second Circuit has gone further. It has indicated that the exemption is available—as it is with formal rulemaking—when an agency must adhere to sections 556 and 557 of the APA.[71] The D.C. Circuit

---

68. *Cf.* Equal Access to Justice Act, 5 U.S.C. § 504, which allows attorney's fees only if a party prevails against the government in an "adversary adjudication," which is defined as a proceeding under section 554 of the APA. *See, e.g., Ardestani v. INS,* 502 U.S. 129 (1991) (explaining that proceedings before the Immigration and Naturalization Service, although including essentially the same procedural components as formal adjudication under section 554, are not covered by the Equal Access to Justice Act because they were not required to be held under section 554).
69. *1978 Guide,* at 27-28.
70. *Philadelphia Newspapers, Inc., supra* p. 68 at 1202-03; Time, Inc., et al. v. United States Postal Service, 667 F.2d 329, 334 (2d Cir. 1981) (hereafter *Time, Inc.*).
71. *Id.* at 334 (the clause includes "all cases for which the procedures of §§ 556 and 557 were required"). APA section 556 requires, for example, that parties are entitled to full opportunity to present their case, including the right to present rebuttal evidence and cross-examine witnesses; that the agency's decision must be based on reliable, probative, and substantial evidence; and, perhaps most important, that the public record is the exclusive basis for the agency's decision. Section 557(d) prohibits *ex parte* communications. Separation of functions is the primary element of the formal hearing that is not included in section 556 or 557 (it is included in section 554 and is appli-

(continued on next page)

has suggested that the exemption is available for all formal proceedings in which the agency agrees to adhere to the strictures of section 554, even if not required by statute to do so.[72] The court reasoned that Congress intended the exemption to apply whenever a proceeding must be decided solely on a formal record and significant aspects of the proceeding are already open to public observation.[73]

Given that the courts have clearly extended Exemption (10) to cover whenever an agency is conducting a proceeding, such as a formal rulemaking, that is decided solely on a formal record, one might ask whether a failure to adhere to separation of functions requirements automatically precludes an agency from invoking Exemption (10).[74] By analogy to formal rulemaking, the answer should be "no." See *Time, Inc., supra* note 70, 667 F.2d at 334, stating that the exemption covers "all cases for which the procedures of §§ 556 and 557 were required." However, in *Philadelphia Newspapers, supra,* Judge Wright believed that off-the-record communications between the agency staff and the commissioners, which are technically a violation of the sepa-

---

(continued from previous page)
cable in cases of formal adjudication but not formal rulemaking). *See generally* STEPHEN BREYER, RICHARD STEWART, CASS SUNSTEIN & MATTHEW SPITZER, ADMINISTRATIVE LAW AND REGULATORY POLICY: PROBLEMS, TEXT AND CASES 565-66 (Aspen Law & Business 4th ed. 1999); JEFFREY S. LUBBERS, A GUIDE TO FEDERAL AGENCY RULEMAKING 3d ed. 43-45 (ABA Publishing 1998).

72. The court in *Philadelphia Newspapers* observed that the Nuclear Regulatory Commission proceeding was "in substance . . . a Section 554 adjudication and thus functionally within Exemption 10." *See* note 70, *supra*, at 1203. *Cf. Time Inc., supra* note 71 at 334 ("The evident sense of Congress was that when a statute required an agency to act as would a court, its deliberations should be protected from disclosure as a court's would be.").

73. *Philadelphia Newspapers, supra* p. 68 at 1203. There is no support, however, in either the Sunshine Act text or its legislative history to support the D.C. Circuit's observation in *Philadelphia Newspapers* that the second clause of Exemption 10 "was meant primarily to encompass formal rulemaking and not adjudication." (The court expressly declined to decide the issue.) *See Philadelphia Newspapers, supra* p. 68 at 1202 n.3 and accompanying text.

74. The separation of functions requirement is contained in section 554(d), not in section 556 or 557.

ration of functions requirement,[75] was central to depriving a proceeding of its "formal" or "on the record" character. *Philadelphia Newspapers,* at 1198, 1201-02.

One of the few illustrations of what procedures may be sufficient to satisfy the requirements of Exemption (10) is District Judge Louis Oberdorfer's examination of an "original jurisdiction" administrative appeal by the United States Parole Commission.[76] The Parole Commission adjudicates individual parole cases. Meetings of the full Commission to determine so-called "original jurisdiction" appeals are considered to be meetings under the Commission's Sunshine Act regulations.[77] An initial parole decision is rendered by a panel of hearing examiners following a hearing at which the prisoner is present. The prisoner has access to information to be considered by the Commission and may testify at the hearing. Disputes concerning the accuracy of information are resolved under a preponderance-of-the-evidence standard. A decision is based on the record established at the hearing and the prisoner receives a statement of reasons for the decision. The prisoner is entitled to an administrative appeal of that decision and appeals considered by the full Commission are denominated "original jurisdiction" appeals. In response to a request from a prisoner for the tape recording of the full Commission's meeting, Judge Oberdorfer upheld the Commission's conclusion that these procedures involved a determination on the record after opportunity for a hearing and thus met the requirements of Exemption (10).

Given the judicial gloss placed on the statute, the exemption would appear to be available for that portion of a meeting that discusses any

---

75. Intra-agency communications to an administrative law judge may constitute an *ex parte* communication under the APA. *See* 5 U.S.C. § 554(d)(1). Otherwise, an *ex parte* communication is limited to communications between an agency decisional official and someone "outside the agency." *See* 5 U.S.C. § 557(d).
76. James v. Baer, Civ. A. No. 89-2841-LFO, 1990 U.S. Dist. LEXIS 5702 (D.D.C. 1990).
77. The description of an "original jurisdiction" administrative appeal is taken from the Government's Motion for Summary Judgment filed in the U.S. District Court for the District of Columbia in Civil Action No. 89-2841 LFO and the accompanying Statement of Material Facts as to which There is No Genuine Issue and Affidavit of Mary E. Cahill, attorney, Office of General Counsel, U.S. Parole Commission (filed March 15, 1990).

"on-the-record" proceeding or a proceeding in which the record is the exclusive basis for decision and the central elements of a trial-type hearing, such as the right to present evidence and argument and receive an explanation of the agency's administrative disposition, are present—whether required by statute or not. However, an agency cannot get the benefit of procedural flexibility ordinarily associated with informal adjudication and later seek to rely on Exemption (10).[78]

While the discussion must relate to a particular case or cases for the exemption to be available,[79] the case need not be pending at the time of the discussion. The Senate Report states that "discussions concerning whether the agency should either bring an action itself or ask the Department of Justice to bring it," S. Rep., 26, are within the exemption, and there is no reason why discussion of possible agency participation in an action as intervenor, defendant, or amicus curiae would not be entitled to similar treatment.[80]

---

78. *See Philadelphia Newspapers, supra* p. 68 at 1196, noting that the NRC created separate yet interrelated proceedings to evaluate whether restarting the undamaged reactor at Three Mile Island would jeopardize public safety. Only one was on-the-record; the other three used informal decisional processes. "In retrospect, it does appear that the [Nuclear Regulatory Commission] was attempting to 'have it both ways,' limiting the scope of the on-the-record adjudication narrowly, while seeking to apply Exemption 10 broadly." *See* Letter from Peter Crane, attorney, Nuclear Regulatory Commission, to Gary Edles, general counsel, Administrative Conference of the United States, p. 9 (Feb. 6, 1995).

79. While "a particular case" is used in Exemption (10) only with respect to agency proceedings, we believe that the references to *a* civil action, and *an* action in a foreign court, etc., likewise contemplate particular cases (emphases added).

80. Agency discussions of whether to institute a civil action or formal adjudication are covered. *Wilkinson, supra* p. 74, 865 F. Supp. at 896 ("adversarial proceedings are imminent"). *See also* A.G. Becker Inc. v. Board of Governors of the Federal Reserve System, 502 F. Supp. 378, 386-87 (D.D.C. 1980) (When an agency must make a decision about institution of a proceeding based on petitions from outside parties, it has a considerable degree of discretion in construing the scope of the outside request in determining whether Exemption (10) is applicable.). However, the qualification that the discussion concern a "particular case" would be emptied of significance if the exemption

(continued on next page)

Most agencies routinely invoke Exemption (10) when discussing formal adjudications. The Federal Mine Safety and Health Review Commission (FMSHRC) is the exception. The FMSHRC is entirely an adjudicatory agency. Nevertheless, its policy is to open almost all its meetings to public observation, including a meeting concerning the disposition of a formal adjudication.[81]

A recurring issue in Exemption 10 cases is whether, and to what degree, an agency may blend its discussion of a particular case with a discussion of broader issues. A threshold inquiry is whether agency deliberations will deal with the specifically enumerated topics that trigger the exemption—for example, whether the agency deliberations will deal with "the agency's participation in a civil action."[82] But the mere fact that an agency meeting may be devoted in part to exempt matters does not automatically permit the agency to close the meeting in its entirety.[83] Agencies are required to "make every reasonable effort to segregate the exempt from the nonexempt."[84] However, the D.C. Circuit has recognized that "[f]or purposes of Exemption 10 . . . there can be no hard-and-fast distinction between litigation strategy and policy questions; what matters is simply that the agency deliberations in ques-

---

(continued from previous page)
were held available for any discussion of legal objections to a proposed course of action. *See also Philadelphia Newspapers, supra* p. 68 at 1201. (The exemption clearly applies if the "particular case of formal agency adjudication" is pending before a subordinate element of the agency, such as an administrative law judge.)

81. *See* 29 C.F.R. § 2701.2(a). The decision to open meetings discussing a formal adjudication was not without controversy. At one stage, one FMSHRC commissioner declined to attend open meetings "in light of his view that there cannot be candid discussions at open meetings." *See* Bob Geiger, *Mine Safety Panelist Won't Go to Meetings,* LEXINGTON (Ky.) HERALD-LEADER, June 11, 1995, at B1, *Marks Continues to Be No-Show at Open Commission Decisional Meetings,* MINE SAFETY AND HEALTH NEWS, April 21, 1995, at 227, and Toby McIntosh, *Where's the Sunshine? Closing the Door on Open Meetings,* 35 COLUMBIA JOURNALISM REVIEW, at 15-16, May/June 1996.
82. *Clark-Cowlitz, supra* note 10 at 502.
83. *Philadelphia Newspapers, supra* p. 68 at 1200-01.
84. *Id.* at 1201. *See also Standards for Closing a Meeting of the Select Commission on Immigration and Refugee Policy,* 43 Op. Att'y Gen. 290 (1980).

tion deal with 'the agency's participation in a civil action.'"[85] In other words, agencies are not required to segregate a discussion of a civil action into the litigation and policy aspects necessarily implicated in that action and open up the discussion of the policy aspect. This is not to say, however, that an agency may avoid public discussion of policy questions merely because the policy developed might be implemented through civil actions. Indeed, the General Counsel of the Federal Trade Commission has suggested that "[t]he conventional wisdom . . . is that the agency may not meet in closed session to develop a consistent approach for application in future cases."[86]

As noted above, for all exemptions, including Exemption (10), the Act establishes a "foreseeability standard."[87] However, when considering the release of transcripts of closed meetings, the agency and reviewing court must base their decisions on the discussions that actually occurred. If the agency is justified in invoking Exemption (10), it need not later release the transcript of that meeting merely because the litigation has concluded.[88]

---

85. *Clark-Cowlitz, supra* note 10 at 502. *See* Shurberg Broadcasting of Hartford, Inc. v. FCC, 617 F. Supp. 825 (D.D.C. 1985) (two matters sufficiently interrelated to justify closure of the entire meeting).
86. Prepared Statement of the Federal Trade Commission presented by Stephen Calkins, General Counsel, before the Special Committee to Review the Government in the Sunshine Act, Administrative Conference of the United States, pp. 2-3. (Sept. 12, 1995).
87. *Common Cause, supra* note 4 at 929. *See also* note 22, *supra*, and accompanying text.
88. *Clark-Cowlitz, supra* note 10 at 503.

Chapter 4

SECTION 552b(d) PROCEDURES FOR CLOSING MEETINGS

REQUIRED MAJORITY VOTE ON CLOSING AND INFORMATION "PROPOSED TO BE WITHHELD UNDER SUBSECTION (C)"	98
Voting to Close by Notation Procedure	98
Meaning of "Portion or Portions" of a Meeting	99
"Series of Meetings" Procedure	100
Recorded Vote and No Proxies	100
REQUESTS TO CLOSE MEETINGS	101
Requests to Close on Other Grounds	103
Procedures Under Subsection (d)(2)	103
Requests to Open Meetings	105
PUBLIC AVAILABILITY OF VOTE, "FULL WRITTEN EXPLANATION" OF CLOSING, AND LIST OF ALL ATTENDEES	106
Availability of Vote	107
"Full Written Explanation" of Closing	107
List of All Expected Attendees	108
EXPEDITED CLOSING PROCEDURE	111
Computing the "Majority"	115
Documentary Justification	117

(d)(1) Action under subsection (c) shall be taken only when a majority of the entire membership of the agency (as defined in subsection (a)(1)) votes to take such action. A separate vote of the agency members shall be taken with respect to each agency meeting a portion or portions of which are proposed to be closed to the public pursuant to subsection (c), or with respect to any information which is proposed to be withheld under

subsection (c). A single vote may be taken with respect to a series of meetings, a portion or portions of which are proposed to be closed to the public, or with respect to any information concerning such series of meetings, so long as each meeting in such series involves the same particular matters and is scheduled to be held no more than thirty days after the initial meeting in such series. The vote of each agency member participating in such vote shall be recorded and no proxies shall be allowed.

REQUIRED MAJORITY VOTE ON CLOSING AND INFORMATION "PROPOSED TO BE WITHHELD UNDER SUBSECTION (C)"

Subsection (d) sets forth the procedures an agency must follow to close a meeting or portions of a meeting and to withhold from the public announcements information relating to the meeting otherwise required by subsections (d) and (e). These procedures are prescribed in considerable detail and have engendered little dispute.

Subsection (d)(1) permits the closing of a meeting or portion of a meeting, or the withholding of information about the meeting, only when "a majority of the entire membership of the agency (as defined in subsection (a)(1)) votes to take such action." The Conference Report indicates that "the reference to the definition of 'agency' . . . is intended to make clear that when a subdivision is authorized to act on behalf of the agency, a majority of the entire membership of the subdivision is necessary to close a meeting." Conf. Rep., 17.

A separate vote must be taken on each meeting, or portion of a meeting, the agency wants to close, or with respect to any information about the meeting the agency wants to withhold.

Voting to Close by Notation Procedure

The legislative history is clear that a vote on whether or not to close a meeting or to withhold information about the meeting need not itself be taken at a gathering of agency members but can be taken by means of a seriatim notation procedure, such as the circulation of a written ballot or tally sheet. H. Rep. I, 3, 13. Where the members do convene to vote, however, this gathering is not a "meeting" within the definition of the Act,[1] and, therefore, none of the Act's requirements regarding meetings are applicable.

Meaning of "Portion or Portions" of a Meeting

Neither the statute nor the legislative history defines "portion or portions" of a meeting. The reference might be to an individual agenda item or to specific issues considered with respect to a particular agenda item. But since the justification for closing a meeting is in most cases the harm to be feared from the public disclosure of particular information, the practical definition of "portion of a meeting" is that part during which it is reasonably anticipated that such information may be discussed. As noted by a former Federal Trade Commission General Counsel: "In practice, a 'portion' of a meeting for Sunshine purposes is that unit of discussion further subdivision of which would interfere with the conduct of agency deliberations. That is to say, a 'portion' is a discussion that could not reasonably be further segregated into an open portion and closed portion."[2] Similarly, former Attorney General Benjamin Civiletti observed that an entire meeting may not be closed "based on the speculation that a free-form exploration of issues . . . might require that some classified information be disclosed."[3] Rather, "the meeting agenda [must] be structured so that classified and other exempt information is considered separately . . . unless such structuring is impossible."[4] However defined, each portion of each meeting stands on its own for purposes of complying with the closing requirements of subsection (d)(1). "The fact that one portion of a meeting may be closed does not justify the closing of any other portion." Conf. Rep., 17.

---

1. See p. 25, *supra*, regarding "Subsection (d) and (e) deliberations."
2. Letter of May 31, 1977, from Michael N. Sohn, general counsel, Federal Trade Commission, commenting on the tentative edition of the *1978 Guide*. See also A. G. Becker Inc. v. Bd. of Governors of the Fed. Reserve System, 502 F. Supp. 378, 387 (D.D.C. 1980) ("Whether the Sunshine Act contemplated segregation of a discussion of a single issue into open and closed portions at the same, or several meetings, is unclear," citing the *1978 Guide*, at 3.) (hereafter *A. G. Becker*).
3. *Standards for Closing a Meeting of the Select Commission on Immigration and Refugee Policy,* 43 Op. Att'y Gen. 290, 4 Op. O.L.C. (Vol. A) 67 (1980).
4. *Id.* at 68.

"Series of Meetings" Procedure

Subsection (d)(1) also permits a single vote to close "a series of meetings, a portion or portions of which are proposed to be closed to the public, or with respect to any information concerning such series of meetings," as long as each meeting in the series "involves the same particular matters and is scheduled to be held no more than thirty days after the initial meeting" in the series.

The Senate Report discusses this single vote closing procedure specifically:

> A single vote can be taken . . . to close a series of meetings where all the meetings will be held within a 30-day period and involve the same "particular matters." The latter phrase means more than general similarity of content. It must involve the same agenda item, such as a particular bank application, a proposal to suspend trading in a particular security, or the like.

S. Rep., 27.

The Senate Report goes on, "This provision was added so that the agency would not have to vote repeatedly on whether to close the same discussion which stretches over more than one meeting."[5]

Recorded Vote and No Proxies

The legislative history says little concerning the requirement of a recorded vote. Nor does it explain the clause "no proxies shall be allowed." Concerning the record vote, the House Government Operations Committee Report states that "the vote of each agency member must be recorded so as to permit identification by name of how each member has voted." H. Rep. I, 13. The Senate Report notes that "the voting procedures specified in paragraph (1) are equally applicable to the other votes an agency may be required to take pursuant to this [Act]." S. Rep., 27. Hence, a recorded vote is also required under subsections

---

5. *Id.* Another example of a situation where closing a series of meetings by a single vote might be appropriate would be where an agency in advance of conducting a public investigatory hearing votes to close off-the-record consultations among members on lines of questioning, issuance of subpoenas, or other problems arising in the course of the hearing.

(d)(2) [voting to close a meeting on the request of an affected individual], (d)(4) [the expedited closing procedure], (e)(1) [scheduling a meeting less than a week in advance], and (e)(2) [changing the subject matter or open-closed status of a previously announced meeting].

With regard to the use of proxies, the legislative history states that "no proxy votes may be cast in a vote on whether to close a meeting." H. Rep. I, 13; *see also* S. Rep., 27. Does this mean that each member must be physically present to vote, or can he or she delegate and instruct a staff assistant to cast the vote?

Because the Sunshine Act permits agency members to conduct business, including the determination whether or not to close agency meetings or portions thereof, by notation procedure, physical presence is not essential and there should be no objection to permitting a staff assistant to cast a vote on a subsection (d)(1) matter under instructions from his or her member. In either case, the decision and the responsibility are the member's. In other contexts courts have upheld a practice by which staff members vote for agency members at their direction. See, e.g., *Eastern Air Lines, Inc. v. CAB*, 271 F.2d 752, 757-58 (2d Cir. 1959), cert. denied, 362 U.S. 970 (1959). However, courts have struck down a practice under which staff personnel cast their members' votes under a general authority. *See, e.g., KFC National Management Corp. v. NLRB*, 497 F.2d 298, 303-06 (2d Cir. 1974). cert. denied, 423 U.S. 1087 (1976); *Flav-O-Rich, Inc. v. NLRB*, 531 F.2d 358 (6th Cir. 1976). We believe that a similar rule should apply here.[6]

REQUESTS TO CLOSE MEETINGS

(d)(2) Whenever any person whose interests may be directly affected by a portion of a meeting requests that the agency close such portion to the public for any of the reasons referred to in paragraph (5), (6), or (7) of subsection (c), the agency,

---

6. *See, e.g.,* regulation of the Federal Trade Commission, 16 C.F.R. § 4.14: "No Commissioner may delegate the authority to determine his or her vote in any matter requiring Commission action, but authority to report a Commissioner's vote on a particular matter resolved either by written circulation, or at a meeting held in the Commissioner's absence, may be vested in a member of the Commissioner's staff."

upon request of any one of its members, shall vote by recorded vote whether to close such meeting.

This "request to close" provision raises a number of questions on which the legislative history provides scanty guidance. The Senate Report provides the only extensive discussion of subsection (d)(2). It notes that:

> [I]n some cases a person may believe that an agency meeting directly affecting him would constitute an invasion of personal privacy [exemption 6], accuse him of criminal charges [exemption 5], or disclose information affecting him in an investigatory file [exemption 7]. The subsection specifically recognizes the right of a person in such circumstances to ask the agency to close the meeting. If one member of the agency concludes that the person may be directly and adversely affected by holding the meeting in public, the entire agency must vote on whether to close the meeting.

S. Rep., 28.

According to the Senate Report:

> [t]he purpose of this clause is to insure that an agency considers any person's legitimate concern that an open meeting may harm him in a direct and personal manner. It should help guarantee, for instance, that an agency does not inadvertently overlook the possibility that a particular discussion, if held in public, would constitute an invasion of personal privacy or disclose the identity of a confidential source. *Id.*

Does subsection (d)(2) give a person whose interests may be adversely affected by disclosure a right to compel the agency to close a meeting? The statute provides simply a procedural right before the agency; however, it does indicate a special concern that the agency strike an appropriate balance between the public interest in openness and the personal interests expressed by exemptions (5), (6), and (7).

Although it is clear that an agency is not required to close a meeting in response to a request under subsection (d)(2) simply because one of those exemptions is available, it is likely that an agency refusal to close a meeting would be reviewable in court under the arbitrary-and-capricious standard, just as an agency refusal to invoke an exemption under the Freedom of Information Act is so reviewable. See, for example, *Pennzoil Co. v. FPC*, 534 F.2d 627, 630-32 (5th Cir. 1976). However, to date, this situation does not appear to have arisen.

Requests to Close on Other Grounds

While subsection (d)(2) requires a procedure to permit agency consideration of requests to close under Exemptions (5), (6), and (7), nothing in the Act prevents an agency from making such procedure available for requests under Exemption (4) or any of the other exemptions. At least three agencies have such a provision in their regulations. The Federal Trade Commission's regulations permit "[a]ny person whose interest may be directly affected if a portion of a meeting is open . . . [to] request that the Commission close that portion for any of the reasons described in 5 U.S.C. § 552b(c)."[7] The vote of one member is sufficient to bring any such request to the Commission for vote. The Federal Mine Safety & Health Review Commission also has a provision permitting a request based on any of the exemptions.[8] The Surface Transportation Board will allow requests under Exemptions (4) and (9)(A) as well as (5), (6) and (7).[9] An agency refusal to close a meeting on grounds other than Exemptions (5), (6), and (7) is probably judicially reviewable at the instance of one who can show he or she is adversely affected or aggrieved by the decision, whether or not the agency has a procedure for entertaining such requests. *See* 5 U.S.C. § 702.[10] However, subsection (d)(2), where applicable, obviates objections based on judicially imposed or so-called "prudential" lack of standing.

Procedures Under Subsection (d)(2)

Neither the Act nor its legislative history provides specific guidance on the nature of the procedures agencies must follow under subsection (d)(2)—whether, for example, an agency must provide an affected per-

---

7. 16 C.F.R. § 4.15(b)(2).
8. 29 C.F.R. § 2701.4.
9. 49 C.F.R. § 1012.6(c).
10. *See* pp. 185-86, *infra*.

son advance notice of a meeting so the person can request a closing under (d)(2). In most cases, agency members will be aware of or may assume the affected person's desire for a closed meeting at the time of the initial vote to close or open the meeting.[11] If, however, the request is made subsequent to the announcement of a decision to hold a meeting, there must be some procedure at the instance of a single member for reconsideration, or for initial consideration by the collegial body if the item was placed on the "open agenda" without collegial action. For example, the Nuclear Regulatory Commission (NRC) provides for reconsideration of any decision to open or close a meeting. The NRC's regulation states that:

> any person may petition the Commission to reconsider its action . . . by filing a petition for reconsideration with the Commission within seven days after the date of such action and before the meeting in question is held . . . . A petition for reconsideration . . . shall state specifically the grounds on which the Commission action is claimed to be erroneous, and shall set forth, if appropriate, the public interest in the closing or opening of the meeting.[12]

Any decision to close under subsection(d)(2), whether initially or on reconsideration, would have to follow all statutory requirements.[13]

---

11. Although the scheme of the Act seems to contemplate that (d)(2) rights are to be exercised between the (e)(1) notice and the meeting, conceivably, a request to close could be made before the notice is issued. The Federal Trade Commission, for example, amended its proposed Sunshine rules to provide in its final regulations that instead of such requests being filed "promptly after the Commission's announcement of an open meeting," they now may be filed "at the earliest practicable time." See 16 C.F.R. § 4.15(b)(2).
12. 10 C.F.R. § 9.106(b), (c). Concern about such a reconsideration procedure resulting in delay of agency meetings is addressed elsewhere in the NRC's regulation. It states, "The filing of such a petition shall not act to stay the effectiveness of the Commission action or to postpone or delay the meeting in question unless the Commission orders otherwise." *Id.*
13. *See, e.g.,* regulations of the Federal Maritime Commission, 46 C.F.R. § 503.75(d)-(g) (requires the statutory certification by the General Counsel and a majority vote of the agency). *See also* regulations of the Federal

(continued on next page)

Requests to Open Meetings

Some agencies provide in their regulations for requests to open as well as to close agency meetings.[14] One agency, the Federal Trade Commission, considered amending its proposed rules to allow requests to open meetings but decided not to do so "because of the potential for delay."[15] Additionally, the Commission said that "because decisions to close meetings will have been examined by the General Counsel and voted on by the Commission, and will be founded on specific expectations that exempt material will be discussed, it is unlikely that a meeting will ever be closed without full consideration."[16]

In contrast, the regulations of the Commodity Futures Trading Commission permit any Commission employee to petition the Commission in writing to open a meeting or portion that might otherwise be closed if that employee's appointment, employment or dismissal is the

---

(continued from previous page)
Communications Commission, 47 C.F.R. § 0.606(b), and the Securities and Exchange Commission, 17 C.F.R. § 200.409, which spell out the procedures to be followed when a person requests that a meeting be closed or open. The regulation of the Federal Communications Commission provides that the agency will vote on the question of closing a meeting if any person directly affected for the reasons listed in exemptions (5), (6) or (7) files a request for closure "at any time prior to the meeting." 47 C.F.R. § 0.606(b)(3). The Postal Rate Commission requires that requests to close be filed "as soon as possible after the issuance of the notice of meeting to which the request pertains." *See* 39 C.F.R. § 3001.43(g)(2) (iii).

While the FMC and the FCC provide for a vote on any proper request to close, it appears more common to require a vote only at the request of one or more agency members. *See, e.g.,* regulations of the Securities and Exchange Commission, 17 C.F.R. § 200.409(a); Federal Energy Regulatory Commission, 18 § C.F.R. 375.206(b); Federal Trade Commission, 16 C.F.R. § 4.15(b)(2); and the National Labor Relations Board, 29 C.F.R. § 102.140(c).

14. *See, e.g.,* regulations of the Federal Communications Commission, 47 C.F.R. § 0.606(b)(3); Surface Transportation Board, 49 C.F.R. § 1012.6; Securities and Exchange Commission, 17 C.F.R. § 200.409; and the Federal Mine Safety and Health Review Commission, 29 C.F.R. § 2701.4.
15. 42 Fed. Reg. 13, 539 (March 11, 1977).
16. *Id. See also* ANNUAL REPORT OF THE SECURITIES AND EXCHANGE COMMISSION ON THE GOVERNMENT IN THE SUNSHINE ACT FOR 2002, p. 9.

subject of the meeting. The Commission will be required to open the meeting upon receipt of a petition from the employee.[17]

The following language in the Senate Report suggests that where the decision to close is based on Exemption (6), a person may waive his or her personal privacy interest and request that the meeting be open:

> The main purpose of this exemption (6) is to protect an individual's privacy. It would clearly not be appropriate, therefore, to invoke this paragraph when the individual involved prefers the meeting to be open.

S. Rep., 22. *See also* H. Rep. I, 11.

The Federal Communications Commission has ruled, however, that an applicant for a broadcasting license was not entitled to demand that its application be considered at an open meeting instead of being disposed of by notation procedure. *See Fifteen-Forty Broadcasting Corp.*, 42 Ad.L. 2d 86 (F.C.C., 77-720, Oct. 21, 1977).

PUBLIC AVAILABILITY OF VOTE, "FULL WRITTEN EXPLANATION" OF CLOSING, AND LIST OF ALL ATTENDEES

(d)(3) Within one day of any vote taken pursuant to paragraph (1) or (2), the agency shall make publicly available a written copy of such vote reflecting the vote of each member on the question. If a portion of a meeting is to be closed to the public, the agency shall, within one day of the vote taken pursuant to paragraph (1) or (2) of this subsection, make publicly available a full written explanation of its action closing the portion together with a list of all persons expected to attend the meeting and their affiliation.

---

17. 17 C.F.R. § 147.5(e).

Availability of Vote

Subsection (d)(3) first requires the agency to "make publicly available" "within one day"[18] a "written copy" of any vote to open or close a meeting or portion of a meeting, or to withhold information about the meeting, taken either on the agency's own initiative under (d)(1) or at the request of an affected person under (d)(2). The Conference Report states that "when such vote is published, the vote of each individual member shall be set forth." Conf. Rep., 17. According to the House Government Operations Committee Report, "[A]ll such votes must be made public in this manner, even if the decision has been to keep the meeting open or to release the information in question." H. Rep. I, 13. The purpose of this requirement is to "enable the general public to be aware of an agency member's overall record on openness questions." Id.[19]

"Full Written Explanation" of Closing

Subsection (d)(3) also requires that if the agency votes to close a meeting or portion of a meeting to the public, it must "make publicly available," again "within one day" of the vote to close, "a full written explanation" of its closing action as well as "a list of all persons expected to attend the meeting and their affiliation." How "full" must the written explanation be? The legislative history indicates that agencies have some discretion in preparing the explanation so as to inform the public without revealing the actual contents of closed meetings. According to the Senate and House Government Operations Reports,

---

18. The regulations of the Commodity Credit Corporation provide that such votes will be made publicly available "within one business day" of being taken, 7 C.F.R. § 1409.6(b), and presumably this is the practical construction of the requirement at most agencies. At the Federal Communications Commission, for example, the agency has no rule defining the meaning of "one day" but has implemented the requirement to mean one business day, since the agency rarely releases any documents on weekends or holidays. Telephone interview of William Caton, Deputy Secretary, Federal Communications Commission, by Stephen Klitzman, Nov. 20, 2003.
19. Subsection (d) does not, of course, require that agency members vote on whether to open or close each meeting. If there is no proposal before the agency to close a particular meeting, no vote need be taken or announced pursuant to subsections (d)(1) and (3).

however, the explanations should be as detailed as possible without revealing exempt information. The Senate Report states:

> The explanation should not only refer to the specific paragraph in subsection (c) that the agency is invoking, but explain why the specific discussion falls within the paragraph cited, the relative advantages and disadvantages to the public of holding the meeting in closed or open session, and why the agency concluded on balance that the public interest would best be served by closing the meeting. The explanation and the accompanying list need not disclose information described in subsection [c], where such disclosure would have the same undesirable effect as opening the meeting itself. In all but the most extraordinary circumstances, however, the agency should be able to give some specific explanation of its action. In such case, the agency must do so in as detailed terms as possible.

S. Rep., 28.

The House Report speaks in similar terms.[20]

In order not to reveal such information, however, the explanation may have to be conclusory in some instances. In fact, the nature of the explanation is likely to depend on, and vary with, the particular exemption and the circumstances of the case.

List of All Expected Attendees

The major interpretive question that has arisen with regard to this requirement is whether or not the listing of "all persons expected to attend the meeting and their affiliation" must include agency staff persons. Most agencies list the names and affiliations of all expected attendees, although at least two agencies, the Federal Trade Commission and the Consumer Product Safety Commission, do not include staff members.[21]

---

20. H. REP. I, at 13-14.
21. *See, e.g.,* the regulations of the Commodity Futures Trading Commission, 17 C.F.R. § 147.5(f), and the Federal Energy Regulatory Commission, 18 C.F.R. § 375.206(c), which list "all persons expected to attend the meeting and their affiliations," and the Federal Communications Commission, 47 C.F.R. § 0.605(d)(3), which expressly includes listing "Commission personnel" as

(continued on next page)

The legislative history is silent on the question. The language of (d)(3), however, refers to "all persons expected to attend" and makes no exception for agency staff. The FTC explained its rationale for not identifying staff as follows:

> The Commission should give notice by rule that the list of expected attendees will not include the names of individual Commission employees or consultants. Besides the fact that the identities of staff attendees cannot always be predicted in advance, we think that the obvious purpose of the (d)(3) listing requirement is to reveal which persons or groups are privy to otherwise closed meetings. The public, however, already knows that the Commission consults with its own staff, and further advance disclosure as to which particular staffers will attend will unnecessarily burden the Commission without generating any public benefit. Also, of course, any comment made at a closed meeting by a staff member that cannot be protected under subsection (c) will appear in the publicly available version of the meeting transcript.

Federal Trade Commission, Office of the General Counsel, "Implementation of the Government in the Sunshine Act: Staff Analysis," 24, reprinted in House Judiciary Oversight Hearing, 56.

A literal reading of subsection (d)(3) would require the specific naming of agency staff members. A practical alternative is generic, organizational identification of staff participants in closed meetings—for example, by bureau or division. The regulations of the Securities and Exchange Commission, for example, allow for such identification. Section 200.404(b)(2) of the SEC's rules provides that the Com-

---

(continued from previous page)
part of "a list of persons expected to attend the meeting . . . together with their affiliations." *Cf.* the regulations of the Federal Trade Commission, which excepts from the listing of expected attendees Commission employees and consultants, as well as any stenographer or court reporter. Furthermore, all FTC employees and consultants may attend nonadjudicative portions of any closed meeting, except as the meeting notice may otherwise provide, 16 C.F.R. § 4.15(c). The Consumer Product Safety Commission's regulations provide for listing "all non-Agency personnel . . . and their affiliations." 16 C.F.R. § 1013.4(c)(4).

mission will make publicly available "a list describing generically or specifically the persons expected to attend the meeting and their affiliation." The SEC explains its use of the word "generically" as follows:

> [It] is intended simply to permit the Commission to refrain from identifying by name all members of its own staff who might attend such a meeting. The Commission believes that the personal privacy and safety of staff members, coupled with the difficulty of predicting which of its employees are likely to attend, justify a provision of this nature.

42 Fed. Reg. 14,692 (March 16, 1977).

In practice, the SEC has indicated that the nature of the identification may vary, depending on whether or not it would indicate the subject matter of the closed meeting. If it would, then the Commission may provide generic description of expected staff attendees by bureau or division. If it would not, the Commission may make the specific names available.[22]

At a minimum, required agency listings should fully identify outside participants in closed meetings and provide in the listings a number or office location where additional information about closed meetings, including further staff identification, may be obtained.

As the Senate Report indicates, however, the listing "need not disclose" the name and title of a staff member if the mere announcement of such information would have the effect of revealing the exempted subject matter of the closed meeting or portions. S. Rep., 28. And agency regulations typically so provide.[23]

Some agencies, apparently relying on the fact that the statute does not specifically require that the list of attendees be included in the meeting notice, merely that it be "publicly available," do not address the issue in their regulations, and simply provide for further information to be supplied in response to specific requests.[24]

---

22. Testimony of Harvey Pitt, general counsel, Securities and Exchange Commission, House Judiciary Oversight Hearing, 81-82.
23. *See, e.g.,* Federal Communications Commission, 47 C.F.R. § 0.605(d)(4), and U.S. Commission on Civil Rights, 45 C.F.R. § 702.54(c)(2)(ii).
24. *See, e.g.,* Federal Maritime Commission, 46 C.F.R. § 503.82, and Equal Employment Opportunity Commission, 29 C.F.R. § 1612.7.

Section 552b(d): Procedures for Closing Meetings

EXPEDITED CLOSING PROCEDURE

(d)(4) Any agency, a majority of whose meetings may properly be closed to the public pursuant to paragraph (4), (8), (9)(A), or (10) of subsection (c), or any combination thereof, may provide by regulation for the closing of such meetings or portions thereof in the event that a majority of the members of the agency votes by recorded vote at the beginning of such meeting, or portion thereof, to close the exempt portion or portions of the meeting, and a copy of such vote, reflecting the vote of each member on the question, is made available to the public. The provisions of paragraphs (1), (2), and (3) of this subsection and subsection (e) shall not apply to any portion of a meeting to which such regulations apply: Provided, That the agency shall, except to the extent that such information is exempt from disclosure under the provisions of subsection (c), provide the public with public announcement of the time, place, and subject matter of the meeting and of each portion thereof at the earliest practicable time.

Subsection (d)(4) permits any agency, "a majority of whose meetings" may properly be closed under the exemptions for trade secrets (4), sensitive financial reports (8), sensitive financial information that might result in speculation (9)(A), or information regarding agency participation in adjudicatory proceedings or civil actions (10), to close such meetings by special regulation and under simplified expediting procedures. Agencies can qualify under this subsection if they may close a majority of their meetings under any of the four cited exemptions, "or any combination thereof."

The expedited closing procedures were originally intended for agencies regulating financial institutions, securities, and commodities, as well as agencies "whose primary or sole responsibility is to conduct adjudicatory proceedings." H. Rep. I, 14; S. Rep., 28-29. Congress recognized that such agencies "often have to conduct their sensitive business in private, and on short notice." S. Rep., 29. Furthermore, this business often concerns generic types of agenda items, each of which could be separately closed, but by a burdensome and unnecessarily repetitive procedure. Therefore, eligible agencies would be allowed to close discussion of such repetitive items by rule and with a reduced number of procedural requirements.

Agencies that the legislative history specifically indicates were expected to be eligible under subsection (d)(4) include the Federal Reserve Board, the Securities and Exchange Commission, and the National Labor Relations Board. S. Rep., 29. As Congress anticipated, expedited procedure is employed by the banking and securities regulatory agencies[25] and by those agencies engaged primarily in adjudicating on-the-record proceedings,[26] as well as by a number of other agencies.[27]

It is important to emphasize that the subsection (d)(4) procedure does not permit an agency to close any meeting that is not otherwise eligible for closure, nor does it permit the agency to omit in each case a determination as to whether the public interest calls for invoking the exemption. It does, however, allow an agency to dispense with most of the closing procedures of subsections (d)(1), (2), and (3), and the announcement procedures of subsection (e). An agency relying on (d)(4) need not take a vote in advance of the meeting on whether or not to close, and while it must make a public announcement of the time, place, and subject matter of the meeting "at the earliest practicable time," this announcement need not be seven days in advance of the meeting; need not include a "full written explanation" of the decision to close, a list of

---

25. Federal Reserve Board, 12 C.F.R. § 261b.7; Federal Deposit Insurance Corp., 12 C.F.R. § 311.6; Export-Import Bank, 12 C.F.R. § 407.2, 407.4; Commodity Credit Corp., 7 C.F.R. § 1409.5; Commodity Futures Trading Commission, 17 C.F.R. § 147.6; Securities and Exchange Commission, 17 C.F.R. § 200.405.
26. National Labor Relations Board, 29 C.F.R. § 102.140(a); Federal Trade Commission, 16 C.F.R. § 4.15(c) (2); Merit Systems Protection Board, 5 C.F.R. § 1206.9; Occupational Safety & Health Review Commission, 29 C.F.R. § 2203.4(b); Federal Labor Relations Auth., 5 C.F.R. § 2413.4; Federal Mine Safety & Health Review Commission, 29 C.F.R. § 2701.7; Postal Rate Commission, 39 C.F.R. § 3001.43(d)(5).
27. *See, e.g.,* Equal Employment Opportunity Commission, 29 C.F.R. § 1612.13; National Mediation Board, 29 C.F.R. § 1209.05; Farm Credit Board, 12 C.F.R. § 604.430; U.S. Postal Service Board of Governors, 39 C.F.R. § 7.4(d); U.S. Parole Commission, 28 C.F.R. § 16.205; and the Federal Housing Finance Board, § 912.5(b).

all expected attendees, or the name and phone number of an agency contact person; and need not be published in the *Federal Register*.[28] Furthermore, no special procedures are required for changing the subject matter of such a meeting. Thus, under (d)(4) procedures, an agency is able routinely to add or delete agenda items on short notice and without prior action by the collegial body.

An agency proceeding under subsection (d)(4) must still comply with certain procedural requirements. These include obtaining a recorded vote for closure by a majority of agency members at the beginning of the meeting or portion, making publicly available a copy of the vote showing how each member voted,[29] and obtaining the General Counsel's certification under subsection (f)(1). Furthermore, the provisions of subsection (f) regarding the maintenance of a transcript, recording, or minutes of a closed meeting, and the making available of non-exempt portions thereof to the public, apply equally to all closed meetings whether closed pursuant to subsection (d)(1) or subsection (d)(4) procedures.

Public announcement of the subsection (d)(4) meeting must be made "at the earliest practicable time." The Conference Report states that "the conferees intend that such announcements be made as soon as possible, which should in few, if any, instances be later than the commencement of the meeting or portion in question." Conf. Rep., 17.[30] Because the members of the agency are not expected to vote on

---

28. The Federal Deposit Insurance Corporation publishes announcement of meetings closed pursuant to subsection (d)(4) in the *Federal Register* "if publication can be effected at least 1 day prior to the scheduled date of the meeting." *See* 12 C.F.R. § 311.6(b). *See also* regulation of the Securities and Exchange Commission, 17 C.F.R. § 200.403(d)(2) (provides for an abbreviated form of announcement to be made publicly available "at the earliest practicable time").
29. The House Government Operations Committee Report notes, however, that "while the vote to close is not required to be made public within one day after it is taken, it must be made public as promptly as is physically possible." H. REP. I, at 14.
30. In *A. G. Becker, Inc.*, *supra* p. 99 note 2, the court held that a Board meeting was properly closed pursuant to subsection (d)(4), but that the Board was wrong in delaying public notice until after the meeting had commenced. "[A]bsent extraordinary circumstances . . . notice that the Board will have a meeting should occur prior to the commencement of the meeting." *Id.* at 385, *citing* the *1978 Guide*, at 41-42.

closing the meeting until the beginning of the meeting itself (and, arguably, must vote at the meeting whether or not they have voted earlier), the public announcement will ordinarily precede the vote. Presumably, the announcement may be made by the official responsible for establishing the agenda and will be to the effect that the agency will meet to consider stated subject matter and that the meeting may or may not be closed.[31]

It must be recognized that, as a practical matter, last-minute decisions to open meetings eligible for closure under subsection (d)(4) are

---

31. The requirement for a majority vote for closure "at the beginning of such meeting" raises a peculiar problem. A vote to close under subsection (d)(1) requires a majority of the entire membership, but that majority may be obtained by notation procedure. If the majority required for closure under subsection (d)(4) must cast their votes at the meeting, and one or more members are absent, it may be harder to obtain a closure vote under subsection (d)(4) than under subsection (d)(1). Yet the theory of subsection (d)(4) is that such closures are expected to be fairly routine. One solution would be to interpret the majority required by subsection (d)(4) as the majority of a quorum. This seems to run counter to the statutory language, although it might be argued that "a majority of the members of the agency" in subsection (d)(4) is not necessarily the same as "a majority of the entire membership of the agency" in subsection (d)(1), and that Congress is unlikely to have intended that absent members be polled on each subsection (d)(4) closing.

Another solution would be to permit some form of absentee voting (subsection (d)(4), unlike subsection (d)(1), does not specifically forbid proxies). Permitting members to note in advance that they favor closing a particular meeting does not seem inconsistent with tallying the votes at the beginning of the meeting. Or the provision for a vote "at the beginning of such meeting" might be interpreted as permissive [in contrast to the procedure under subsection(d)(1), which requires a vote at least a week in advance of the meeting] and not as precluding an earlier vote so long as that vote is taken with respect to the particular meeting. At least two agencies, the National Labor Relations Board, 29 C.F.R. § 102.140, and the National Mediation Board, 29 C.F.R. § 1209.06, permit a closure vote by "a majority of the members of the Board who will participate in the meeting"; these provisions appear to apply to all closure votes, although both agencies use expedited procedures.

bound to be extremely rare.[32] Agency members are certainly unlikely to reexamine in the context of a routine agenda item the decision reflected in the agency regulation to close discussions of such items. Furthermore, if the public has not previously been made aware that the meeting may be open, interested persons will not be in a position to attend.

It may be suggested that an agency's adoption of a subsection (d)(4) regulation does not necessarily demonstrate a determination to close any particular class of meetings, but merely makes available a more convenient procedure for doing so if the agency should so desire. In requiring a vote to close each meeting, Congress presumably did not intend a meaningless formality. But where a meeting is scheduled under expedited procedure, unless an agency member has raised the issue of closure in advance, it does not come up until the beginning of the meeting, and at this point the members are unlikely to decide to deviate suddenly from the accepted practice.[33]

Computing the "Majority"

How are agencies to compute the required majority of meetings eligible for closure for purposes of invoking subsection (d)(4)? The *1978 Guide* suggested three methods of computation: "The computation might be made (1) by counting toward the majority of meetings any meeting, any portion of which could be closed under one of the

---

32. Personnel contacted at several (d)(4) agencies were unable to recall a single instance. We were told of one case where a three-member agency, which had had a policy of closing meetings to consider adjudications, was operating with one vacancy. The two remaining members were divided on the question of opening, but the member who had favored open meetings voted to continue to close out of deference to the established policy.
33. A number of agencies have stated frankly in their regulations that meetings subject to expedited procedure will ordinarily be closed. Merit Systems Protection Board, 5 C.F.R. § 1206.9(a)(2); Export-Import Bank, 12 C.F.R. § 407.2(b); Federal Deposit Insurance Corporation, 12 C.F.R. § 311.6(a); Federal Labor Relations Authority, 5 C.F.R. § 2413.4(a). On the other hand, the Federal Mine Safety & Health Review Commission, while providing for expedited procedure, announced that as a general policy it would open to the public even those meetings subject to closure, 29 C.F.R. § 2701.7(a), and it has continued to adhere to this policy. *See also* p. 94, *supra* note 81.

(d)(4) exemptions; (2) by counting exempt agenda items, as a proportion of total agenda items; or (3) by computing the amount of time devoted to exempted agenda items, or making a qualitative judgment on the basis of time and relative significance of exempt items."[34]

The Act and its legislative history offer little or no guidance on the question of how to compute the "majority" of meetings as required under (d)(4). The Conference Report simply notes "[t]he fact that one portion of a meeting may be closed does not justify the closing of any other portion." Conf. Rep., 17. This might be read as rejecting a computation based on the first method, although it is not clear that the statement is addressed to the computation problem. In any event, the first method is subject to the objection that it would permit an entire meeting to be counted as closed even if it contained only one exempted agenda item. This would seem to permit a skewed result and distort the apparent intent of subsection (d)(4).

The second method, measuring by exempted agenda items, would seem consistent with the Act's general approach of treating each portion of a meeting on its own merits for purposes of closure. However, this approach might conceivably result in a manipulated tabulation of eligible agenda items.

The third method might, in the abstract, appear to be the best. However, supporting documentation, such as the percentage of meeting time devoted to items exempted under the (d)(4) exemptions or the portions of staff preparation time devoted to such subjects, etc.,

---

34. *See 1978 Guide,* at 42-43. *See also* FTC Staff Analysis, 25-26, House Judiciary Oversight Hearing, 56-57. The FTC counts as a closed meeting any meeting that contained any discussion eligible for Exemption (10). The final FTC rule allows for subsection (d)(4) procedures only with regard to Exemption (10) items, 16 C.F.R. § 4.15(c)(2). Notwithstanding that subsection (d)(4) does not require that agency eligibility be established separately for each of the four exemptions, the FTC Staff Analysis recommended, at least for the time being, "against using (d)(4) procedures for (c)(4) items without a better record basis showing the regularity with which (c)(4) information is discussed at meetings." FTC Staff Analysis, 26. The Commission has not revised its original rule in this respect. The Equal Employment Opportunity Commission, like the FTC, limits subsection (d)(4) procedures to Exemption (10) cases based on its prior experience. *See* 29 C.F.R. § 1612.13(c).

Section 552b(d): Procedures for Closing Meetings 117

would be relatively difficult to compile, and any evaluation of the significance of exempt items is likely to be subjective.

What appears to be called for, in the last analysis, is a good faith calculation based on a review of past agency meetings and a reasonable expectation of future agency business.[35] The question of computing the majority, however, may be largely academic, since by and large the agencies invoking (d)(4) are the ones that were expected to invoke it, and there may not be any agency for which eligibility for subsection(d)(4) procedures depends on the method of computation.

In making the required computation, the agency may confine its consideration to whether the subject matter of the meetings surveyed was within the enumerated exemptions; it need not make a retrospective determination as to whether closure would have been in the public interest. The test is whether a majority of meetings may properly be closed, not whether they were, in fact, closed.

Documentary Justification

An agency invoking subsection (d)(4) should set out in documentary detail in its regulation (or preambular statement) exactly how it made its computation. The legislative history is clear that such documentary justification is necessary in order for an agency to demonstrate its legitimate reliance on the expedited closing procedures. Thus, the Senate Report notes that:

> the regulations should fully document on the basis of the past history of agency meetings the likelihood that [the agency] will have to close a majority of its meetings pursuant to [exemptions (4), (8), (9)(A), or (10)]. The regulation should also specify in detail the types of meetings to which the regulations apply and which exemption is relied upon as the grounds for closing each type of meeting.

S. Rep., 29.

Agency regulations have addressed this subject in different ways. Several agencies set out in their regulations how they arrived at the

---

35. *See* testimony of Rep. Abzug, House Judiciary Committee Hearings, at 18.

determination of eligibility to use subsection (d)(4).[36] Others state that a majority of meetings may be closed under one or more of the four exemptions, but do not elaborate.[37] Still others do not specifically state that they meet the majority test, but simply provide for expedited procedure.[38]

In any event, the agency's determination that it is eligible to invoke subsection (d)(4) should be periodically reexamined in the light of current experience. Historically, one way to test eligibility was to use the agency's annual reports to Congress formerly required under subsection (j).[39] In *A. G. Becker*,[40] the court relied in part on the tabulation in the Federal Reserve Board's annual report to uphold the Board's use of expedited procedure. If Congress were to reenact this requirement, one benefit would be to provide more information to evaluate agency eligibility to invoke (d)(4) closing procedures.[41]

---

36. *See, e.g.,* Equal Employment Opportunity Commission, 29 C.F.R. § 1612.13(c) (based on review of meetings over past two years); Federal Mine Safety & Health Review Commission, 29 C.F.R. § 2701.7(a); Occupational Safety & Health Review Commission, 29 C.F.R. § 2203.4(b) (Commission responsibilities almost entirely involve formal adjudication); Securities and Exchange Commission, 17 C.F.R. § 200.405(a) (based on review of meetings over several months).
37. *See, e.g.,* Federal Deposit Insurance Corp., 12 C.F.R. § 311.6 (a); Federal Housing Finance Board, 12 C.F.R. § 912.5(b); Postal Rate Commission, 39 C.F.R. § 3001.43(d)(5).
38. *See, e.g.,* Federal Trade Commission, 16 C.F.R. § 4.15 (c); Export-Import Bank, 12 C.F.R. § 407.2(b); Federal Labor Relations Authority, 5 C.F.R. § 2413.4(a); National Labor Relations Board, 29 C.F.R. § 102.139(a); National Mediation Board, 29 C.F.R. § 1209.05(a).
39. These reports included a tabulation of open and closed meetings, together with information as to the grounds for closure. However, Congress terminated the report requirement in subsection (j) effective May 2000. Nevertheless, some Sunshine agencies have continued to file annual reports with the Senate Committee on Governmental Affairs. *See* p. 231, *infra.*
40. *See supra* p. 99 note 2, 502 F. Supp. at 384.
41. *See also* p. 231, *infra,* for our recommendation to Congress to reinstate the Sunshine Act annual reporting requirement at least for a limited period of time so the Congress can evaluate whether or not to reinstate the reporting requirement permanently.

Chapter 5

SECTION 552b(e) PROCEDURES FOR ANNOUNCING MEETINGS

CONTENTS AND TIMING OF ADVANCE NOTICE	120
Withholding Notice Information	123
Providing Shorter Notice	124
Providing No or Limited Notice	130
CHANGING THE TIME, PLACE, SUBJECT MATTER, OR DECISION TO OPEN OR CLOSE	133
Changing the Time or Place	133
Cancellation	133
Changing the Subject Matter or Decision to Open or Close; Addition, Deletion or Carry-Over of Agenda Items	134
CONTENTS AND SUBMISSION OF NOTICE TO FEDERAL REGISTER	138
Use of "Reasonable Means" to Circulate Public Announcements	140

(e)(1) In the case of each meeting, the agency shall make public announcement, at least one week before the meeting, of the time, place, and subject matter of the meeting, whether it is to be open or closed to the public, and the name and phone number of the official designated by the agency to respond to requests for information about the meeting. Such announcement shall be made unless a majority of the members of the agency determines by a recorded vote that agency business requires that such meeting be called at an earlier date, in which case the agency shall make public announcement of the time, place, and subject matter of such meeting, and whether open or closed to the public, at the earliest practicable time.

This subsection generally requires advance public notice of all agency meetings, whether open or closed, and of changes in meetings previously announced. Agencies must make such information available "in order to make the public's right to attend a meeting meaningful." S. Rep., 29.

CONTENTS AND TIMING OF ADVANCE NOTICE

Subsection (e)(1) requires that for each of its meetings, an agency must "make public announcement, at least one week before the meeting," of (1) the time of the meeting; (2) the place of the meeting; (3) the subject matter of the meeting; (4) whether the meeting is to be open or closed to the public; and (5) the name and phone number of the official designated by the agency to respond to requests for information about the meeting.

Although the majority of agency regulations repeat the seven-day advance notice requirement, some agencies initially provided a longer notice period. For example, the United States International Trade Commission (USITC) set a 10-day notice period. Explaining its action, the Commission stated that its experience under the one-week notice provision in its proposed rules "demonstrated that a 1-week period may not be sufficient in order to insure that notices will be published in time for subscribers to the *Federal Register* to receive them and make plans to attend Commission meetings or that [notices] will be otherwise available."[1] In 1993, however, the USITC amended its Sunshine

---

1. 42 Fed. Reg. 11,242 (Feb. 28, 1977). *See also* 19 C.F.R. § 201.35, 42 Fed. Reg. 11,244 (Feb. 28, 1977). Eight-day notice periods have been established by the Inter-American Foundation, 22 C.F.R. § 1004.6(c), 42 Fed. Reg. 20,462 (March. 28, 1977); and the Commission on Civil Rights, 45 C.F.R. § 702.55, 42 Fed. Reg. 14,109 (March 15, 1977). The regulations of the Foreign Claims Settlement Commission provide that notice shall be published "[a]t the earliest practicable time, which is estimated to be not later than eight days" before the meeting. *See* 45 C.F.R. § 504.25(d), 42 Fed. Reg. 1,101 (Feb. 25, 1977). On the other hand, the Federal Trade Commission rejected a suggestion that it issue public announcements 10 days before meetings. "The Commission believes that one week's advance notice, as specified in the Sunshine Act, is adequate, and that increasing the amount of advance notice would result in more changes in announcements." 42 Fed. Reg. 13,539 (March 11, 1977). For current FTC regulation on this point, *see* 16 C.F.R. §
(continued on next page)

Act regulations to change the time to submit a Sunshine notice of a meeting to the *Federal Register* from 10 days to seven days. According to its General Counsel, "the USITC made the change to bring the agency's rule into conformity with the practices of most other agencies."[2]

By sending meeting notices to the *Federal Register* only a week in advance, agencies may provide inadequate notice, especially because of the lag between submission to and publication in the *Federal Register*.[3] Consequently, agencies should attempt to ensure at least seven days advance notice in the *Federal Register*. They also should—and

---

(continued from previous page)
4.15, which provides for notice "at least one week" before the meeting. Prior issues of the *Federal Register* from 1994 to the present are available online at www.gpoaccess.gov/fr/index.html, and www.westlaw.com. Pre-1994 *Federal Register*s are available online at http://heinonline.org/Federal Register library, or for public inspection in the Office of the Federal Register, 800 North Capitol Street NW, 7th Floor, Washington, D.C. 20002, (202) 741-6000.

2. Letter from Lyn M. Schlitt, general counsel, USITC, to Stephen Klitzman, dated Sept. 26, 2001. Two notable exceptions to the usual seven-days advance notice practice of most agencies are the 30-day advance notice periods provided by the Mississippi River Commission, Corps of Engineers, Department of the Army, and the National Commission on Libraries and Information Science (NCLIS). *See* ANNUAL REPORT OF THE MISSISSIPPI RIVER COMMISSION ON COMPLIANCE WITH THE GOVERNMENT IN THE SUNSHINE ACT FOR CALENDAR YEAR 2000, submitted to the Congress (Senate Committee on Governmental Affairs) Feb. 12, 2001, at 2, and e-mail from Judith Russell, executive secretary, NCLIS, to Stephen Klitzman, Nov. 19, 2001.

3. Normally, a document is published in the *Federal Register* on the third or fourth workday after it is received. The *Federal Register*, however, for many years has provided an expedited service on Sunshine meeting notices. Provided an agency submits its notice by 4 p.m., the *Federal Register* publishes all such notices two working days after receipt rather than the usual three to four working days for all other documents. *See* 42 Fed. Reg. 15,482 (March 22, 1977) (announcement of 90-day trial program); 42 Fed. Reg. 31,205 (June 20, 1977) (90-day trial program made permanent); *and* 1 C.F.R. § 17.2(d) (54 Fed. Reg. 9680, March 7, 1989) (final rule). Telephone interview by Stephen Klitzman of Barbara Suhre, former supervisor, Scheduling Unit, Office of the Federal Register, Dec. 11, 2001 (hereafter Suhre Interview). *See also* Appendix M, *Sample Agency Meeting Notices*.

often do—use additional means of notification that may reach the interested public more quickly and effectively than *Federal Register* notice. In this electronic Internet age, this will mean the placement of agency Sunshine Act meeting notices on agency Web sites, as well as on telephone "hot news" lines, or on other technologies providing similar instantaneous information.

Providing Sunshine Act notices other than in the *Federal Register* may be preferred by some agencies, especially smaller ones. Publication in the *Federal Register* of all information may impose a burden on small agencies. They may want to change meeting dates or give other changed meeting information quickly and without incurring additional costs. One option would be to note initially in the *Federal Register* that other announcements concerning such schedule changes will be posted on agency Web sites. This would be not only a quicker way to get information to the public but also a considerable cost saving. An amendment that clarified that this is possible would be beneficial to most agencies.[4]

Concerning the contents of the announcement, the Senate Report states:

> The identification of the subject matter must be adequate to inform the general public thoroughly, referring, for example, to a specific docket number, the name of the applicant, the identity of the proposed rule, and the like. Reference to a generic subject matter, such as "consumer complaints," or "ap-

---

4. The Postal Rate Commission makes a similar point but does not call for a legislative remedy: "The Commission's chief problem in implementing Sunshine Act procedures remains the administrative challenge of conforming notices to the Commission's actual calendar of meetings, which can change abruptly due to unforeseeable developments in Commission business. Inasmuch as this problem is administrative in nature, and procedures are available to address it, the Commission has not proposed any legislative remedy." Letter from Stephen L. Sharfman, general counsel, Postal Rate Commission, to Stephen Klitzman, Sept. 19, 2001. *See also* comments of the NCLIS at note 2, *supra*: "The only practical problem with Sunshine Act compliance is timely publication of advance notice in the *Federal Register*. We provide 30 days advance notice whenever possible. We have not sought any legislative remedy as this is a minor problem." *Id.*

plications for new routes," does not meet the requirements of this subsection. S. Rep., 29-30.

Withholding Notice Information

Any description of the subject matter can be withheld "for the same reasons that may require the agency to close the meeting in the first place," S. Rep., 10. Section 552b(c) permits basic "information pertaining" to a meeting, otherwise required by subsections (d) and (e) to be made public, to be withheld from the public if disclosure "would disclose the very information that the meeting itself was closed to protect." S. Rep., 20.

A decision to withhold information otherwise required for the public announcement is, of course, subject to the procedural requirements of subsection (d)(1), S. Rep., 27, and must be based on one or more of the exemptions in subsection (c).[5] While the decision as to what information to withhold will unquestionably depend on the circumstances of the particular case, the better agency practice is not to dispense with all the public notice requirements of subsections (d)(3) and (e), except under the most extraordinary circumstances. For example, the Federal Communications Commission stated that it would proceed as follows: First, "notice of all open and closed meetings will be given," 42 Fed. Reg. 12,868 (March 7, 1977), now codified at 47 C.F.R. § 0.605(a). Second, if the meeting is closed, "the agency may omit from the announcement information usually included, if and to the extent that it finds that disclosure would be likely to have any of the consequences listed in [the exemptions section]." 47 C.F.R. § 0.605(d)(4), 42 Fed. Reg. 12,868 (March 7, 1977). Third, the FCC noted that it does not read the exemption language in 5 U.S.C. § 552b(c) "as permitting an agency to withhold notice of a meeting," 42 Fed. Reg. 12,868 (March 7, 1977). However, the Commission does interpret the language "to mean that certain of the information usually contained in the notice may be omitted if there is a valid basis for omitting such information under subsection (c) of the Act." *Id.* The Commission then went on to explain the requirements and circumstances under which it will withhold some, but not all, notice information:

---

5. *See, e.g.,* regulation of the Nuclear Regulatory Commission, 10 C.F.R. § 9.105(c), 42 Fed. Reg. 12,876, 12,878 (March 7, 1977).

A separate vote to withhold information is required, and the basis for withholding information must be reasonably related to the act of withholding as opposed to the act of closing the meeting. For example, if the meeting involved accusing a person of a crime, we would announce the time and place of the meeting, the fact that it involved a criminal accusation and was being closed for that reason, the vote on the question of closing the meeting and on that of withholding information, and the name and phone number of the Public Information Officer. The name of the person involved would be withheld. To take a more extreme example, if a meeting involved a freeze on the filing of applications and notice of the fact would frustrate the purpose of the freeze, the subject matter of the meeting would be withheld; the other information would be set out in the notice. *Id.*

We believe this is a correct interpretation regarding the withholding of Sunshine Act information. An agency cannot simply act as if the subject matter was not on an agency's agenda at all but it can withhold specific, identifying information about the subject matter under circumstances suggested above by the FCC.

Providing Shorter Notice

Subsection (e)(1) also allows an agency to shorten the one-week advance notice of its meetings if "a majority of the members of the agency" votes by recorded vote "that agency business requires" the meeting to be held with less than seven days notice. In such a case, the requisite public announcement of the time, place, subject matter, and open-closed status of the meeting must still be provided "at the earliest practicable time."

Legislative history indicates that this "escape clause" allowing for shorter notice is not to be relied upon routinely, but should be primarily used to deal with emergency, late-breaking items. Thus, the Senate Report notes:

> This provision allows agencies to schedule a meeting where consideration of an emergency matter can not be delayed seven days. It recognizes that the public interest in obtaining rapid agency action may at times override the public interest in re-

ceiving advance notice of meetings. This clause does not, however, allow an agency to wait until the last moment to schedule a meeting when agency business truly requires it, if the meeting could have been scheduled in time to give the public a week's notice.

S. Rep., 30.

Citing these points from the *1978 Guide*, the court in *Coalition for Legal Services v. Legal Services Corporation*, 597 F. Supp. 198, 201 (D.D.C. 1984) (hereafter *Legal Services*), considered the plaintiff's allegation that the Board of Directors of the Legal Services Corporation (LSC) violated the Sunshine Act by not providing seven days advance notice of a meeting of the LSC Board. "While falling short of requiring the LSC to publicly announce all of its meetings via publication in the *Federal Register*, the court found that the LSC had violated the Sunshine Act as to the particular meeting at issue by not publishing timely notice of the meeting in the *Federal Register*."[6]

---

6. Letter from Victor M. Fortuno, general counsel and corporate secretary, Legal Services Corporation, to Stephen Klitzman, Oct. 23, 2001. *Cf.* R.J. Reynolds Tobacco Co. v. F.T.C., 1999 WL 816699 (D.D.C. 1999) (hereafter *R.J. Reynolds*) (court did not find a violation of the notice provision in 5 U.S.C. § 552b(e)(1)). The *R.J. Reynolds* court distinguished the case from the *Legal Services* case: "Unlike the instant case . . . the agency in *Legal Services* had issued multiple cancellation notices, one of which was issued in error. The court emphasized that these contradictory notices heightened the Corporation's duty to clarify the time and place of the meeting and that the Corporation's failure to use any additional methods of announcement exacerbated the 'climate of confusion.' Here, by contrast, the FTC posted three notices concerning the May 28 meeting." The *R.J. Reynolds* court went on to note that "although the first meeting was [scheduled] in order to rescind the second notice regarding the agenda for the meeting, the fact that the FTC acted three times to inform the public about the May 28 meeting distinguishes this case from *Legal Services*. Moreover, unlike *Legal Services*, the meeting in this case was not moved or postponed, but rather held in accordance with the May 9, 19 and 23 notices. Accordingly, the court finds that the FTC provided ample notice of the May 28, 1997 meeting and that *RJR's* complaint should be dismissed on

(continued on next page)

A 1989 Senate oversight report on agency implementation of the Sunshine Act—the last such report, it should be noted— highlighted the importance of the public notice provisions of the Act. It summarized the facts of the *Legal Services* case at length and critiqued the LSC as follows:

> In September 1983, the LSC placed notice in the *Federal Register* that a meeting of the Corporation's Board was to be held on October 4, 1983, in Washington, D.C. At the meeting, the Board was to discuss several proposed regulations which would substantially change the nature of legal services. The items set for discussion included eligibility requirements, private bar involvement and policies regarding legal services program fund balances, and instructions regarding how local programs would set priorities in the types of cases handled. Given the significance of the issues to be considered, beneficiaries of the legal services program, legal services advocates, members of the media and other interested parties planned to attend the meeting to voice their opinions and concerns.[7]

The 1989 Senate Report continues:

(continued from previous page)
this count." *Id.* For two other cases in which courts have not found violations of the notice provision in 5 U.S.C. § 552b(e)(1), *see* Consolidated Aluminum Corp. v. T.V.A., 462 F. Supp. 464 (M.D. Tenn. Civ. No. 78-3210, June 30, 1978), and A. G. Becker, Inc. v. Board of Governors of Federal Reserve System, 502 F. Supp. 378 (D.D.C. 1980). *See also* American Federation of Gov't Employees v. EEOC, Case No. 1:05CV01035 (D.D.C. May 20, 2005) (AFGE alleges that the EEOC violated 5 U.S.C. § 552b(e)(1) and 29 C.F.R. § 1612.7(c) (1) by not taking a recorded vote to waive the required seven-days advance notice of an EEOC meeting. AFGE further alleges that the EEOC did not give adequate advance public notice of the meeting in the *Federal Register,* on its Web site or telephone hot line in violation of 5 U.S.C. § 552b(e)(3) and 29 C.F.R. § 1612.7(a), (d). The EEOC has denied the complaint and the Department of Justice is seeking to dismiss it. As of October 2005, a Motion to Dismiss or in the Alternative for Summary Judgment is pending before the U.S. District Court in the District of Columbia.).
7. *See* 1989 S. Rep., at 28-30, p. 33 note 8, *supra.*

On October 3, the Corporation indefinitely postponed the October 4 meeting with a notice to that effect placed in the *Federal Register* on October 5. A few days later, the Corporation rescheduled the October 3 meeting for October 13, to be held in Salt Lake City, Utah, providing no notice to the interested public. As of October 12, the Corporation had not published notice in the *Federal Register*. It was fairly clear that the Corporation changed the date and site of the meeting to avoid public opposition to the proposed regulations.[8]

The Sunshine Act requires that covered agencies give adequate public notice, at least one week in advance, of any meeting to be held either open or closed to the public. When a meeting is legitimately rescheduled, the Act requires such change be announced at the earliest practicable time. If a meeting is held in a location many miles from where meetings are ordinarily held, agencies should ideally demonstrate good faith by giving the public at least the 7-day notice required by the Act. The Legal Services Corporation did not comply with these Sunshine Act requirements.[9]

The Coalition for Legal Services and the National Council of Senior Citizens requested that the Corporation either postpone the Salt Lake City meeting until reasonable advanced notice was provided or hold the meeting in Washington, D.C. The Corporation did neither, and the two groups sought a temporary restraining order to prevent the October 13 meeting from proceeding.[10]

On October 12, the United States District Court for the District of Columbia granted the restraining order, blocking the October 13 meeting. As District Court Judge Barrington Parker stated: "Congress' intent in enacting the Sunshine Act was to afford persons who are interested in and affected by an agency's work an opportunity to attend the agency's meetings. In this case, the fact that a *Federal Register* notice regarding the Salt Lake City meeting will not be circulated until . . . October 12, at the earliest, one day before the scheduled meeting, supports

---

8. *Id.*
9. *Id.*
10. *Id.*

the conclusion that the public will not receive adequate notice of the meeting in violation of the letter and spirit of the Sunshine Act." On October 13, the United States Court of Appeals upheld the lower court's decision.[11]

The 1989 Senate Report concluded that "the important point in this case was not simply that the Legal Services Corporation failed to give adequate public notice. The point . . . was that the Corporation abruptly (and perhaps deliberately) cancelled a highly publicized and controversial meeting that had been scheduled for weeks and tried to hold it unannounced, over a thousand miles from the clients and organizations planning to attend. . . . A number of major policy changes were to be discussed. The Corporation deliberately attempted to discourage public access and inhibit public attendance [at] its meeting. This tactic was a blatant contravention of the Sunshine Act. . . ."[12]

The court in *Legal Services* noted that "[a]lthough publication in the *Federal Register* is not an exclusive means for communicating notice of Sunshine Act meetings to the public, it assumes special importance in this instance since the Corporation chose not to take steps it had routinely followed in the past to inform the public of its meetings"—for example, mailing notice of meetings to the press, and giving notice to other interested groups. The LSC argued that it had no duty to take these steps. But the court said the LSC did "have a duty to reasonably and fully inform the public of its meetings. The avenues used in the past had helped the agency fulfill its duty and, with respect to this meeting, might have countered the reliance on the *Federal Register* announcements."[13]

The court concluded that "if an agency may reschedule a meeting for reasons not based upon an emergency situation requiring swift agency decision, then the Sunshine Act loses much of its force. Sensibly, Congress could not have given the public the entitlement to the 'fullest practicable information regarding the decisionmaking processes of the Federal Government,' Pub. L. No. 94-409, Sec. 2, and then in

---

11. *Id.*, quoting Temporary Restraining Order issued by U.S. District Judge Barrington Parker, Oct. 12, 1983.
12. *Id.*
13. *Legal Services, supra* p. 125 , 597 F. Supp at 200.

the same penstroke taken that entitlement away by giving the agency the broad 'escape clause' which" the [LSC claimed].[14]

A few agencies reflected this emergency rationale for providing shorter notice in their final regulations implementing 5 U.S.C. § 552b(e)(1).[15] Most, however, merely repeat the statutory language and do not emphasize the emergency nature of the clause.

The better agency practice would be to place procedural limits on, or to establish criteria regarding, the use of the shorter notice. For example, the Federal Communications Commission provides in the announcement of any last-minute meeting the vote of each agency member on the decision to give less than seven days notice. The announcement also "specif[ies] the nature of the emergency situation if it is not clear from the subject matter."[16] "In the rare circumstance when the International Trade Commission calls a meeting on short notice, it apprises interested members of the public of the meeting by (1) promptly posting a notice in a public display rack, (2) posting a notice on the agency's Web site, and (3) telephoning interested persons."[17]

The public announcement required under the "shorter notice" clause of (e)(1) must be made "at the earliest practicable time." The legislative intent as expressed in the Conference Report on the Sunshine Act is that "such announcements be made as soon as possible, which should, in few, if any, instances, be later than the commencement of the meeting or portion in question." Conf. Rep., 18. The Senate Report states:

> If the need is genuine, however, the announcement may be made only hours in advance of the meeting. In the unusual case, the announcement may have to be issued simultaneously with the convening of the meeting. Or a meeting which has already started as an open one may suddenly have to be closed if some sensitive matters unexpectedly arise.

S. Rep., 30.

---

14. *Id.* at 202.
15. *See, e.g.,* regulations of the former Civil Service Commission, 42 Fed. Reg. 13,011 (March 8, 1977), and the former United States Railway Association, 42 Fed. Reg. 14,114 (March 15, 1977).
16. 47 C.F.R. § 0.605(e), 42 Fed. Reg. 12,864, 12,868 (March 7, 1977).
17. Telephone interview by Stephen Klitzman of Marilyn R. Abbott, secretary, USITC, Jan. 12, 2005.

The Senate Report adds, however, that "even if, in such circumstances, the public does not in fact learn of the meeting until after it has occurred, the announcement must be made to provide a record of such meetings." *Id.*

The last-minute announcement must be posted by the agency as well as published in the *Federal Register* under subsection (e)(3). Legislative history indicates that the vote to conduct the last-minute meeting should also "be made public as promptly as it [is] physically possible." H. Rep. I, 15.

The Sunshine Act exempts from the term "meetings" deliberations about whether to schedule future meetings on shorter notice.[18]

Providing No or Limited Notice

Some agencies that close all or the vast majority of their meetings under the expedited closing procedures of 5 U.S.C. § 552b(d)(4) because they deal with sensitive business, banking or investigatory matters may routinely give less than the usual seven days advance notice of their closed meetings. And in some cases, these agencies have given no notice at all. The Federal Deposit Insurance Corporation, for example, in its Annual Reports to Congress on its compliance with the Sunshine Act for 1994-1998, acknowledged it had never given seven days advance notice for any of its closed meetings.[19] The agency noted in its reports to Congress that the designation "o" indicated "that no advance notice equal to a full day's notice was given of a meeting. In those cases, notice was given hours or minutes before, during, or shortly

---

18. *See also* WATCH v. FCC, 665 F.2d 1264 (D.C. Cir. 1981). In this case, the FCC Commissioners held a meeting without giving seven days' notice to decide whether or not to meet to resolve an application for transfer of control of a radio station at an open meeting to be held on less than seven days' notice. The court held that the Sunshine Act did not require seven days' notice of meetings whose sole purpose is to consider whether to schedule a future meeting with less than seven days' notice.
19. *See* ANNUAL REPORTS OF THE FEDERAL DEPOSIT INSURANCE CORPORATION ON COMPLIANCE WITH THE GOVERNMENT IN THE SUNSHINE ACT, FOR CALENDAR YEARS 1994-1998, submitted to the Congress (Senate Committee on Governmental Affairs). *See also* FDIC rule at 12 C.F.R. § 311.6(a).

following the meeting."[20] In 1999 and 2000, however, following two complaints filed against it in 1998, the FDIC did increase the advance notice it gave of its closed meetings from zero to as much as five days.[21]

Similarly, the Federal Trade Commission in its Annual Report to Congress for 2000 noted its practice not to publish any meeting notice in the *Federal Register* for meetings closed pursuant to 5 U.S.C. § 552b(c)(10) and (d)(4).[22]

The Occupational Safety and Health Review Commission (OSHRC), a multimember adjudicatory agency, has gone even further in reducing or eliminating notice of its "regularly scheduled" meetings in the *Federal Register.* OSHRC explains that under its earlier Sunshine regulations:

> the Commission was required to follow formal procedures for announcing all Commission meetings, even though the regularly-scheduled meetings were almost always closed to the public because they involved only the disposition of contested cases. The Commission determined that the costly and time-consuming public announcement procedures of those regulations were unnecessary and wasteful. As a result, in December of 1985, the Commission revised its regulations in order to allow it to use a less costly and less formal procedure when the

---

20. *See* FDIC ANNUAL REPORT for 1995, at 5.
21. *See* FDIC ANNUAL REPORT for 1999, at 3, and FDIC ANNUAL REPORT for 2000, at 3. *Cf.* Sunshine Act practices of the Securities and Exchange Commission. Of the 58 meetings it closed in 2004, pursuant to many of the same exemptions invoked by the FDIC and the FTC, the SEC provided public notice of 46 of these closed meetings a week or more in advance. *See* ANNUAL REPORT OF THE SECURITIES AND EXCHANGE COMMISSION ON THE GOVERNMENT IN THE SUNSHINE ACT FOR CALENDAR YEAR 2004, Exhibit C.
22. *See* ANNUAL REPORT OF THE FEDERAL TRADE COMMISSION ON COMPLIANCE WITH THE GOVERNMENT IN THE SUNSHINE ACT FOR CALENDAR YEAR 2000, submitted to the Congress (Senate Committee on Governmental Affairs), at 4. *See also* 16 C.F.R. § 4.15(c)(2) (Commission announces closure of meetings at the beginning of meeting.).

meeting will be closed. 50 *Federal Register* 51, 678 (Dec. 19, 1985).[23]

Under the revised regulations, the categories of "regularly scheduled meetings" and "other Commission meetings" were created. Regularly scheduled meetings are held at 10 a.m. every Thursday, except for legal holidays, in the Commission's hearing room. *See* 29 C.F.R. § 2203.4(c). That notice is supplemented by posted notices only when the Commission cancels a regularly scheduled meeting or reschedules it for another time or day. Notice of the Commission's regularly scheduled meetings are no longer published in the *Federal Register*.[24]

Other Commission meetings that involve official business and that cannot be conducted in a regularly scheduled meeting are now scheduled for a special meeting or meetings for the purpose of conducting that business. The public announcement of those meetings and decisions to close these meetings in whole or in part will be made in accordance with the Sunshine Act's formal procedures, including publication of the meetings in the *Federal Register*. *See* 29 C.F.R. § 2203.5.[25]

Another cutback in *Federal Register* notice was adopted in 1997 by the U.S. Postal Service. It deleted a self-imposed requirement that it publish in the *Federal Register* a notice of the vote to close a meeting immediately after the vote is taken. The Postal Service notes that the Sunshine Act, 5 U.S.C. § 552b(d)(3), requires making publicly available a notice of votes to close future meetings, but does not require publication in the *Federal Register*.[26]

We do not think that the Sunshine Act permits blanket notices, for example, in the agency's regulations contained in the *Code of Federal Regulations*. May OSHRC lawfully publish a generalized "we meet every Thursday" notice? There would appear to be no problem with such a generic notice in the Code as long as the public is directed to where it

---

23. Letter from Earl R. Ohman, Jr., General Counsel, OSHRC, to Stephen Klitzman, Nov. 20, 2001.
24. *Id.*
25. *Id.*
26. Letter from Mary Ann Gibbons, Vice President-General Counsel, U.S. Postal Service, Aug.15, 2001, to Stephen Klitzman, at pp. 1-2.

can get information on the subject matter of individual meetings. (In fact, the Code may be a better place than the *Federal Register* to provide practitioners with real Sunshine notice because it is often the first reference practitioners consult, especially those inexperienced in agency procedures.) We also believe the Act does not allow general notices of meetings routinely closed—for example, adjudications by OSHRC.

CHANGING THE TIME, PLACE, SUBJECT MATTER, OR DECISION TO OPEN OR CLOSE[27]

(e)(2) The time or place of a meeting may be changed following the public announcement required by paragraph (1) only if the agency publicly announces such change at the earliest practicable time. The subject matter of a meeting, or the determination of the agency to open or close a meeting, or portion of a meeting, to the public may be changed following the public announcement required by this subsection only if (A) a majority of the entire membership of the agency determines by a recorded vote that agency business so requires and that no earlier announcement of the change was possible, and (B) the agency publicly announces such change and the vote of each member upon such change at the earliest practicable time.

Subsection (e)(2) allows for changes in the time, place, subject matter, or open-closed status of a meeting after the agency has already scheduled the meeting and publicly announced it.

Changing the Time or Place

The agency may change the time or place of a meeting after the public announcement "only if the agency publicly announces [the] change at the earliest practicable time." Agency members, however, need not vote on the change of meeting time or place. Conf. Rep., 18.

Cancellation

The question of the cancellation of a meeting is not considered in the Act or its legislative history. If a cancellation is viewed as a change in the time or place, rather than the subject matter, of a meeting, it would

---

27. *See* Appendix M, *Sample Agency Meeting Notices.*

not require a recorded vote of the agency but would necessitate an announcement of the cancellation "at the earliest practicable time." Similarly, if an agency passes over an already scheduled and announced agenda item, the rescheduling of the item may most practically be considered a change in the time or place of the meeting portion and need only be announced "at the earliest practicable time."

Changing the Subject Matter or Decision to Open or Close; Addition, Deletion or Carry-Over of Agenda Items

The second sentence of subsection (e)(2) permits an agency, after it has scheduled and announced a meeting, to change the subject matter, or the decision to open or close the meeting. The agency may make such changes "only if (A) a majority of the entire membership of the agency determines by a recorded vote that agency business so requires and that no earlier announcement of the change was possible, and (B) the agency publicly announces such change and the vote of each member upon such change at the earliest practicable time." The Senate Report elaborates on this provision:

> This procedure anticipates cases when agency business requires that a matter be added to the agenda on a few days or even a few hours notice. For example, a motor carrier may apply for an emergency temporary operating license in order to provide fuel, food, clothing or the like to those who need it immediately. Agency action within days or hours may be necessary. In such a case, the matter could be added to the already announced agenda of the meeting, or the agency could call a separate meeting to consider the matter. The decision to close a meeting previously open to the public might also occur on short notice, or even at the meeting itself, when a new subject or new facts arise. The provision is designed to provide the flexibility necessary to insure expeditious agency action.

S. Rep., 30.[28]

The question has arisen whether agencies may add, delete, or carry over agenda items without complying with the voting and notice requirements of subsections (e)(2) and (e)(3).

---

28. *See also* Conf. Rep., at 18.

Additions of agenda items should comply with the voting and notice requirements of subsections (e)(2) and (e)(3). That (e)(2) was intended to be used for such last-minute additions is clear from the legislative history quoted above and consistent with the basic purpose that notice serves. Deletion and carry-over of agenda items raise more difficult questions of interpretation. On the one hand, not providing advance notice that an item will not be discussed might be regarded as unfair and inconvenient to those planning to attend a meeting because of the announced discussion of a specific item. Furthermore, a concern about agencies issuing "dummy" agendas and notices and then changing them at will without providing adequate public notice would argue for compliance with the voting and notice requirements of subsection (e)(2) and (e)(3) when deleting, as well as adding, agenda items.

On the other hand, practical considerations of conducting agency business appear to require some flexibility for agencies to delete agenda items without voting or providing notice as required in subsection (e)(2). A collegial vote on each decision to delete or postpone an agenda item seems a needlessly complicated procedure, especially since in many, if not most, agencies the agenda is not set initially by collegial action.[29] It can be argued that a decision to postpone an item, either to a date certain or date to be determined, is a change in time and not a change in subject matter, and consequently need not be made by the collegium.[30] Such an interpretation of subsection (e)(2) might yield practical advantages both to the agency and to the public, since it would permit prompt notice of agenda changes, whereas requiring collegial action is likely to result in pro forma approval of postponements by the collegium in the course of the meeting itself.

---

29. In his study of the respective roles of chairmen and members at seven major regulatory commissions, Prof. David M. Welborn pointed to the chairman's responsibility for organizing the meeting agenda as a significant source of his or her authority. See WELBORN, GOVERNANCE OF FEDERAL REGULATORY AGENCIES 120-21 (Univ. of Tenn. Press 1977).
30. See regulation of the Board of Governors, Federal Reserve System, 12 C.F.R. § 261b.9 (changes in subject matter or whether to open or close a meeting made by a majority of members; changes in time of meeting, postponements, cancellations announced by Board Secretary). See also 42 Fed. Reg. 13,299 (March 10, 1977).

Whether deletion of an agenda item is viewed as a change in subject matter or a change in time, the language of subsection (e)(2) appears to require public notice as soon as practicable after the decision to delete is made. Providing such notice would, of course, always be of value in the case of open meetings. With regard to closed meetings, however, the deletion of agenda items without prior notice would not inconvenience members of the public, who would not be attending in any case, and it may be that the test of practicability can take this into account. This is, in essence, the position of both the Securities and Exchange Commission and the United States Parole Commission. The regulation of the Parole Commission permits the deletion of agenda items without notice only with respect to closed meetings.[31] The SEC's deletion provision states that notwithstanding the requirements of subsection (e)(2), "matters which have been announced for Commission consideration may be deleted, or continued in whole or in part to the next scheduled Commission meeting, without notice."[32] In the preamble to its rules, however, the SEC qualifies this deletion provision as follows:

> [t]he Commission does not intend that this provision will be invoked as to items previously announced for consideration at a meeting open to the public except in extraordinary circumstances. The Commission recognizes that members of the public may arrange to attend particular open meetings, and will make every effort to afford reasonable notice of any alterations in previously noticed open meetings should such alterations be necessary. In the case, however, of closed meetings the Commission believes it important that it retain a measure of flexibility to respond to contingencies requiring the omission or rescheduling of agenda items. Since the public would not, in any event, be in attendance at such meetings, the Commission does not believe that [the deletion provision] will inconvenience interested persons.

42 Fed. Reg. 14,692 (March 16, 1977).

---

31. 28 C.F.R. § 16.204(c), 42 Fed. Reg. 14,715 (March 16, 1977).
32. 17 C.F.R. § 200.403(c)(2), 42 Fed. Reg. 14,696 (March 16, 1977).

In contrast, the Federal Energy Regulatory Commission is adhering to the policy expressed by its predecessor agency, the Federal Power Commission, of deleting individual agenda items without notice.[33]

The FPC stated in the order adopting its Sunshine rules:

To eliminate flexibility with respect to deletions of agenda items would serve no useful purpose, while creating additional administrative burdens. The proposed procedure gives adequate notice to the public that a particular matter may be considered at a meeting. The agenda is subject to further check with the agency contact person designated in the notice. We therefore believe that retaining the proposed [deletion] procedure best serves the needs of the public.

42 Fed. Reg. 14,698 (March 16, 1977).

Concerning the continuation or carry-over of agenda items, legislative history is once again silent. If an agency votes to adjourn a meeting and put all unfinished business over to the next day or next meeting, it could announce and submit a notice to that effect to the *Federal Register*. Where the agendas of several meetings have been announced in advance, however, it would seem more efficient to allow matters listed for one agenda but not disposed of to be carried over automatically to the agenda of the next meeting. This automatic carry-over could be listed in each meeting notice and could be supplemented by the listing of an agency contact person for more information about the status of meeting agendas.[34] If the agenda of the next meeting has not been announced at the time the decision to carry over items is made, these items should be listed in the subsequent announcement.

Finally, subsection (e)(2) allows an agency to reconsider and change its decision to open or close a meeting. Such a change might be made

---

33. 18 C.F.R. § 375.204(b), 42 Fed. Reg. 14,701 (March 16, 1977).
34. *See, e.g.,* meeting notices of the Board of Governors, Federal Reserve System, 42 Fed. Reg. 16,208 (March 25, 1977); the Foreign Claims Settlement Commission, 42 Fed. Reg. 17,940 (March 25, 1977); and the USITC, 66 Fed. Reg. 35,268 (July 3, 2001).

at the request of a "directly affected" person under subsection (d)(2), or at the instance of an agency member. In either case, the change in the status of the meeting can be made only if the agency members cast the required majority vote and the change and the vote are announced "at the earliest practicable time."

With regard to the majority vote requirement, the subsection requires a "majority of the entire membership of the agency" to vote to change the meeting subject matter or a decision to open or close the meeting. Just as under subsections (d)(1), (d)(2), (d)(4), and (e)(1), the vote of a simple majority of a quorum is not sufficient to take action.

CONTENTS AND SUBMISSION OF NOTICE TO *FEDERAL REGISTER*

(e)(3) Immediately following each public announcement required by this subsection, notice of the time, place and subject matter of a meeting, whether the meeting is opened or closed, any change in one of the preceding, and the name and phone number of the official designated by the agency to respond to requests for information about the meeting, shall also be submitted for publication in the Federal Register.

Subsection (e)(3) requires that, immediately after each public announcement required by subsections (e)(1) and (e)(2), the agency must submit for publication in the *Federal Register* notice of the time, place, and subject matter of a meeting, whether the meeting is open or closed, change in any of these items, and the name and phone number of an agency person to contact for additional information. These seven items are the minimum contents of the meeting notice, to be published in the *Federal Register* whether the meeting is to be open or closed, unless the meeting is covered by the expediting procedures of subsection (d)(4).[35] A few agencies include in their *Federal Register* notices information required to be made public by subsections (d)(3) and (f)(1), such as the votes of members on closings, explanations of closings,

---

35. The provisions of subsection (e) are not applicable to meetings subject to subsection (d)(4) procedures, whether or not such meetings are actually closed.

Section 552b(e): Procedures for Announcing Meetings 139

lists of expected attendees and the certifications of the General Counsel.[36] Some agencies have also included in (e)(3) notices a paragraph informing the public of the procedure to request a closing under subsection (d)(2).[37]

These additional items of information are not required to be published in the *Federal Register*, nor are they included in the standardized format for Sunshine Act meeting notices adopted right after enactment of the GISA by the *Federal Register* as a means of cutting the time lag between submission and publication of notices. This format includes only the minimum information required by subsection (e)(3). According to an official in the Office of the *Federal Register*, notices identified by agencies as Sunshine Act notices submitted to the Office by 4 p.m. will be published two working days after receipt rather than the usual three working days, even if they are in regular text rather than the standardized format. Notices, however, that are not clearly identified either in the title or body of the document as Sunshine Act notices will not receive expedited publication.[38]

The publication of the additional information cited in subsections (d)(3) and (f)(1) does, of course, provide the public with a fuller explanation and more complete notice of closed agency meetings. Where an agency opts not to submit a notice in the standardized format, it would be practical and efficient to issue a single document complying with subsections (d)(3) and (e)(3), and referring as well to the General Counsel's certification required in subsection (f)(1). Agencies submitting standardized notices to the *Federal Register*, pursuant to subsection (e)(3), should issue and make available the (d)(3) information—members' votes, explanations of closings, and lists of expected attendees—using agency Internet Web sites, bulletin boards, press releases, or whatever additional means of notification or public announcement they have adopted. While the certification of the General Counsel need not be published in the *Federal Register*, it too should

---

36. *See, e.g.*, meeting notices of the Federal Communications Commission, 42 Fed. Reg. 13,342 (March 10, 1977), and the Securities and Exchange Commission, 42 Fed. Reg. 17,580 (April 1, 1977).
37. *See, e.g.*, meeting notices of the Commodity Futures Trading Commission, 42 Fed. Reg. 15,359 (March 21, 1977), and the USITC, 42 Fed. Reg. 18,687 (April 8, 1977).
38. *See* Suhre Interview, p. 121 note 3, *supra*.

be issued or made available by the agency. See, for example, regulations of the Federal Trade Commission that make the General Counsel's certification "publicly available within one day," 16 C.F.R. § 4.15(c), and the regulations of the National Credit Union Administration that the General Counsel's certification will be made "promptly available to the public," 12 C.F.R. § 791.18(d).

The legislative history is clear that the *Federal Register* need not actually publish the notice prior to the meeting it announces. Indeed, in some cases publication in advance of the meeting will be impossible. Submission for publication is required by subsection (e)(3) nevertheless. For, as the Senate Report notes, "In any event, the information must be printed in the *Federal Register* as soon as possible following the first public announcement. Even if this does not occur until after the meeting, such notice will provide a record of all agency meetings in a single publication widely available to members of the public." S. Rep., 31.

Use of "Reasonable Means" to Circulate Public Announcements

Publication of the notice in the *Federal Register* is only part of an agency's responsibility to notify the public of forthcoming meetings. The Act itself does not define "make publicly available" [(d)(3)], "public announcement" [(d)(4), (e)(1)-(e)(3)], or "publicly announce" [(e)(2)]. However, Congress was well aware that publication in the *Federal Register* would often fail to provide timely and effective notice. The Conference Report states clearly that "reasonable means" besides publication in the *Federal Register* must be "used to assure that the public is fully informed of public announcements" under the Act. Conf. Rep., 19. These additional methods of publicity include posting notices on agency Web sites or bulletin boards, making notices available in a Public Affairs or Secretary's Office or in the agency's headquarters lobby area, publishing and distributing to a general or specialized mailing list a weekly or monthly calendar of agency meetings, issuing press releases to various special interest, trade and daily newspaper publications, and using recorded telephone announcements. Conf. Rep., 19; S. Rep., 30-31; H. Rep. I, 14.

A number of agency regulations specify the "reasonable means" by which public announcements will be issued and by which the public can obtain agency notices. For example, the Nuclear Regulatory Commission provides that its public announcement of a meeting shall include a posting on the agency's Web page and, to the extent appropriate, mailing a copy to persons on a mailing list, submitting a copy to at least two Washington newspapers of general circulation, and "any other means which the Secretary believes will serve to further inform any persons who might be interested."[39] The Securities and Exchange Commission, in addition to giving notice of its Sunshine Act meetings in the *Federal Register*, provides public notice of its meetings in the *SEC News Digest,* which is available on the SEC's Web site. According to the SEC, "Publishing meeting notices on the WorldWide Web provides timely and wider circulation of Commission notices to interested members of the public."[40] Similarly, the Postal Rate Commission "views Internet posting as a valuable adjunct to public announcements in the *Federal Register,* physical posting in the Commission's reading room, press releases and recorded telephone announcements, and commends the practice to other agencies."[41]

---

39. 10 C.F.R. § 9.107(d). *See also* regulations of the Commodity Futures Trading Commission, 17 C.F.R. § 147.4(d), 42 Fed. Reg. 13,705 (March 11, 1977); USITC, 19 C.F.R. § 201.35(e), 42 Fed. Reg. 11,244 (Feb. 20, 1977). The CFTC maintains a mailing list of individuals or groups wishing to receive a copy of each agency's calendar. The CFTC specifically indicates that the mailing service is free of charge. *See* 17 C.F.R. § 147.4(d)(1). The USITC discontinued its mailing list and now makes its calendar available on its Web site. Telephone message from Marilyn R. Abbott, secretary, USITC, April 26, 2005.
40. *See* Memorandum from Andrew Glickman, attorney, Office of General Counsel, to David M. Becker, general counsel, Securities and Exchange Commission, Dec. 3, 2001, at 6 (hereafter SEC Memo). The SEC also posts notices of meetings outside its Secretary's office and maintains a mailing list. *See* 58 Fed. Reg. 64,120 (Dec. 6, 1993).
41. *See* letter from Stephen L. Sharfman, general counsel, Postal Rate Commission, to Stephen Klitzman, Sept. 19, 2001. For other comprehensive statements of agency public notice procedures used to publicize Sunshine Act meetings, *see* the ANNUAL REPORTS ON COMPLIANCE WITH THE GOVERNMENT IN THE SUNSHINE ACT FOR CALENDAR YEAR 2000 submitted to the Congress (Senate Committee on Governmental Affairs) by the agencies, *e.g.,* the Equal Employment Opportunity Commission, at 3; the Federal Communications Commission, at 3; the Federal Reserve System, Board of Governors, at 4-5; the Federal Trade Commission, at 4; and the Tennessee Valley Authority, at 4-5.

Whatever methods of dissemination of notice are adopted, agencies should keep in mind that the Sunshine Act encourages the widest possible circulation of meeting information. In the words of the former Interstate Commerce Commission, "The provision for comprehensive public notice of agency meetings is the keystone to fulfillment of the congressional policy expressed in the Act." 42 Fed. Reg. 13,796-97 (March 11, 1977). Meetings will be effectively open only to those interested persons who have notice of them.

Chapter 6

SECTION 552b(f)
GENERAL COUNSEL CERTIFICATION; PREPARATION AND PUBLIC AVAILABILITY OF TRANSCRIPTS, RECORDINGS, AND MINUTES OF CLOSED MEETINGS

GENERAL COUNSEL CERTIFICATION	144
Effect of Refusal to Certify	144
Delegation	147
Timing	149
Certification and the Public Interest Determination	150
Contents of the Certification	150
RETENTION OF CERTIFICATION, PRESIDING OFFICER'S STATEMENT	150
MAINTENANCE OF TRANSCRIPT, RECORDING OR MINUTES	152
DESCRIPTION OF MINUTES	152
PUBLIC ACCESS TO AND AGENCY PROVISION AND RETENTION OF TRANSCRIPTS, RECORDINGS, OR MINUTES	153
Obligation of Agency to Make Meeting Record "Promptly Available"	153
Standard for Deletion; Extent of Agency's Duty to Edit the Record	157
Procedural Requirements and Delegation	161
Subsequent Review of Transcript Material	163
Administrative Appeal Procedures	167
Fees for Furnishing Copies	168
Maintenance and Use of Verbatim Copies of Transcripts, Recordings, or Minutes	171

(f)(1) For every meeting closed pursuant to paragraphs (1) through (10) of subsection (c), the General Counsel or chief legal officer of the agency shall publicly certify that, in his or her opinion, the meeting may be closed to the public and shall state each relevant exemptive provision. A copy of such certification, together with a statement from the presiding officer of the meeting setting forth the time and place of the meeting, and the persons present, shall be retained by the agency. The agency shall maintain a complete transcript or electronic recording adequate to record fully the proceedings of each meeting, or portion of a meeting, closed to the public, except that in the case of a meeting, or portion of a meeting, closed to the public pursuant to paragraph (8), (9)(A), or (10) of subsection (c), the agency shall maintain either such a transcript or recording, or a set of minutes. Such minutes shall fully and clearly describe all matters discussed and shall provide a full and accurate summary of any actions taken, and the reasons therefor, including a description of each of the views expressed on any item and the record of any roll call vote (reflecting the vote of each member on the question). All documents considered in connection with any action shall be identified in such minutes.

GENERAL COUNSEL CERTIFICATION

Subsection (f)(1) first requires that "for every meeting closed" pursuant to the exemptions of subsection (c), whether the agency closes under subsection (d)(1) or (d)(4), "the General Counsel or chief legal officer of the agency shall publicly certify that, in his or her opinion, the meeting may be closed to the public and shall state each relevant exemptive provision." This provision concerning the role of the General Counsel raises several questions of interpretation.

Effect of Refusal to Certify

The most difficult question raised by the certification requirement is whether certification by the General Counsel or chief legal officer is a prerequisite to a legally closed meeting. Can an agency decide to close a meeting despite the refusal of the General Counsel to certify the closing? Or can the General Counsel, in effect, exercise a veto over the agency's decision to close the meeting?

Section 552b(f): General Counsel Certification

The Act itself does not specifically address the contingency of a refusal to certify, but a literal reading of the first sentence of subsection (f)(1) suggests that certification is a prerequisite. Proponents of that position might also cite the Conference Report, which states that "before a meeting may be closed, the General Counsel or chief legal officer of the agency must certify that, in his or her opinion, the meeting may properly be closed and state each relevant exemptive provision."[1] Based on this language, some agencies have adopted regulations that make certification a prerequisite for closing a meeting.[2] However, other agencies have interpreted this language in a temporal sense, as requiring that the certification take place prior to closing the meeting but not that a favorable determination by the General Counsel is a prerequisite for the holding of a closed meeting. For example, the Federal Trade Commission (FTC) regulation reads:

> Whenever the Commission votes to close a meeting . . . it shall make publicly available . . . notices both of such vote and the General Counsel's determination regarding certification.[3]

In the preamble to its rule, the FTC observed that the determination regarding certification must be made in advance of the meeting but did not believe that the agency is barred from holding a closed meeting if the General Counsel declines to certify.[4] The FTC indicated:

---

1. Conf. Rep., at 19. *See also* Appendix N, *Sample Agency General Counsel Certification Forms.*
2. *See, e.g.,* regulations of the Consumer Product Safety Commission, 16 C.F.R. § 1013.4(c)(3) ("Before the Commission may hold a closed meeting the General Counsel must certify that in his or her opinion, the meeting may properly be closed to the public."), and the U.S. International Trade Commission, 19 C.F.R. § 201.39 (Before a Commission meeting may be closed . . . the General Counsel . . . shall . . . certify that in his or her opinion the meeting may be closed to the public.").
3. 16 C.F.R. § 4.15(c)(1). *See also* regulations of the Export-Import Bank of the United States, 12 C.F.R. § 407.5 (the General Counsel "will be asked to certify" that the meeting may be closed); and the Tennessee Valley Authority, 18 C.F.R. § 1301.45(d) ("[T]here shall be a certification by the General Counsel of TVA stating whether, in his or her opinion, the meeting may be closed to the public.").
4. 42 Fed. Reg. 13,539 (March 11, 1977).

Public disclosure of the General Counsel's refusal to certify should be sufficient to conform with congressional intent. The legality of closing any given meeting depends on the matters to be discussed at the meeting, not on the procedures followed. While the Commission expects generally to follow the advice of its General Counsel as reflected in his decision whether or not to certify, the Commission does not believe that Congress intended the General Counsel, an advisor to the Commission, to have veto authority over the decisions of Presidential appointees who are ultimately accountable to Congress and the public.[5]

A number of policy and practical considerations support the FTC's interpretation.[6] To begin with, if a General Counsel can veto closings, eventually he or she will either accommodate to the views of the agency with pro forma certifications or be replaced by a counsel who will. In neither case will the independent opinion contemplated by the statute be obtained. Indeed, the certification requirement will not work as a safeguard unless such independent judgment is expected and applied. (On any reading, the certification requirement makes it difficult for the General Counsel to give a completely objective opinion, but if the failure to certify must be made public but will not override the agency's determination, an agency could presumably get along with a General Counsel who occasionally refused to certify.) Second, in the event of a challenge, the courts will make an independent assessment of whether a meeting was properly closed. It is, of course, possible that a court will agree with the agency rather than the General Counsel. By interpreting the certification to be an independent, prior determination, though not a prerequisite, the agency is still required to obtain legal advice from its General Counsel or chief legal adviser. Finally, it is anomalous for a General Counsel, an advisory employee of the agency, to be in a position to overturn the considered decision of a majority of

---

5. *Id.*
6. Consultations with agencies under subsection (g) in connection with preparation of the *1978 Guide* indicated a strong consensus in favor of this interpretation, even though most agency regulations did not address the issue squarely. *See* testimony of Richard K. Berg, House Judiciary Oversight Hearing, at 7.

the collegial body. Only the clearest language in the statute could be construed to compel such a result. Without such language, it is difficult to conclude that the congressional intent was to grant a veto power to the General Counsel over the actions of his or her agency.[7]

As a practical matter, General Counsels play a significant role in ensuring agency compliance with the Act. Based on interviews with agency staff officials, a 1984 study of Sunshine Act implementation undertaken for the Administrative Conference of the United States (ACUS) noted:

> [G]eneral counsels tend to be vigorous in their application of the law at this stage, more so at times than members and staff appreciate. In one agency the role played by the general counsel's staff in relation to line staff was described as "adversarial" in closure decisions. General counsels also have been known to cut off discussion among members in closed meetings when it veers toward subjects that are not closable. Instances are also reported in which the general counsel's office advises against the use of notation voting on important items and encourages open consideration of matters that could probably be closed. Nevertheless, there seems to be a general tendency, often stronger now than in the immediate period after the act was passed, to close discussions when an exemption applies.[8]

Delegation

Can the certification responsibility be delegated? The answer is not apparent from the Act or the legislative history. However, because the

---

7. If the General Counsel's certification had been accepted as an alternative to requiring a transcript of every closed meeting (*see* remarks of Rep. Horton, 122 Cong. Rec. 24,204-205 (July 28, 1976)), it would have made more sense to regard it as a prerequisite for closing a meeting. Because the evidence of the meeting would be beyond recall, reliance would have to have been placed on the General Counsel's determination. But as a supplement to the transcript requirement, it is not the final test of the propriety of closing, but rather a procedural step to emphasize to the agency members the gravity of the determination to close.
8. *See* Welborn Report, *supra* p. 34 note 9, and Appendix G, *infra*.

certification is presumably intended as an assurance by the agency's chief legal adviser[9] that closure is proper, the requirement carries an implication that certification by a lower-level official does not suffice.[10] The agency regulations reflect a consensus that the function of certification may not simply be delegated. However, in the absence of the General Counsel it may be performed by one who is designated or otherwise acting as General Counsel.[11] Where the agency has no General Counsel or chief legal officer, the certification should be performed by whoever is responsible for furnishing legal advice to the agency or, if necessary, by a lawyer member of the agency, or by the head of the agency.[12]

---

9. At the National Labor Relations Board, for example, the General Counsel is an independent official charged with litigating cases before the Board. The Board's legal adviser is its Solicitor, who is the appropriate official to perform the certification. *See* 29 C.F.R. § 102.140(e).
10. *Cf.* United States v. Giordano, 416 U.S. 503, 514 (1974).
11. *See, e.g.,* regulations of the Securities and Exchange Commission, 17 C.F.R. § 200.21(c), and the Federal Deposit Insurance Corporation, 12 C.F.R. § 311.7, which create a descending hierarchy of senior-level lawyers who may issue the certification in the absence of the General Counsel.
12. *See, e.g.,* the National Museum Services Board, 45 C.F.R. § 1180.88(c). Prior to 1981, the Board was part of the Department of Health, Education and Welfare or the Department of Education, and the certification was by the Department's General Counsel. Following the transfer of the Board to the National Foundation for the Arts and Humanities, the certification has been issued by "the attorney responsible for providing advice with regard to matters under the Government in the Sunshine Act rather than by the General Counsel of the Department of Education because [the Board] is no longer part of the Department." *See* 49 Fed. Reg. 3182 (Jan. 26, 1984) *and* 45 C.F.R. § 1180.88(c) ("The Board addresses requests for the certification required by Section 552b to the individual responsible for providing legal services to the [Board]."). On occasion, an agency lacking a legally trained officer or access to legal services will assign the certification functions to someone else. *See, e.g.,* National Commission on Libraries and Information Service, 45 C.F.R. § 703.203(b) (certification by chairman). Such agencies may nonetheless coincidentally have a lawyer or legally trained individual among its members and could, in such circumstances, assign this responsibility to such individual.

Timing

The Act is not clear as to the timing of the certification, stating only that "for every meeting closed pursuant to . . . subsection (c)," the certification shall be made. The statute does not require that the General Counsel be in the deliberation that votes to close the meeting, although such participation may be practical. Yet the apparent purpose of the certification requirement is to provide for an independent assessment by the General Counsel as a safeguard against improper closings, and at most agencies the certification precedes or is coincident with the determination regarding the holding of a closed meeting.[13] But the statute does not preclude the possibility that the vote to close may precede consultation with the General Counsel, and some agencies explicitly recognize this possibility.[14] The 1984 ACUS study

---

13. For example, the regulation of the Federal Energy Regulatory Commission provides that the General Counsel's certification occur "prior to a determination that a meeting should be closed," 18 C.F.R. § 375.206(d), and the regulation of the Federal Trade Commission likewise provides that the General Counsel's certification "shall be made prior to the Commission vote to close a meeting," 16 C.F.R. § 4.15 (c).
14. The Commodity Credit Corporation regulation leaves open the possibility that certification may occur after a decision is made to close a meeting but before the meeting is held. 7 C.F.R. § 1409.5(c). Indeed, because the agency retains the authority to reconsider its decision to close, it is acceptable for an agency to vote to close pursuant to subsection (d)(1) in advance of certification. Because the General Counsel may be unable to attend personally every meeting at which members proceed under subsection (d)(1) to vote to close a future meeting, to permit the certification to be made in the interval between the vote and the holding of the closed meeting may be both more practical and more consistent with the intent of subsection (f)(1) than to have an acting general counsel certify at the time of the vote. The Federal Election Commission takes the position that the certification "need not be provided before the meeting is held. This permits the certification to be prepared after the meeting is held in cases where time does not permit its preparation earlier." 50 Fed. Reg. 39,968, 39,970 (Oct. 1, 1985). The Export-Import Bank closes most of its regularly scheduled meetings to the public. *See* 12 C.F.R. § 407.2(b). Its regulations provide that the certification must be posted in the Secretary's Office, but not that it be part of the (d)(3) or (e)(i) documents. 12 C.F.R. § 407.5. Thus, certification can be obtained in the interval between the meeting announcement and the meeting.

found that the recommendation for consideration of a matter at a closed meeting is typically made by the staff unit initiating the action and that General Counsels "tend to be vigorous" in ensuring proper application of the law at that stage.[15] Although the General Counsel's advice is ordinarily given at the time that the agency members must make their judgment as to the suitability of a meeting for closure, General Counsels will also occasionally cut off discussion at the meeting where it drifts into areas that should be open.[16]

Certification and the Public Interest Determination

Does the certification by the General Counsel include a "public interest" determination under subsection (c)? To the extent that the public interest determination is distinct from the availability of the exemption, it is a policy question that seems more appropriate for the agency than the General Counsel to resolve. In our view, the General Counsel need certify only that the meeting may be closed under one or more specified exemptions; he or she need not certify that the public interest does not require that the meeting be open.

Contents of the Certification

As a matter of good practice, the General Counsel's certification should cite multiple exemptions if they are available—it should "state each relevant exemptive provision." The certification should cite both the exemptions relied upon under 5 U.S.C. § 552b(c) and the equivalent citations under agency regulations.

RETENTION OF CERTIFICATION, PRESIDING OFFICER'S STATEMENT

The second sentence of subsection (f)(1) requires that a copy of the General Counsel's certification, as well as "a statement from the presiding officer of the meeting setting forth the time and place of the meeting, and the persons present, shall be retained by the agency." The

---

15. *See* Welborn Report, *supra* p.34 note 9.
16. *Id.* The regulations of the Chemical Safety and Hazard Investigation Board also require that a lawyer from the General Counsel's office attend sessions that do not constitute "meetings" in order to ensure that the agency members do not drift into deliberative activity. *See* 40 C.F.R. § 1603.5.

legislative history has little to say about this requirement. The Conference Report simply indicates that the certification and the statement, including the date of the meeting, must be retained by the agency as part of the transcript, recording, or minutes of the meeting.[17]

It is not clear that the General Counsel's certification must be posted or published as well as retained. Certainly, it need not be part of the *Federal Register* notice required by subsection (e)(3). However, one might infer an affirmative duty of issuance from the words "publicly certify." Some agencies provide that the certification will be part of the statement or announcement required by subsections (d)(3) and (e)(1).[18] In view of the statutory goal of providing the public "the fullest practicable information regarding the decisionmaking processes of the Federal Government,"[19] the better practice is for agencies to post or publish the General Counsel's certification, as well as retain it in public agency files.

With regard to the presiding officer's statement, the only interpretive question is whether the statutory requirement for listing "the persons present" applies to staff as well as outside persons. Like the similar provision of subsection (d)(3) requiring the agency to list all expected attendees, subsection (f)(l) refers to "the persons present" and makes no exception for agency personnel.[20] Many regulations simply repeat the statutory language. The Federal Election Commission expressly includes staff employees but by institutional title rather than name.[21] But others, such as the Federal Communications Commission, expressly exclude the names of staff members,[22] and the Federal Trade Commission excludes the names of both agency staff members and consultants.[23]

---

17. Conf. Rep., at 20.
18. *See, e.g.,* regulations of the Federal Election Commission, 11 C.F.R. § 2.5(b), *and* the Federal Trade Commission, 16 C.F.R. § 4.15(c), which provide for the certification to be part of, or attached to, the subsection (d)(3) statement. The regulations of the U.S. International Trade Commission, 19 C.F.R. § 201.35(b), make the certification part of the subsection (e)(1) public notice.
19. Government in the Sunshine Act, Pub. L. No. 94-409, § 2.
20. 5 U.S.C. § 552b(f)(1).
21. 11 C.F.R. § 2.5(d)(iii).
22. 47 C.F.R. § 0.607(d).
23. 16 C.F.R. § 4.15(c)(1).

152 *An Interpretive Guide to the Government in the Sunshine Act, 2d Ed.*
Chapter 6

If agencies issue a notice of meeting in advance that includes the names of individuals expected to attend, they should amend the list if, in fact, other individuals actually attend.[24]

MAINTENANCE OF TRANSCRIPT, RECORDING OR MINUTES

The third sentence of subsection (f)(1) requires each agency to make and maintain a complete verbatim transcript or electronic recording of each meeting or portion closed to the public, "except that for a meeting closed under Exemptions (8) (bank reports), (9)(A) (information likely to lead to financial speculation), and (10) (adjudicatory proceedings or civil actions), the agency may elect to make a transcript, a recording, or minutes."[25] If the material is made available in the form of a recording, the agency must also see to it that listeners can identify each speaker.[26] The Senate Report contemplated that the taped record of the closed meeting must be "adequate to identify each speaker,"[27] but Congress did not contemplate that agencies had to use a court reporter or person with similar skills to make a transcript of the meeting.[28]

There is no requirement that a transcript, recording, or minutes be kept of each open as well as closed agency meeting. However, a few agencies do so.[29]

DESCRIPTION OF MINUTES

The final sentence of subsection (f)(1) describes the minutes that are to be kept if the agency elects to maintain them instead of a

---

24. *See, e.g.*, the regulations of the Federal Energy Regulatory Commission, which provide that the notice of closure list "all persons expected to attend the meeting and their affiliation," 18 C.F.R. § 375.206(c), but also provide that the presiding officer's statement set out "the persons present," 18 C.F.R. § 375.206(d).
25. Conf. Rep., at 20.
26. S. Rep., at 32.
27. *Id.* at 31.
28. *See id.* at 40.
29. *See, e.g.*, regulations of the Consumer Product Safety Commission, 16 C.F.R. § 1012.5(c) (transcripts); U.S. International Trade Commission, 19 C.F.R. § 201.40(c) (transcript or recording); Federal Trade Commission, 16 C.F.R. § 4.9(b)(8)(iv) (minutes); Marine Mammal Commission, 50 C.F.R. § 560.7(a) (transcript or electronic recording).

transcript or recording of any meeting or portion closed pursuant to Exemptions (8), (9)(A), or (10). "If minutes are kept, they must fully and clearly describe all matters discussed, provide a full and accurate summary of any actions taken and the reasons expressed therefor, and include a description of each of the views expressed on any item. The minutes must also reflect the vote of each member on any roll call vote taken during the proceedings and must identify all documents considered at the meeting." Conf. Rep., 20.

PUBLIC ACCESS TO AND AGENCY PROVISION AND RETENTION OF TRANSCRIPTS, RECORDINGS, OR MINUTES

(f)(2) The agency shall make promptly available to the public, in a place easily accessible to the public, the transcript, electronic recording, or minutes (as required by paragraph (1)) of the discussion of any item on the agenda, or of any item of the testimony of any witness received at the meeting, except for such item or items of such discussion or testimony as the agency determines to contain information which may be withheld under subsection (c). Copies of such transcript, or minutes, or a transcription of such recording disclosing the identity of each speaker, shall be furnished to any person at the actual cost of duplication or transcription. The agency shall maintain a complete verbatim copy of the transcript, a complete copy of the minutes, or a complete electronic recording of each meeting, or portion of a meeting, closed to the public, for a period of at least two years after such meeting, or until one year after the conclusion of any agency proceeding with respect to which the meeting or portion was held, whichever occurs later.

Obligation of Agency to Make Meeting Record "Promptly Available"

The agency must make the non-exempt transcripts, recordings, or minutes of meetings "promptly available" for free inspection, as well as provide copies for a fee, and the public must be granted access to such materials in a public reading room or some other "easily accessible," unrestricted place within the agency. S. Rep., 32. The language of the first sentence of subsection (f)(2) implies and the legislative history confirms that agencies are expected to make the meeting record materials available on their own initiative, prior to the receipt of public requests for such materials. The Senate Report also expressed the expectation that "[w]here a meeting was unnecessarily closed to the public it should take the agency a week or less to make the record available to the public."[30]

A number of agency regulations comply strictly with the legislative intent concerning public availability of, and access to, non-exempted transcripts, recordings, or minutes. For example, the Federal Energy Regulatory Commission regulations provide that "within a reasonable time after the adjournment of a meeting closed to the public, the Commission shall make available to the public . . . the transcript, electronic recording, or minutes of the discussion of any item on the agenda" except for those exempt from disclosure.[31] The Nuclear Regulatory Commission places the "transcript, electronic recording, or minutes" of non-exempt portions of closed meetings on its Web site,[32] and the Federal Reserve Board regulations indicate that non-exempt materials "will promptly be made available to the public in the Freedom of Information Office."[33]

Some agency regulations, however, provide for the availability of, and access to, non-exempted material only "upon request." For example, the Securities and Exchange Commission regulations provide:

> Within 20 days (excluding Saturdays, Sundays, and legal holidays) of the receipt by the Commission's Freedom of Information Act Officer of a written request, or within such extended period as may be agreeable to the person making the request, the Secretary shall make available for inspection

---

30. S. Rep., at 32.
31. 18 C.F.R. § 375.206(f). Similarly, the U.S. International Trade Commission regulations require that, except for the discussion of items properly withheld from public disclosure, the Commission's Secretary "shall promptly make available to interested members of the public the transcript or electronic recording of the discussion of any item on the agenda of a Commission meeting . . . ," except for items exempt from disclosure. 19 C.F.R. § 201.41(a).
32. 10 C.F.R. § 9.108 (b).
33. 12 C.F.R. § 261b.11(c).

by any person in the Commission's Public Reference Room, the transcript, electronic recording, or minutes . . . of the discussion of any item on the agenda, except for such item or items as the Freedom of Information Act Officer determines to involve matters which may be withheld . . . .[34]

The National Credit Union Administration promptly posts on its Web site a brief summary of the items discussed at closed sessions but awaits public requests for the actual transcripts or minutes.[35]

Some agencies are understandably reluctant to undertake a process of review of transcripts or recordings of closed meetings until it becomes necessary to do so. Explaining why it decided not to make materials available prior to request, the National Science Foundation stated:

> The Board has been conducting its meetings under the Act for several months, during which no request for a transcript or recording has yet been made. Preparation of a transcript or recording for release, with accompanying decisions on what will and will not be withheld, is costly. The Board's experience thus far indicates that anticipatory expenditure of the taxpayer's money for this purpose would be unjustified. Should the frequency of requests for transcripts materially increase, however, the Board will reconsider this matter.[36]

One agency, the Federal Communications Commission, has adopted a somewhat different approach. After a meeting, the respon-

---

34. 17 C.F.R. § 200.408(a). *See also* the regulations of the Harry S Truman Scholarship Foundation, 45 C.F.R. § 1802.7(d)(1) (material provided within 10 days of a request, Saturdays, Sundays and legal holidays excluded); the Overseas Private Investment Corporation, 22 C.F.R. § 708.6(d) (material provided within 10 days of a request, Saturdays, Sundays and legal holidays excluded); and the National Science Board, 45 C.F.R. § 614.4(b) (informal requests will be handled "informally and expeditiously," while written requests will be treated as formal FOIA requests).
35. Letter of Sheila A. Albin, associate general counsel, NCUA, to Stephen Klitzman, Sept. 13, 2001.
36. 42 Fed. Reg. § 14,719 (March 11, 1977).

sible Bureau or Office Chief determines, in light of the actual discussion, whether the meeting could have been open or that the reason for withholding information no longer pertains. If the information can be made public, it is placed in the public file.[37] The Commission explained:

> If, after the meeting, the responsible Bureau or Office Chief decides, in light of the discussion which in fact took place, that the meeting could have been open to the public or that the reason for withholding information no longer pertains, he will direct the Secretary to place the transcript in the public file. If the sole reason for closing the meeting was to avoid frustrating a Commission action, for example, the transcript will be placed in the public file after the action is taken. In addition, if a request for inspection of a transcript is granted, in whole or in part, the transcript, or portion thereof, which is made available will thereafter be maintained in the public file. Where the transcript is not maintained in the public file, requests for copies must be reviewed by the responsible Bureau or Office Chief and in some cases, possibly, by the Commission.

42 Fed. Reg. 12,866 (March 7, 1977).

The FCC's procedure, which it continues to use, deals satisfactorily with the situation where the transcript contains discussion of only one exempt item. Given the FCC's practice of generally closing meetings only for one item, the need to edit transcripts rarely, if ever, arises. Moreover, the discussion is reviewed to ensure that the meeting was properly closed and that the initial reason for closure continues to be valid. Provisions for individual requests under the FCC's FOIA rules provide a further procedure for considering factors that may justify release of the entire transcript, or exempt portions of such transcript, even when all of the materials could otherwise be withheld under the Sunshine Act.[38]

Of course, the critical question is not whether the agency will make the materials available only upon request (presumably any procedure for making materials available in a public document room will involve

---

37. 47 C.F.R. § 0.607(b).
38. *See* 47 C.F.R. §§ 0.607(b) *and* 0.461.

at least a written or oral request to the file clerk), but how promptly the agency is prepared to respond to the request.[39] This will ordinarily depend on whether the agency has reviewed the materials in advance of the request and determined which matters are to be made available to the public and which withheld.

Those rules providing for availability "upon request" appear to place the burden upon the member of the public to ask an agency, in effect, to "declassify" and release transcripts, recordings, or minutes of closed meetings. The Act, however, places the burden on the agency to quickly review its meeting records to determine what can be released. This burden is consistent with the obligation imposed on the agency to justify its closed meetings and the withholding of information.

Standard for Deletion; Extent of Agency's Duty to Edit the Record

Subsection (f)(2) requires disclosure of "the discussion of any item on the agenda, or of any item of the testimony of any witness received at the meeting, except for such item or items of such discussion or testimony as the agency determines to contain information that may be withheld under subsection (c)." The general standard governing deletion of information from a closed meeting transcript, recording, or minutes is that the deleted material must be exempt under subsection (c). Conf. Rep., 20; S. Rep., 31; H. Rep. I, 15. This standard presumably also requires the agencies to determine whether the public interest requires disclosure, notwithstanding the availability of an exemption.

Obviously, the determination of what may be deleted differs somewhat from the determination whether to close the meeting in the first place; the decision on closure is based on expectations of the course of discussion at the meeting—what one court has described as a "foreseeability standard."[40] Thus, an agency may properly close a meeting on the basis of what it fears may be disclosed, and yet conclude after

---

39. For discussion of the definition of "promptly available" under the Freedom of Information Act, see Aviation Consumer Action Project v. CAB, 418 F. Supp. 638 (D.D.C. 1976).
40. Common Cause v. NRC, 674 F.2d 921, 929 (D.C. Cir. 1982). *See also* ch. 3, pp. 71-72 note 22, and accompanying text, *supra*.

the event that the entire transcript may be released.[41] Of course, the decision whether or not to delete also involves an estimate of the consequences of disclosure, but the agency is on firmer ground in knowing what in fact would be disclosed.[42]

To what extent must the agency segregate exempt from non-exempt material in the transcript or recording? Subsection (f)(2) permits the agency to withhold any "item or items" that contain information that may be withheld, and it is at least arguable that "item" refers back to "item on the agenda."[43] The legislative history establishes certain guideposts. The occasional reference to sensitive matters does not justify withholding the entire contents of a meeting, but the agency need not engage in line-by-line redaction of the kind required by the FOIA. The Senate Report said:

> If only one or two brief references to sensitive matters were made in a lengthy discussion of an item on the agenda, the record of the discussion, minus the one or two references, must be made public. Agencies need not edit a transcript or electronic recording of the Commission's discussion of a particular matter word by word so as to make abbreviated portions of the record of the meeting available to the public. Where sensitive matters are an integral part of the record of the discussion of a matter, no part of the record need be made public. . . . Subsection [(f) (2)] should be used to inform the public about the bulk of the discussion of any item on the agenda where the consideration of sensitive matters occurs in an easily identifiable segment of the discussion occupying only a small portion of the time devoted to the entire agenda item.

S. Rep., 31.

---

41. *Id. See also* S. REP., at 31-32
42. In rejecting a criticism of its standard of "likely" harm as applied to withholding of transcripts, the Federal Trade Commission said, "One comment suggests that since the nature of the information disclosed in transcripts is certain, deletions should be made only where disclosure will have the enumerated effects, and not merely where it is 'likely to.' The Commission believes this analysis is incorrect since it is never possible to know for certain in advance what effects will result from disclosure of information. The Commission therefore has determined that its rule need not be revised." 42 Fed. Reg. 13,539 (March 11, 1977).

Moreover, the bill, as reported by the Senate Government Operations Committee and passed by the Senate, provided:

> The agency shall make promptly available to the public, in a place easily accessible to the public, the complete transcript or electronic recording of the discussion at such meeting of any item on the agenda, or of the testimony of any witness received at such meeting, where no significant portion of such discussion or testimony contains any information specified in paragraphs (1) through (10) of subsection (b).

It is this language to which the Senate Report quoted above was addressed. On the Senate floor Senator Chiles further explained the above provision as follows:

> The discussion of an item on the agenda could be withheld from the public if any substantial part of it involved confidential matters. Word-by-word editing would not be necessary.[44]

The *1978 Guide* indicated that an agency may regard the discussion of each agenda item as a unit, and if there is exempt material in the discussion of that item, the whole discussion may be withheld.[45] It noted that Senator Javits expressed concern that the bill might be read to require release of the complete transcript where the references to confidential matters were less than significant. He urged "that it be made clear that [the subsection] requires only that the non-sensitive portion of a closed meeting be released in its entirety, allowing the agency to withhold from public disclosure the admittedly less than significant portion of a transcript relating to sensitive subject matter protected by the act." Senator Chiles concurred that "the public benefit results obviously intended by the transcript requirements . . . do not logically call for release by an agency of the complete recording of a closed meeting, but should be limited to disclosure of the total portion of such discussion not covered by one of the bill's exemptions."[46]

---

43. *See* Conf. Rep., at 20.
44. 121 Cong. Rec. 35,325 (Nov. 6, 1975) (statement of Senator Chiles).
45. *1978 Guide*, at 70.
46. 121 Cong. Rec. 35,329 (Nov. 6, 1975) (statement of Senator Chiles).

On the House side, the bill reported by the Government Operations Committee imposed a more stringent standard for deletion:

> The agency shall make promptly available to the public, in a location easily accessible to the public, the complete transcript or electronic recording of the discussion at such meeting of any item on the agenda, or of the testimony of any witness received at such meeting, *except for such portion or portions of such discussion or testimony as the agency, by recorded vote taken subsequent to the meeting and promptly made available to the public, determines to contain information specified in paragraphs (1) through (10) of subsection (c)*. In place of each portion deleted from such a transcript or transcription the agency shall supply a written explanation of the reason for the deletion, and the portion of subsection (c) and any other statute said to permit the deletion (emphasis added).

However, the requirement for a recording or transcript of closed meetings was deleted on the floor of the House and replaced with requirements for minutes of the meeting and for General Counsel certification that closure was proper.[47]

The eventual language defining the agency's right to withhold was placed in the bill in the House-Senate Conference. The Conference version eschewed the "significant portion" test that had raised problems for Senator Javits and is similar in structure to the bill of the House Government Operations Committee. However, where the latter version said "except for such portion or portions of such discussion or testimony," the Conference version substituted "item or items" for "portion or portions." The Conference Report also describes the exception as "for agenda items or items of the discussion or testimony." Conf. Rep., 20. Bearing in mind that the Conference was seeking to reconcile the Senate version with a House-passed bill that contained no requirement for a transcript, one must conclude that the use of the phrase "item or items of such discussion or testimony" was intended to impose on the agencies a less onerous editing responsibility than the House Government Operations Committee formulation or even than the "reasonably segregable" test applicable under the Freedom

---

47. 122 Cong. Rec. 25,202-08 (July 28, 1976).

of Information Act, 5 U.S.C. § 552(b).[48] The D.C. Circuit's en banc decision in *Clark-Cowlitz Joint Operating Agency v. FERC*[49] is consistent with this approach. Quoting from the Senate Report, the court observed:

> [U]nder the Sunshine Act agencies need not edit a transcript or electronic recording of the Commission's discussion of a particular matter word by word so as to make abbreviated portions of the record of the meeting available to the public. Where sensitive matters are an integral part of the record of the discussion of [an item on the agenda], no part of the record need be made public.[50]

The practical necessities of making the edited recording or transcript "promptly available" also mitigate in favor of a standard that permits a fairly rough-and-ready differentiation between material that must be disclosed and material that may be withheld. However, agencies ought not to withhold entire portions of a discussion in reliance on isolated references to exempt material, but should apply a common-sense approach consistent with the Act's overall policy of "fullest practicable" disclosure.[51]

Procedural Requirements and Delegation

The agency's determination to withhold portions of the recording, transcript or minutes of a closed meeting is not governed by the procedures of subsection (d)(1) and does not require a recorded vote of the agency members. Indeed, the determination need not be made by

---

48. In view of the obvious analogy between the two situations, it is perhaps significant that the Conference Report, which elsewhere makes several references to experience under the Freedom of Information Act, does not refer to the FOIA on this point.
49. 798 F.2d 499 (D.C. Cir. 1986) (en banc).
50. *Clark-Cowlitz,* 798 F.2d 502 n.3.
51. *See, e.g.,* the deletion practices of the Federal Reserve Board, which "has been following informally a conservative, FOIA-like approach of 'reasonably segregable' for [withholding] portions of a transcript or minutes." Informal Comments on Revised Sunshine Guide re: Standard for deletion from transcripts, p. 6, Jan. 4, 2005.

the agency members at all. As a result of the legislative give-and-take over the transcript provision of the statute, Congress ultimately decided that the determination to withhold material from the public may be delegated to staff if the agency has general authority to delegate.[52] A majority of agencies delegate the deletion determination to their General Counsel,[53] Secretary,[54] a director of public information,[55] or other staff official.[56] On the other hand, a few agencies, such as the Occupational Safety and Health Review Commission,[57] the United States Postal Service,[58] the Federal Election Commission,[59] and the Rural Telephone Bank,[60] provide that the agency members themselves will make the decision to withhold closed meeting information.

---

52. The legislative history of subsection (f)(2) indicates that the procedures of subsection (d)(1) and its predecessor provisions were not regarded as governing the decision to withhold portions of the transcript. The report of the Senate Government Operations Committee said with respect to the transcript provision that "[t]he subsection does not require the agency to follow any specified procedure in determining whether to make the record of a meeting available to the public." S. REP., 31. Furthermore, the bill as reported by the House Government Operations Committee had a separate requirement for a recorded agency vote on withholding material in the transcript, notwithstanding that there was a provision on procedure for closing meetings substantially identical to subsections (d)(1). The House subsequently deleted the transcript requirement entirely. It was restored in the Conference in a somewhat revised form from that approved by the Senate, but with no indication that a recorded vote by agency members was necessary on questions of withholding transcript materials.
53. *See, e.g.,* regulations of the Harry S Truman Scholarship Foundation, 45 C.F.R. § 1802.7(d)(1), and the Federal Trade Commission, 16 C.F.R. § 4.9(c)(3).
54. *See, e.g.,* regulations of the U.S. International Trade Commission, 19 C.F.R. § 201.41(a) and (c); Overseas Private Investment Corporation, 22 C.F.R. § 708.6(d); Commodity Credit Corporation, 7 C.F.R. § 1409.8(a).
55. *See, e.g.,* regulations of the Federal Energy Regulatory Commission, 18 C.F.R. § 375.206(f)(1).
56. *See, e.g.,* regulations of the Securities and Exchange Commission, § 17.200.408(a) (Freedom of Information Act Officer).
57. 29 C.F.R. § 203.7(b).
58. 39 C.F.R. § 7.6(c).
59. 11 C.F.R. § 2.6(b)(1).
60. 7 C.F.R. § 1600.8(c).

Subsequent Review of Transcript Material

The agency's duty under subsection (f)(2) to make materials promptly available includes a review of the recording, transcript, or minutes contemporaneous with, or shortly after, the meeting itself. Generally, the considerations of confidentiality that justified closing the meeting will continue to be present when the transcript is reviewed. However, with the passage of time, the need for confidentiality may in some cases disappear. The Senate Report contemplates that agencies will release transcript material once the need for confidentiality disappears. S. Rep., 32.[61]

A determination as to when the need for confidentiality comes to an end depends not merely on the passage of time but on the underlying purpose of the exemption as well. In its en banc decision in the *Clark-Cowlitz* case, the D.C. Circuit noted that the Senate Report's reference to information that may subsequently lose its sensitivity was limited to information withheld pursuant to Exemption 9.[62] So there will clearly be circumstances in which the passage of time will not eliminate the need for confidentiality. In examining Exemption (10), the D.C. Circuit in *Clark-Cowlitz* observed that where a meeting is closed pursuant to Exemption (10) to permit an agency to address its participation in pending litigation, release of the transcript at a subsequent date would frustrate an underlying purpose of Exemption (10)— that is, "to facilitate the candid exchange of views between client and counsel necessary for effective participation in adversary proceedings. Exposing such communications *ex post* would tend to inhibit free and open discussion nearly as much as would contemporaneous disclosure."[63] Although the court's decision involved the agency's use of Exemption (10) in the context of court litigation and relied on the analogy to the attorney-client privilege, the underlying rationale plainly applies to other Exemption (10) closures as well. Indeed, one agency— the Federal Energy Regulatory Commission (FERC)—has extended

---

61. For example, where a meeting is closed pursuant to Exemption (9)(B) to prevent frustration of a proposed agency action, public announcement of the agency action would ordinarily end the need to maintain the confidentiality of the deliberations.
62. *Clark-Cowlitz,* 798 F.2d 501-02.
63. *Id.* at 503.

the *Clark-Cowlitz* rationale to justify withholding the transcript of a closed meeting pursuant to Exemption (10) after completion of an administrative investigation.[64] *Cf. Time, Inc. v. U.S. Postal Service* ("The evident sense of Congress was that when a statute required an agency to act as would a court, its deliberations should be protected from disclosure as a court's would be.").[65]

Because the court's decision was undergirded by the view that subsequent release of the transcript would inhibit free and open discussion, its rationale appears to apply with equal force to material withheld pursuant to all exemptions except Exemption (9). In his dissenting statement in *Clark-Cowlitz*, Judge Wright complained that reliance on the attorney-client privilege "flies in the face of congressional resolve to avoid such a broad exemption from the Sunshine Act."[66] The majority flatly rejected that assertion, noting that there was no necessary inconsistency between Congress's decision to take into account the "chilling effects" of public discussion when enacting certain exemptions and its refusal to create a general Sunshine Act exemption for predecisional deliberations.[67]

The D.C. Circuit's subsequent opinion in *Natural Resources Defense Council, Inc. v. Defense Nuclear Facilities Safety Board*, involving Exemption (3), provides a curious twist.[68] Under its enabling statute, the Defense Nuclear Facilities Safety Board must transmit its recommendations regarding the safety of the government's nuclear facilities to the Secretary of Energy and, in some cases, to the President. The statute provides that "after receipt by the Secretary of Energy" or "after receipt by the President," the Board "promptly shall make such recommendations available to the public." In drafting its regulations implementing the Government in the Sunshine Act, the Board determined that it may close meetings pursuant to Exemption (3) involving deliberations on Board recommendations. The court, over a dissent by Judge Williams, concluded that, pursuant to Exemption (3), the Board may

---

64. PJM Interconnection, L.L.C. et al., 97 F.E.R.C. P61,319 (Dec. 20, 2001) (hereafter *PJM*).
65. 667 F.2d 329, 334 (2d Cir. 1981).
66. *Clark-Cowlitz*, 798 F.2d at 505.
67. *Id.* at 502-03, especially n.4.
68. 969 F.2d 1248, 1252 (D.C. Cir. 1992), *request for rehearing en banc denied*, 969 F.2d 1248, 1255, *cert. denied*, 508 U.S. 906 (1993).

close meetings at which it discusses its recommendations so as not to disturb what it described as "the time-controlled disclosure of its recommendations."[69] In the final paragraph of its decision, the court took pains to remind the Board that it may only close meetings during which recommendations that will be sent to the Secretary or the President are likely to be discussed. However, it then observed that "after a closed meeting, the Board must provide the public with a transcript, electronic recording, or minutes of all portions of the meeting *not devoted to the Board's recommendations*."[70] Does that allow the Board to refuse indefinitely to release the record of that portion of a meeting devoted to the Board's recommendations? Even assuming that the underlying substantive statute is intended to protect the timing of disclosure so as to justify closing the meeting to the public, the only value that might be protected by the underlying statute once the Board's recommendations are made public is the need for confidential discussion. Yet neither the majority nor the dissent mentions the *Clark-Cowlitz* decision. When dealing with exemptions other than Exemption (10), agencies should determine on a case-by-case basis whether they believe the need for confidentiality continues.[71]

To review transcripts, recordings or minutes on a systematic basis would require some procedure for review of previous determinations to withhold in the light of changed circumstances. Senator Chiles addressed this problem briefly on the Senate floor, stating:

> I might further add that an agency will not have to review continually the sensitivity of the transcripts of its board meeting. A periodic review at reasonable intervals is all that is needed.

121 Cong. Rec. 35329.

A few agency regulations recognize this need to review closed meeting records and to release initially exempted and withheld infor-

---

69. *Id.* at 1251.
70. *Id.* at 1252 (emphasis added).
71. We note, in this regard, that when FERC relied on both Exemptions (7) and (10) to close its meeting dealing with an administrative investigation, it thereafter relied solely on Exemption (10) with respect to its refusal to release the transcript. *PJM, supra* note 64.

mation.[72] The regulations of the National Museum Services Board, for example, provide that transcripts or recordings previously withheld will be released "when the Chairman (or the Chairman's designee) determines that the grounds for withholding no longer apply."[73] Most agencies presumably rely on their procedures for handling requests for transcripts to provide the occasion for reconsideration of previous decisions to withhold. Thus, the Federal Communications Commission, in rejecting as "impracticable" a suggestion that transcripts of closed meetings be reviewed regularly to determine whether they could be made available, stated, "[t]ranscripts may be placed in the public file just after the meeting is held, but otherwise will be reviewed only when requests for copies are received."[74] Once such a review leads to release of a transcript, it is placed in the public file. However, the FCC declines to "undertake to issue a public notice every time a transcript of a closed meeting is released."[75]

It is doubtful that there is a single ideal procedure for handling the problem of reconsideration of decisions to withhold transcript material in the light of changed circumstances. The needs and experiences of agencies vary. Where the demands for such materials are frequent, it would be unreasonable to expect agencies to reexamine their previous decisions each time a request is made. A procedure for systematic and periodic review appears preferable. On the other hand, where demands are few, an agency, having fulfilled its initial responsibility to make non-exempt material available, might then review its determination only in response to a request. In any event, once it decides to release material previously withheld, an agency should provide some means for bringing this action to the attention of the interested public.

---

72. See, e.g., regulations of the National Science Board, 45 C.F.R. § 614.4 (non-exempt material made available on request); Nuclear Regulatory Commission, 10 C.F.R. § 9.108(d) ("If at some later time the Commission determines that there is no further justification for withholding" previously withheld information, "such information shall be made available. ").
73. 45 C.F.R. § 1180.91(b).
74. 42 Fed. Reg. 12,867 (March 7, 1977).
75. Id.

Administrative Appeal Procedures

A number of Sunshine Act regulations provide either for administrative appeals from determinations to withhold closed meeting transcripts, recordings, or minutes under subsection (f)(2) or, more generally, for administrative review of any agency action under the Act and regulations. Agencies that have delegated the initial review of transcripts to a staff member typically provide for administrative appeals to a different member of the staff[76] or the agency members themselves.[77] Because the Sunshine Act exemptions are permissive and not mandatory,[78] those making agency determinations on appeal may, of course, waive any exemptions initially relied upon to withhold closed meeting records.[79]

The time limits in these regulations differ, reflecting division among the agencies over whether or not to apply FOIA time limits to requests for access to, and appeals from, withholding of Sunshine Act transcripts, recordings or minutes. As noted in Chapter 10, some agencies have adopted procedures and limits akin to those in the FOIA, some

---

76. *See, e.g.,* regulations of the Federal Energy Regulatory Commission, 18 C.F.R. § 375.206(f)(2) (decision by the director of the Division of Public Information may be appealed to the General Counsel or his designee); Tennessee Valley Authority, 18 C.F.R. § 1301.48(c) (decision by the manager, Media Relations, may be appealed to TVA's senior vice president, Communications and Employee Development).
77. *See, e.g.,* the regulations of the Securities and Exchange Commission, 17 C.F.R. § 200.408 (b) (action by agency Freedom of Information Act Officer may be appealed to the Commission). The Nuclear Regulatory Commission provides for agency member participation in the staff review process. The Commission's regulations set forth a procedure for determining at the end of each closed meeting which portions of the transcript, recording, or minutes of the meeting should be withheld pursuant to section 552b(f)(2). In the case of a request for information not initially made public, the Commission's Secretary "upon the advice of the General Counsel and after consultation with the Commission" determines which portions of the record, transcript or minutes should be withheld. 10 C.F.R. § 9.108(c).
78. *See* S. REP., at 20.
79. *See, e.g.,* regulations of the Tennessee Valley Authority, 18 C.F.R. § 1301.48(d).

have established special Sunshine Act procedures and limits,[80] and some do not specify any procedures or limits.[81] In our subsequent discussion of subsection (k), we conclude that the Freedom of Information Act should govern requests for access under subsection (f)(2). Hence, an agency's access and appeals procedures should be consistent with those procedures, particularly the time limits, of the FOIA.

Besides prescribing the form for the requests (generally, in writing and with reasonable detail) and to whom they should be sent (the agency members, the chairman, a general manager, etc.) a few of the regulations also specify the form to be taken by the agency's response to the request for appeal or review. These regulations provide that if the final determination on appeal is to deny all or part of the request, written notice will be provided to the requester, including a statement of the reasons for the denial, short of disclosing exempt information, and a notice of the person's right to seek judicial review under 5 U.S.C. § 552b(h).[82]

Fees for Furnishing Copies

The second sentence of subsection (f)(2) provides that the agency shall furnish copies of a closed meeting transcript, transcription of a

---

80. The FOIA requires that an agency inform a requester within 20 days (Saturdays, Sundays, and legal public holidays excepted) of its intent to comply with or deny a request. 5 U.S.C. § 552(a)(6)(A)(i). The requester may appeal a denial and the appeal official must decide the appeal within 20 days. 5 U.S.C. § 552(a)(6)(A)(ii). In unusual circumstances, either time limit may be extended for 10 working days. 5 U.S.C. § 552(a)(6)(B)(i). There is no statutory time period within which a requester is required to appeal. However, the Tennessee Valley Authority's regulations provide that an appeal must be taken within 30 days after receipt of a determination to withhold a closed meeting record. 18 C.F.R. § 1301.48(d). The regulations of the Securities and Exchange Commission provide that any person who has not received a response to his or her request, or is unsatisfied with the response, "may appeal the adverse determination or failure to respond" within 20 days. 17 C.F.R. § 200.408(b).
81. *See, e.g.,* regulations of the Mississippi River Commission, 33 C.F.R. § 209.50.
82. *See, e.g.,* regulations of the Consumer Product Safety Commission, 16 C.F.R. § 1013.6(b)(5)(iii).

recording, or minutes "at the actual cost of duplication or transcription."[83]

At the time the Sunshine Act was enacted, the Freedom of Information Act authorized agencies to recover the "direct costs" for search and duplication of records; it also gave agencies the option of waiving or reducing fees if the information sought would benefit the general public as well as the requester.[84] Significantly, however, section 11(a) of the Federal Advisory Committee Act provided that "[e]xcept when prohibited by contractual agreements entered into prior to [October 6, 1972], agencies shall make available to any person, at actual cost of duplication, copies of transcripts of agency proceedings."[85]

The Senate and House Reports accompanying the Sunshine Act anticipated regulations establishing a uniform fee schedule, with provision for waiver or reduction of fees when such action is in the public interest. *See* S. Rep., 32; H. Rep. I, 15; H. Rep. II, 16. The fees were to be "limited to reasonable standard charges for duplication . . . ." S. Rep., 32. "In no instance should fees be set with the purpose of discouraging public requests for transcripts or transcriptions; their sole purpose is to permit recovery of some or all of the direct cost of providing them." H. Rep. I, 16. But Congress ultimately failed to provide any fee waiver or reduction provision in the Sunshine Act.

Congress amended the fees and fee waiver provisions of the FOIA significantly in the Freedom of Information Reform Act of 1986.[86] The statute established three levels of fees, depending on the status of the requester,[87] and particularized the "public interest" standard for fee waiv-

---

83. The transcription must disclose "the identity of each speaker." 5 U.S.C. § 552b(f)(2). The Senate Report also states that "if a person requests a copy of a tape, rather than a transcription of it, this should also be provided at the actual cost of copying." S. REP., at 32.
84. Pub. L. No. 93-502, §§ 1-3, 88 Stat. 1561-64 (1974).
85. Pub. L. No. 92-463, 86 Stat. 775 (1972). The term "proceeding" has the same meaning as contained in the Administrative Procedure Act, because it includes rulemaking, adjudication, and licensing—virtually all activity in which an agency engages. It is not limited to the proceedings of Federal Advisory Committees. This provision remains on the statute books at section 11(a) of 5 U.S.C. Appendix (2000 ed.).
86. Pub. L. No. 99-570, §§ 1801-1804, 100 Stat. 3207.
87. 5 U.S.C. § 552(a)(4)(A)(ii).

ers.[88] It also required the Office of Management and Budget to formulate guidelines that provide for a uniform schedule of fees for all agencies.[89] Congress further amended the FOIA in the Electronic Freedom of Information Act Amendments of 1996[90] but made no changes in the fee or fee waiver provisions. On neither occasion did Congress modify the fee provisions of the Sunshine Act. Moreover, the FOIA specifically provides that fees under FOIA are superseded by fees chargeable "under a statute specifically providing for setting the level of fees for particular types of records."[91] In the circumstances, the fee provisions of the Sunshine Act and section 11(a) of the Federal Advisory Committee Act would appear to govern the release of the transcript, electronic recording, or minutes of closed agency meetings.[92]

Because the requirement of subsection (f)(2) of the Sunshine Act that copies of any transcript, minutes or transcription be furnished at the actual cost of duplication or transcription is limited to transcripts, minutes or transcriptions of closed meetings, the FOIA fee provisions apply where agencies voluntarily maintain a transcript, electronic recording, or minutes of their open meetings.[93]

---

88. 5 U.S.C. § 552(a)(4)(A)(iii).
89. 5 U.S.C. § 552(a)(4)(A)(i). The OMB uniform FOIA fee schedule and guidance can be found at 52 Fed. Reg. 10,011 (March 27, 1987). As part of its general statutory responsibility "to encourage agency compliance with" the FOIA, 5 U.S.C. § 552(e)(5), the Department of Justice in 1983 issued fee waiver guidelines for federal agencies. It amended those guidelines following enactment of the Freedom of Information Reform Act of 1986, now codified at 5 U.S.C. § 552(a)(4)(A). The current guidelines can be found at the DOJ FOIA Web site: www.usdoj.gov/oip/fees.html.
90. Pub. L. No. 104-231, 110 Stat. 3048.
91. 5 U.S.C. § 552(a)(4)(A)(vi).
92. *See* note 85, *supra,* and accompanying text.
93. In addressing the issue of costs to be charged when releasing the recording of a closed meeting, the Defense Nuclear Facilities Safety Board decided that a recording released at the Board's own initiative, and placed in its Public Reading Room, will be made available at the actual cost to the Board. The Board does not consider requests for a waiver or reduction of fees for such recording. When it determines in response to an FOIA request that a recording should be released, it will consider any accompanying fee waiver or reduction request. 10 C.F.R. § 1703.106, 56 Fed. Reg. 21,259 (May 8, 1991).

Most agency regulations provide simply that copies of transcripts of meetings, transcriptions of recordings, or minutes will be provided at the actual cost of transcription or duplication.[94]

Explicit provisions for waiver or reduction of fees are rare. However, the Federal Energy Regulatory Commission treats requests for transcripts, recordings or minutes as it would FOIA requests.[95] So the FOIA fee waiver and reduction provisions apply.[96] The National Science Foundation treats requests as they would FOIA requests but automatically waives fees for search or transcription.[97] The Consumer Product Safety Commission waives all fees unless they exceed $25 and calculates fees exceeding $25 to reflect the $25 reduction.[98] The Federal Communications Commission will waive all charges if it serves "the financial or regulatory interests of the United States."[99] Where an agency has decided to reduce its fees or permit a waiver, it should explicitly set forth the procedures and standards in its regulations so that members of the public may make the necessary request for the waiver or reduction.

Maintenance and Use of Verbatim Copies of Transcripts, Recordings, or Minutes

The final sentence of subsection (f)(2) requires the agency to maintain a complete, verbatim copy of the transcript, minutes, or recording of a closed meeting "for at least two years after the meeting or one year after the conclusion of the agency proceeding that was the sub-

---

94. The regulations of the National Transportation Safety Board, 49 C.F.R. § 804.10, and the Postal Service, 39 C.F.R. § 7.6(c), are typical.
95. 18 C.F.R. § 388.109(a)(3).
96. 18 C.F.R. § 388.109(c).
97. 45 C.F.R. § 614.4(d).
98. 16 C.F.R. § 1013.6(b)(6).
99. *See* 47 C.F.R. § 0.607(b). The FCC explains in the preamble to its final regulations: "It would serve the regulatory interests of the Commission to waive the fee if the party seeking the transcript can use it to make a contribution to a proper public interest determination and cannot afford to pay the duplicating charges." 42 Fed. Reg. 12,867 (March 7, 1977). The FCC's regulations provide that copies of meeting transcripts may be obtained from the agency's duplicating contractor but that there is no charge for a record search or transcription. 47 C.F.R. § 0.607(b), *supra.*

ject of the meeting, whichever occurs later." Conf. Rep., 20. Most agency regulations repeat this provision.[100] The only elaboration on this section in any of the legislative reports is contained in the Senate Report, which adds that "[I]f an agency discusses the initiation of a proposed investigation at a closed meeting, the record should be retained until the investigation, and any agency adjudication arising from it, is completed and final agency action taken." S. Rep., 32.

---

100. *See, e.g.,* regulations of the Federal Communications Commission, 47 C.F.R. § 0.607(c), and the National Transportation Safety Board, 49 C.F.R. § 804.10.

Chapter 7

SECTION 552b(g)
JUDICIAL REVIEW OF AGENCY RULES

(g) Each agency subject to the requirements of this section shall, within 180 days after the date of enactment of this section, following consultation with the Office of the Chairman of the Administrative Conference of the United States and published notice in the Federal Register of at least thirty days and opportunity for written comment by any person, promulgate regulations to implement the requirements of subsections (b) through (f) of this section. Any person may bring a proceeding in the United States District Court for the District of Columbia to require an agency to promulgate such regulations if such agency has not promulgated such regulations within the time period specified herein. Subject to any limitations of time provided by law, any person may bring a proceeding in the United States Court of Appeals for the District of Columbia to set aside agency regulations issued pursuant to this subsection that are not in accord with the requirements of subsections (b) through (f) of this section and to require the promulgation of regulations that are in accord with such subsections.

Section 6(a) of the Government in the Sunshine Act provided that the provisions of the Act would take effect 180 days after enactment—on March 12, 1977. During that 180-day period subsection (g) required the agencies to promulgate regulations to implement the provisions of section 552b.[1] The subsection further required that the

---

1. Subsection (g) was, of course, not applicable to agency regulations issued to implement section 4 of the Act, regarding *ex parte* communications, or section 5, which made certain conforming amendments in the Freedom of Information Act, the Federal Advisory Committee Act, and the Postal Service legislation.

rulemaking process include consultation with the Office of the Chairman of the Administrative Conference of the United States and at least a 30-day period for notice of the proposed rules and opportunity for written public comment. These provisions of subsection (g) have long since been executed and require no further comment.[2]

The rulemaking procedures prescribed by subsection (g) apply, in our view, only to the initial promulgation of rules and not to subsequent amendments. This conclusion is consistent with a literal reading of the language of the subsection and is supported by practical considerations and subsequent agency practice. Because amendments to these regulations are not governed by subsection (g), the only statutory authority that might apply to the amendment process, absent special provision in the agency's organic legislation, is the Administrative Procedure Act, 5 U.S.C. § 553 (APA). However, because these regulations are "rules of agency organization, procedure or practice" within section 553(b)(A), the APA does not require the agencies to follow notice-and-comment procedures in amending them. Nevertheless, agencies should bear in mind that the Sunshine Act assumes a broad public interest in the openness of agency decision-making processes and in how the requirements of section 552b are implemented. Consequently, we believe that agencies should comply voluntarily with the procedures for notice and comment set forth in section 553(b) and (c), except where the agency finds, pursuant to section 553(b)(B), that

---

2. Newly created agencies should, of course, follow notice-and-comment procedure in issuing their initial Sunshine regulations. *See, e.g.,* regulations of the Chemical Safety and Hazard Investigation Board, 67 Fed. Reg. 35,445 (May 20, 2002). *See* Appendix C for a list of agencies that have issued Sunshine Act regulations, with citations to their rules. Although not required to do so, new agencies typically consulted with the Administrative Conference before proposing their Sunshine regulations. *See, e.g.,* proposed regulation of the former United States Enrichment Corp., privatized in 1996, 59 Fed. Reg. 9150 (Feb. 25, 1994). However, the Administrative Conference was terminated in 1995 when Congress failed to renew its appropriation. *But see* Pub. L. No. 108-401, 118 Stat. 2255, the Federal Regulatory Improvement Act of 2004, which President Bush signed into law on October 30, 2004. The bill reauthorizes ACUS, though Congress will still have to appropriate the authorized funds. *See also* p. 214 note 3, *infra.*

notice and public procedure are "impracticable, unnecessary, or contrary to the public interest."[3]

The last sentence of subsection (g) provides that "any person" may challenge an agency rule issued under section 552b in the United States Court of Appeals for the District of Columbia. Subsection (g) assumes a challenge of the rule on its face and not a dispute arising out of its application to a particular meeting. (Such litigation would be brought under subsection (h).)[4] The Act deliberately eschews any requirement that the plaintiff be able to demonstrate that he or she is directly affected or "aggrieved" by the challenged regulation. *See* S. Rep., 32-33; *see also United States v. Students Challenging Regulatory Agency Procedures (SCRAP)*, 412 U.S. 669, 684-89 (1973).[5] On

---

3. *See, e.g.,* rulemaking notices of the U.S. International Trade Commission, 58 Fed. Reg. 49,452 (Sept. 23, 1993), and the U.S. Commission on Civil Rights, 67 Fed. Reg. 17,528 (April 10, 2002). Notice and public procedure are generally omitted for such minor rules changes as changes in address, official titles, authority citations, etc. *See, e.g.,* 64 Fed. Reg. 53,264 (Oct. 1, 1990) (Surface Transportation Board); 64 Fed. Reg. 40,286 (July 26, 1999) (National Mediation Board); and 65 Fed. Reg. 48,886 (Aug. 10, 2000) (Merit Systems Protection Board).

4. *Johnston v. Nuclear Regulatory Comm'n*, 766 F.2d 1182 (7th Cir. 1985), illustrates the interplay of subsections (g) and (h). The plaintiffs sought to challenge in a suit in the U.S. District Court under subsection (h)(1) a rule of the NRC providing that the Sunshine Act did not apply to meetings of the Commission's Atomic Safety and Licensing Boards. The district court upheld the rule on the merits, but the court of appeals concluded that inasmuch as the ASLB had not closed the meeting plaintiffs sought to have opened and was not proposing to hold a subsequent closed meeting, plaintiffs' cause of action did not arise out of a particular meeting. Therefore, the district court lacked jurisdiction under subsection (h)(1), and the plaintiffs' challenge to the regulation could be brought only in the Court of Appeals for the D.C. Circuit under subsection (g). *See also* discussion at p. 180 note 1, *infra*.

5. Any person has standing to bring an action, since the bill is designed to protect the right of the general public to attend agency meetings. *See* S. REP., at 33. *See also* Rushforth v. Council of Economic Advisers, 762 F.2d 1038, at 1039 n.3 (D.C. Cir. 1985). Congress cannot, of course, override constitutional limits on standing through legislation. *See* PETER L. STRAUSS, ADMINISTRATIVE JUSTICE IN THE UNITED STATES 314-15 (Carolina Academic Press 2002*), citing* Lujan v. Defenders of Wildlife, 504 U.S. 555 (1992).

the other hand, the Senate report suggests, "If an issue is too speculative or remote, the Court of Appeals may refuse to entertain the suit."[6]

A suit under the last sentence of subsection (g) must be brought "[s]ubject to any limitations of time provided by law." This is a reference to those statutes that set a time limit on challenging a rulemaking order of an agency. Examples cited in the House Report include the Administrative Orders Review Act, 28 U.S.C. § 2344, and the Communications Act of 1934, 47 U.S.C. § 402(c). H. Rep. I, 16. Reference to these statutory review procedures suggests potential problems of interpretation. While it is settled that the Administrative Orders Review Act, which provides for review of the orders of specified agencies in the U.S. Courts of Appeals, applies to orders issuing rules of general applicability, *United States v. Storer Broadcasting Co.*, 351 U.S. 192, 195-200 (1956), courts have differed over the application of the *Storer* rationale to analogous statutes. *Compare PBW Stock Exchange v. SEC*, 485 F.2d 718, 729-31 (3d Cir. 1973), *cert. denied*, 416 U.S. 989 (1974), *with Investment Company Institute v. Bd. of Governors, Federal Reserve System,* 551 F.2d 1270, 1276-78 (D.C. Cir. 1977). Nor is it clear that such statutory review provisions, which usually specify the agency actions to which they apply (*see, e.g.,* 28 U.S.C. § 2342), impose by their terms any limitations of time on review of an agency's Sunshine regulations. Accordingly, it may be difficult to ascertain which statutory periods of limitation are brought into play by subsection (g).

There is little reason for courts to construe broadly the phrase "subject to any limitations of time provided by law." The time limitations in the statutory provisions cited were imposed on the assumption that the order to be reviewed was issued on an administrative record and in a proceeding participated in by the party seeking review. *See Gage v. United States Atomic Energy Commission,* 479 F.2d 1214, 1217-19 (D.C. Cir. 1973). These considerations are not relevant to review under subsection (g), where there is no requirement for prior participa-

---

6. S. REP., at 33. A critic of this provision might observe that the ordinary ripeness and standing requirements swept aside by the last sentence of subsection (g) have traditionally been used by the courts to avoid "speculative" and "remote" issues. *See, e.g.,* Metcalf v. Nat'l Petroleum Council, 553 F.2d 176, 187-90 (D.C. Cir. 1977).

tion in the rulemaking proceeding before the agency and where there is not likely to be an evidentiary administrative record.[7]

However, it does not appear that uncertainty as to the availability of subsection (g) review has posed a significant problem. Challenges to agency Sunshine rules on their face have been relatively few, largely because the agency rules generally hew very closely to the statute,[8] and even where a dispute involves the validity of an agency rule, an adequate remedy is usually available under subsection (h)(1).[9]

---

7. Where the statutory period for challenging a rule under the Administrative Orders Review Act has run, some courts have suggested that a new period may run from the agency's denial of a party's request for amendment or waiver of the rule. *See* Baltimore Gas & Electric Co. v. ICC, 672 F.2d 146, 149-50 (D.C. Cir. 1982); FUNK, LUBBERS & POU, FEDERAL ADMINISTRATIVE PROCEDURE SOURCEBOOK 176 (3d ed. 2000).
8. Furthermore, controversial amendments to agency Sunshine rules have been rare, with the notable exception of the NRC's rule defining a "meeting." *See* pp. 23-24, *supra*.
9. *But see Johnston, supra* note 4, which involved a somewhat unusual fact situation.

Chapter 8

SECTION 552b(h)
JUDICIAL REVIEW OF PARTICULAR AGENCY ACTIONS

INDEPENDENT ENFORCEMENT SUITS; JURISDICTION AND REMEDIES	181
Suits to Obtain Access to Transcripts	184
"Reverse Sunshine" Cases	185
JUDICIAL REVIEW PROCEEDINGS	186
Relief Under 5 U.S.C. § 552b(h)(2)	188
Use of the Transcript for Judicial Review	192

(h)(1) The district courts of the United States shall have jurisdiction to enforce the requirements of subsections (b) through (f) of this section by declaratory judgment, injunctive relief, or other relief as may be appropriate. Such actions may be brought by any person against an agency prior to, or within sixty days after, the meeting out of which the violation of this section arises, except that if public announcement of such meeting is not initially provided by the agency in accordance with the requirements of this section, such action may be instituted pursuant to this section at any time prior to sixty days after any public announcement of such meeting. Such actions may be brought in the district court of the United States for the district in which the agency meeting is held or in which the agency in question has its headquarters, or in the District Court for the District of Columbia. In such actions a defendant shall serve his answer within thirty days after the service of the complaint. The burden is on the defendant to sustain his action. In deciding such cases the court may examine in camera any portion of the transcript, electronic recording, or minutes of a meeting closed to the public, and may take such additional evidence as it deems necessary. The court, having due regard for orderly administration and the

public interest, as well as the interests of the parties, may grant such equitable relief as it deems appropriate, including granting an injunction against future violations of this section or ordering the agency to make available to the public such portion of the transcript, recording, or minutes of a meeting as is not authorized to be withheld under subsection (c) of this section.

Subsection (h) provides for judicial enforcement of the provisions of section 552b where agency actions, including failures to act, relating to a meeting are asserted to be in violation of the provisions of the section. Subsection (h) is not available for pre-enforcement review of an agency's Sunshine regulation; such an action must be brought under subsection (g). However, if a dispute over a particular act of alleged noncompliance, such as the use of improper procedure in closing a meeting, involves the validity of the agency regulation, this issue may be resolved in an action brought under subsection (h).[1] Subsec-

---

1. *See* Johnston v. Nuclear Regulatory Comm'n, 766 F.2d 1182, 1185-87 (7th Cir. 1985) (hereafter *Johnston*). Citing the *1978 Guide* at 82, 85-86, and 90, the court held that a complaint asking the court to declare that the Atomic Safety and Licensing Board (ASLB) of the NRC may not close licensing hearings except in full compliance with the Sunshine Act, and seeking injunctive relief to prevent the NRC from unlawfully closing any of the licensing hearings concerning a particular nuclear plant, failed to state a claim under section 552b(h)(1) and dismissed the action. The court noted that the complaint did not allege that any meeting was actually scheduled to be a closed meeting or actually closed pursuant to NRC's implementing regulations, which thus excluded the ASLB from the open-meeting requirements of the Sunshine Act. Instead, the court found the complaint was actually a challenge to NRC's implementing regulations and, as such, was within the exclusive jurisdiction of the Court of Appeals for the District of Columbia pursuant to 552b(g). *See also* p. 175 note 4, *supra*. The *Johnston* court reasoned that because the plaintiff had requested prospective relief and had failed to base its claim on the closure of a specific meeting, the complaint was not "an action . . . brought by any person against any agency . . . within 60 days after the meeting out of which the violation of this section arose . . ." under section 552b(h)(1). The *Johnston* court also distinguished the case from *Hunt v. Nuclear Regulatory Comm'n*, 611 F.2d 332 (10th Cir. 1979), *cert. denied*, 445 U.S. 906 (1980) (hereafter *Hunt*). The court noted that, whereas the *Johnston* plaintiffs had failed to base their complaint on an actual closure of

(continued on next page)

tion (h)(1) provides for an independent suit in federal district court to enforce the Sunshine provisions; subsection (h)(2) provides for the raising of Sunshine Act violations in a proceeding for judicial review of an agency action taken under procedures that did not comply with the Act.

INDEPENDENT ENFORCEMENT SUITS; JURISDICTION AND REMEDIES

Subsection (h)(1) confers jurisdiction on district courts to enforce the requirements of subsections (b) through (f) of the Act "by declaratory judgment, injunctive relief, or other relief as may be appropriate." As with suits under subsection (g), there is no statutory standing requirement, but subsection (h)(1) does provide a 60-day statute of limitations. An action may be brought "by any person," "prior to, or within sixty days after the meeting out of which" the alleged violation of the Act arose.[2] However, if proper public announcement of the meeting was "not initially provided by the agency in accordance with the requirements" of the Act, the enforcement action may be brought within 60 days after the required announcement is made. "If an agency provides no public announcement at all, the 60-day requirement is inapplicable." S. Rep., 33. The report of the House Government Operations Committee adds that "[a]s in subsections (d) and (e), any public announcement must be made in a manner calculated to assure its wide

---

(continued from previous page)
an ASLB hearing, "in *Hunt*, the ASLB actually closed a construction permit hearing to consider a report prepared by the company under contract to construct part of the nuclear power plant and the plaintiffs challenged that specific closure." *Johnston,* at 1187 n.5.

For further discussion of the *Johnston* case and other cases interpreting sections 552b(g), (h)(1), and (h)(2), see Eunice A. Eichelberger, *Availability of Judicial Review of Agency Compliance with Sunshine Act* (5 U.S.C.A. § 552b(g) and (h)), 84 A.L.R. Fed. 251, 254-56 (1987).

2. *See* Clark-Cowlitz Joint Operating Agency v. Fed. Energy Regulatory Comm'n, 775 F.2d 359 (D.C. Cir. 1985), *vacated on reh'g en banc,* 798 F.2d 499 (D.C. Cir. 1986). Note that in this case the suit to obtain access to the transcript was brought under 552b(h)(1) and not under the FOIA. Also of interest here is that the court in this case does not seem to have considered the objection that 60 days had already elapsed since the meeting.

dissemination in order to qualify as a 'public announcement' as that term is used herein." H. Rep. I, 16.

The Sunshine Act does not require a plaintiff to exhaust his or her administrative remedies within the agency prior to bringing suit under subsection (h). The Conference Committee explicitly rejected a Senate provision requiring resort to administrative remedies. Conf. Rep., 22. However, the conferees stated that they "expect and encourage potential plaintiffs or their attorneys to communicate informally with the agency before bringing suit." *Id.* A number of agencies promulgated administrative review procedures,[3] but no court to date appears to have required resort to such agency procedures as a prerequisite to suit.

A plaintiff may bring an action under subsection (h)(1) in the district court for the district "where the agency meeting was or is to be held, where the agency has its headquarters, or in the District of Columbia." Conf. Rep., 22. The Senate Report notes: "It is important that actions brought under this subsection be handled expeditiously in order for public participation to be meaningful." S. Rep., 33. Thus, "[the agency] must serve [its] answer within 30 days after the service of the complaint, and the court is not given discretion . . . to extend that time limit." Conf. Rep., 22. The burden of proof is on the agency to sustain its closing, withholding of information, or other challenged conduct. The Senate Report declares:

> This is in accord with the presumption of openness established in the bill. Those who wish to operate in secrecy should have to justify it. Furthermore, in most cases the agency will be the only party in possession of information that might justify closing the meeting. The burden must therefore be on the agency to produce any facts that may support its action.

S. Rep., 33.

---

3. *See* pp. 167-68, *supra*. Only a few agency regulations, however, make any reference to the judicial review and enforcement provisions of subsections (g) and (h). *See, e.g.,* regulations of the Consumer Product Safety Commission, 16 C.F.R. § 1013.6(b)(5)(iii) (denial of request for records of closed meeting shall inform the requester of right to seek judicial review under section 552b(h)); and the U.S. Postal Service, 39 C.F.R. § 7.7.

The reviewing court is authorized to examine in camera any portion of the transcript, recording, or minutes of a closed meeting, "and may take such additional evidence as it deems necessary." The Senate Report adds that "in appropriate cases [the court] may also permit attorneys for all parties to examine the record of the meeting and argue the case in camera." S. Rep., 33.

District courts acting under subsection (h)(1) are authorized only to correct Sunshine Act violations, the remedy, in effect, being generally more "Sunshine." Thus, they may grant "appropriate" equitable relief, including an injunction against future violations of the Act, a declaratory judgment that a certain practice or policy is unlawful, an order that the agency open a meeting it had planned to close or make available to the public such portion of the transcript, recording, or minutes of a meeting as is not authorized to be withheld under subsection (c) of the Act,[4] or even an injunction against holding a meeting. 5 U.S.C. § 552b(h)(1); H. Rep. I, 17; S. Rep., 33-34.[5] However, as the second sentence of subsection (h)(2) makes clear, a federal court proceeding under subsection (h)(1) is not authorized "to set aside, enjoin, or invalidate any agency action (other than an action to close a meeting or to withhold information under this section) taken or discussed at any agency meeting out of which the violation of this section arose." 5 U.S.C. § 552b(h)(2). Such a remedy, to the extent it is available at all, is available exclusively in a proceeding under subsection (h)(2). *But see Investment Co. Institute v. Federal Deposit Insurance Corp.,* 728 F.2d 518 (D.C. Cir. 1984) ("Sunshine Act alone could not support setting aside the FDIC decision.") (hereafter *Investment Co.*).

---

4. "The power of the court to release the non-exempt portion of a transcript, recording, or transcription of an unlawfully closed meeting points up another reason for requiring such records to be made. Since a judicial determination that a meeting was unlawfully closed will in most instances come long after the meeting has been held, and since the substantive action taken at the meeting cannot be nullified when the court is acting solely under this subsection, the possibility of finding out what transpired at the meeting represents the only realistic remedy available to a plaintiff." H. Rep., at 1, 17.
5. The Senate Report states that "normally, it should not be necessary for a court to enjoin the holding of a meeting in order to correct violations" of the Act. "The court may do so, however, where, for example, the agency's violation is flagrant," or "when the matter does not demand immediate action, and the public interest in the matter is great." S. Rep., at 34.

Any relief the district court does decide to grant pursuant to subsection (h)(1) must comport with a standard of "due regard for orderly administration and the public interest, as well as the interests of the parties." 5 U.S.C. § 552b(h)(1).[6]

Suits to Obtain Access to Transcripts

Subsection (h)(1) grants the district courts jurisdiction "to enforce the requirements of subsections (b) through (f)," which, read literally, would include suits to obtain access to transcripts, recordings, and minutes pursuant to subsection (f)(2). On the other hand, a suit under subsection (h)(1) must be brought within 60 days after the meeting in question, whereas an improper refusal to grant access may occur at any time. Consequently, a suit under the Freedom of Information Act, 5 U.S.C. § 552(a)(4), is the appropriate remedy in such a situation. Subsection (h)(1) should be regarded either as inapplicable to suits to obtain access to materials required to be made available by subsection (f)(2), or as an alternative remedy.[7] To permit such suits to be brought under

---

6. *See, e.g.*, the way the district court struck this balance and applied the remedy in *A.G. Becker, Inc. v. Board of Governors of the Federal Reserve System*, 502 F. Supp. 378, 388 (D.D.C. 1980):

    Becker having prevailed as to the failure of the Board to comply with the notice requirement contained in the expedited procedures, the question then focuses on the relief, if any, to which the plaintiff is entitled under 5 U.S.C. § 552b(h)(1). Since it has been held . . . that three exemptions . . . were properly invoked by the Board, it would be pointless to remand the cause to the Board for its further consideration. Accordingly, while plaintiff shall be entitled to a declaratory judgment that the Board violated the notice requirements relevant to the July 16 and August 22 meetings, it is entitled to no more. . . . Congress wisely recognized that while the commandment of advance notice and openness is vital to free, democratic processes, absoluteness without limited constraints could be highly injurious, if not totally destructive, to the rights of many. *Id.*

7. The practical result is likely to be the same, since the venue and attorney fees provisions of the FOIA are somewhat more favorable to plaintiffs than those of section 552b. However, unlike under the Sunshine Act, a plaintiff under the FOIA must demonstrate that he, she, or it has exhausted administrative remedies, as exhaustion is defined in that Act. 5 U.S.C. § 552(a)(6)(C); Open

(continued on next page)

the Freedom of Information Act is consistent with section 552b(k), which defines the relationship between the FOIA and the Sunshine Act.[8]

"Reverse Sunshine" Cases

We have previously expressed the view that agency refusals to close meetings in response to requests made pursuant to subsection (d)(2) or otherwise are judicially reviewable. *See* pp. 102-03, *supra*. What is less clear is whether an action to review such a refusal may be brought under subsection (h)(1). The alternative would be to permit a suit for so-called "non-statutory review" under the Administrative Procedure Act, 5 U.S.C. §§ 701-706, with district court jurisdiction based on the existence of a federal question, 28 U.S.C. § 1331.[9]

A similar problem has arisen under the Freedom of Information Act, where courts have held that the jurisdictional basis for "reverse FOIA" suits is not in the Act itself, but rather in 28 U.S.C. § 1331. *Planning Research Corp. v. Federal Power Comm'n*, 555 F.2d 970,

---

(continued from previous page)
America v. Watergate Special Prosecution Force, 547 F.2d 605, 609-10 (D.C. Cir. 1976). Because requests for access to records of closed meetings are governed by the procedures of the FOIA, *see* pp. 207-09, *infra*, the FOIA is the exclusive remedy for an improper refusal of access. However, in a suit brought under subsection (h)(1) for injunctive or declaratory relief with respect to an agency's action in closing a meeting, a court would clearly be authorized to require that the transcript be made available in addition to, or in lieu of, other relief.

8. *See* pp. 207-09, *infra*.
9. The Administrative Procedure Act provides that "[a] person suffering legal wrong because of agency action, or adversely affected or aggrieved by agency action within the meaning of a relevant statute, is entitled to judicial review thereof," 5 U.S.C. § 702. In the absence of a special statutory review proceeding, review may be sought by "any applicable form of legal action, including actions for declaratory judgments or writs of prohibitory or mandatory injunction or habeas corpus, in a court of competent jurisdiction," 5 U.S.C. § 703. Such review is usually referred to as "non-statutory review." However, until 1977, there was a long-standing conflict of views as to whether the APA was itself a grant to the federal district courts of jurisdiction over non-statutory review proceedings. In 1977, the Supreme Court answered the question in the negative. Califano v. Sanders, 430 U.S. 99 (1977). Consequently, the jurisdictional basis for non-statutory review proceedings must be found elsewhere, notably in 28 U.S.C. § 1331.

977 (D.C. Cir. 1977). The leading Supreme Court case is *Chrysler Corp. v. Brown,* 441 U.S. 281 (1979). The Court held that review was available under the APA because the release in that case arguably violated the Trade Secrets Act and therefore might not have been "in accordance with law" within the meaning of 5 U.S.C. § 706(2). However, the judicial review provision of the FOIA, 5 U.S.C. § 552(a)(4), applies by its terms only to complaints about agency records improperly withheld. The first sentence of subsection (h)(1) of the Sunshine Act, on the other hand, grants the district courts jurisdiction to enforce the requirements of subsections (b) through (f), which could be interpreted to include authority to review decisions to open meetings as well as decisions to close them. However, there are other provisions in subsection (h) that are inconsistent with the literal application of subsection (h)(1) to "reverse Sunshine" cases. First, the entire thrust of subsection (h)(1) is directed toward suits to open meetings. A good illustration of this point is the *in camera* language of (h)(1), which only makes sense in the context of closed meetings. Moreover, the language about a court's authority to enjoin future violations applies most often to closed meetings, although a court could conclude that opening future meetings would violate Exemptions (1) or (3) concerning, respectively, national security or a matter exempted from disclosure by statute. Second, the fifth sentence of subsection (h)(1) provides that "the burden is on the defendant [agency] to sustain [its] action." This, too, is consistent with a suit to open a meeting, but inconsistent with a suit to close a meeting because there is a statutory presumption in favor of open meetings. *See* p. 39, *supra*; H. Rep. I, 17. Since reading subsection (h)(1) as inapplicable to "reverse Sunshine" suits would leave plaintiffs an adequate remedy under the APA and 28 U.S.C. § 1331, there seems to be no need for a strained interpretation of subsection (h)(1) to accommodate such suits.

JUDICIAL REVIEW PROCEEDINGS

> *(h)(2) Any Federal court otherwise authorized by law to review agency action may, at the application of any person properly participating in the proceeding pursuant to other applicable law, inquire into violations by the agency of the requirements of this section and afford such relief as it deems appropriate. Nothing in this section authorizes any Federal*

court having jurisdiction solely on the basis of paragraph (1) to set aside, enjoin, or invalidate any agency action (other than an action to close a meeting or to withhold information under this section) taken or discussed at any agency meeting out of which the violation of this section arose.

Subsection (h)(2) authorizes any federal court "otherwise authorized by law" to review an agency action to "inquire into" Sunshine Act violations in the proceeding leading to such agency action. The Senate Report cites as an example that "a company challenging the validity of an agency rule may include in its challenge the fact that the agency adopted the rule in a meeting improperly closed to the public." S. Rep., 34. The court may be either the court of appeals or the district court, depending on the form of proceeding for judicial review of the agency action in question. *See* 5 U.S.C. § 703.

Since subsection (h)(2) does not create an independent right of action, it may be invoked only by one who is "properly participating in the proceeding pursuant to other applicable law"—that is, by one who has standing to challenge the underlying agency action.[10] Presumably, the "proceeding" referred to is the judicial review proceeding. Whether participation in the agency proceeding is necessary for participation in the judicial review proceeding depends on the law governing review of the action in question. *See, e.g., Gage v. United States Atomic Energy Commission*, 479 F.2d 1214, 1217-19 (D.C. Cir. 1973). The Senate Report also notes, "If the action an agency took at a closed meeting was not otherwise reviewable by the court, [subsection (h)(2)] would not make that action, or the agency's compliance with this subsection reviewable." S. Rep., 34.

---

10. *See Johnston, supra* note 1, at 1187, citing this point in the *1978 Guide*, at 90; Washington Ass'n for Television & Children v. FCC, 665 F.2d 1264 (D.C. Cir. 1981) ("challenge to the FCC definition of 'agency' included in challenge to FCC approval of transfer of control of television station"); Communications Systems, Inc. v. FCC, 595 F.2d 797 (D.C. Cir. 1978) ("challenge to FCC practice of conducting business by circulating papers rather than holding a meeting included in petition for review of refusal by FCC of authorization to convert a radio station from a Class B to a Class C station").

The limitations of time, however, that apply to acting under subsection (h)(1) are inapplicable under subsection (h)(2). H. Rep. I,17. Less clear is whether subsection (h)(2) is available at an intermediate stage of the agency proceeding. Subsection (h)(2) contemplates raising Sunshine violations only within a judicial review proceeding otherwise properly brought, so that if there is not yet a final agency action to review, resort to subsection (h)(2) would ordinarily be premature under the doctrine of exhaustion of administrative remedies. *Cf. Renegotiation Board v. Bannercraft Clothing Co.*, 415 U.S. 1, 24 (1974) and *Bristol-Myers Co. v. FTC*, 469 F.2d 1116 (2d Cir. 1972). Of course, a party to an agency proceeding who thinks his or her interests are threatened by Sunshine Act violations would also be able to invoke subsection (h)(1). At least one federal district court found no grounds for an interlocutory appeal that raised a Sunshine Act claim and declined to hear the claim pursuant to section 552b(h)(2).[11]

Relief Under 5 U.S.C. § 552b(h)(2)

The court acting under subsection (h)(2) is authorized to inquire into Sunshine violations and "afford such relief as it deems appropri-

---

11. In *R.J. Reynolds Tobacco Co. v. Federal Trade Commission*, 14 F. Supp. 2d 757 (M.D. N.C. 1998) (hereafter *Reynolds*), the court granted the FTC's motion to dismiss for lack of subject matter jurisdiction a complaint filed by the R.J. Reynolds Tobacco Co. against the FTC for its decision to issue a complaint against the company alleging that its "Joe Camel" advertising campaign violated section 5 of the FTC Act, 15 U.S.C. § 45. Among its counts, Reynolds had alleged in its complaint that the FTC had violated the Sunshine Act by failing to announce a particular meeting, failing to make public its vote at the beginning of the meeting to close it, and failing to make public any part of the transcript of the meeting.

The *Reynolds* court held that it was precluded from asserting subject matter jurisdiction by the holding in *FTC v. Standard Oil Co. of California*, 449 U.S. 232 (1980) (holding that the FTC's issuance of a complaint did not constitute final agency action and was not judicially reviewable before the conclusion of the administrative adjudication). *Id.*

The *Reynolds* court also found "no grounds for interlocutory appeal," and concluded that "lacking jurisdiction over the subject matter to review the Commission's actions, the court lacks jurisdiction under 5 U.S.C. § 552b(h)(2) to hear Reynolds' Sunshine Act claims," and granted the FTC motion to dismiss the tobacco company's complaint. *Id.*

ate." Presumably, this includes the full range of remedies available under subsection (h)(1). In addition, it may include the setting aside of the agency action under review. Indeed, the unique feature of subsection (h)(2) is the possibility it offers for attacking the underlying agency action. Yet, Congress evidently granted this authority with some reluctance:

> The conferees do not intend the authority granted to the Federal courts by the first sentence of subsection (h)(2) to be employed to set aside agency action taken other than under section 552b solely because of a violation of section 552b in any case where the violation is unintentional and not prejudicial to the rights of any person participating in the review proceeding. Agency action should not be set aside for a violation of section 552b unless that violation is of a serious nature.

Conf. Rep., 23.

Similarly, the Senate Report states: "It is expected that a court will reverse an agency action solely on [the ground that it was taken at an improperly closed meeting] only in rare instances where the agency's violation is intentional and repeated, and the public interest clearly lies in reversing the agency action." S. Rep., 34. See also H. Rep. I, 17.

This reluctant congressional grant of authority to set aside an agency action solely because of a Sunshine Act violation is clearly reflected in the case law decided since enactment of the Sunshine Act in 1976. In fact, there does not appear to be any case decided since enactment in which a court reversed an agency action on the merits due just to a Sunshine Act violation. Instead, the " 'release of transcripts, not invalidation of the agency's substantive action,' is the remedy generally appropriate for disregard of the Sunshine Act."[12]

---

12. *See* Braniff Master Executive Council of the Airline Pilots Ass'n Int'l v. Civil Aeronautics Board, 693 F.2d 220 (D.C. Cir. 1982), *citing* Pan American World Airways, Inc. v. CAB, 684 F.2d 31, 35-37 (D.C. Cir. 1982) (hereafter *Pan American*). In the *Pan American* case, the court found that the CAB violated the Sunshine Act by closing a meeting in which it granted to American and Continental Airlines interim authority to operate two international air routes abandoned by a bankrupt Braniff Airways, Inc. The court even described the violation in this case to be "of a serious nature" and "prejudicial" to Pan
(continued on next page)

(continued from previous page)
American. Nonetheless, the court said the release of the transcript of a meeting had removed the prejudice to the parties. The court noted that "failure to comply with the Sunshine Act ... provides no basis ... to set aside the agency's action. Section 552b(h)(2), while it does not forbid us to vacate [an] order, strongly indicates a congressional policy that release of transcripts, not invalidation of the agency's substantive action, shall be the normal remedy for Sunshine Act violations." *Pan American,* at 36.

In striking contrast, some state open meeting laws, as in Ohio, invalidate any formal agency action taken even in an open meeting that results from prior private deliberations. *See, e.g.,* State *ex rel.* Delph v. Barr, 44 Ohio St. 3d 77, 541 N.E.2d 59 (1989). State sanctions for violating open meeting laws also include fines and even removal from office. For example, "in Florida between 1977 and 1992, 86 officials were fined, many [were] sentenced to community service and to studying the law, and one was removed." *See* "Brechner Center (release of Oct. 12, 1993)," cited by PETER L. STRAUSS, TODD D. RAKOFF & CYNTHIA R. FARINA, GELLHORN AND BYSE'S ADMINISTRATIVE LAW— CASES AND COMMENTS, 10th Edition, Chapter 6, Section 4—"Government in the Sunshine," at p. 765 (Foundation Press 2003). *See also* p. 218 note 13, *infra.*

The court in the *Pan American* case "did observe, in reviewing the legislative history of the Sunshine Act, that circumstances might exist in which agency action should possibly be set aside ... where the violation was intentional, prejudicial, and of a serious nature, *see id.* at 36 (citing H.R. REP. No. 1441, 94th Cong., 2d Sess. 23 (1976))," *see also* Railroad Comm'n of Texas v. United States, 765 F.2d 221, 231 (D.C. Cir. 1985) (hereafter *Railroad Comm'n*). However, the *Pan American* court continued, "[i]n the unique circumstances of the case, the violation may have been 'unintentional.'" The court explained that the fact that no party had asked the CAB to open its meeting did not make closure any less a violation of the act, but it [did] bear on the willfulness of the violation. The court concluded that as long as the CAB's awards of temporary route authority were reasonable, it would not set them aside because they were reached in closed session. The court noted also that until oral argument, no party had asked it to base its decision on Sunshine Act violations, and the court [further] pointed out that section 552b(h)(2), unlike section 552(b), premises inquiring into Sunshine Act violations on "the application of any person properly participating in the proceeding." E. Eichelberger, *supra* note 1, at 256-57.

Since 1982, several other courts have reached conclusions similar to those of the *Braniff* and *Pan American* courts, and have held that release of transcripts rather than invalidation or reversal of an agency's substantive action is the appropriate, normal remedy for Sunshine Act violations pursu-
(continued on next page)

The efficacy of any relief under subsection (h)(2), however, is questionable. Since the improper closure of a meeting is unlikely to have had any demonstrable effect on the decision itself, a remand to the agency to consider the matter again at an open meeting would probably accomplish little. To require the agency to go through the entire proceeding again would be a needless burden on all concerned.[13] Perhaps where a case is otherwise close on the merits, a court might regard Sunshine violations as the "tipping factor" justifying a remand, but it seems doubtful that a court should do so unless there is some reason to believe that additional proceedings before the agency might lead to a different result.[14]

(continued from previous page)
    ant to 5 U.S.C. § 552b(h)(2). *See, e.g., Investment Co.*, p. 183, *supra*; *Railroad Comm'n, supra*; and The Hoke Co., Inc. v. Tenn. Valley Auth., 661 F. Supp. 740 (W.D. Ky. 1987).

    For further discussion of the *Braniff* and *Pan American* cases, see also Larry W. Thomas, *The Courts and the Implementation of the Government in the Sunshine Act*, 37 ADMIN. L. REV. 259, 276-78 (1985) ("By unlawfully closing the meeting and offering no explanation for its action, the court stated that the CAB had come 'perilously close' to forcing the court to set aside the agency's decision. The court declared, however, that the CAB's failure to comply with the Sunshine Act did not provide a basis for invalidating the agency's action. The court noted that such a decision would be to the detriment of American Airlines, Continental Airlines, and the traveling public, none of whom was directly involved in the Board's 'illegal closure.' The court concluded that the release of transcripts would be the proper remedy for the Sunshine Act violations." *Id.*).

13. *See* comments of Federal Communications Commission, House Government Operations Hearings, at 392.
14. *Cf.* Justice Fortas's plurality opinion in NLRB v. Wyman-Gordon Co., 394 U.S. 759, 767 n.6 (1969): "To remand would be an idle and useless formality. . . . There is not the slightest uncertainty as to the outcome of a proceeding before the Board, whether the Board acted through a rule or an order. . . ." *See also* Time, Inc. v. United States Postal Service, 667 F.2d 329 (2d Cir. 1981) (Court declined to "set aside and enjoin or invalidate" an action of the Board of the U.S. Postal Service pursuant to 5 U.S.C. § 552b(h)(2) because it found the administrative record was sufficient to support the Board's closing of the meeting in contention as well as its substantive findings in the case.).

Use of the Transcript for Judicial Review

In proceedings under subsection (h)(2) the court will, of course, have access to the transcript or recording of the closed meeting. A question not squarely addressed by the Act is whether the court may consider that transcript, or a transcript or recording of an open meeting,[15] for any purpose other than to determine whether there has been compliance with the Sunshine Act. In other words, is the transcript part of the administrative record? Prior to the Sunshine Act, there would have been no question that the deliberations of the agency members, even if known or accessible, would not be appropriate for consideration on judicial review. As the *Braniff* court noted:

> It is "not the function of the court to probe the mental processes" of administrative officers, *Morgan v. United States*, 304 U.S. 1, 18 (1938). A strong presumption of regularity supports the inference that when administrative officials purport to decide weighty issues within their domain they have conscientiously considered the issues and adverted to the views of their colleagues. . . . Agencies are no more bound to enter for the record the time, place, and content of their deliberations than are courts. *Braniff Airways, Inc. v. CAB*, 379 F.2d 453, 460 (D.C. Cir. 1967).

A major reason for the courts' declining to probe the mental processes of officers is the practical difficulty of doing so. This difficulty, however, would largely disappear where meeting transcripts and recordings are available.

It might be argued that such probing would be all to the good, that the courts should not defer to legal presumptions of agency expertise and impartiality where the facts are at hand to demonstrate otherwise. It

---

15. Of course, transcripts or recordings are required only where the meeting is closed, but some agencies are maintaining transcripts or recordings of open meetings as well. *See, e.g.,* p. 152 note 29, *supra*, and accompanying text. Indeed, in view of the difficulty of preventing tape recordings by members of the public (even where the agency seeks to do so, *see* pp. 48-49, *supra*), an official agency transcript or recording would serve to avoid disputes over an inaudible or inaccurate record produced unofficially by others.

might even be argued that such a broadening of the scope of judicial review would exert some pressure toward raising the quality of the decision-making process and, at the least, enable the courts to overturn some bad decisions that would survive review under present standards.

Against these advantages, however, must be weighed the impact on the administrative process and on the judicial review process of a procedure in which the lawyers comb the record of the meeting for evidence that a member acted arbitrarily, that he or she misunderstood an argument or misstated a fact in the record, that he or she cast his vote to please the chairman and not out of conviction, etc. The dangers arising from this kind of inquiry and this multiplication of issues surely outweigh the advantages of permitting the meeting transcript to become part of the record on review.

There is some legislative history indicating that Congress did not intend that transcripts be considered part of the administrative record. Thus, when a Department of Justice witness suggested that a transcript containing discussion between agency members and staff might become part of the administrative record for judicial review, Rep. Bella Abzug stated:

> That is an interesting question. We have not regarded that as additional history which would enable a court to expand its review of the ultimate rulemaking and the decision making by the agency.[16]

Perhaps more significant is that the strongest proponents of the transcript requirement appear to have viewed it exclusively as a means of making available to the public information that is not exempt under subsection (c) and of obtaining judicial review of unlawful closings.[17] There is no indication in the legislative history of an intent that transcripts of closed meetings or evidence of deliberations at open meetings should routinely become part of the administrative record of a proceeding.

---

16. House Government Operations Hearings, at 197. A warning against using transcripts for expanded judicial review was voiced by the Association of the Bar of the City of New York. *Id.* at 221, 245.
17. *See, e.g.*, remarks of Rep. Abzug, 122 Cong. Rec. H7891 (daily ed. July 28, 1976).

A few agencies have attempted to deal with this problem in their rules. The former Civil Aeronautics Board, for example, provided that the transcripts and minutes required by the Sunshine Act will be kept for Sunshine purposes only and "do not constitute the official record of Board action. The official record of the Board continues to be the Minutes . . . maintained by the Office of the Secretary."[18] The Securities and Exchange Commission, meanwhile, noted in the explanatory statement preceding its rule:

> [t]he Commission also stresses that the expanded right to observe Commission meetings (and the possibility of obtaining transcripts or recordings of discussion at closed meetings) should not be viewed as creating new grounds for challenging the basis and rationale for Commission action. Observations made by individual members of the Commission during the course of deliberations may not necessarily reflect the reasoning underlying the Commission's final action on a given matter. Thus, the legal sufficiency of Commission action must, as in the past, be judged solely on the basis of the action itself and any official supporting statement released by the Commission—not on the basis of remarks or observations made prior thereto.

42 Fed. Reg. 14,692 (March 16, 1977).

Similarly, the Federal Communications Commission states on the front of every news release of a substantive FCC action that "this is an

---

18. 14 C.F.R. § 310b.10(e), published at 42 Fed. Reg. 14,683 (March 16, 1977). The CAB Sunshine regulations also addressed the closely analogous problem of whether parties to agency proceedings may file responses to matters discussed at open meetings:

    > The right of the public to observe open discussions at Board meetings shall not include a right to participate at the meeting, or the right to file motions, pleadings, or other documents based on the comments of Board Members or staff at open discussions. The open meeting procedure is not an appropriate vehicle for persons to supplement records in matters before the Board. Such motions, pleadings or documents shall not be accepted by the Board.

    14 C.F.R. § 310b.9(c), published at 42 Fed. Reg. 14,682 (March 16, 1977).

unofficial announcement of a Commission action. Release of the full text of a Commission order constitutes official action. *See MCI v. FCC*, 515 F.2d 385 (D.C. Cir. 1974)."[19]

Finally, one federal appellate court has ruled on the issue of the use of transcripts on judicial review. In *Kansas State Network v. FCC*, 720 F.2d 185 (D.C. Cir. 1983) (hereafter *Kansas State Network*), the petitioner, to support its contention that it was "the victim of an unfair Commission policy," submitted, as part of the Joint Appendix to its brief, a transcript it had made of an open meeting of the FCC held on February 11, 1982, pursuant to the Sunshine Act. Its petition for an FCC tax certificate was discussed at that meeting. The FCC moved to strike the transcript, arguing that it was not part of the administrative record on review.[20] The court granted the FCC's motion to strike, holding that "where an agency has issued a formal opinion or a written statement of its reasons for acting, transcripts of agency deliberations at Sunshine Act meetings should not routinely be used to impeach that written opinion."[21]

Should the fact that agency deliberations are now made public make a difference? One court has suggested that it does. In *Pan American*, the court observed:

> The CAB contends that we may not examine this transcript. This contention is meritless. . . . The cases prohibiting "inquiry into the mental processes of administrative decision-

---

19. In this *MCI* case, a petition sought review of an order of the FCC after the Commission denied applications seeking rehearing. The court held that the statutory period for filing a petition for review of an order refused rehearing by the Commission commenced on the date when the text of the order was released to the litigants, rather than the date a news report of the order was issued by the FCC information office. Court held as correct FCC's construction of "public notice" as having been given only when complete text of order and any accompanying decision became available to litigants. *Id.*
20. 720 F.2d 185 (1983), at 191.
21. *Id. See also* Deukmejian v. NRC, 751 F. 2d 1287, 1324 (D.C.Cir. 1984) (rejected petitioner's Sunshine Act claim against the Nuclear Regulatory Commission because "confidential transcripts and documents are not properly a part of the record of these proceedings").

makers" [citations omitted] present no bar to our examination of the transcript. Those cases involve attempts to gain insight into the decisionmaker's mind by obtaining otherwise unavailable documents or by questioning the decisionmaker. . . . [citations omitted] Congress, through the Sunshine Act, has dictated that a transcript of this meeting be made available to the entire public. We will not close our eyes to it.[22]

The *Pan American* decision, however, misperceives the transcript requirement. First, there is no requirement of a transcript for open meetings. So one cannot presume that Congress intended that the public deliberations be memorialized as part of the official agency record. Moreover, maintenance of an official transcript of closed meetings is for the purpose of permitting a court to determine whether a meeting was properly closed. Ever since the famous *Morgan* case in the 1940s,[23] courts have declined to examine an agency's internal decisional processes. For example, the D.C. Circuit was specifically asked to examine transcripts of closed agency meetings that allegedly demonstrated that the agency relied on extra-record material in reaching its decision and then misinterpreted the facts to the court. Citing the *Morgan* case, the court noted that such review would be "an extraordinary intrusion into the realm of the agency." *San Luis Obispo Mothers for Peace v. U.S. Nuclear Regulatory Commission,* 789 F.2d 26, 44 (D.C. Cir. 1986) (en banc), *cert. denied,* 479 U.S. 923 (1986) (hereafter *San Luis Obispo Mothers for Peace*). The court did not categorically exclude examination of transcripts in every case but stated that "there must be a strong showing of bad faith or improper behavior before [inquiry into the mental processes of the administrative decision-maker] may be made." *Id.* at 44-45. Four of the nine participating judges concluded that the evidence of bad faith or improper behavior must be established by independent information before the court would look at the transcripts themselves. Judge Mikva, concurring, argued that a strong allegation of bad faith or improper purpose could be supported by the record, affidavits or the transcripts. *Id.* at 45-46. It is not apparent why a different rule should apply to transcripts of open meetings voluntarily

---

22. 684 F.2d 31, 37 n.12 (D.C. Cir. 1982); *see also* note 12, *supra.*
23. United States v. Morgan, 313 U.S. 409 (1941).

maintained by an agency. In the well publicized "God Squad" case, the Ninth Circuit expressly distinguished between its legitimate examination of prohibited *ex parte* communications between the White House and members of a special, statutorily created committee and the inappropriate judicial examination of "the internal decisional processes of the agency . . . [or] the mental processes of individual agency members" at issue in the case of *San Luis Obispo Mothers for Peace. See Portland Audubon Society v. Oregon Lands Coalition,* 984 F.2d 1534, 1549 (9th Cir. 1993).

The D.C. Circuit has offered a further explanation for rejecting examination of transcripts in *LO Shippers Action Committee (LOSAC) v. Interstate Commerce Commission.*[24] In that case, it declined to evaluate the transcript of the discussion that occurred at an open meeting and relied instead on the ICC's subsequent formal written decision. The court distinguished its earlier *Pan American* decision as follows:

> LOSAC argues that the vote at this public conference was the decision and that we must, therefore, scrutinize the transcript and disregard the subsequent published decision as a *post hoc* rationalization. This we decline to do. The ICC's formal opinion is its decision because the commissioners retained full authority to approve, disapprove, or modify until published. . . . This is . . . the critical difference between this case and our decision . . . in *Pan American.* . . .
>
> In *Pan Am,* the Civil Aeronautics Board, after an unlawfully closed board meeting, issued an emergency order that lacked statutorily required findings of fact. Those followed twelve days later. On review of the order, this court considered both the subsequently issued findings and a transcript of the preceding board meeting. . . . While we recognized in that case that *Pan Am* had involved our review of a transcript, we noted that the agency in *Pan Am* had not supplied a contemporaneous statement of reasons necessitating a review of the transcript in order "to dispose of the issue of whether the agency had complied with the Sunshine Act." *Kansas State Network,* 720 F.2d at 192. We further noted that the agency's failure in

---

24. 857 F.2d 802 (D.C. Cir. 1988).

Pan Am to provide a written decision made it impossible for us to assess the reasonableness of the board's action without an examination of the transcript. None of these factors prevails here. Following in the footsteps of *Kansas State,* we limit our review to reasons given in the ICC's published decision and, absent a compelling indication of error, we must defer to the Commission's interpretation of the statute, with the administration of which it is charged (citations omitted).[25]

---

25. *Id.* at 805-06. *See also Kansas State Network, supra,* at 195, 720 F.2d at 192, which also distinguished its reasoning from that of the *Pan American* decision as follows:

> This case is unlike *Pan American* [citation omitted] where the Board failed to comply with the Sunshine Act and did not write a contemporaneous statement of reasons. In that case, review of the transcript was necessary to dispose of the issue of whether the agency had complied with the Sunshine Act. Moreover, given the lack of a written decision, the court could not assess the "reasonableness" of the Board's action without examining the transcript. No such necessity exists here [in the *Kansas State Network* case] because the agency's rationale has been clearly articulated.

See also Checkosky v. S.E.C., 23 F.3d 452, 485 (D. C. Cir. 1994) (citing *Kansas State Network, supra,* and *San Luis Obispo Mothers for Peace, supra,* court noted that "in passing on final agency action, we . . . have refused to consider transcripts of closed agency meetings . . . requiring an agency to produce such internal materials and allowing litigants to depose agency officials about such matters would be warranted only in the rarest of cases. . . ."); and Public Utility District No. 1 of Snohomish County, Washington v. Federal Energy Regulatory Commission, 270 F. Supp. 2d 1 (D.D.C. 2003), in which court refused to order discovery regarding alleged Sunshine Act violation in absence of a transcript of a telephone conversation between agency members.

Chapter 9

SECTION 552b(i) ASSESSMENT OF COSTS

"REVERSE SUNSHINE" CASES 201

(i) The court may assess against any party reasonable attorney fees and other litigation costs reasonably incurred by any other party who substantially prevails in any action brought in accordance with the provisions of subsection (g) or (h) of this section, except that costs may be assessed against the plaintiff only where the court finds that the suit was initiated by the plaintiff primarily for frivolous or dilatory purposes. In the case of assessment of costs against an agency, the costs may be assessed by the court against the United States.

The Sunshine Act, like the Freedom of Information Act (FOIA), 5 U.S.C. § 552(a)(4)(E), and the Privacy Act, 5 U.S.C. § 552a(g)(2)(B) and 3(B), contains a provision for the assessment of "reasonable attorney fees and other litigation costs" against the United States where the plaintiff has "substantially prevail[ed]." As a general rule, the courts have construed in a similar fashion fee-shifting statutes that use identical language and have similar congressional purposes.[1] For example,

---

1. *See, e.g.*, Buckhannon Board & Care Home, Inc. v. W. Va. Dep't of Health and Human Resources, 532 U.S. 598, 603 n.4 and accompanying text (2001) (Court interprets similar fee-shifting provisions consistently); Oil, Chem. and Atomic Workers Int'l Union, AFL-CIO v. Dep't of Energy, 288 F.3d 452, 454-55 (D.C. Cir. 2002) (noting that courts treat "prevailing party" and "substantially prevails" language of various fee-shifting statutes similarly and interpret fee-shifting statutes "consistently"); Gowan v. U.S. Dep't of the Air Force, 148 F.3d 1182, 1194 (10th Cir.), *cert denied,* 525 U.S. 1042 (1998); Clarkson
(continued on next page)

the Department of Justice and at least one academic observer have assumed that fees and costs are available under the Sunshine Act in much the same fashion as under the FOIA.[2] So, despite the apparent lack of litigation directed solely to section 552b(i), it is generally assumed that fees and costs are available under the Sunshine Act as under the FOIA.

Both the Senate-passed bill and the bill reported by the House Government Operations Committee contained a provision for assessing costs against individual agency members who "intentionally and repeatedly" violate the open-meeting requirements. But this provision was stricken by the House Judiciary Committee "because it was concluded that it is not desirable or even possible to assess costs against individual members for actions taken by a collegial body." H. Rep. II, 7. The Judiciary Committee position was sustained by the House and in Conference. Conf. Rep., 23.[3]

Unlike the FOIA or Privacy Act, the Sunshine Act also provides for an assessment of costs against the plaintiff but "only where the court finds that the suit was initiated . . . primarily for frivolous or dilatory purposes."[4] We have been unable to uncover any cases in which the government has sought fees or costs under this provision.

(continued from previous page)
v. Internal Revenue Service, 678 F.2d 1368, 1371 (11th Cir. 1982) (applying the analysis of "prevailing party" consistently under the FOIA and the Privacy Act). *But see* Blazy v. Tenet, 194 F.3d 90, 96 (D.C. Cir. 1999) (declining to read the Privacy Act and FOIA fee provisions in a similar fashion because the statutory purposes are different).

2. *See* Oil, Chem. and Atomic Workers v. U.S. Dep't of Energy, 141 F. Supp. 2d 1, 4 n.4 (D.D.C. 2001), *rev'd on other grounds*, 288 F.3d 452 (D.C. Cir. 2002); Gregory Sisk, *A Primer on Awards of Attorney's Fees Against the Federal Government*, 25 Ariz. St. L.J. 733, 776 (1993) (brief discussion of fees under the Sunshine Act refers the reader to the section on fees under the FOIA).

3. It might be argued that costs might nevertheless be assessed against the agency members if they are named as individual defendants. However, subsection (h)(1) provides for suit against the agency in its own name and not for suit against its members. *See* 5 U.S.C. § 703; H. Rep. No. 94-1656, 94th Cong. 2d Sess., at 18; 1976 U.S. Code Cong. & Ad. News 6138.

4. The "costs" that may be assessed against the plaintiff include reasonable attorney fees. There is no reason to believe that the term "costs" in the "ex-
(continued on next page)

"REVERSE SUNSHINE" CASES

We have concluded elsewhere that subsection (h)(1) is not applicable to a suit to require an agency to close a meeting.[5] It follows that subsection (i) regarding fees and costs is not applicable to "Reverse Sunshine" cases, either. However, some other statutes—although not 28 U.S.C. § 1331 or the judicial review provisions of the APA—may provide a basis for assessment of fees and costs.

(continued from previous page)
cept" clause is used in contradistinction to attorney fees. *See* S. Rep. 34-35; H. Rep. I, at 18. Such costs could be awarded to the United States but would not accrue to the benefit of the particular agency under government accounting practices. *See* 31 U.S.C. § 3302. *See generally Letter to the Chairman, National Labor Relations Board*, 47 Comp. Gen. 70 (1967).

5. *See* ch. 8, pp. 185-86, *supra,* where we note that suits seeking to close meetings may nonetheless be brought pursuant to other statutes, such as 28 U.S.C. § 1331, that give the district courts federal question jurisdiction.

Chapter 10

SECTION 552b(k)[1] RELATIONSHIP TO FREEDOM OF INFORMATION ACT

CONFIDENTIALITY OF INTERNAL MEMORANDA	204
APPLICABILITY OF FOIA PROCEDURES TO REQUESTS FOR ACCESS TO TRANSCRIPTS	206
RECORDS DISPOSAL	209

(k) Nothing herein expands or limits the present rights of any person under section 552 of this title, except that the exemptions set forth in subsection (c) of this section shall govern in the case of any request made pursuant to section 552 to copy or inspect the transcripts, recordings, or minutes described in subsection (f) of this section. The requirements of chapter 33 of title 44, United States Code, shall not apply to the transcripts, recordings, and minutes described in subsection (f) of this section.

Subsection (k) provides that "nothing herein[2] expands or limits the present rights of any person" under the Freedom of Information Act, except that the agency authority to withhold material in the transcripts, recordings or minutes of closed meetings will be governed by the Sunshine Act exemptions rather than by the exemptions in the

---

1. We omit discussion of subsections (l) and (m), which are self-explanatory. *See also* pp. 230-31, *supra,* for discussion of the amendment in 1995 and, later, the expiration in May 2000 of the requirement in subsection (j) that each Sunshine agency submit an annual report to Congress.
2. "Herein," of course, refers to the open meeting provisions, section 552b, and not to the entire Government in the Sunshine Act. Section 5(b) of the Act does alter rights under the FOIA by narrowing the third exemption. *See* pp. xxxiv, *supra.*

FOIA. Hence, nothing in the open meeting provisions is intended to increase or decrease the public's access to documents or other records under the FOIA.[3] "Access to the actual documents or other written matter discussed or referred to at a meeting subject to [section 552b] will continue to be governed, as before, by the Freedom of Information Act." S. Rep., 39.

CONFIDENTIALITY OF INTERNAL MEMORANDA

The status of inter-agency and intra-agency memoranda, such as staff recommendations, that are considered at open agency meetings remains a controversial question.[4] Such memoranda are exempt from disclosure as documents under the fifth exemption of the FOIA, 5 U.S.C. § 552(b)(5). However, since there is no Sunshine exemption comparable to 552(b)(5), meetings may not be closed in order to protect the confidentiality of internal memoranda. Moreover, if the meeting is closed on other grounds, the agency may not withhold from the public that portion of the transcript that includes discussion of internal memoranda, unless the discussion falls within one of the Sunshine Act exemptions. Of course, if preservation of the confidentiality of the memorandum, or aspects of it (such as the identity of the author), is

---

3. The requirement in the last sentence of subsection (f)(1) that agency minutes of a closed meeting must identify "all documents considered in connection with any action" may facilitate FOIA requests, but does not by itself expand any rights under the FOIA.
4. This question was at issue in the first lawsuit to be brought under the Government in the Sunshine Act. *See* Consumers Union of the United States, Inc. v. Board of Governors of the Federal Reserve System (D.D.C. Civ. A. #77-1800, Jan. 28, 1978). Consumers Union sought to compel the Board to make available a document to be discussed in an open meeting. Consumers Union argued that without the document, it was difficult to understand what was being discussed at the meeting, and that, therefore, the discussion was not meaningfully open to the public. The Board denied that its discussion of the document was incomprehensible. The case was dismissed on agreement of both parties. The Board's present policy is to release most of the staff memoranda considered at open meetings, providing them at the meeting and through its FOIA office and Web site, www.federalreserve.gov/Board/Docs/meetings/sunshine.html. *See also* Federal Reserve Board, *A Guide to the Meetings of the Board of Governors of the Federal Reserve System*, Appendix L, *infra,* and pp. 61-62, *supra.*

important to the agency, the participants in the meeting can no doubt contrive to refer to it obliquely, even though to do so may make it difficult for observers of the meeting to follow the course of the discussion. There is an unavoidable tension between FOIA exemption (5), which recognizes a legitimate governmental interest in protecting the agency deliberative process as such, see *Environmental Protection Agency v. Mink*, 410 U.S. 73, 86-90 (1973), and the Sunshine Act, which aims at maximum exposure of that process, at least at the collegial level.[5] However, a common-sense approach by the agency can in most cases achieve a satisfactory resolution of the conflict.

The Federal Trade Commission has addressed this problem. Responding to a public comment calling for making staff memoranda available to the public observing a meeting, the Commission declined to provide for routine duplication of all memoranda to the Commission "both because of cost and of certain remaining requirements of confidentiality." However, the Commission has undertaken "to make available before open meetings summaries of matters on the agenda in order to facilitate the public's understanding of open discussions," 42 Fed. Reg. 13,539 (March 11, 1977).[6] But staff memoranda are usually not made public, except where the staff recommendation was otherwise expected to be made public or has already been placed on the public record.[7]

---

5. It should be recalled, however, that the drafters of the Sunshine Act recognized that the considerations favoring exposure to public scrutiny of the deliberations of agency heads do not necessarily apply to the deliberative process at the staff level. S. REP., 17. *See* p. 6, *supra*. *See also* Common Cause v. NRC, 674 F.2d 921, 930 n.24 (D.C. Cir. 1982) (describes the *1978 Guide* as a "leading commentary on the Sunshine Act" and cites it here for its recognition of the "unavoidable tension between FOIA exemption (5), which recognizes a legitimate governmental interest in protecting the agency deliberative process as such," and the Sunshine Act, "which aims at maximum exposure of that process, at least at the collegial level"). *See also* p. 63, *supra*.
6. *See also* p. 60 note 88, *supra*.
7. FTC GOVERNMENT IN THE SUNSHINE ACT ANNUAL REPORT FOR 2001, at 3. The question is somewhat academic because the FTC has in recent years rarely held an open meeting. In 2002, for example, the FTC held one open meeting and in 2003 two open meetings, all oral arguments. Fax to Stephen Klitzman from Rachel Miller Dawson, assistant general counsel, Federal Trade Commission, Feb. 2, 2004.

Where the agency's concern is simply to preserve in confidence the identity of the authors of staff memoranda in the interest of encouraging candid expression by staff members, it may be feasible to release the memoranda with the names or other identifying material deleted. *See Tax Reform Research Group v. IRS*, 419 F. Supp. 415, 423-24 (D.D.C. 1976).

APPLICABILITY OF FOIA PROCEDURES TO REQUESTS FOR ACCESS TO TRANSCRIPTS

Another question raised by the interaction of subsection (f)(2) and subsection (k) is whether agency procedures for handling subsection (f)(2) requests are governed by the FOIA, the Sunshine Act, or both. The principal difference between the two statutes is that the FOIA, 5 U.S.C. § 552(a)(6), prescribes time limits for agency handling of requests—20 working days for an initial determination and 20 working days for disposition of an administrative appeal.[8] The Sunshine Act does not.[9] In addition, the FOIA, section 552(a)(4)(A), provides that agencies shall furnish documents "without charge or at a reduced charge where the agency determines that waiver or reduction of the fee is in the public interest because furnishing the information can be considered as primarily benefiting the general public." The Sunshine Act contains no such provision, although the legislative history indicates that such waivers are encouraged. S. Rep., 32. *See also* pp. 168-71, *supra*.

The agencies are divided over whether to follow FOIA procedures. Some agencies will consider requests for transcripts, recordings, or

---

8. The Electronic Freedom of Information Act Amendments of 1996 increased the FOIA's time limit for initial responses from 10 to 20 working days. Pub. L. No. 104-231, 8(b), 110 Stat. 3048, 3052 (codified as amended at 5 U.S.C. § 552(a)(6)(A)(i)). The period for resolving administrative appeals remains 20 working days.
9. The FOIA limits serve to define the requester's duty to exhaust administrative remedies, whereas the Sunshine Act contains no exhaustion requirement. *See* p. 184 note 7, *supra*. Therefore, it is doubtful that an agency may obtain more time to process requests by adopting Sunshine Act procedures distinct from its FOIA procedures.

minutes under FOIA procedures and time limits,[10] some under Sunshine Act procedures, with or without specified time limits,[11] while some regulations do not specify procedures for considering such requests.[12] Where a Sunshine Act procedure is not otherwise specified, the agency's FOIA procedure is presumably applicable.

The language and the legislative history of subsection (k) indicate that Congress intended the Freedom of Information Act to govern requests for access under subsection (f)(2) of the Sunshine Act. First, the plain meaning of the clause "except that the exemptions set forth in subsection (c) . . . shall govern in the case of any request made pursuant to section 552 to copy or inspect the transcripts," etc., is that such requests should be made pursuant to section 552, the FOIA. It thus seems a fair inference that the reference to the "exemptions" in the Sunshine Act is intended to negate a broader applicability of that Act to the processing of such requests. It is true that there is legislative history suggesting that Congress contemplated procedures distinct from, though similar to, those under the FOIA.[13] But this legislative

---

10. *See, e.g.,* regulations of the Federal Trade Commission, 16 C.F.R. § 4.15(c)(3); Federal Communications Commission, 47 C.F.R. §§ 0.461, 0.607(b); Federal Energy Regulatory Commission, 18 C.F.R. § 375.206(f); and the Federal Maritime Commission, 46 C.F.R. § 503.86(b). The regulation of the Securities and Exchange Commission, 17 C.F.R. § 200.408, conforms to its FOIA procedure, except that requests to review an initial denial of access are to be addressed to the Secretary of the Commission rather than to the General Counsel. It is understandable that members of the agencies may wish to be consulted on determinations to release transcripts of closed meetings.
11. *See* regulations of the Consumer Product Safety Commission, 16 C.F.R. § 1013.6 (response within 10 working days); Commodity Futures Trading Commission, 17 C.F.R. § 147.8; Federal Reserve System, Board of Governors, 12 C.F.R. § 1261b.12; Federal Deposit Insurance Corporation, 12 C.F.R. § 311.8(d); and the Nuclear Regulatory Commission, 10 C.F.R. § 9.108.
12. *See* regulations of the Defense Nuclear Facilities Safety Board, 10 C.F.R. § 1704.9; Merit Systems Protection Board, 5 C.F.R. § 1206.9(d); the National Labor Relations Board, 29 C.F.R. § 102.142; and the USITC, 19 C.F.R. § 201.41.
13. "When people ask for copies of the records of meetings available to the public, agencies should follow procedures similar to those adopted under the Freedom of Information Act. . . . " S. REP., at 32. *See also* H. REP. I, at 18.

history referred to Senate and House bills that stated that, with respect to requests for transcripts, etc., "the provisions of this Act shall govern . . . ."[14] The Conference rephrased the subsection, substituting "exemptions" for "provisions," Conf. Rep., 24, presumably in order to leave the FOIA in effect for other purposes.

There do not seem to be any serious practical difficulties in conforming to the FOIA the processing of requests under subsection (f)(2). It has been suggested that the agency's duty under subsection (f)(2) to make transcript material "promptly available" is inconsistent with the time period provided in FOIA section 552(a)(6) for processing requests for information. This difficulty disappears on examination, however. The agency does indeed have a duty under subsection (f)(2) to make transcript material available in advance of a specific request, *see* pp. 153-54, *supra*, just as agencies are required under section 552(a)(2) to make certain materials "available for public inspection and copying." It is true that under the FOIA the category of records to which a requester is entitled is considerably broader than the category the agency is required to make available in advance of a request, whereas under the Sunshine Act the agency should, in theory, make available in the first instance all meeting records that it is not entitled to withhold. But in practice an agency's initial decision to withhold meeting record material may be altered on reconsideration in the light of a particular request, or on review by a higher level of authority, or simply because of the passage of time. *See* pp. 163-66, *supra*.

Therefore, compliance with the duty to make meeting record material promptly available does not eliminate the need for a procedure for handling individual requests, and this procedure should be that provided by the FOIA. This does not mean, of course, that the agency's procedure for disposing of subsection (f)(2) requests must be identical

---

14. The language of the House bill, ". . . except that the provisions of this Act shall govern in the case of any request made pursuant to [section 552] to copy or inspect the minutes [the bill did not require recordings or transcripts] described in subsection (f) of this section," seems clearly to have contemplated separate Sunshine Act procedures. The language of the Senate bill, "in the case of any request made pursuant to section 552 . . . the provisions of this Act shall govern whether such transcripts or electronic recordings shall be made available in accordance with such request," is more ambiguous, and the report seems to point both ways. *Cf.* S. Rep., at 32, 39.

to the procedure it follows for other FOIA requests. For example, the agency members may desire greater involvement in decisions to release meeting record material than they would have in decisions respecting documents. Or agencies might wish to expedite processing of subsection (f)(2) requests by requiring that they be distinctively identified or addressed to an office other than that which handles other FOIA requests. It will, in our view, suffice that the procedure employed is consistent with the requirements of the FOIA.

There are provisions for judicial enforcement in both the FOIA, 5 U.S.C. § 552(a)(4)(B), and the Sunshine Act, 5 U.S.C. § 552b(h)(1), and apparently a party seeking access to transcript materials may seek relief under either statute.[15]

RECORDS DISPOSAL

The last sentence of subsection (k) provides that the records disposal requirements of the Federal Records Act. 44 U.S.C. §§ 3301-3314, shall not apply to the records of the proceedings at closed meetings required by subsection (f). Such materials need not be kept beyond the period specified in subsection (f)(2). S. Rep., 40. The Report added, "The committee expects, however, that in accordance with the principles established in the Federal Records Act, the agency will choose to permanently retain transcripts or electronic recordings of meetings of special interest." *Id.*

---

15. We have previously discussed the advantages of applying the judicial review procedures of the FOIA rather than those of the Sunshine Act to requests for meeting record materials. *See* pp. 184-85, *supra*.

Chapter 11

SUNSHINE ACT PERCEPTIONS, PROBLEMS, AND PROPOSALS

GENERAL CONSIDERATIONS	211
NEED FOR CONGRESSIONAL REVIEW	219
The Dilemma of Openness vs. Collegiality	219
Lack of Collegiality	219
Definition of "Meeting"	226
FEES AND FEE WAIVERS	228
ANNUAL REPORTING REQUIREMENT	230

GENERAL CONSIDERATIONS

The federal government was late to enact a Government in the Sunshine Act. By the time Congress enacted the statute in 1976, all states except New York already had their own open-meeting laws.[1] However, in the nearly 30 years since passage of the federal law, affected agencies have thoroughly integrated the law into their regular procedures and the public and the media have come to expect openness or, to use a more contemporary term, "transparency," in agency

---

1. Christopher W. Deering, *Closing the Door on the Public's Right to Know: Alabama's Open Meetings Law After Dunn v. Alabama State University Board of Trustees*, 28 CUMB. L. REV. 361, 366 (1997). Although most state statutes address the same common issues, they vary widely in terms of agencies covered, the definition of "meeting," procedural requirements, and the remedies for violation. *See generally* Teresa Dale Pupillo, Note, *The Changing Weather Forecast: Government in the Sunshine in the 1990s— An Analysis of State Sunshine Laws*, 71 WASH. U. L. Q. 1165 (1993). *See also* CHARLES H. KOCH, ADMINISTRATIVE LAW AND PRACTICE, 2D ED., § 3.61. "State open meeting statutes," 306-09 (West Publishing Co. 1997). State agencies, of course, are not subject to the federal Sunshine Act. *See* Proffitt v. Davis, 707 F. Supp. 182, 188 (E.D. Pa. 1989).

deliberations. There is little support for repeal of the Sunshine Act. Yet, there is a growing call by some agency members and administrative law experts for Congress to reexamine the law and possibly to amend it to allow agencies more flexibility to close their meetings.[2]

---

2. *See, e.g.,* Appendix O for Letter from Michael K. Powell, Chairman, and Michael J. Copps, Commissioner, Federal Communications Commission, to the Honorable Ted Stevens, Chairman, Senate Committee on Commerce, Science and Transportation, Feb. 2, 2005. The letter was also sent to the FCC's other congressional "overseers"—the ranking member of the Senate Commerce Committee and the chairmen and ranking members of the House Committee on Energy and Commerce and its Subcommittee on Telecommunications and the Internet. In the letter, Republican Chairman Powell and Democratic Commissioner Copps argued that the Sunshine Act has not "achieved its goal of . . . Commissioners . . . shap[ing] each others' views in the course of public deliberations." To the contrary, they asserted that the open-meeting requirement "is a barrier to the substantive exchange of ideas among commissioners, hampering our abilities to obtain the benefit of each others' views, input or comments, and hampering efforts to maximize consensus on the complex issues before us. Due to the prohibition on private collective deliberations, we rely on written communications, staff, or one-on-one meetings with each other. These indirect methods of communicating clearly do not foster frank, open discussion, and they are less efficient than in-person interchange among three or more commissioners would be. Finally, and perhaps most significantly, Commission decisions are in some cases less well informed and well explained than they would be if we each had the benefit of the others' expertise and perspective." *Id.* Therefore, they recommended that the Congress permit more "closed deliberations among Commissioners in appropriate circumstances," with "safeguards" such as "brief summaries of topics discussed at meetings between all decisionmakers . . . recorded and placed in relevant administrative records." *Id.*

According to an Associated Press article, "[n]ewspaper groups and free speech advocates bristled at [this FCC] request and said it would lead to less transparency. 'It's basically arguing that it is inconvenient for them to have open meetings,' said Steve Sidlo, managing editor of the *Dayton Daily News* and chairman of the First Amendment Committee for the Associated Press Managing Editors Association. 'If you're going to have a transparent government that's accountable for decision-making, that allows people to understand why decisions are made, then you have to have open meetings,' Sidlo said." *See* Genaro C. Arnas, *FCC Members Ask for Some Closing of Rules that Require Open Meetings,* CLEVELAND PLAIN DEALER, Feb. 10, 2005,

(continued on next page)

(continued from previous page)
and OMB Watch, *FCC Requests Exemption in Open Meetings Law,* Feb. 22, 2005. As of October 2005, the FCC had yet to receive a response from Capitol Hill to its February 2005 letter.

For an even more frank agency critique calling for a complete exemption from the statute, see testimony of then FCC Commissioner Michael Powell before the House Subcommittee on Telecommunications, Trade, and Consumer Protection, House Committee on Commerce, Oct. 26, 1999:

> The proposal to exempt the Commission from the Government in the Sunshine Act should be considered. I recognize that at first blush, it seems fantastic to support less openness. But the fact is that the Sunshine Act not only has failed in its purpose, it may have had the opposite effect. The notion that substantive decisions are debated by Commissioners in public meetings and voted after such deliberations is fiction. The press of business requires that most items be voted on circulation. Moreover, even the votes at open meetings are ceremonial, the decision having been debated and determined in advance. The Sunshine Act, in fact, impedes efficient decision-making. Because three Commissioners may not discuss a substantive matter (except at a public forum), questions are filtered through and among layers of Commission staff and then are communicated back and forth to the Commissioners. This produces a lengthy and often chaotic decision-making process. Our decisions certainly should not be cloaked in the shadows, but they are presently being scorched by sunshine.

See also pp. 22-24, 33 note 8, and 35-36 note 14, *supra,* and pp. 219-28, *infra.*

FCC Commissioner Copps, a Democratic appointee by President George W. Bush, has been particularly outspoken about the impact of the Sunshine Act on agency collegiality. He has called for repeal of the law as an "anachronistic throwback to the Watergate era." Short of abolition, which he grants may not be politically feasible, Commissioner Copps also supports congressional oversight hearings to examine how the Sunshine Act is, or is not, working, and especially its impact on the collegiality of the Sunshine agencies. In addition, the commissioner supports the 1995 recommendation of the ACUS Special Committee to Review the Government in the Sunshine Act to allow for more closed meetings to discuss substantive agency matters in exchange for less reliance on the use of notation procedure or circulation of agency items and the release of general public summaries of closed meeting discussions, but a summary that "would not identify specific positions with specific agency members." Interview of FCC Commissioner Michael J. Copps by Stephen Klitzman, June 18, 2003.

This lack of motivation to repeal the law is because implementation of the statute has satisfied all relevant constituencies. It is a useful tool by which the political branches of government have rendered multimember government agencies more accountable by enhancing their transparency. At the same time, despite some complaints, agencies have implemented the statute's requirements in a way that has not undermined their ability to manage their missions. Perhaps most important, the affected public—primarily the media, public interest organizations, and the regulated sector—find that they can monitor agency operations and gain insight into agency decision-making somewhat better than they could in pre–Sunshine Act days. Indeed, individuals below the age of 50 most likely have no experience operating in a pre–Sunshine Act era. The only serious criticism of the Act is that it has undoubtedly compromised the collegiality that is supposed to be the cornerstone of the decisional process at multimember agencies.

Implementation of the Sunshine Act began smoothly. The statute provided a six-month period before its effective date to allow agencies to develop implementing regulations and expressly required that agencies, in preparing their regulations, consult with the Administrative Conference of the United States (ACUS). Until abolished by Congress in 1995, ACUS was the government's non-partisan, expert advisory agency on administrative procedure.[3] ACUS staff held a se-

---

3. For a general discussion of the role of ACUS, the reasons for its demise, and suggestions for its revival, *see* Gary J. Edles, *The Continuing Need for an Administrative Conference*, 50 ADMIN. L. REV. 101 (1998); and Jeffrey S. Lubbers, *If It Didn't Exist, It Would Have to Be Invented—Reviving the Administrative Conference*, 30 ARIZ. ST. L. J. 147 (1998). The Lubbers article is part of a Symposium issue devoted to ACUS. *See also* Pub. L. No. 108-401, 118 Stat. 2255, the Federal Regulatory Improvement Act of 2004, which President Bush signed into law on October 30, 2004. The bill reauthorizes the Administrative Conference of the United States. As of October 2005, however, ACUS's "resurrection [was] not yet complete." Congress had yet to appropriate the authorized funds. Public Law 108-401 authorized "appropriations of not more than $3 million for fiscal year 2005, $3.1 million for fiscal year 2006, and $3.2 million for fiscal year 2007, providing a lean but reasonable budget, since the Conference's highest budget was just over $2 million in the early 1990s." Jeffrey S. Lubbers, *Consensus-Building in Administrative Law: The Revival of the Administrative Conference of the U.S.*, 30 ADMIN. & REG. L., NEWS, at 3 (Winter 2005).

ries of meetings with representatives of affected agencies, circulated drafts and other materials supplied by the agencies, offered oral and written comments on proposed regulations, and generally served as an impartial clearinghouse for Sunshine Act information for agencies in the process of preparing their Sunshine Act regulations. This consultative process also led to publication of the 1978 *Interpretive Guide*. As noted throughout this volume, the *1978 Guide* has been relied upon for guidance by the courts, the agencies, the media, and the public. This process was so effective that, to this day, many of the 67 Sunshine agencies we list in Appendix C use essentially the same regulations they enacted in 1977, right after passage of the Sunshine Act.

Implementation of the Sunshine Act contrasts with the initial execution of the Freedom of Information Act, enacted in 1966. In part, that reflects the broader coverage of the FOIA—the Sunshine Act was applicable to only about 50 multimember entities at the time of its enactment, many of which had relatively small public constituencies. Key parts of the government, including the cabinet departments and important independent bodies such as EPA and the CIA, are not covered by the Sunshine Act. Writing in 1978, and pointing to the Senate Report that accompanied passage of the Sunshine Act,[4] Professor Kenneth Culp Davis, "the father of U.S. administrative law,"[5] noted that if Congress were genuinely to ensure governmental openness, it would have to require all executive branch officials to make their decisions in public. "Collegial bodies make only a tiny fraction of the decisions that are made for the government. To carry out the goal stated by the

---

4. *See* S. REP., at 1: The Sunshine Act "is founded on the proposition that the government should conduct the public's business in public," and at 11, that the law "establishes as the policy of the United States the principle that the public should have the fullest practicable knowledge about the decisionmaking process of the Government. It is the purpose of the bill to implement this policy without infringing upon the rights of individual citizens and the ability of the Government to carry out its responsibilities. The provision thus reaffirms the intent of this bill that openness is desirable in a democratic Government. It is the intent of this bill that governmental bodies conduct their deliberations in public to the greatest extent possible."

5. *See* PIERCE, *supra* p. 19 note 28, at xv.

Senate committee, the other ninety percent or more will have to be included."[6]

The documents that are the targets of FOIA requests are often far more significant or controversial than the subjects examined at meetings of multimember agencies. One public interest litigator has noted that "most public-interest organizations have generally regarded access to documents (including transcripts of meetings) as more valuable than access to meetings."[7] Significantly, the Sunshine Act was enacted a decade after the FOIA, when notions of openness were better established. Some agencies resisted the FOIA at the outset, but the courts and Congress responded to such resistance with vigor. Professor Davis argued that the original FOIA had many infirmities and that the Attorney General's Memorandum of 1967, by interpreting most doubtful questions "in the direction of nondisclosure, set the tone for agency noncompliance." By 1976 that had largely changed. Professor

---

6. KENNETH CULP DAVIS, I ADMINISTRATIVE LAW TREATISE 441 (K.C. Davis Pub. Co., 2d ed. 1978). Professor Davis noted that:

> [t]he Government in the Sunshine Act [GSA] fails to connect with the most important government operations. The GSA provides for about five percent of the government in the sunshine and leaves about 95 percent in the darkness.
>
> The Commission on Civil Rights and the Commission on Fine Arts, neither of which has power to take governmental action of any kind, must have open meetings, but the President and his Cabinet, or the President and his White House advisers, are not required to have open meetings. That is what is called, in its present stage of development, "government in the sunshine." The most vital parts are not in the sunshine. A step has been taken, and a journey of a thousand miles begins with one step, but whatever value the idea may have, its realization has not yet been achieved. *Id.* at 446.

7. Letter from Eric R. Glitzenstein to Jeffrey Lubbers, ACUS Special Committee to Review the Government in the Sunshine Act (Sept. 12, 1995) (on file with the authors) (hereafter *Glitzenstein Letter*). *See also* Stephen H. Klitzman, *Government in the Sunshine Act—Nuts, Bolts and Tacks: A Summary of Statutory Provisions, Judicial Interpretations, and Pending Issues*, 38 FED. B. J. 114, 115 (Fall 1979) (citing among the reasons "for the present paucity of Sunshine Act litigation" compared with voluminous FOIA litigation "a greater interest in obtaining tangible agency documents than in hearing possibly pre-orchestrated agency discussions").

Davis noted that the courts rejected most of the Attorney General's interpretations, that the 1974 FOIA amendments "changed the basic spirit, and the 1975 Attorney General's Memorandum diligently upheld the new spirit."[8] FOIA continues to be the source of significant litigation and its practical implementation is subject to changes in the political winds.[9] Congress has returned to the FOIA on several occasions to make modifications in light of experience.

In short, agencies follow the Sunshine Act's requirements as a matter of course. Daily agency activity under the Sunshine Act is thoroughly routine and reasonably noncontroversial. As a consequence, Sunshine Act litigation is rare. Individual court decisions reflect the tension between openness, on the one hand, and effective agency administration, on the other.[10] But the Supreme Court has found it necessary to tackle a Sunshine Act issue only once.[11] Over 25 years, the courts have played a useful role by interpreting the statute so as not to

---

8. KENNETH C. DAVIS, I ADMINISTRATIVE LAW TREATISE 309 (K.C. Davis Pub. Co. 2d ed. 1978).
9. *Compare* Memorandum of President Clinton to Heads of Federal Departments and Agencies (Oct. 4, 1993) and Memorandum to Heads of Departments and Agencies from Attorney General Janet Reno (Oct. 4, 1993) (in deciding whether to defend an agency's nondisclosure decision, Justice Department will apply a presumption of disclosure and defend only those cases where the agency can reasonably foresee that disclosure would be harmful to the interest protected by the exemption) *with* Memorandum to Heads of All Federal Departments and Agencies from Attorney General John Ashcroft (Oct. 21, 2001) (rescinding Clinton Administration FOIA Memorandum. Enhancing the effectiveness of law enforcement agencies and protecting national security, sensitive business information, and personal privacy are equally important as disclosure, so Justice Department will defend decisions not to disclose unless they lack a sound legal basis or present an unwarranted risk of adverse impact on the ability of other agencies to protect important records.).
10. *Compare* the Supreme Court's decision in FCC v. ITT World Communications, 466 U.S. 463 (1984), (according the term "meeting" a narrow construction to foster congressional intent not to "impair normal agency operations") *with* the D.C. Circuit's decision it reversed, 699 F.2d 1219, 1243 (D.C. Cir. 1984) (noting that "[t]he Act's presumption of openness requires that all doubts be resolved against closure").
11. *See* FCC v. ITT World Communications, Inc., *supra*.

compromise either the fundamental openness objective of the law or the agencies' practical ability to conduct their operations efficiently. During this period the government has won some cases and lost others. The lower courts early on resolved some key practical issues under the statute in a manner favorable to agencies.[12] For example, the courts have consistently held that the remedy for an improperly closed meeting is the release of the transcript of the meeting, not vacating the agency's substantive action, thus significantly reducing the incentives for litigation.[13]

Notwithstanding the limited litigation under the Sunshine Act, the statute has still been the subject of some academic interest. But many of those who write about the subject focus on a single issue or a single agency.[14] Meanwhile, Congress has found no need to amend the stat-

---

12. For example, several cases, such as *Railroad Comm'n of Texas v. United States*, 765 F.2d 221, 230-31 (D.C. Cir. 1985) (hereafter *Railroad Comm'n*) and *Communications Systems v. FCC*, 595 F.2d 797 (D.C. Cir. 1978), upheld the continued use of notation voting. Moreover, two cases determined that certain types of multimember governmental entities are not covered by the Act. *Symons v. Chrysler Corp. Loan Guarantee Board*, 670 F.2d 238 (D.C. Cir. 1981), decided that agencies whose presidential appointees serve only ex officio do not come within the definition of "agency," while *Hunt v. Nuclear Regulatory Commission*, 611 F.2d 332 (10th Cir. 1979), *cert. denied*, 445 U.S. 906 (1980), concluded that staff tribunals with power to act on behalf of the agency do not constitute "agencies" for purposes of the statute.

13. *See, e.g., Railroad Comm'n, supra* n.12, *and* Braniff Master Executive Council v. CAB, 693 F.2d 220 (D.C. Cir. 1982). *See generally* chapter 8 for a discussion of judicial review of particular agency actions. Notably, many state Sunshine laws permit a court to invalidate an agency's substantive action if taken in derogation of open-meeting requirements. *See* Teresa Dale Pupillo, Note, *The Changing Weather Forecast: Government in the Sunshine in the 1990s—An Analysis of State Sunshine Laws*, 71 Wash. U. L. Q. 1165, 1173-74, 1182-84 (1993). *See also* pp. 189-91 note 12, *supra*.

14. *See, e.g.,* James H. Cawley, *Sunshine Law Overexposure and the Demise of Independent Agency Collegiality*, 1 Widener J. P. L. 43 (1992); James T. O'Reilly & Gracia M. Berg, *Stealth Caused by Sunshine: How Sunshine Act Interpretation Results in Less Information for the Public About the Decision-Making Process of the International Trade Commission*, 36 Harv. Int'l L. J. 425 (1995); Michael A. Lawrence, *Finding Shade from the "Government in*

(continued on next page)

ute, despite the passage of time, except to eliminate the requirement that agencies file annual Sunshine Act reports.[15] In sum, the Sunshine Act has become a key element of open government in the United States, a statute that 67 covered agencies have by now thoroughly integrated into their agency cultures.

NEED FOR CONGRESSIONAL REVIEW

Perhaps because of the widespread agency acceptance of the Sunshine Act and its relatively straightforward implementation, compared with the more difficult implementation of the FOIA, Congress has not undertaken a thorough review of the operation of the Government in the Sunshine Act since 1989. Despite the relatively routine manner, however, in which the statute now operates, it would be useful for Congress to conduct such an oversight review. This is because, as discussed below, there is ample evidence that the statute has, to a significant degree, compromised the collegiality of the decisional process at multimember agencies. Congress should now evaluate to what extent the Sunshine Act has adversely affected collegial decision making at federal agencies and whether any limitation on the effectiveness of the decisional process occasioned by the Sunshine Act can be corrected in a fashion that will not undermine the openness objective of the statute.

The Dilemma of Openness vs. Collegiality

Lack of Collegiality

The most serious attack on implementation of the Sunshine Act is the claim that it has compromised the collegiality that is supposed to be the cornerstone of the decisional process at multimember agen-

---

(continued from previous page)
the Sunshine Act": A Proposal to Permit Private Informal Background Discussions at the U.S. International Trade Commission, 45 CATH. U. L. REV. 1 (1995) (hereafter Lawrence Article); and Kathy Bradley, *Do You Feel the Sunshine? Government in the Sunshine Act: Its Objectives, Goals and Effect on the FCC and You*, 49 FED. COMM. L. J. 473 (1997).

15. While 5 U.S.C. § 552b(j) remains on the statute books, the filing requirement was terminated, effective May 15, 2000. *See* 5 U.S.C. § 552b note and 31 U.S.C.S. § 1113 note, and pp. 230-31, *infra*.

cies.[16] However, it is important to recognize that agency statutes and

---

16. *See, e.g.,* pp. 22-23, 33-36, 212-13, *supra.* The impact of open meeting laws on collegial decision making has caused some to rethink Justice Louis Brandeis's oft-quoted declaration at the height of the Progressive Era in 1914 that "[P]ublicity is justly commended as a remedy for social and industrial disease. Sunlight is said to be the best disinfectant and electric light the most efficient policeman." *See* LOUIS D. BRANDEIS, OTHER PEOPLE'S MONEY AND HOW THE BANKS USE IT, 92 (1914). As Professor Arthur Bonfield, former chairman, ABA Section of Administrative Law and Regulatory Practice, noted in 1988, while "mould does not grow where there is light . . . too much sunshine causes sunburn." *See* Arthur Bonfield, *Chairman's Message*, 40 ADMIN. L. REV. iii-iv (1988), quoted in Nicholas Johnson, *Open Meetings and Closed Minds: Another Road to the Mountaintop,* 53 DRAKE L. REV. 11 (Fall 2004). This is one of the most recent articles calling for a reexamination of open-meeting laws by a former liberal Democrat FCC Commissioner, 1966-1973, appointed by President Lyndon Johnson. He argues that the legal requirement for open meetings, especially as implemented in practice, is actually inconsistent with the goals of rational decision making, enhanced public accessibility, and confidence. Discussing the Iowa open-meeting law, Johnson asserts that the purposes of Sunshine laws "are, in some contexts, often better served by less rather than more openness. The objectives of these laws can still be served—indeed, better served in those instances—by affording agency members the freedom to engage in closed discussions that alone can produce the quality of creativity and analysis the laws seek to promote." 52 DRAKE L. REV., at 14. *Cf.* Public Citizen v. National Economic Commission, 703 F. Supp. 113, 125 (D.C.D.C. 1989), *citing* Common Cause v. Nuclear Regulatory Commission, 674 F.2d 921, 928 (D.C. Cir. 1982) ("Congress, in enacting the Sunshine Act, believed that 'increased openness would enhance citizen confidence in government, encourage higher-quality work by government officials, stimulate well- informed public debate about government programs and policies, and promote cooperation between citizens and government.").

See also Glitzenstein Letter, supra p. 216 note 7. The public interest litigator notes that the open meeting requirement "is most useful and illuminating to the public when there is at least one 'dissident member' of a commission or board" who uses "the open meeting obligation as a legally sanctioned opportunity to share with concerned members of the public a much more frank and candid understanding of the pertinent issues." Accordingly, Glitzenstein asserts that "any easing up of the rules on when meetings must be held in public . . . should provide for an exception which allows any member of a board or commission to trigger the requirement of an open meeting."

(continued on next page)

traditions, and the personality of agency members, especially the chair, are dominant factors that also help determine the level of collegiality at a particular agency.[17] The Sunshine Act, nonetheless, exacerbates these circumstances.

> *(continued from previous page)*
> *Id. See, e.g.,* such agency procedures noted *supra* at p. 38 note 21, which already authorize any agency member to direct that an item circulated for consideration and voting by notation procedure be placed instead on the agenda of an agency meeting for joint deliberation.
>
> 17. *See generally* Marshall Breger & Gary Edles, *Established by Practice: The Theory and Operation of Independent Federal Agencies*, 52 ADMIN. L. REV. 1111, 1164-82 (2000), quoting statements by former FCC member Glen Robinson that "the FCC's Chairman and a handful of staff—usually selected by the Chair—can and usually do exercise nearly total control over that agency's basic policy agenda. . . ." *Id.* at n.329; by former FTC Chair Miles Kirkpatrick that "in the management of the Commission's day-to-day affairs, there are no collegial decisions. . . . *Id.*; by Professors Martha Derthick and Paul Quirk that at three regulatory agencies they studied, "Commission members tended in general to defer to the chairman. . . ." *Id.* at 1177; and by Professor David Welborn, relying on a survey of decisions at seven independent agencies in the pre-Sunshine era, that "[w]ith only a few exceptions, the number of times chairmen dissent during their tenure can be counted on the fingers of one hand. . . ." *Id.* at n.331. *See also* the Lawrence Article, *supra* note 14, noting that at the International Trade Commission (ITC), commissioners at one time did not circulate draft opinions to their colleagues before they were publicly released. A former acting ITC chair lamented that "I therefore do not know whether . . . [my colleagues'] arguments might have swayed me." Lawrence Article at 2-3. This practice at the ITC was not required by the Sunshine Act. According to Paul R. Bardos, assistant general counsel, USITC, "Currently, ITC Commissioners generally share a draft of each opinion with their colleagues before it is publicly released." E-mail to Stephen Klitzman, Feb. 23, 2005. Items are also circulated in writing at the EEOC and recirculated in the event of a divided vote, so that commissioners may change their votes if they wish. *See* REPORT OF THE EQUAL EMPLOYMENT OPPORTUNITY COMMISSION ON ITS ADMINISTRATION OF THE GOVERNMENT IN THE SUNSHINE ACT FOR CALENDAR YEAR 2000, attached to Letter of Sylvia Anderson, assistant director for legislative affairs, to the Honorable Richard Cheney (Feb. 6, 2001). At the Federal Election Commission, some matters are circulated in writing but may be placed on the agency's meeting agenda for discussion at the behest of a single
> *(continued on next page)*

There is clear evidence to support the view that while the Sunshine Act has reduced collegiality, it has, as a corollary, served to enhance the influence of agency chairmen and staff.[18] Yet, it is also clear that the

---

(continued from previous page)
commissioner. *See* REPORT OF THE FEDERAL ELECTION COMMISSION, IMPLEMENTATION OF THE GOVERNMENT IN THE SUNSHINE ACT, CALENDAR YEAR 2000, appended to Letter from Chairman Danny Lee McDonald to the Honorable Dick Cheney (July 25, 2001). *See also* p. 38 note 21 and p. 220 note 16, *supra*.

18. *See, e.g.,* PETER STRAUSS, ADMINISTRATIVE JUSTICE IN THE UNITED STATES 286-87 (2d ed. Carolina Academic Press 2002), citing the 1984 study for the Administrative Conference by Professors Welborn, Lyons, and Thomas and the 1995 Administrative Conference study by the Special Committee to Review the Government in the Sunshine Act. *See* Appendix G and Appendix I, *infra*. *See also* comments of former SEC commissioner Bevis Longstreth that "[t]he Act tends to shift power in a multi-headed agency from the collegial body to its chairman. . . . [T]he Chairman typically meets with staff or outsiders alone, formulating policy without the benefit of timely and meaningful comment from other members of the collegial body. . . . In particular, the chairman's meetings with the staff have a powerful tendency to shape the staff's responses and recommendations, which might well be different if it were possible for the other members to be present," quoted in GELLHORN & BYSE'S ADMINISTRATIVE LAW, CASES AND COMMENTS (Foundation Press 2003), at 764. A 1986 report prepared by the Congressional Research Service (CRS) for Senator Lawton Chiles attempting to rebut the findings of the 1984 ACUS study claimed that there was "no clear evidence to indicate that the quality of collegial decision making has deteriorated." The CRS Report stated that "it might be argued that because members are better prepared, the quality of collegial decision making has improved." Report of Rogelio Garcia, Analyst in American National Government, Congressional Research Service, to Honorable Lawton Chiles (May 8, 1986), at 11 (on file with the authors).

But cf. comments of NRC attorney Peter Crane: "If one believes that the multi-member agency is too unwieldy a format for effective management of a regulatory staff, then it can be argued that the Sunshine Act's diminution of agency collegiality has been a sound development, because it concentrates power in the hands of the Chairman and the staff. If, on the other hand, one attaches greater importance to the interaction of differing viewpoints among diverse Commissioners, then the Sunshine Act appears in a different light: as an inhibitor of communication and a barrier to the collegial exchanges that are the reason for creating multi-member agencies in the first place." *See* Letter from Peter Crane, attorney, Nuclear Regulatory Commission, to Gary Edles, general counsel, Administrative Conference of the United States, p. 10 (Feb. 6, 1995).

Sunshine Act can compromise the quality of agency deliberations.[19] Some agencies engage in so-called "round robin" meetings among agency members so that a quorum of the full membership is never present at the same time.[20] And there has been an increased use of notation voting at some agencies instead of holding open meetings.[21] Indeed, one observer who has noted the negative effects of the Government in the Sunshine Act expressed concerns that "neither openness nor collegiality values are being served by the present operation of the Act and . . . many of the open meetings under the Act are *pro forma* or overly rehearsed and scripted sessions that provide the public with less information than it deserves."[22] Comments we received from agency staff in response to our questionnaire on agency practice under the Sunshine Act confirmed their concern about the lack of collegiality.[23]

---

19. *See* comments of former FERC Commissioner Charles Stalon, *Conference: Harvard Electricity Policy Group: Regulatory Decisionmaking Reform,* 8 ADMIN. L.J. AM. U. 789, 798 (1995). He notes the "iron-clad" rule that "the staff shall not embarrass a Commissioner in public," whereas staff can and do correct or help shape a Commissioner's positions on issues in private meetings.
20. *Id.* at 796-97.
21. *See* chapter 2, *supra,* at notes 8-19 and accompanying text. A popular treatise refers to the testimony of a former Interstate Commerce Commission chairman that, starting in the late 1970s through the mid-1980s, his agency had not held regularly scheduled public meetings. Prodded by a Senate panel, the agency thereafter held two public meetings. RICHARD J. PIERCE, JR., SIDNEY A. SHAPIRO & PAUL R. VERKUIL, ADMINISTRATIVE LAW AND PROCESS 448 n.83 2d ed. (Foundation Press 1992).
22. Letter from Jeffrey S. Lubbers, former Research Director, ACUS, to Carl Rupert, Raleigh Research Director, Clean Water Fund of North Carolina (Nov. 21, 2001) (on file with the authors).
23. *See* Appendix B, *infra.* The problem of lack of collegiality is not unique to the federal government. *See, e.g.,* Kennedy v. Upper Milford Twp. Zoning Board, 834 A.2d 1104, 1115 (Pa. 2003) ("The necessity of collegiality to group decision-making of the highest quality is well established as is the degree to which collegiality and public deliberations are incompatible."). *See also* comments of former California Public Utilities Commissioner Daniel Fessler, *Conference: Harvard Electricity Policy Group: Regulatory Decisionmaking Reform,* 8 ADMIN. L.J. AM. U. 789, 801 (1995) (describing "a dysfunctional distance between myself and my four colleagues").

Professors Pierce, Shapiro, and Verkuil have succinctly summarized the effect of the Sunshine Act. They observe:

> Open decision-making is a concept that is attractive to those who seek to reform the administrative process. But it is not an unqualified virtue. The perverse effect of the concept upon the process of collegial decision-making is indicative of a more general problem. Notions of fairness (implicit in the openness principle) have the potential to trammel upon equally important principles of political accountability. At this time, the Sunshine Act has earned only two cheers.[24]

A more specific and colorful critique came from the pen of Professor Pierce, who was asked by the late K.C. Davis to write the third and subsequent editions of Davis's *Administrative Law Treatise:*

> GSA [the Government in the Sunshine Act], renders collegiality impossible in a collegial body that heads an agency. . . . Because of GSA, meetings among members of multi-member

---

24. RICHARD J. PIERCE, JR., SIDNEY A. SHAPIRO, PAUL R. VERKUIL, ADMINISTRATIVE LAW AND PROCESS 479 (Foundation Press 1999). Professor Richard Merrill notes, in the context of the Consumer Product Safety Commission, that the Sunshine Act has impeded the interaction between Commission members and the agency's technical staff. Richard A. Merrill, *CPSC Regulation of Cancer Risks in Consumer Products: 1972-1981*, 67 VA. L. REV. 1261, 1267-68 (1981). *See also* Toby McIntosh, *Where's the Sunshine? Closing the Door on Open Meetings*, 35 COLUMBIA JOURNALISM REVIEW 15, May/June 1996:

> Many reporters who cover regulatory agencies say that most open meetings now resemble scripted scenes. Prepared statements precede planned motions and predictable votes. Some say they go mostly for the occasional candid moments or flashes of debate that illuminate official thinking, or for staff briefings after a meeting is over.
> Sunshine Act critics argue that if the act is being ignored, and can't be enforced, it might as well be changed. Alan Morrison, for one, a Ralph Nader associate who has litigated many open-government cases and served on the ACUS [Sunshine Act reform] panel, has concluded that the act is 'a charade,' and he concurs in the panel's recommendations.

See pp. 212-13, *supra*, and pp. 227-28 and Appendix I, *infra*.

agencies are infrequent; such agencies often make important decisions through notational voting with *no* prior deliberation; and communications at open meetings are grossly distorted by the presence of the public. Commissioners are reluctant to express their true views for fear that they will expose their ignorance or uncertainty with respect to issues of fact, policy, and law. They attempt to disguise their uncertainties with stilted and contrived discussions that greatly impede the kind of frank exchange of views that is essential to high-quality decisionmaking by a collegial body.

It is peculiar that multimember agencies are singled out for a type of public exposure that inevitably impairs their ability to act in effective and informed ways. There can be no doubt that GSA has this effect. It is highly unlikely, for instance, that the Supreme Court would have issued its unanimous, bold decision in *Brown v. Board of Education,* 347 U.S. 483 (1954), if the Justices had been required to conduct the decade-long debate that preceded *Brown* only in public meetings. It is tempting to indulge the cynical assumption that Congress enacted GSA for the purpose of crippling multi-member agencies. Whatever may have been Congress's intent, GSA certainly has that effect (emphasis in original).[25]

---

25. PIERCE, *supra* p. 19 note 28, at 294, 296. For more favorable views of open meeting laws and the Sunshine Act, *see* Bensch, *supra* p. 33 note 8, citing, at 1513 n.3, Larry W. Thomas, *The Courts and the Implementation of the Government in the Sunshine Act*, 37 ADMIN. L. REV. 259-60 (1985) (arguing that "democracy is dependent upon a well informed citizenry, which in turn necessitates a firsthand view of the governmental decision-making process"); David A. Barrett, Note, *Facilitating Government Decision Making: Distinguishing Between Meetings and Nonmeetings Under the Federal Sunshine Act*, 66 TEX. L. REV. 1195-96 (1988) (discussing the benefits of open government to the democratic system); Maurice Baskin, Note, *The Federal "Government in the Sunshine Act": A Public Access Compromise*, 29 U. FLA. L. REV. 881-83 n.13 (1977) (citing historical sources for the idea that open government is an essential part of the democratic process); Susan T. Stephenson, Comment, *Government in the Sunshine Act: Opening Federal Agency Meetings*, 26 AM. U. L. REV. 154, 156-57 (1976) (reviewing the positive effects openness has on the democratic system). *See also* Bradley, *supra* note 14,

(continued on next page)

Definition of "Meeting"

The negative impact of the Sunshine Act on agency collegiality is intimately tied to the statutory definition of what constitutes a "meeting" of the agency. As discussed in chapter 1, the definition of "meeting" adopted in the Supreme Court's 1984 decision in *FCC v. ITT World Communications*,[26] which approved the approach taken in the *1978 Guide,* created a general dichotomy between deliberative sessions, on the one hand, and general or preliminary discussions that merely clarify issues or expose varying views, on the other. Although the Supreme Court's interpretation is now accepted doctrine relied on by agencies and remains the most authoritative exposition of the statute, its decision left open the precise circumstances in which agency members may or may not discuss issues in private. In their responses to our survey, the agencies have noted the uncertainties this creates. Agency general counsels understandably caution against discussion among members that may tilt toward deliberation. And at least some agency members are reluctant to test out preliminary ideas or reveal any lack of information or understanding in public sessions. Both of these tendencies impede collegial discussion. When coupled with a chairman's management of the agency's docket, they can have the effect of further centralizing control of the agency's decisional course in the hands of the chairman or staff. So any effort to enhance collegiality while retaining the essential objective of openness will inevitably entail some elucidation of the definition of "meeting."

(continued from previous page)
citing, at 475 n.7, 133 CONG. REC. 5177 (1987) (statement of Senator Lawton Chiles, author of the Sunshine legislation, on 10th anniversary of the Sunshine Act that "there is no common-sense reason why citizens shouldn't be able to watch how Government spends their money and reaches decisions affecting their businesses, their communities and their future. Citizens cannot hold Government officials accountable if they don't know what those officials are doing." *See also* Jessica M. Natale, *Exploring Virtual Legal Presence,* 1 J. HIGH TECH. L. 157-58 (2002) (stating that the primary purpose of open-meetings laws "is to maintain or restore confidence in the political process through disclosure").
26. 466 U.S. 463 (1984), *reversing* ITT World Communications v. FCC, 699 F.2d 1219 (D.C. Cir. 1983).

Both the American Bar Association[27] and the Administrative Conference of the United States have made useful recommendations concerning the definition of "meeting" and methods of improving collegiality without compromising openness. Shortly before it went out of business in 1995, an ACUS special committee took testimony from current and former agency officials and members of the private bar seeking to address the question of collegiality. Although there was no opportunity for the usual ACUS consideration by a full plenary session, the committee's recommendations were published. *See* Randolph May, *Reforming the Sunshine Act*, 49 Admin. L. Rev. 415 (1997). The committee was concerned that "the public is neither receiving the enhanced access to the governmental decisionmaking process that the Act envisioned, nor . . . is it receiving the benefit of better agency decisions through collegial decisionmaking."[28] The committee's central proposal was a five- to seven-year pilot program that would allow Sunshine Act agency members to meet in private as long as such meetings were memorialized and a "detailed summary" of the meeting was made public five days later "that would indicate the date, time, participants, subject matters discussed, and a review of the nature of the discussion," but without identifying positions of individual commissioners. In exchange for such relaxation of Sunshine Act requirements, a participating agency would have to agree to hold periodic open meetings at which members could address issues discussed in private sessions or items disposed of by notation voting and refrain, to the extent practicable, from using notation voting procedures for such matters. However, agencies would not be relieved of the Act's requirements to conduct votes and take other official actions on important substantive matters in public meetings (absent an applicable

---

27. *See* pp. 22-23, *supra,* and Appendix F, *infra,* for the ABA's February 1987 *Report and Recommendation* about Sunshine Act reform.
28. *Report and Recommendation by the Special Committee to Review the Government in the Sunshine Act, reprinted in* 49 ADMIN. L. REV. at 421, 424 (1997). (The ACUS Special Committee noted, for example, that "true collective decisionmaking does not occur at agency public meetings," that instead the Act "promotes inefficient practices" like seriatim, notation voting of agency items, which erodes collegial decision making and the ultimate quality of agency decisions. *Id.* at 423.) *See also* Appendix I, *infra.*

exemption). The Special Committee's Report and Recommendation are set out in full as Appendix I.

Appropriate congressional committees should closely examine the ABA's 1987 Report and Recommendation and the 1995 ACUS Special Committee Report and Recommendation and give them serious consideration.

FEES AND FEE WAIVERS

Because of the relationship between the FOIA and the Sunshine Act, some agencies consider requests for copies of transcripts, minutes, or recordings under FOIA procedures while others consider them under the Sunshine Act. *See generally* chapter 10, *supra*. It is not uncommon for agencies to require the public to obtain meeting transcripts from their transcription or reporting companies. However, the Sunshine Act, which predates the 1986 FOIA amendments, provides simply that the transcript, minutes, or recordings be furnished "to any person at the actual cost of duplication or transcription."[29] Similarly, section 11 of the Federal Advisory Committee Act provides that "[e]xcept where prohibited by contractual agreements entered into prior to . . . [1972], agencies . . . shall make available to any person, at actual cost of duplication, copies of transcripts of agency proceedings . . . ."[30] Those statutory provisions prohibit an agency or any reporting company from charging fees that include any profit element.

Moreover, the policy elements that underlie the 1986 amendments to the fee provisions of the FOIA[31] would appear to apply equally to the Sunshine Act. For fee purposes, the 1986 FOIA amendments create three categories of requester: commercial requesters; educational or noncommercial scientific institutions and representatives of the news media; and all others.[32] The FOIA fixes different fees for different categories of requester and provides that all requesters except commercial requesters under the FOIA receive the first two hours of search

---

29. 5 U.S.C. § 552b(f)(2).
30. 5 U.S.C. Appendix (2000 ed.).
31. Freedom of Information Reform Act of 1986, Pub. L. No. 99-570, 100 Stat. 3207.
32. 5 U.S.C. § 552(a)(4)(A)(ii).

time and the first 100 pages of material without charge.[33] In contrast with the Sunshine Act, commercial requesters under the FOIA can be charged for the time that it takes to review documents. On the other hand, the 1986 FOIA amendments provide that agencies furnish documents "without any charge or at a charge reduced below the fees established . . . [by agency regulation] if disclosure of the information is in the public interest because it is likely to contribute significantly to public understanding of the operations or activities of the government and is not primarily in the commercial interest of the requester."[34] The Sunshine Act contains no explicit fee waiver or reduction provision, although the legislative history indicates that waivers are encouraged. S. Rep., 32.

The 1986 FOIA amendments required the Office of Management and Budget to promulgate a uniform schedule of fees, and agencies are required to conform their fee regulations to these OMB guidelines.[35] The statute also required agencies to establish specific procedures and guidelines for determining when fees should be waived or reduced,[36] and the Department of Justice has issued fee waiver policy guidance to all departments and agencies.[37] Congress also particularized the "public interest" standard for fee waivers.[38] Congress has not reexamined the comparable provisions of the Sunshine Act. Although

---

33. 5 U.S.C. § 552(a)(4)(A)(iv)(II). In addressing the issue of costs to be charged when releasing the recording of a closed meeting, the Defense Nuclear Facilities Safety Board decided that a recording released at the Board's own initiative, and placed in its Public Reading Room, will be made available at the actual cost to the Board—$3. The Board does not consider requests for a waiver or reduction of fees for such recording. When it determines in response to an FOIA request that a recording should be released, it will consider any accompanying fee waiver or reduction request. 10 C.F.R. § 1703.103(b)(5) and 56 Fed. Reg. 21,259 (May 8, 1991).
34. 5 U.S.C. § 552(a)(4)(A)(iii).
35. 5 U.S.C. § 552(a)(4)(A)(i).
36. 100 Stat. 3207-49.
37. 28 C.F.R. § 16.11.
38. *See, e.g.,* Judicial Watch, Inc. v. Rossotti, 326 F.3d 1309 (D.C. Cir. 2003) (evaluating four nonexclusive fee waiver factors); and McClellan Ecological Seepage Situation v. Carlucci, 835 F.2d 1282, 1286 (9th Cir. 1987) (applying four fee waiver factors).

the Sunshine Act poses far fewer practical problems, it would appear consistent with overall congressional policy governing openness to divide Sunshine Act requesters by category as the FOIA now does, and explicitly provide for the elimination or reduction of fees in appropriate circumstances.[39]

ANNUAL REPORTING REQUIREMENT

In the Federal Reports Elimination and Sunset Act of 1995,[40] Congress deleted the requirement that agencies file annual reports outlining their activities under the Government in the Sunshine Act, effective May 2000. It did so in a curious way. Section 3002 of the statute modified the reporting requirement slightly. The new language appears at 5 U.S.C. § 552b(j), and reads as follows:

> (j) Each agency subject to the requirements of this section shall annually report to the Congress regarding the following:
> 1) The changes in the policies and procedures of the agency under this section that have occurred during the preceding 1-year period.
> 2) A tabulation of the number of meetings held, the exemptions applied to close meetings, and the days of public notice provided to close meetings.
> 3) A brief description of litigation or formal complaints concerning the implementation of this section by the agency[; and]
> 4) A brief explanation of any changes in law that have affected the responsibilities of the agency under this section.

However, Section 3003(a) of the statute provided for the termination, effective May 15, 2000, of those provisions of law that required the submittal to Congress of certain reports listed in House Document

---

39. As a practical matter, there should be no significant search time involved to uncover transcripts, recordings or minutes of meetings where, for one reason or another, an agency subsequently releases the contents of closed sessions. Moreover, in light of the case law interpreting the Sunshine Act provisions governing transcripts, agencies are not likely to have to undertake the type of intensive, line-by-line review of meeting transcripts required by FOIA. The principal cost is duplication.
40. Pub. L. No. 104-66, 109 Stat. 734, 31 U.S.C. § 1113 note.

No. 103-7. The Sunshine Act reports to Congress required by subsection 552(j) are listed on page 151 of House Document 103-7. So the reporting requirement, as modified, was in effect from 1995 until May 2000 but is no longer in effect, although 5 U.S.C. § 552b(j) remains on the statute books.[41]

Since 2000, despite the elimination of the annual report requirement, some Sunshine Act agencies have continued to submit annual reports to Congress.[42] In connection with the oversight review we believe Congress should undertake regarding the Sunshine Act, it should require at a minimum a one-time submission by each Sunshine Act agency of the information heretofore included in each agency's annual report submission. Based on its review of this information, Congress should then also consider whether or not to reenact the annual reporting requirement for all Sunshine Act agencies.[43]

---

41. See 5 U.S.C. § 552b note and 31 U.S.C. § 1113 note.
42. The following 21 agencies continued to submit annual Sunshine Act reports between 2000 and 2004, despite the May 15, 2000 expiration of the annual reporting requirement: Equal Employment Opportunity Commission, Export-Import Bank, Farm Credit Administration, Federal Communications Commission, Federal Election Commission, Federal Energy Regulatory Commission, Federal Housing Finance Board, Federal Maritime Commission, Federal Reserve System, Board of Governors, Federal Trade Commission, Foreign Claims Settlement Commission, Legal Services Corporation, Merit Systems Protection Board, Mississippi River Commission, National Credit Union Administration, National Science Board, Nuclear Regulatory Commission, Railroad Retirement Board, Securities and Exchange Commission, Tennessee Valley Authority, and U.S. Postal Service. Telephone interview of Tom Eisinger, former archivist, Senate Committee on Governmental Affairs, by Stephen Klitzman, Oct. 8, 2002; e-mail to Stephen Klitzman from Tom Eisinger, Oct. 24, 2002; and a fax from the current archivist of this Senate Committee, Elizabeth F. Butler, Nov. 16, 2004.
43. "Congress may one day decide to reinstate the Sunshine Act annual report requirement in order to undertake more effective oversight of Sunshine Act implementation, as well as to provide the public with an annual source of information about agency compliance with the Sunshine law." Telephone interview of Harold Relyea, specialist, American National Government, Congressional Research Service, by Stephen Klitzman, Oct. 8, 2002.

SELECTED BIBLIOGRAPHY

An Interpretive Guide to the Government in the Sunshine Act, Richard K. Berg & Stephen H. Klitzman, Administrative Conference of the United States, Office of the Chairman, June 1978 ("the leading commentary on the Act and its history," Peter L. Strauss, *Administrative Justice in the United States, Second Edition,* 285 n.48 (Carolina Academic Press 2002)).

Source Book

Government in the Sunshine Act – S.5 (Public Law 94-409) – Source Book: Legislative History, Texts, and Other Documents, 94th Cong., 2d Sess. (Comm. Print 1976). This "source book," a Joint Committee Print issued by the Senate and House Committees on Government Operations, is a definitive compilation of legislative history materials.

Law Review Articles, Annotations, Books, and Dissertations

David A. Barrett, *Facilitating Government Decision Making: Distinguishing Between Meetings and Nonmeetings Under the Federal Sunshine Act,* 66 Tex. L. Rev. 1195 (1988).

Jennifer A. Bensch, *Government in the Sunshine Act—Seventeen Years Later: Has Government Let the Sun Shine In?,* 61 Geo. Wash L. Rev. 1475 (1993).

Richard K. Berg, Stephen H. Klitzman & Gary J. Edles, *Government in the Sunshine Act (1976)* in "Major Acts of Congress," (Macmillan Reference USA 2002).

Kathy Bradley, Note, *Do You Feel the Sunshine? Government in the Sunshine Act: Its Objectives, Goals, and Effect on the FCC and You*, 49 Fed. Comm. L. J. 473 (1997).

Kevin W. Brown, Annotation, *What Is an 'Agency' Within the Meaning of Federal Sunshine Act (5 USC 552b)?*, 68 A.L.R. Fed. 842 (1984).

James H. Cawley, *Sunshine Law Overexposure and the Demise of Independent Agency Collegiality*, 1 Widener J. Pub. L. 43 (1992).

Eunice A. Eichelberger, Annotation, *Construction and Application of Exemptions Under 5 U.S.C.A. § 552(c) to Open Meeting Requirements of Sunshine Act*, 82 A.L.R. Fed. 465 (1987).

Eunice A. Eichelberger, Annotation, *Availability of Judicial Review of Agency Compliance with Sunshine Act (5 U.S.C.A. § 552b(g) and (h))*, 84 A.L.R. Fed. 251 (1987).

Harry A. Hammitt, David L. Sobel & Tiffany A. Stedman, eds., *Litigation Under the Federal Open Government Laws, 22nd Edition*, Chapter 22 - "Government in the Sunshine Act," pp. 403-20, 525-28 (2004).

Terry W. Hartle, *The Implementation of the Government in the Sunshine Act of 1976*, unpublished Ph.D. Dissertation, George Washington University, Washington, D.C. (1981).

Stephen H. Klitzman, *Government in the Sunshine Act—Nuts, Bolts, and Tacks: A Summary of Statutory Provisions, Judicial Interpretations, and Pending Issues*, 38 Fed. B. J. 114 (Fall 1979).

Michael A. Lawrence, *Finding Shade from the 'Government in the Sunshine Act': A Proposal to Permit Private Informal Background Discussions at the United States International Trade Commission*, 45 Cath. U. L. Rev. 1 (1995).

David Marblestone, *The Relationship Between the Government in the Sunshine Act and the Federal Advisory Committee Act*, 30 Fed. B. J. 65 (1977).

Randolph J. May, *Reforming the Sunshine Act,* 49 Admin. L. Rev. 415 (1997).

Randolph J. May, *Taming the Sunshine Act: Too Much Exposure Inhibits Collegial Decision Making,* Legal Times (Feb. 5, 1996), p. 24.

Jessica M. Natale, *Exploring Virtual Legal Presence: The Present and the Promise,* 1 J. High Tech L. 157 (2002).

James T. O'Reilly & Gracia M. Berg, *Stealth Caused by Sunshine: How Sunshine Act Interpretation Results in Less Information for the Public About the Decision-Making Process of the International Trade Commission,* 36 Harv. Int'l L.J 425 (Spring 1995).

Lisa A. Reilly, *The Government in the Sunshine Act and the Privacy Act,* 55 Geo. Wash. L. Rev. 955 (1987).

Robert W. Sloat, *Government in the Sunshine Act: A Danger of Overexposure,* 14 Harv. J. on Legis. 620 (1977).

Stuart M. Statler, *Let the Sunshine In?,* 67 A.B.A. J. 573 (1981).

Peter L. Strauss, Todd D. Rakoff & Cynthia R. Farina, *Gellhorn and Byse's Administrative Law—Cases and Comments, 10th Edition,* Chapter 6, Section 4, "Government in the Sunshine," pp. 762-66, 998-99 (Foundation Press 2003).

Susan T. Stephenson, Comment, *Government in the Sunshine Act: Opening Federal Agency Meetings,* 26 Amer. U. Int'l L. Rev. 154 (1976).

Larry W. Thomas, *The Courts and the Implementation of the Government in the Sunshine Act,* 37 Admin. L. Rev. 259 (1985).

Thomas H. Tucker, Commentary, *"Sunshine"—The Dubious New God,* 32 Admin. L. Rev. 537 (1980).

David M. Welborn, William Lyon, Larrry Thomas, *The Federal Government in the Sunshine Act and Agency Decisionmaking*, 20 Admin. & Soc'y 465 (1989).

Note, *Government in the Sunshine Act*, [1978] Ann. Surv. Am. L. 305.

Note, *The Government in the Sunshine Act—An Overview*, [1977] Duke L. J. 568.

Reports

Rogalia Garcia, *Public Access to Sunshine Act Meetings, 1979-1984*, Congressional Research Service, Library of Congress (May 8, 1986).

Government in the Sunshine Act: History and Recent Issues, Senate Committee on Governmental Affairs, S. Rep. No. 101-54, 101st Cong., 1st Sess. (1989).

Report and Recommendation by the Special Committee to Review the Government in the Sunshine Act, Administrative Conference of the United States, *reprinted in* 49 Admin. L. Rev. 421 (1997).

Congressional Hearings

Hearing before the Subcommittee on Government Management, Information, and Technology, Committee on Government Reform and Oversight, House of Representatives, 104th Cong., 2nd Sess., "Federal Information Policy Oversight," June 13, 1996, pp. 121, 137-54, 184-89, 232-54 (As of 2005, this is the most recent congressional hearing that received testimony on implementation of the Government in the Sunshine Act, but only as part of a broader oversight hearing on federal information policy.).

Hearing before the Subcommittee on Energy Conservation and Power, Committee on Energy and Commerce, House of Representatives, 99th Congress, 1st Sess., "Nuclear Regulatory Commission Sunshine Act Regulations," May 21, 1985, Serial No. 99-39.

Law Review Articles and Annotations on State Sunshine Laws

James Bowen, *Behind Closed Doors: Re-Examining the Tennessee Open Meetings Act and Its Inapplicability to the Tennessee General Assembly*, 35 Colum. J. L. & Soc. Probs. 133 (2002).

Brian J. Caveney, *More Sunshine in the Mountain State: The 1999 Amendments to the West Virginia Open Governmental Proceedings Act and Open Hospital Proceedings Act*, 102 W. Va. L. Rev. 131 (1999).

Meri K. Christensen, *Open and Public Meetings: Authorize Attorney General to Bring Civil or Criminal Actions to Enforce Georgia Open and Public Meetings Laws*, 15 Ga. St. U. L. Rev. 242 (1998).

Meri K. Christensen, *Open the Door to Access: A Proposal for Enforcement of Georgia's Open Meetings and Open Records Laws*, 15 Ga. St. U. L. Rev. 1075 (1999).

Christopher W. Deering, *Closing the Door on the Public's Right to Know: Alabama's Open Meetings Law After* Dunn v. Alabama State University Board of Trustees, 28 Cumb. L. Rev. 361 (1998).

Margaret S. DeWind, *The Wisconsin Supreme Court Lets the Sun Shine In: State v. Showers and the Wisconsin Open Meeting Law*, 1988 Wis. L. Rev. 827.

Nicholas Johnson, *Open Meetings and Closed Minds: Another Road to the Mountaintop*, 53 Drake L. Rev. 11 (Fall 2004).

Charles H. Koch, *Administrative Law and Practice, 2d ed.*, § 3.61, "State open meeting statutes," 306-09. (West Publishing Co. 1997).

John F. O'Connor and Michael J. Baratz, *Some Assembly Required: The Application of State Open Meeting Laws to E-Mail Correspondence*, 12 Geo. Mason L. Rev. 719 (2004).

Teresa Dale Pupillo, *The Changing Weather Forecast: Government in the Sunshine in the 1990s—An Analysis of State Sunshine Laws*, 71 Wash. U. L. Q. 1165 (1993).

Stephen Schaeffer, *Sunshine in Cyberspace? Electronic Deliberation and the Reach of Open Meeting Laws*, 48 St. Louis L. J. 755 (2004).

R.J. Shortridge, *The Incidental Matters Rule and Judicially Created Exceptions to the Nebraska Public Meetings Law: A Call to the Legislature in* Meyer v. Board of Regents, 510 N.W.2d 450 (Neb. App. 1993), 73 Neb. L. Rev. 456 (1994).

Lucille E. Turner, *Florida's Open Government Laws: No Exception for Attorney-Client Communications*, 13 Fla. St. U. L. Rev. 389 (1985).

APPENDICES

Appendix A
The Government in the Sunshine Act Pub. L. No. 94-409, 90 Stat. 1241 (94th Cong., 2d Sess., S.5, Sept. 13, 1976 as amended)   241

Appendix B
Letter-Questionnaire to Sunshine Act Agencies from the Authors, July, 2001   255

Appendix C
Government in the Sunshine Act: Agency Meeting Regulations in the *Code of Federal Regulations*   259

Appendix D
Definition of "Meeting" in the Government in the Sunshine Act: A Chronological Chart   264

Appendix E
Department of Justice Letter to Covered Agencies, April 19, 1977   266

Appendix F
American Bar Association, Report and Recommendation on the Government in the Sunshine Act, February 1987   269

Appendix G
Administrative Conference of the United States Report and Recommendation 84-3 Improvements in the Administration of the Government in the Sunshine Act 49 FR 29937 (1984)   283

Appendix H
Letter from Steven M.H. Wallman, Commissioner, Securities and Exchange Commission, to Thomasina Rogers, Chairperson, Administrative Conference of the United States, February 17, 1995   286

Appendix I
Administrative Conference of the United States, Report and Recommendation by the Special Committee to Review the Government in the Sunshine Act, as reprinted at 49 Admin. L. Rev. 421 (Spring 1997) 299

Appendix J
Memorandum for J. Virgil Mattingly, Jr., General Counsel for the Board of Governors of the Federal Reserve System Re: Permissibility of Federal Reserve Board Efforts to Control Access to Buildings and Open Meetings, from M. Edward Whelan III, Principal Deputy Assistant Attorney General, July 9, 2002 308

Appendix K
Letter from J. Virgil Mattingly, Jr., General Counsel for the Board of Governors of the Federal Reserve System, to Paul Colborn, Esq., Special Counsel, Department of Justice, Office of Legal Counsel, April 10, 2002 316

Appendix L
Federal Reserve Board, "A Guide to the Meetings of the Board of Governors of the Federal Reserve System," 2004 321

Appendix M
Sample Agency Meeting Notices 329

Appendix N
Sample Agency General Counsel Certification Forms 340

Appendix O
Letter from Michael K. Powell, Chairman, and Michael J. Copps, Commissioner, Federal Communications Commission, to the Honorable Ted Stevens, Chairman, Senate Committee on Commerce, Science and Transportation, February 2, 2005 343

Appendix A
The Government in the Sunshine Act
Pub. L. No. 94-409, 90 Stat. 1241
(94th Cong., 2d Sess., S.5, Sept. 13, 1976 as amended)

An Act

To provide that meetings of Government agencies shall be open to the public, and for other purposes.

Be it enacted by the Senate and House of *Representatives of the United States* of *America in Congress assembled,* That this Act may be cited as the "Government in the Sunshine Act". Government in the Sunshine Act, § 552b note. 5 USC 552b note.

DECLARATION OF POLICY

Sec. 2. It is hereby declared to be the policy of the United States that the public is entitled to the fullest practicable information regarding the decisionmaking processes of the Federal Government. It is the purpose of this Act to provide the public with such information while protecting the rights of individuals and the ability of the Government to carry out its responsibilities.

OPEN MEETINGS

Sec. 3. (a) Title 5, United States Code, is amended by adding after section 552a the following new section:

§ 552b. Open meetings 5 USC 552b. Definitions.

"(a) For purposes of this section—

"(1) the term 'agency' means any agency, as defined in section 2(e) of this title, headed by a collegial body composed of two or more individual members, a majority of whom are appointed to such position by the President with the advice and consent of the Senate, and any subdivision thereof authorized to act on behalf of the agency; 5 USC 552.

"(2) the term 'meeting' means the deliberations of at least the number of individual agency members required to take action on behalf of the agency where such deliberations determine or result in the joint conduct or disposition of official agency business, but does not include deliberations required or permitted by subsection (d) or (e); and

"(3) the term 'member' means an individual who belongs to a collegial body heading an agency.

"(b) Members shall not jointly conduct or dispose of agency business other than in accordance with this section. Except as provided in subsection (c), every portion of every meeting of an agency shall be open to public observation.

"(c) Except in a case where the agency finds that the public interest requires otherwise, the second sentence of subsection (b) shall not apply to any portion of an agency meeting, and the requirements of subsections (d) and (e) shall not apply to any information pertaining to such meeting otherwise required by this section to be disclosed to the public, where the agency properly determines that such portion or portions of its meeting or the disclosure of such information is likely to—

"(1) disclose matters that are (A) specifically authorized under criteria established by an Executive order to be kept secret in the interests of national defense or foreign policy and (B) in fact properly classified pursuant to such Executive order;

"(2) relate solely to the internal personnel rules and practices of an agency;

"(3) disclose matters specifically exempted from disclosure by statute (other than section 552 of this title), provided that such statute (A) requires that the matters be withheld from the public in such a manner as to leave no discretion on the issue, or (B) establishes particular criteria for withholding or refers to particular types of matters to be withheld;

"(4) disclose trade secrets and commercial or financial information obtained from a person and privileged or confidential;

"(5) involve accusing any person of a crime, or formally censuring any person;

"(6) disclose information of a personal nature where disclosure would constitute a clearly unwarranted invasion of personal privacy;

"(7) disclose investigatory records compiled for law enforcement purposes, or information which if written would be continued in such records, but only to the extent that the production of such records or information would (A) interfere with enforcement proceedings, (B) deprive a person of a right to a fair trial or an impartial adjudication, (C) constitute an unwarranted invasion of personal privacy, (D) disclose the identity of a confidential source and, in the course of a record compiled by a criminal law enforcement authority in the course of a criminal investigation, or by an agency conducting a lawful national security intelligence investigation, confidential information furnished only by the confidential source, (E) disclose investigative techniques and procedures, or (F) endanger the life or physical safety of law enforcement personnel;

"(8) disclose information contained in or related to examination, operating, or condition reports prepared by, on behalf of, or for the use of an agency responsible for the regulation or supervision of financial institutions;

"(9) disclose information the premature disclosure of which would—

"(A) in the case of an agency which regulates currencies, securities, commodities, or financial institutions, be likely to (i) lead to significant financial speculation in currencies, securities, or commodities, or (ii) significantly endanger the stability of any financial institution; or

"(B) in the case of any agency, be likely to significantly frustrate implementation of a proposed agency action, except that subparagraph (B) shall not apply in any instance where the agency has already disclosed to the public the content or nature of its proposed action, or where the agency is required by law to make such disclosure on its own initiative prior to taking final agency action on such proposal; or

"(10) specifically concern the agency's issuance of a subpoena, or the agency's participation in a civil action or proceeding, an action in a foreign court or international tribunal, or an arbitration, or the initiation, conduct, or disposition by the agency of a particular case of formal agency adjudication pursuant to the procedures in section 554 of this title or otherwise involving a determination on the record after opportunity for a hearing.

[5 USC 554.]

[Recorded voting.]

"(d)(1) Action under subsection (c) shall be taken only when a majority of the entire membership of the agency (as defined in subsection (a)(1)) votes to take such action. A separate vote of the agency members shall be taken with respect to each agency meeting a portion or portions of which are proposed to be closed to the public pursuant to subsection (c), or with respect to any information which is proposed to be withheld under subsection (c). A single vote may be taken with respect to a series of meetings, a portion or portions of which are proposed to be closed to the public, or with respect to any information concerning such series of meetings, so long as each meeting in such series involves the same particular matters and is scheduled to be held no more than thirty days after the initial meeting in such series. The vote of each agency member participating in such vote shall be recorded and no proxies shall be allowed.

"(2) Whenever any person whose interests may be directly affected by a portion of a meeting requests that the agency close such portion to the public for any of the reasons referred to in paragraph (5), (6), or (7) of subsection (c), the agency, upon request of any one of its members, shall vote by recorded vote whether to close such meeting.

"(3) Within one day of any vote taken pursuant to paragraph (1) or (2), the agency shall make publicly available a written copy of such vote reflecting the vote of each member on the question. If a portion of a meeting is to be closed to the public, the agency shall, within one day of the vote taken pursuant to paragraph (1) or (2) of this subsection, make publicly available a full written explanation of its action closing the portion together with a list of all persons expected to attend the meeting and their affiliation. *[Copies, availability.]*

"(4) Any agency, a majority of whose meetings may properly be closed to the public pursuant to paragraph (4), (8), (9)(A), or (10) of subsection (c), or any combination thereof, may provide by regulation for the closing of such meetings or potions thereof in the event that a majority of the members of the agency votes by recorded vote at the beginning of such meeting, or portion thereof, to close the exempt portion or portions of the meeting, and a copy of such vote, reflecting the vote of each member on the question, is made available to the public. The provisions of paragraphs (1), (2), and (3) of this subsection and subsection (e) shall not apply to any portion of the meeting to which such regulations apply: *Provided*, That the agency shall, except to the extent that such information is exempt from disclosure under the provisions of subsection (c), provide the public with public announcement of the time, place, and subject matter of the meeting and of each portion thereof at the earliest practicable time. *[Meeting closure, regulation. Public announcement.]*

"(e)(1) In the case of each meeting, the agency shall make public announcement, at least one week before the meeting, of the time, place, and subject matter of the meeting, whether it is to be open or closed to the public, and the name and phone number of the official designated by the agency to respond to requests for information about the meeting. Such announcement shall be made unless a majority of the members of the agency determines by a recorded vote that agency business requires that such meeting be called at an earlier date, in which case the agency shall make public announcement of the time, place, and subject matter of such meeting, and whether open or closed to the public, at the earliest practicable time. *[Scheduling, public announcement.]*

Scheduling changes, public announcement.

"(2) The time or place of the meeting may be changed following the public announcement required by paragraph (1) only if the agency publicly announces such change at the earliest practicable time. The subject matter of a meeting, or the determination of the agency to open or close a meeting, or portion of a meeting, to the public, may be changed following the public announcement required by this subsection only if (A) a majority of the entire membership of the agency determines by a recorded vote that agency business so requires and that no earlier announcement of the change was possible, and (B) the agency publicly announces such change and the vote of each member upon such change at the earliest practicable time.

Scheduling notice, publication in Federal Register.

"(3) Immediately following each public announcement required by this subsection, notice of the time, place, and subject matter of a meeting, whether the meeting is open or closed, any change in one of the preceding, and the name and phone number of the official designated by the agency to respond to requests for information about the meeting, shall also be submitted for publication in the Federal Register.

Closed meetings, certification.

"(f)(1) For every meeting closed pursuant to paragraphs (1) through (10) of subsection (c), the General Counsel or chief legal officer of the agency shall publicly certify that, in his or her opinion, the meeting may be closed to the public and shall state each relevant exemptive provision. A copy of such certification, together with a statement from the presiding officer of the meeting setting forth the time and place of the meeting, and the persons present, shall be retained by the agency. The agency shall maintain a complete transcript or electronic recording adequate to record fully the proceedings of each meeting, or portion of a meeting, closed to the public, except that in the case of a meeting, or portion of a meeting, closed to the public pursuant to paragraph (8), (9)(A), or (10) of subsection (c), the agency shall maintain either such a transcript or recording, or a set of minutes. Such minutes shall fully and clearly describe all matters discussed and shall provide a full and accurate summary of any actions taken, and the reasons therefor, including a description of each of the views expressed on any item and the

Transcripts, recordings or minutes.

record of any rollcall vote (reflecting the vote of each member on the question). All documents considered in connection with any action shall be identified in such minutes.

"(2) The agency shall make promptly available to the public, in a place easily accessible to the public, the transcript, electronic recording, or minutes (as required by paragraph (1)) of the discussion of any item on the agenda, or of any item of the testimony of any witness received at the meeting, except for such item or items of such discussion or testimony as the agency determines to contain information which may be withheld under subsection (c). Copies of such transcript, or minutes, or a transcription of such recording disclosing the identity of each speaker, shall be furnished to any person at the actual cost of duplication or transcription. The agency shall maintain a complete verbatim copy of the transcript, a complete copy of the minutes, or a complete electronic recording of each meeting, or portion of a meeting, closed to the public, for a period of at least two years after such meeting, or until one year after the conclusion of any agency proceeding with respect to which the meeting or portion was held, whichever occurs later.

"(g) Each agency subject to the requirements of this section shall, within 180 days after the date of enactment of this section, following consultation with the Office of the Chairman of the Administrative Conference of the United States and published notice in the Federal Register of at least thirty days and opportunity for written comment by any person, promulgate regulations to implement the requirements of subsections (b) through (f) of this section. Any person may bring a proceeding in the United States District Court for the District of Columbia to require an agency to promulgate such regulations if such agency has not promulgated such regulations within the time period specified herein. Subject to any limitations of time provided by law, any person may bring a proceeding in the United States Court of Appeals for the District of Columbia to set aside agency regulations issued pursuant to this subsection that are not in accord with the requirements of subsections (b) through (f) of this section

Public availability.

Retention.

Regulations, Notice, publication in Federal Register.

Judicial proceeding.

and to require the promulgation of regulations that are in accord with such subsections.

"(h)(1) The district courts of the United States shall have jurisdiction to enforce the requirements of subsections (b) through (f) of this section by declaratory judgment, injunctive relief, or other relief as may be appropriate. Such actions may be brought by any person against an agency prior to, or within sixty days after, the meeting out of which the violation of this section arises, except that if public announcement of such meeting is not initially provided by the agency in accordance with the requirements of this section, such action may be instituted pursuant to this section at any time prior to sixty days after any public announcement of such meeting. Such actions may be brought in the district court of the United States for the district in which the agency meeting is held or in which the agency in question has its headquarters, or in the District Court for the District of Columbia. In such actions a defendant shall serve his answer within thirty days after the service of the complaint. The burden is on the defendant to sustain his action. In deciding such cases the court may examine in camera any portion of the transcript, electronic recording, or minutes of a meeting closed to the public, and may take such additional evidence as it deems necessary. The court, having due regard for orderly administration and the public interest, as well as the interests of the parties, may grant such equitable relief as it deems appropriate, including granting an injunction against future violations of this section or ordering the agency to make available to the public such portion of the transcript, recording, or minutes of a meeting as is not authorized to be withheld under subsection (c) of this section.

"(2) Any Federal court otherwise authorized by law to review agency action may, at the application of any person properly participating in the proceeding pursuant to other applicable law, inquire into violations by the agency of the requirements of this section and afford such relief as it deems appropriate. Nothing in this section authorizes any Federal court having jurisdiction solely on the basis of paragraph (1) to set aside, enjoin, or invalidate any agency action (other than an action to close a meeting or to withhold information under this section) taken or discussed at any agency meeting out of which the violation of this section arose.

"(i) The court may assess against any party reasonable attorney fees and other litigation costs reasonably incurred by any other party who substantially prevails in any action brought in accordance with the provisions of subsection (g) or (h) of this section, except that costs may be assessed against the plaintiff only where the court finds that the suit was initiated by the plaintiff primarily for frivolous or dilatory purposes. In the case of assessment of costs against an agency, the costs may be assessed by the court against the United States. *Litigation costs, assessment.*

"(j) Each agency subject to the requirements of this section shall annually report to Congress regarding the following: *Report to Congress.*

(1) The changes in the policies and procedures of the agency under this section that have occurred during the preceding 1-year period.

(2) A tabulation of the number of meetings held, the exemptions applied to close meetings, and the days of public notice provided to close meetings.

(3) A brief description of litigation or formal complaints concerning the implementation of this section by the agency.

(4) A brief explanation of any changes in law that have affected the responsibilities of the agency under this section.

"(k) Nothing herein expands or limits the present rights of any person under section 552 of this title, except that the exemptions set forth in subsection (c) of this section shall govern in the case of any request made pursuant to section 552 to copy or inspect the transcripts, recordings, or minutes described in subsection (f) of this section. The requirements of chapter 33 of title 44, United States Code, shall not apply to the transcripts, recordings, and minutes described in subsection (f) of this section. *5 USC 552.*

44 USC 3301.

"(l) This section does not constitute authority to withhold any information from Congress, and does not authorize the closing of any agency meeting or portion thereof required by any other provision of law to be open.

"(m) Nothing in this section authorizes any agency to withhold from any individual any record, including transcripts, recordings, or minutes required by this section, which is otherwise accessible to such individual under section 552a of this title.".

(b) The chapter analysis of chapter 5 of title 5, United States Code, is amended by inserting:
"552b. Open meetings."
immediately below:
"552a. Records about individuals.".

EX PARTE COMMUNICATIONS

Sec. 4. (a) Section 557 of title 5, United States Code, is amended by adding at the end thereof the following new subsection:

"(d)(1) In any agency proceeding which is subject to subsection (a) of this section, except to the extent required for the disposition of ex parte matters as authorized by law—

"(A) no interested person outside the agency shall make or knowingly cause to be made to any member of the body comprising the agency, administrative law judge, or other employee who is or may reasonably be expected to be involved in the decisional process of the proceeding, an ex parte communication relevant to the merits of the proceeding;

"(B) no member of the body comprising the agency, administrative law judge, or other employee who is or may reasonably be expected to be involved in the decisional process of the proceeding, shall make or knowingly cause to be made to any interested person outside the agency an ex parte communication relevant to the merits of the proceeding;

"(C) a member of the body comprising the agency, administrative law judge, or other employee who is or may reasonably be expected to be involved in the decisional process of such proceeding who receives, or who makes or knowingly causes to be made, a communication prohibited by this subsection shall place on the public record of the proceeding:

"(i) all such written communications;

"(ii) memoranda stating the substance of all such oral communications; and

"(iii) all written responses, and memoranda stating the substance of all oral responses, to the materials described in clauses (i) and (ii) of this subparagraph;

"(D) upon receipt of a communication knowingly made or knowingly caused to be made by a party in violation of this subsection, the agency, administrative law judge, or other employee presiding at the hearing may, to the extent consistent with the interests of justice and the policy of the underlying statutes, require the party to show cause why his claim or interest in the proceeding should not be dismissed, denied, disregarded, or otherwise adversely affected on account of such violation; and

"(E) the prohibitions of this subsection shall apply beginning at such time as the agency may designate, but in no case shall they begin to apply later than the time at which a proceeding is noticed for hearing unless the person responsible for the communication has knowledge that it will be noticed, in which case the prohibitions shall apply beginning at the time of his acquisition of such knowledge.

Applicability.

(2) This subsection does not constitute authority to withhold information from Congress.".

(b) Section 551 of title 5, United States Code, is amended—

(1) by striking out "and" at the end of paragraph (12);

(2) by striking out the "act" at the end of paragraph (13) and inserting in lieu thereof "act; and"; and

(3) by adding at the end thereof the following new paragraph:

"Ex parte communication."

"(14) 'ex parte communication' means an oral or written communication not on the public record with respect to which reasonable prior notice to all parties is not given, but it shall not include requests for status reports on any matter or proceeding covered by this subchapter.".

(c) Section 556(d) of title 5, United States Code, is amended by inserting between the third and fourth sentences thereof the following new sentence: "The agency may, to the extent consistent with the interests of justice and the policy of the underlying statutes administered by the agency, consider a violation of section 557(d) of this title sufficient grounds for a decision adverse to a party who has knowingly committed such violation or knowingly caused such violation to occur.".

5 USC 557.

CONFORMING AMENDMENTS

Sec. 5. (a) Section 410(b)(1) of title 39, United States Code, is amended by inserting after "Section 552 (public information)," the words "section 552a (records about individuals), section 552b (open meetings).".

(b) Section 552(b)(3) of title 5, United States Code, is amended to read as follows:

"(3) specifically exempted from disclosure by statute (other than section 552b of this title), provided that such statute (A) requires that the matters be withheld from the public in such a manner as to leave no discretion on the issue, or (B) establishes particular criteria for withholding or refers to particular types of matters to be withheld;".

5 USC app. I.

(c) Subsection (d) of section 10 of the Federal Advisory Committee Act is amended by striking out the first sentence and inserting in lieu thereof the following: "Subsections (a)(1) and (a)(3) of this section shall not apply to any portion of an

Appendices 253

advisory committee meeting where the President, or the head of the agency to which the advisory committee reports, determines that such portion of such meeting may be closed to the public in accordance with subsection (c) of section 552b of title 5, United States Code.".

EFFECTIVE DATE

Sec. 6. (a) Except as provided in subsection (b) of this section, the provisions of this Act shall take effect 180 days after the date of its enactment.

5 USC 552b note.

(b) Subsection (g) of section 552b of title 5, United States Code, as added by section 3(a) of this Act, shall take effect upon enactment.

Approved September 13, 1976.

LEGISLATIVE HISTORY:

HOUSE REPORTS: No. 94-880, Pt. I and No. 94-880, Pt. 2, accompanying H.R. 11656 (Comm. on Government Operations) and No. 94-1441 (Comm. of Conference).

SENATE REPORTS: No. 94-354 (Comm. on Government Operations), No. 94-381 (Comm. on Rules and Administration) and No. 94-1178 (Comm. of Conference).

CONGRESSIONAL RECORD:
- Vol. 121 (1975): Nov. 5, 6, considered and passed Senate.
- Vol. 122 (1976): July 28, considered and passed House, amended, in lieu of H.R. 11656.
  Aug. 31, House and Senate agreed to conference report.

WEEKLY COMPILATION OF PRESIDENTIAL DOCUMENTS:
  Vol. 12, No. 38 (1976); Sept. 13, Presidential statement.

AMENDMENTS

1995 Congress, in enacting the Federal Reports Elimination and Sunset Act of 1995, Pub. L. No. 104-66, 109 Stat. 734, altered requirements under subsection (j) regarding the reporting requirements of agencies, but also provided for the termination of annual Sunshine Act reports to Congress, effective May 15, 2000. Prior to amendment, subsec. (j) read as follows: "Each agency subject to the requirements of this section shall annually report to Congress regarding its compliance with such requirements, including a tabulation of the total number of agency meetings open to the public, the total number of meetings closed to the public, the reasons for closing such meetings, and a description of any litigation brought against the agency under this section, including any costs assessed against the agency in such litigation (whether or not paid by the agency)."

See 5 U.S.C. §552 note and 31 U.S.C. §1113 note, and pp. 230-31, *supra*.

Appendix B
Letter-Questionnaire to Sunshine Act Agencies
from the Authors, July, 2001

AMERICAN BAR ASSOCIATION

Defending Liberty
Pursuing Justice

Section of Administrative Law and
Regulatory Practice
740 15th Street NW
Washington, DC 20005-1022
(202) 662-1528
Fax: (202) 662-1529
www.abanet.org/adminlaw

July 2, 2001

United States Postal Service
Board of Governors
MaryAnne Gibbons, General Counsel and Vice President
475 L'Enfant Plaza West, S.W.
Washington, D.C. 20260-0010

Dear Ms. Gibbons:

In June 1978, the Administrative Conference of the United States (ACUS) published *An Interpretive Guide to the Government in the Sunshine Act* to assist agencies in complying with the Sunshine Act enacted by Congress in 1976.

Twenty-three years have elapsed since the publication of the *Guide*. It has long been relied upon and cited as a leading authority on the Sunshine Act by the Supreme Court, other courts, commentators, and agencies. In 1995, ACUS commissioned a revised and updated Second Edition of the *Guide* in the light of subsequent judicial and administrative authority and practice. However, Congress abolished ACUS in October 1995, and the project was never completed. This year, under the sponsorship of the Section on Administrative Law and Regulatory Practice, American Bar Association, we are reviving this project, and are writing to seek your assistance.

The undersigned, Richard K. Berg and Stephen H. Klitzman, are the co-authors of the 1978 edition of the *Guide.* (Mr. Berg is the former Executive Secretary and General Counsel of ACUS, and Mr. Klitzman is a former ACUS Staff Attorney.) We are joined in this Second Edition project by Gary J. Edles, former ACUS General Counsel and currently Professor of Law, Washington College of Law, the American University, and Visiting Professor of Law at the University of Hull Law School in England.

We intend the Second Edition of the *Guide,* like its predecessor, to be an objective compilation of legal authority and administrative practice. To facilitate this project, we are seeking from each agency the following information:

1. Does your agency generally conduct its meetings in public? If so, does it do so because (i) it is an agency that meets the definition of "agency" contained in the Government in the Sunshine Act, 5 USC Sec. 552b(a), (ii) it is subject to the Sunshine Act as a result of separate legislation, or (iii) it complies with the Sunshine Act voluntarily?

2. Please cite your current Sunshine regulations. What major changes have been made in your agency's Sunshine regulations since their initial adoption, and why were they made? (Please omit merely housekeeping changes, such as change of addresses, meeting days, designations of responsible officials, etc.)

3. What significant changes in Sunshine procedures have you made which are not reflected in your regulations?

4. How, if at all, has the Sunshine Act impacted your agency's use of notational voting and the number of open meetings held by your agency?

5. How, if at all, has the Sunshine Act impacted your Members' use of e-mail to communicate with each other on official agency business?

6. Has your agency been involved in any litigation under the Sunshine Act? Please list and briefly describe the cases.

7. What legal, administrative, or other practical problems does your agency encounter or perceive in its implementation of the Sunshine Act? Has your agency ever proposed or supported legislation to address these problems? If so, please describe the legislation, and provide us with any related testimony or other public communications with Congress about these Sunshine-related problems.

8. Do you have any recommendations of Sunshine Act procedures which other agencies might find useful?

9. Do you have recommendations of any Sunshine Act reforms?

10. What features in the present *Guide* have you found particularly useful and what would you like to see improved?

11. Please designate a staff member familiar with your agency's Sunshine Act implementation whom we can contact with additional questions.

To assist you in your response, we enclose a copy of the response your agency submitted to a similar questionnaire sent by ACUS in the 1995 project.

Please send your response by September 10, 2001, to:

Stephen H. Klitzman
Associate Director, Office of Legislative and Intergovernmental Affairs
Federal Communications Commission
Room 8C-468
445 12th St., S.W.
Washington, D.C. 20554

You can also e-mail your response to sklitzma@fcc.gov.

Finally, if you have any questions, please call Steve Klitzman at 202/418-1913.

We look forward to hearing from you.

>Sincerely,
>
>Richard K. Berg
>
>Stephen H. Klitzman
>
>Gary J. Edles

Cc: Fred Eggleston, Attorney
     Room 6626

Appendix C
Government in the Sunshine Act:
Agency Meeting Regulations
in the *Code of Federal Regulations**

1. Advisory Board for Cuba Broadcasting — None[1]
2. African Development Foundation — 22 CFR 1500.1 et seq.
3. Barry Goldwater Scholarship and Excellence in Education Foundation — None[2]
4. Broadcasting Board of Governors — 22 CFR 507.1 et seq.
5. Chemical Safety and Hazard Investigation Board — 40 CFR 1603.1 et seq.
6. Commission of Fine Arts — 45 CFR 2102.1 et seq.[3]
7. Commodity Credit Corporation (Board of Directors) — 7 CFR 1409.1 et seq.
8. Commodity Futures Trading Commission — 17 CFR 147.1 et seq.
9. Consumer Product Safety Commission — 16 CFR 1013.1 et seq.
10. Copyright Office, Library of Congress (Copyright Arbitration Royalty Panels) — 37 CFR 251.11 et seq.[4]

---

* Unless otherwise noted, agencies meet the statutory definition of 5 U.S.C. 552b(a)(1), *i.e.*, they are "a collegial body composed of two or more individual members, a majority of whom are appointed to such position by the President with the advice and consent of the Senate . . .." Current through December 2004.

1. Agency meets statutory definition. See 22 U.S.C. 1465c(a). See also 66 FR 15073 (2001).
2. Agency meets statutory definition. Conducts meetings pursuant to the statute only. See, e.g., 68 FR 8490 (2003).
3. Members are not subject to Senate confirmation. See 40 U.S.C. 9101. Complies voluntarily with the Sunshine Act.
4. A legislative branch agency. Proceedings subject to provisions of the Administrative Procedure Act pursuant to 17 U.S.C. 802(c).

11.	Corporation for National and Community Service	45 CFR 2505.1 et seq.
12.	Council on Environmental Quality	40 CFR 1517.1 et seq.
13.	Delaware River Basin Commission	None[5]
14.	Defense Nuclear Facilities Safety Board	10 CFR 1704.1 et seq.
15.	Equal Employment Opportunity Commission	29 CFR 1612.1 et seq.
16.	Export-Import Bank of the United States (Board of Directors)	12 CFR 407.1 et seq.
17.	Farm Credit Administration (Office of the Board)	12 CFR 604.400 et seq.
18.	Federal Communications Commission	47 CFR 0.601 et seq.
19.	Federal Deposit Insurance Corporation (Board of Directors)	12 CFR 311.1 et seq.
20.	Federal Election Commission	11 CFR 2.1 et seq.
21.	Federal Energy Regulatory Commission	18 CFR 375.201 et seq.
22.	Federal Housing Finance Board	12 CFR 912.1 et seq.
23.	Federal Labor Relations Authority	5 CFR 2413.1 et seq.
24.	Federal Maritime Commission	46 CFR 503.70 et seq.
25.	Federal Mine Safety and Health Review Commission	29 CFR 270 1.1 et seq.

---

5. Commission created by Compact of states of Delaware, New Jersey, New York and Pennsylvania, and the federal government. Pub. L. No. 87-328, 75 Stat. 688. Section 14.4(a) of the Compact provides that "[a]ll meetings . . . shall be open to the public." The Commission has no regulations but issues notices and all meetings are open to the public. See also 18 CFR 401.105, which provides for public access to official minutes of Commission meetings.

Appendices

26.	Federal Open Market Committee	12 CFR 281.2[6]
27.	Federal Reserve System (Board of Governors)	12 CFR 26lb.1 et seq.
28.	Federal Retirement Thrift Investment Board	5 CFR 1632.1 et seq.
29.	Federal Trade Commission	16 CFR 4.9-4.11, 4.14-4.15
30.	Foreign Claims Settlement Commission	45 CFR 503.20 et seq.
31.	Foreign Service Labor Relations Board	22 CFR 1413.1 et seq.[7]
32.	Harry S. Truman Scholarship Foundation (Board of Trustees)	45 CFR 1802.1 et seq
33.	Inter-American Foundation	22 CFR 1004.1 et seq.
34.	Legal Services Corporation	45 CFR 1622.1 et seq.
35.	Marine Mammal Commission	50 CFR 560.1 et seq.
36.	Merit Systems Protection Board	5 CFR 1206.1 et. seq.
37.	Millennium Challenge Corporation	None[8]
38.	Mississippi River Commission	33 CFR 209.50
39.	National Commission on Libraries and Information Science	45 CFR 1703.102 et seq.

---

6. Committee is an independent statutory body composed of the 7 members of the Board of Governors of the Federal Reserve System and 5 representatives of the Federal Reserve Banks and is not a Sunshine Act agency within the meaning of 5 U.S.C. 552b. See 12 U.S.C. 263. All meetings are closed but the agency indicates that its "procedures and timing of public disclosure" are conducted "in accordance with the spirit of the Sunshine Act." See 12 CFR 281.2.
7. Three-member board composed of chairman of Federal Labor Relations Authority and two members appointed by the chairman and is not a Sunshine Act agency within the meaning of 5 U.S.C. 552b. See 22 USC 4106. Complies voluntarily with the Sunshine Act.
8. Agency meets statutory definition. See 22 U.S.C. 7703. Meetings held pursuant to Government in the Sunshine Act. See Section 13 of Corporation Bylaws. See also 69 FR 41852 (2004).

262 *An Interpretive Guide to the Government in the Sunshine Act, 2d Ed.*

40.	National Council on Disability	None[9]
41.	National Council on the Arts	None[10]
42.	National Credit Union Administration	12 CFR 791.1 et seq.
43.	National Labor Relations Board	29 CFR 102.137 et seq.
44.	National Mediation Board	29 CFR 1209.04 et seq.
45.	National Museum Services Board	45 CFR 1180.80 et seq.
46.	National Science Foundation (National Science Board)	45 CFR 614.1 et seq.
47.	National Transportation Safety Board	49 CFR 804.1 et seq.
48.	Neighborhood Reinvestment Corporation (Board of Directors)	24 CFR 4100.2[11]
49.	Nuclear Regulatory Commission	10 CFR 9.1 10 CFR 9.100 et seq.
50.	Occupational Safety and Health Review Commission	29 CFR 2203.1 et seq.
51.	Overseas Private Investment Corporation (Board of Directors)	22 CFR 708.1 et seq.
52.	Pacific Northwest Electric Power and Conservation Planning Council	None[12]
53.	Postal Rate Commission	39 CFR 3001.43

---

9. Agency meets statutory definition. See 9 U.S.C. 780(a)(1). Conducts meetings pursuant to the statute only. See, e.g., 69 FR 62917 (2004).
10. Agency meets statutory definition. See 20 U.S.C. 955. However, it operates as both a Sunshine Act agency and a Federal Advisory Committee and issues notices of meetings pursuant to the Federal Advisory Committee Act. See, e.g., 67 FR 41278 (2002).
11. Board of Directors composed of officials of other government agencies. See 42 U.S.C. 8103(a). Proceedings subject to provisions of the Sunshine Act pursuant to 42 U.S.C. 8103(i).
12. Commission composed of representatives of states of Idaho, Montana, Oregon and Washington. Pub. L. No. 96-501, 94 Stat. 2697. Meetings subject to the same open meeting requirements as are applicable to the Federal Energy Regulatory Commission. See 16 U.S.C. 839b (a) (4).

Appendices 263

54.	Railroad Retirement Board	20 CFR 200.6
55.	Rural Telephone Bank	7 CFR 1600.1 et seq.[13]
56.	Securities and Exchange Commission	17 CFR 200.400 et seq.
57.	State Justice Institute	None[14]
58.	Surface Transportation Board	49 CFR 1012.1 et seq.
59.	Susquehanna River Basin Commission	None[15]
60.	Tennessee Valley Authority (Board of Directors)	18 CFR 1301.41 et seq.
61.	Uniformed Services University of the Health Sciences (Board of Regents)	32 CFR 242a.1 et seq.
62.	United States Institute of Peace	None[16]
63.	United States Postal Service (Board of Governors)	39 CFR 7.1 et seq.
64.	U.S. Commission on Civil Rights	45 CFR 702.50 et seq.[17]
65.	U.S. Election Assistance Commission	None[18]
66.	U.S. International Trade Commission	19 CFR 201.34 et seq.
67.	U.S. Parole Commission	28 CFR 16.200 et seq.

---

13. Members are not subject to Senate confirmation. See 7 U.S.C. 945(b). Proceedings subject to provisions of the Sunshine Act pursuant to 7 U.S.C. 945(j).
14. Agency meets statutory definition. See 42 U.S.C. 10703(a). Conducts meetings pursuant to the statute only. See, e.g., 68 FR 43415 (2003).
15. Commission created by Compact of states of New York, Maryland and Pennsylvania, and the federal government. Pub. L. 91-575, 84 Stat. 1509. Section 15.4(a) of the Compact provides that "[a]ll meetings of the Commission shall be open to the public." Commission issues notices of its meetings 20 days in advance by posting a notice at its offices and publication in newspapers. See also 18 CFR 801.2(b)(6), providing that the Commission's regular meetings are announced in advance and open to the public.
16. Agency meets statutory definition. See 22 U.S.C. 4605(h)(3). See also 69 FR 62935 (2004).
17. Majority of members not appointed by the President. Members are not subject to Senate confirmation. See 42 U.S.C. 1975. Complies voluntarily with the Sunshine Act.
18. Agency meets statutory definition. See 42 U.S.C. 15323. Conducts meetings pursuant to the statute only. See, e.g., 69 FR 65415 (2004).

Appendix D
Definition of "Meeting" in the Government in the Sunshine Act: Pub. L. No. 94-409, 90 Stat. 1241, 5 U.S.C. §552b: A Chronological Chart

A. Senate
1. S.260, §201(a) as introduced Jan. 9, 1973 (Chiles): No definition.
2. S.5, §201(a) as introduced Jan. 15, 1975 (Chiles):
". . . any procedure by which official agency business is considered or discussed by at least the number of agency members (or of members of a subdivision of the agency authorized to take action on behalf of the agency), required to take action on behalf of the agency. . ."
3. S.5, §201(a) Committee Print No. 2, May 2, 1975:
". . . a gathering, electronically or in person, of at least the number of agency members required to take action on behalf of the agency where such gathering results in the consideration or disposition of official agency business. . ."
4. S.5, §201(a) Committee Print No. 3, June 18, 1975:
". . . a gathering, electronically or in person, of at least the number of agency members required to take action on behalf of the agency where such gathering results in the joint consideration or disposition of official agency business. Informal discussions between only two members of an agency which do not result in the disposition of official agency business shall not constitute a meeting for purposes of this section. . ."
5. S.5, §201(a) as reported July 31, 1975:
". . . the deliberations of at least the number of individual agency members required to take action on behalf of the agency where such deliberations concern the joint conduct or disposition of official agency business. . ."
6. S.5, §4(a) as passed Nov. 6, 1975: Same as 5. above.

B. House, Conference and Final Enactment

7. H.R. 9868, §4(a) as introduced Sept. 26, 1975 (Fascell):
   ". . . the deliberations of at least the number of individual agency members required to take action on behalf of the agency where such deliberations concern the joint conduct or disposition of official agency business . . ."
8. H.R. 10315, §552b(a)(2) as introduced Oct. 22, 1975 (Abzug):
   ". . . the deliberations of at least the number of individual agency members required to take action on behalf of the agency where such deliberations concern the joint conduct or disposition of official agency business, but does not include deliberations solely for the purpose of taking an action required or permitted by this section . . ."
9. H.R. 11656, §552b(a)(2) as reported March 8, 1976 (Cmte. on Govt. Ops.):
   ". . . the deliberations of at least the number of individual agency members required to take action on behalf of the agency where such deliberations concern the joint conduct or disposition of agency business . . ."
10. H.R. 11656, §552b(a)(2) as reported April 8, 1976 (Cmte. on Judiciary):
    ". . . an assembly or simultaneous communication concerning the joint conduct or disposition of agency business by two or more, but at least the number of individual agency members required to take action on behalf of the agency, but does not include meetings required or permitted by subsection (d) . . ."
11. H.R. 11656, §552b(a)(2) as amended and passed on the House floor, July 28, 1976 (Horton):
    ". . . a gathering to jointly conduct or dispose of agency business by two or more, but at least the number of individual agency members required to take action on behalf of the agency, but does not include gatherings required or permitted by subsection (d) . . ."
12. **S.5, §552b(a)(2) as enacted Aug. 31, 1976:**
    ". . . the deliberations of at least the number of individual agency members required to take action on behalf of the agency where such deliberations determine or result in the joint conduct or disposition of official agency business, but does not include deliberations required or permitted by subsection (d) or (e) . . ."

Appendix E
Department of Justice Letter to
Covered Agencies, April 19, 1977*

ASSISTANT ATTORNEY GENERAL
CIVIL DIVISION

Mr. Harry E. Webb, Jr.
General Counsel
Indian Claims Commission
1730 K Street, N.W.
Room 630
Washington, D.C. 20006

Dear Mr. Webb:

In conjunction with the Civil Division's responsibilities for the defense of litigation under the Sunshine Act, 5 U.S.C. § 552b, I think it might be helpful to comment from time to time on matters which may raise potential litigation issues. This is the first such letter. I hope that you will consider the discussion in this letter as a part of our joint responsibility to insure that the Sunshine Act works and to avoid litigation whenever possible. Please feel free too to distribute the letter to your staff so that our offices can cooperate and work together toward effective implementation of the Sunshine Act.

Recently promulgated agency regulations bring to light a number of matters of interest which may merit consideration within your office:

1. Several agencies define the term "meeting" as used in subsection (a)(2) of the Sunshine Act (5 U.S.C. § 552b (a) (2)) in such way as to

---

* Copies of this letter were addressed to all 47 agencies then covered by the Sunshine Act.

limit the joint deliberations which are subject to the Act. For instance we believe that in order to avoid ultimately fruitless litigation, a briefing session attended by at least the number of agency members required to take action on behalf of the agency, where the members attending have an opportunity to ask questions or seek clarification of matters of concern, should be included within the purview of regulations or practices applying the term "meeting". Where the deliberations do determine or result in the joint conduct or disposition of official agency business, and except as specified in subsection (d) or (e) of the Act. such deliberations are meetings subject to the Act. Should your agency have drawn a more narrow regulation, it leaves the agency's proceedings subject to continuous attack. Subsection (h) (1) of the Act (5 U.S.C. § 552(b)(h)(1)) provides that suits challenging agency action may be brought prior to the action challenged or within 60 days after the meeting out of which the violation allegedly arises "except that if public announcement of such meeting is not initially provided by the agency in accordance with the requirements of this said section, such action may be instituted pursuant to this section at any time prior to sixty days after any public announcement of such meeting." I suggest that you insure that the term "meeting" is broadly defined in practice so that the statute of limitations can come into play and so that the potential for litigation can be reduced.

2. The Act requires that agency meetings shall be open to "public observation" (5 U.S.C. § 552b(b)). Obviously public observation does not include the right to participate in the meeting. Likewise, the right to observe does not include any right to disrupt a meeting. Within these limits, I suggest that you accommodate members of the public desiring to attend open meetings. Meetings should be held in a room that has ample space, sufficient visibility, and adequate acoustics. Again, in order to avoid needless litigation over issues which do not go to the heart of the Act, the public should be permitted to take notes and photographs (without flash aids) and should be permitted to make sound recordings in a non-obtrusive manner. Each of these measures will enhance the public's ability to observe meetings and still permit the agency's business to proceed. If your agency has regulations not consistent with the foregoing, I suggest that you consider amending them. Of course, any person may attend a meeting without indicating

his identity and/or the person, if any, whom he represents and no requirement of prior notification of intent to observe a meeting may be required.

3. A number of agency regulations explicitly provide that meetings will be open although an exemption may permit the closing of the meeting or portion thereof. I can add that a general practice of opening meetings to the fullest extent practicable will not only reduce litigation under the Act but will likely place us in a better posture in litigation, if and when any litigation occurs. I am certain that a vote of the membership of your agency on whether to close a meeting or portion thereof would, of course, take the public interest into account.

I hope that the foregoing discussion is of assistance to you. I would welcome any suggestions you may have for matters appropriate for discussion in future, similar letters.

Very truly yours,

BARBARA ALLEN BABCOCK
Assistant Attorney General

Appendix F
American Bar Association, Report and Recommendation on the Government in the Sunshine Act, February 1987

Section of Administrative Law (Midyear Meeting 1987)

The Section's recommendation was approved by voice vote. It reads:

BE IT RESOLVED, That the American Bar Association offers the following guidelines to federal agencies and courts with respect to the interpretation of the term "meeting" as used in the Government in the Sunshine Act:

1. So long as discussions are not sufficiently focused on discrete proposals or issues as to cause or be likely to cause the individual participating (agency) members to form reasonably firm positions regarding matters pending or likely to arise before the agency, the definition of "meeting" does not include: (a) spontaneous casual discussions among agency members of a subject of common interest; (b) briefings of agency members by staff or outsiders; a key element would be that the agency members be primarily receptors of information or views and only incidentally exchange views with one another; (c) general discussions of subjects which are relevant to an agency's responsibilities but which do not pose specific problems for agency resolution; and (d) exploratory discussions, so long as they are preliminary in nature, there are no pending proposals for agency action, and merits of any proposed agency action would be open to full consideration at a later time.

2. If agencies intend to hold discussions described in subsection (b), (c), and (d), appropriate mechanisms, such as monitoring by general counsel or other agency representatives, should be undertaken to ensure that such discussions do not proceed to the point of becoming "meetings." In addition, agencies should memorialize such discussions through notes, minutes or recording as assurance to the public of compliance with the Act.

REPORT

The Government in the Sunshine Act, 5 U.S.C. §552b, was enacted in September 1976, to take effect on March 12, 1977. The Act, one of several statutes enacted in the 1970s to provide greater "openness" in government, requires in general that meetings of the members of collegial agencies be open to the public unless the meeting has been formally closed because the matters to be discussed fall within one of the statutory exemptions.

In September, 1985, the Administrative Law Section formed a Steering Committee (Task Force on Government in the Sunshine) to conduct a review of current issues under the Sunshine Act and to report back to the Council. This examination was undertaken primarily in response to the events in the past two years which have drawn attention to the Sunshine Act and certain problems which have arisen in its administration.

First, the Administrative Conference of the United States concluded, after a comprehensive study of experience with the Act, that "one of the clearest and most significant results of the Government in the Sunshine Act is to diminish the collegial character of the agency decisionmaking process. The open meeting requirement has generated reluctance to discuss certain important matters; and discussions, when they occur, may not contribute to achieving a consensus position. In some agencies the pattern of decisionmaking has shifted from collegial exchanges to one-on-one encounters, transmission of views through staff, and exchanges of memoranda or notation procedure. The inhibition of collegial exchanges . . . tends to weaken the role of the collegium vis-a-vis that of the staff and the agency chairman." In a carefully restrained recommendation, however, the Conference did not call directly for relaxation of the Act's open meeting requirements, but urged Congress to consider whether the Act's restrictions are advisable and if not, how they might best be revised without undercutting the basic principle of the public's access to the fullest practicable information about the government's decisionmaking process. The Conference further suggested that there might be some relaxation in the requirement for open meetings "when discussions are preliminary in nature or pertain to matters, such as budget or legislative proposals, which are to be considered in a public forum prior to final action."[1]

---

[1] Administrative Conference Recommendation 84.3, 1 C.F.R. §305.84-3 (adopted June, 1984).

Second, in April 1984 the Supreme Court in *Federal Communications Commission v. ITT World Communications Inc.*, 461 U.S. 463, adopted a narrower definition of the term "meeting" for purposes of the open meeting requirement than had been employed by the Court of Appeals for the D.C. Circuit and urged by proponents of a broad interpretation of the Act. At issue in the *ITT* case was the participation of three members of the Federal Communications Commission in a series of conferences with their European counterparts "intended to facilitate joint planning of telecommunications facilities through an exchange of information on regulatory policies," 466 U.S. at 465. The three members were not a quorum of the full Commission, and the statutory definition of "meeting" requires the presence of a quorum, but they were a quorum of a subdivision of the Commission, the Telecommunications Committee. On this basis the Court of Appeals for the D.C. Circuit had concluded that the discussion of telecommunications policy by a quorum of a subdivision of the Commission with their foreign counterparts was a covered meeting. The Supreme Court disagreed, and set forth a narrower test of a "meeting".

> [The] statutory language contemplates discussions that "effectively predetermine official actions." [citation omitted]. Such discussions must be sufficiently focused on discrete proposals or issues as to cause or be likely to cause the individual participating members to form reasonably firm positions regarding matters pending or likely to arise before the agency." R. Berg & S. Klitzman, An Interpretive Guide to the Government in the Sunshine Act 9 (1978) . . . . ITT alleged neither that the [Telecommunications] Committee formally acted upon applications for certification at the Consultative Process sessions nor that those sessions resulted in firm positions on particular matters pending or likely to arise before the Committee. Rather, the sessions provided general background information to the Commissioners and permitted them to engage with their foreign counterparts in an exchange of views by which decisions already reached by the Commission could be implemented. As we have noted, Congress did not intend the Sunshine Act to encompass such discussion. [466 U.S. at 471-72.]

Third, the Nuclear Regulatory Commission, in response to the Supreme Court's *ITT* decision, acted to revise the definition "meeting" in its Sunshine Act regulation to incorporate the key language from the Supreme Court's opinion, and in so doing served notice that it read that case to permit "informal preliminary briefings" and "generalized background discussions [in which) Commissioners can decide what topics should become the subject of more particularized proposals," 50 F.R. at 20890 (May 21, 1995). The NRC action inspired considerable unfavorable comment in the news media and in Congress, and although the rule change was effected on an interim basis, the NRC has not, so far as we know used the more liberal provisions.

While these events have served both as background and as catalysts, the Steering Committee was given a broad charge to consider the experience under the Sunshine Act and, in particular, what the American Bar Association might usefully recommend to the agencies and to Congress on the basis of that experience. In pursuing this task we have not engaged in much original research but have relied primarily on the report to the Administrative Conference by Professors Welborn, Lyons and Thomas, and the reported cases, particularly *FCC. v. ITT World Communications*. We have, in addition, solicited written comments from agencies and other interested groups, and met once with a group of agency general counsels and their representatives and once with a group of public interest group and media representatives.

We have broken down our inquiry into four parts: First, an examination of the ITT World Communications case and its impact, actual and potential, on agency practices. Second, a look at whether a statutory exemption should be created under the Sunshine Act for agency deliberations on proposed legislation, budgets and the like.

Finally, general consideration of whether the Sunshine Act as a whole should be reevaluated after ten years of operation.

I. ITT World Communications and Its Implications for Administration of the Sunshine Act

The Nuclear Regulatory Commission's revision of its Sunshine regulation to conform to or, perhaps, to test the limits of what is permitted by the Supreme Court's decision raises the initial question—Will *ITT* make a significant change in the administration of the Act? In fairness to NRC it must be emphasized that while most agencies have from the beginning simply tacked the statutory definition of "meeting" in their regulations, the NRC in 1977 had defined "meeting" in terms which appeared to go beyond the general understanding of the meaning of the Act even before the *ITT* decision.[2] It is understandable that given the context in which the NRC operates and the broad public interest in its deliberations, the amendment of its rules would provoke interest and controversy. It does not follow, however, that the *ITT* opinion has broad implications for all agencies administering the Sunshine Act (or even for the NRC), and this question was the first we sought to address.

It is important to note that whether a given "gathering" of agency members is a "meeting" has significant consequences for administration of the Act. Although there are a variety of grounds upon which a meeting may be legally closed, somewhat elaborate procedures must be followed to close a meeting,[3] and even then a transcript or, in some cases, detailed minutes must be maintained,[4] and the circumstances under which such materials must later be made available to the public are by no means clear.[5] Furthermore, even if a meeting is not closed to the public, some formalities must be followed, including public announcement, ordinarily, at least a week in advance, and notice in the Federal Register.[6] On the other hand, if a "gathering" is not a "meeting," no announcement or procedures are required because the Act has no application.

The Sunshine Act defines a "meeting'" as "the deliberations of at least the number of individual agency members required to take action on behalf of the agency <u>where such deliberations determine or result in the joint conduct or disposition of official agency business....</u>" (Emphasis added). The first part of the definition is simple enough; it is the passage we have underlined which has presented problems or, from the agencies' point of view, opportunities.

The Supreme Court's language quoted earlier in this report constitutes a gloss on the underlined passage of the definition. It draws on the language

---

[2] The definition had excluded "gatherings of a social or ceremonial nature" and briefings by representatives of other agencies or departments or representatives of foreign governments or international bodies "where such briefings or discussions are informational in nature and are not conducted with specific reference to any particular matter then pending before the Commission." See 50 F.R. 20889. The language, therefore, impliedly included staff briefings within the definition of meeting although a number of other agencies excluded them. See note 12 *infra*.
[3] 5 U.S.C. §552b(d).
[4] 5 U.S.C. §552b(f).
[5] See *Clark-Cowlitz Joint Operating Agency v. FERC,* 775 F.2d 359 (D.C. Cir. 1985), *petition for rehearing granted.*
[6] 5 U.S.C. §552b(e).

of the Administrative Conference's *Interpretive Guide*, but it must be borne in mind that the controlling question is what the Court meant and not what the authors of the Guide meant by this language.

It has been suggested that the Supreme Court's opinion should be limited to the facts before the Court. Concededly, when the Supreme Court construed "official agency business" in the context of the case as measured by the subject matter formally delegated to the Telecommunications Committee (thus rejecting the D.C. Circuit's essentially circular definition that it meant anything the members were expressly or impliedly authorized to do in the course of their official duties), it was relatively easy to conclude that whatever else the Consultative Process was, it was not part of the decisionmaking process of the Telecommunications Committee. But it cannot be assumed that the Supreme Court got carried away or that it was unaware that the definition of "meeting" was controversial and "one of the most troublesome problems in interpreting and applying the Sunshine Act."[7] We conclude, therefore, that the Supreme Court meant what it said in *ITT World Communications*, and that it intended to provide guidance to the agencies and the sources in applying the definition of "meeting."

There are, nevertheless, obstacles to translating the opinion into guidelines for determining when a given gathering is a "meeting." First, the definition of what is not a meeting is negative. Whether stated in terms of the statutory language, i.e., any discussions that do not "determine or result in the joint conduct of official agency business," or in terms of the Supreme Court's gloss, any discussions not "sufficiently focused on discrete proposals," etc., it will cover a multitude of different situations which are beyond the periphery of the definition of what *is* a meeting.

The problem is compounded by the fact that there are a number of variables exceedingly difficult to state in the abstract, for example, the range of circumstances surrounding the discussion and the relationship of the subject matter of the discussion to anticipated or possible agency action.

But undoubtedly most frustrating to efforts to state firm guidelines is the fact that any description of hypothetical gatherings is likely to be stated in conclusory terms which do not really resolve practical problems. For example, there is general agreement, even among strong advocates of open meetings, that "casual" conversations are not covered. Indeed, the Conference Report explained the final revision of the definition of meeting as "intended to permit casual discussions between agency members." But

---

[7] *Interpretive Guide* 3.

"casual" is not a very precise term. It's dictionary meanings include "produced as a result of chance," "occurring without specific motivation," "occasional," "informal," "without significance," etc. Chance and infrequency are not meaningful qualifications with respect to members of a collegium who presumably see each other nearly every day, so that the essential element of a *casual* discussion would appear to be its informality or lack of significance. "Informal" is another word frequently called upon to explain what kinds of discussion are not covered in "informal background discussions [that] clarify issues and expose varying views."[8] Yet informality, with its reference to the form of the discussion, seems an inappropriate test, given that the Act's legislative history indicates the test of a meeting is what actually happens rather than the members' purpose in coming together. Other terms that have been used to limn the statutory distinction, such as "preliminary," "exploratory," and "tentative," may provide somewhat more guidance, but they are likewise largely conclusory and their applicability to a particular discussion is more easily determined in retrospect than at the time the discussion commences.

The difficulty of specifying *in advance* those characteristics of a particular discussion which will cause it to fall short of becoming a meeting has been urged by opponents of the NRC rule as a reason for not importing the Supreme Court's view of the Act into agency rules. Even if that view is correct, they argue, the test can only be applied retrospectively and is not a reliable basis for deciding whether to hold a gathering which is not to be treated as a meeting. This argument seems to us to prove too much for its logic points to permitting *no* discussion of agency business among the requisite number of agency members without treating it as a meeting. Yet this result seems to us clearly not to have been intended by Congress,[9] and it would have a serious impact on the ability of agencies to conduct day-to-day business.

---

[8] *FCC v. ITT World Communications*, 466 U.S. at 469, *quoting from* the Senate Committee Report.

[9] The argument, on analysis, seems to be saying that although Congress, after much deliberation, wrote a higher threshold test, "deliberations [which] determine or result in the joint conduct or disposition of official agency business," agencies should apply the statute as if it read "discussions which are about official agency business," lest a given discussion unintentionally drift over the line. But Congress can hardly have gone to such pains to articulate a narrower standard had it not expected the agencies to use the leeway such a standard provides, and if they are to do so, they must attempt to set out in advance, whether by regulation or internal guidelines, the elements or characteristics of a discussion which will cause it to fall short of being a meeting.

Therefore, without minimizing the difficulties in the task, we believe it is worthwhile to attempt to set forth in some detail those types of gathering which are not meetings, as the Supreme Court has defined the term. We should recall that a meeting first of all consists of "deliberations," and "deliberation" is defined as the act of weighing and examining reasons for and against a choice or measure; a discussion and consideration by a number of persons of the reasons for and against a measure (Webster's Third Intl. Dictionary). It is the element of the participants trying to reach a decision (whether or not they do so) which distinguishes deliberations from more "casual" or "informal" discussions. To quote the *Interpretive Guide,* "the question is whether the discussion is decision-oriented."[10]

This analysis certainly does not sweep away the difficulties, but at least it helps us to know what to look for. It seems to us that there are at least three paradigmatic situations which are clearly or arguably outside the definition of meeting:

1. The casual, in the sense of spontaneous or unplanned, discussion among colleagues of a subject of common interest. Examples are given in NRC General Counsel Plaine's memorandum of December 6, 1985: "I read an article in _____ the other day about the nuclear industry and I wonder whether any of the rest of you read it and what you thought of it." "I just got back from visiting _____ and I'd like to tell you my perceptions of how they run the regulatory program in that country, and some of their perceptions of how we do business, and discuss with you whether anything I learned suggests areas we ought to explore further in a more formal setting." A key element of this type of discussion is its spontaneity. While it may include all the members of the agency it seems to us that with respect to this kind of gathering it is essential that there be no conscious policy of involving all the members, simply because such a requirement would be inconsistent with the casual nature of the discussion.

2. The briefing of agency members, whether by staff or by outsiders.[11] Indeed, briefings have long been fairly generally recognized as outside

---

[10] *Interpretive Guide* 9n.
[11] While a briefing may be outside the "meeting" definition, we do not mean to suggest that limitations on ex parte communications would not be applicable.

the scope of the term "meeting." The original NRC regulation excluded "briefings of the Commission by representatives of other agencies ... or representatives of foreign governments or international bodies where such briefings or discussions are informational in nature and are not conducted with specific reference to any particular matter then pending before the Commission." Several other agencies have long excluded briefings from the definition of meeting.[12] The key elements here are that the members are primarily receptors of information or views and only incidentally exchanging views with each other. Obviously, a briefing can very easily turn into a serious exchange of views, particularly if the briefing relates to a discrete issue before the agency. Consequently, an important variable in this situation is the subject matter of the briefing and how directly it is related to possible agency action.

3. The serious "general" discussion among agency members. By hypothesis, this discussion is not casual; it is likely to have been planned, perhaps with a written agenda, and announced and scheduled to secure maximum member attendance. The key element, therefore, is that it is not "focused on discrete proposals or issues." Obviously, this kind of "non-meeting" presents the hardest case and the rationale for recognition draws very heavily on the Supreme Court's decision. It is also extremely difficult to describe in hypothetical terms because the presence of the key element essentially depends on the relationship of the subject matter to what the agency is or might be doing about it. The category might be broken down into two subcategories:

a) The general discussion of subject which is relevant to the agency's responsibilities but does not pose specific problems for agency resolution. For example, a discussion of general foreign trade or balance of payments problems by the International Trade Commission would be permissible if the Commission acts only with respect to specific industries or products, whereas a general discussion by the members of the SEC of insider trading would be a more difficult case because it might be impossible to separate the subject of insider trading from the question of what the SEC should do about it.

b) Closest to the borderline is the "exploratory" discussion of a problem area. The key element here is that the discussion is preliminary

---

[12] See 12 C.F.R. §505b.2 (FHLBB); 49 C.F.R. §804. 3 (Natl. Transportation Safety Board); 12 C.F.R. §311.2(b) (FDIC).

in the sense that there are not hard proposals for action before the agency and consequently the merits of anything the agency decides to do would be open to full consideration at a later time. Thus, the discussion cannot "predetermine" agency action and the members are not deliberating in the sense of confronting and weighing choices. Yet in any such discussion there is always the possible resolution of deciding not to do anything, so that the "issue" of whether the agency ought to turn its attention and resources to the problem may be sufficiently discrete to come within the statutory definition. In short, the status of "preliminary" or "exploratory" discussions of a problem within the agency's authority to address is the hardest case, for even if one accepts a particular verbal formulation, such as that set out in the *Interpretive Guide*[13] the difficulties of application are intimidating, Yet inasmuch as whether a particular discussion is exploratory or decision-oriented depends on the total factual context; it is likely to be more difficult to resolve a hypothetical situation than a real one. In other words one may say of a meeting, as Justice Stewart said of obscenity, "I know it when I see it."

Summary

Thus, we may conclude that agencies are free to treat certain discussions of agency business, certainly, casual discussions and briefings, and probably, "general" and "exploratory" discussions, as not covered by the Sunshine Act. Should they do so? We must emphasize that it is not our purpose to urge agencies to close any discussions now open. Open meetings serve valuable functions. Furthermore, while this study has not focused on the adequacy of the available grounds for closing meetings, we believe that, putting aside the problems of legislative and budget discussions, discussed later in this report, the exemptions in the Act are sufficient to protect *information* for which there is a legitimate need for confidentiality.

But the fact is that the Sunshine Act *has* had an inhibiting effect on the initiation of discussions among agency members. This is the conclusion

---

[13] "A discussion which significantly furthers the decisional process by narrowing issues, discarding alternatives, etc., should be treated as a meeting even though it does not and is not expected to achieve a complete resolution. On the other hand, those exchanges of views which are not of a nature to foreclose or narrow discussion at subsequent collegial gatherings might be treated as outside the definition without loss to the values the Sunshine Act seeks to achieve." *Interpretive Guide* 10n.

of the Welborn report, and it is confirmed by our meeting with agency general counsels. Quite apart from the evident preference of many members for closed meetings, the sheer logistical difficulties in invoking the machinery of the Act has made difficult if not impossible the maintenance of close day-to-day working relationships in those agencies, by far the majority, where three or even two members constitute a quorum.[14]

We believe that a sensible and sensitive application of the principles announced in the *ITT* case can ease the somewhat stilted relationships that exist in some agencies. However, it is important to establish procedures which provide, insofar as possible, credibility for the agency process and assurance to the public that these principles are not being abused. The first sentence of section 552b(b) enjoins agency members *not* to "jointly conduct or dispose of agency business other than in accordance with" the requirements of the Act, and if this prohibition is to an extent redundant, it is a reminder to the members that when they are in a gathering which is not being treated as a meeting, they have a duty to conduct themselves accordingly.

Therefore. we believe it is the obligation of each agency, and particularly its general counsel's office, to brief the members on the requirements of the Act and to provide guidance on what kinds of discussion are permissible outside the meeting context.

It was suggested in our meetings that if agencies are to use the added flexibility that the *ITT* decision provides, there should be policing mechanisms designated to provide a record of what was discussed so as to assure the public that the discussions did not rise to the threshold of a "meeting." Obviously, there are problems in proceduralizing "non-meeting meetings." For example, casual discussions would cease to be casual if each one was to be attended by a representative of the general counsel or extensively memorialized. Briefings and general discussions present somewhat less of a problem in this respect. Certainly, they could be monitored by the general counsel or his representative and notes taken.

---

[14] One agency general counsel reported the agency members were very concerned about complying with the Act. As a result three members, a quorum, did not even go to lunch together. The members were reluctant to discuss among themselves even housekeeping matters. The result has been to increase *staff* power, because it is at the staff level that discussions may occur.

It remains to be considered whether a broad reading of the *ITT* case would check the loss of collegiality which the Administrative Conference pointed to and which has been confirmed by our discussions with agency counsels. It was the well nigh unanimous view of those to whom we spoke, both proponents and critics of Sunshine, that the impact of the case on collegiality is likely to be slight. It is true that to the extent it would contribute to more normal interpersonal relationships among agency members, it would have some tendency to increase collegiality. But since the line between "preliminary" or "general" discussions and "meetings" is likely to remain hazy, conscientious agency members are likely to feel inhibited whenever such discussions move to address agency choices. Ultimately, it is those exchanges of views which are part of the process of reaching a group decision where collegiality is most important, and those discussions are clearly meetings under the Act.

II. Possible Statutory Exemption for Agency Deliberations on Proposed Legislation, Budgets and the Like

In *Common Cause v. Nuclear Regulatory Commission*, 674 F.2d 921 (D.C. Cir. 1982), the Court ruled that none of the Sunshine Act's exemptions provides a blanket exemption for discussions at any stage of the budget preparation process. The Court specifically refused to apply Exemption 9(B) (protection of premature disclosure), Exemption 2 (matters relating solely to internal personnel rules and practices) and Exemption 6 (protection of personal privacy).

Absent future consideration of this basic issue by the Supreme Court, it appears likely that an agency's consideration of budget proposals generally will not be exempt from the Sunshine Act. The same general approach would seem to apply to an agency's consideration of legislative proposals. Under these circumstances, the Task Force solicited written and oral comments from a number of agencies as well as public interest and media organizations. No clear consensus emerged from the oral and written comments received. In some instances, agencies closed meetings to discuss budget proposals where they would impact upon law enforcement policies (Exemption 7). Other agencies indicated that they did not consider the budget and legislative area to be of particular sensitivity. Public interest groups and media organizations, on the other hand, felt that the public had a compelling interest in access to information on budget discussions. For example, because the decrease in the size of an enforcement or oversight office could dramatically affect an agency's performance, such groups felt the public should be a party to that process. In addition, faced with the fiscal constraints of Gramm-Rudman, such groups believed that the allocation of limited monies will become all the more critical. Accordingly, strong opposition was voiced to any change in the law that would alter the public's access to information on budgetary matters. Similar, although less vocal, opposition was expressed toward exempting legislative discussions.

We understand the reluctance of some agencies to hold candid budget discussions in open meetings, and we realize that the alternative to closed meetings on the budget may be no meetings at all. Yet this argument appears to prove too much, for there is ample evidence that Sunshine requirements have discouraged the holding of meetings on a broad range of subjects and inhibited the freedom of expression at such meetings as are held. We do believe that there are few, if any, subjects of more moment to the agency than how it plans to allocate its resources and prioritize its tasks. While it is true, as the Welborn report points out, that the agency's decision on its proposed budget is preliminary in the sense that the proposal must first be passed upon by OMB and then by the Appropriations Committees of Congress, nevertheless, it is doubtful that these reviews are, in effect, *de novo*. As a practical matter the agency decision sets parameters to the subsequent reviews. Consequently, unless the entire Sunshine principle is to be reconsidered, we cannot recommend a special exemption for budget discussions.

We reach a similar conclusion with respect to discussion of legislative proposals, recognizing that the elements of the equation are somewhat different. On the one hand, the formulation of the agency position is likely to be more preliminary to the ultimate legislative decision than in the case of the budget, simply because the Congressional examination is likely to be more thorough and more open. But for this very reason we do not see why the agency members cannot candidly consider the pros and cons of a legislative proposal, as they would of a proposed rule. In short, we do not believe the case has been made for a special exemption.

III. Reevaluation of the Sunshine Act

In our discussion with agency general counsels and their representatives, it became obvious that the provision of guidelines on what constitutes a "meeting" (*see* Part I above) would not address the broader question of the impact the Sunshine Act has had upon collegiality in multimember agencies. For that reason, the Task Force was urged to reevaluate the Sunshine Act as a whole, particularly in view of the fact that the Act is about to have its 10th anniversary.

The Task Force has carefully considered whether it should urge a general reevaluation of the Sunshine Act. In so doing, it has examined in detail the Welborn Report prepared for the Administrative Conference as well as the resulting Recommendation 84-3, adopted on June 28, 1984.

The examination undertaken by the Administrative Conference was extremely thorough and spanned a considerable period of time. Drafters of the Welborn Report submitted detailed questionnaires to affected agencies in an attempt to determine the Sunshine Act's impact on those agencies. Although the Task Force has met with agency general counsels and representatives of interested groups, it has not had the time nor the inclination for the type of comprehensive examination undertaken by the Administrative Conference. Based on the informal discussions the Task Force has had with interested persons, it has concluded that it has little to add to the thorough analyses undertaken by the Administrative Conference and that no clear consensus has emerged on whether the Act is in need of any significant revision. Under the circumstances, the Task Force believes the most meaningful contribution the Section of Administrative Law can make is to provide guidance, within the constraints of existing law, on what types of informal gatherings and discussions are permitted without bringing into play the requirements of the Sunshine Act. To go beyond that point and to attempt to strike a balance between the public's need for access to information and the need for collegiality among agency members is an extremely difficult and delicate question and one which the Task Force finds itself unable to resolve. Accordingly, the Task Force does not urge that the Sunshine Act be reevaluated at the present time.

Respectfully submitted,
EDWARD J. GRENIER, JR.
Chairman
Section of Administrative Law
February, 1987

Appendix G
Administrative Conference of the United States
Report and Recommendation 84-3
Improvements in the Administration
of the Government in the Sunshine Act
49 FR 29937 (1984)

Administrative Conference of the United States
Recommendation No. 84-3
Improvements in the Administration of the
Government in the Sunshine Act

49 FR 29937
(July 25, 1984)

A. *Periodic Agency Review of Sunshine Practices.* Members of the public voice several criticisms of the manner in which agencies employ the Government in the Sunshine Act and conduct open meetings. Among the most significant are that meetings are often closed on technical legal grounds without substantive reason for doing so, that at times discussion in meetings is inadequate to allow those in attendance to understand fully the proceedings, and that frequently members of the public have insufficient access to explanatory materials and underlying documents to allow them to follow the discussion and comprehend the content of meetings. At issue is not so much compliance with the letter of the law as progress toward fuller realization of its general objective of enlarged, meaningful public access to information. To the extent that problems exist, they are a function of agency practice and are appropriately addressed in their particulars on an agency-by-agency basis.

B. *Impact of Sunshine on the Collegiality of Agency Decisionmaking.* The desirability of the collegial form of agency organization, as opposed to the agency headed by a single executive, has long been the subject of debate. Congress has, however, chosen to delegate certain administrative functions to collegial bodies.

One of the most frequently offered justifications for collegial decisionmaking is that stated by the First Hoover Commission's Committee on Independent Regulatory Commissions:

> A distinctive attribute of commission action is that it requires concurrence by a majority of members of equal standing after full discussion and deliberation. At its best, each decision reflects the combined judgment of the group after critical analysis of the relevant facts and divergent views. This provides both a barrier to arbitrary or capricious action and a source of decisions based on different points of view and experience * * * . The member of the commission must expose his reasons and judgments to the critical scrutiny of his fellow members and must persuade them to his point of view. He must analyze and understand the views of his colleagues if only to refute them.

Though no generally accepted standard for measuring the quality of agency decisions under the Government in the Sunshine Act has been devised, one of the clearest and most significant results of the Government in the Sunshine Act is to diminish the collegial character of the agency decisionmaking process. The open meeting requirement has generated reluctance to discuss certain important matters; and discussions, when they occur, may not contribute to achieving a consensus position. In some agencies the pattern of decisionmaking has shifted from collegial exchanges to one-on-one encounters, transmission of views through staff, and exchanges of memoranda or notation procedure. The inhibition of collegial exchanges, in turn, impedes the members in the collective exercise of their responsibilities, and tends to weaken the role of the collegium vis-a-vis that of the staff and the agency chairman.

Congress was aware of the inherent and unavoidable tension between the values of openness in government and collegiality in decision making when it enacted the Government in the Sunshine Act, and it consciously chose a result that would maximize openness. Concessions were made in the statute to the need for maintaining the confidentiality of certain categories of information under discussion, but few if any concessions were made to the needs of the deliberative process as such. Although the legislative history indicates Congress believed that, after the initial period of adjustment, sunshine would not have a significant inhibiting effect on collegial exchanges, unfortunately this has not been the case.

Recommendation

1. Agencies should continually strive to reflect fully in their activities the basic purpose of the Government in the Sunshine Act, which is to enlarge public access to information about the operations of government. Agencies are strongly encouraged to review periodically their sunshine policies and practices in light of experience and the spirit of the law for the purpose of making adjustments that would enlarge public access to meaningful information, such as (a) invoking the exemptions of the Act to close meetings only when there is substantial reason to do so; and (b) making open meetings more useful through comprehensible discussion of agenda items and provision of background material and documentation pertaining to the issues under consideration.

2. Under the Government in the Sunshine Act the degree of collegiality in the multi-member agencies has diminished. Congress should consider whether the present restrictions on closing agency meetings are advisable and, if not, how they might best be revised without undercutting the basic principle of the Act that "the public is entitled to the fullest practicable information regarding the decision making processes of the Federal Government."

If a new balance is to be struck between the values of collegiality and openness, the Administrative Conference suggests that agency members be permitted some opportunity to discuss the broad outlines of agency policies and priorities (including enforcement priorities) in closed meetings, when the discussions are preliminary in nature or pertain to matters, such as budget or legislative proposals, which are to be considered in a public forum prior to final action.

This recommendation was adopted in Plenary Session June 28-29, 1984 and issued July 19, 1984.

Appendix H
Letter from Steven M.H. Wallman, Commissioner, Securities and Exchange Commission, to Thomasina Rogers, Chairperson, Administrative Conference of the United States, February 17, 1995

UNITED STATES
SECURITIES AND EXCHANGE COMMISSION
450 FIFTH STREET, N.W.
WASHINGTON, D.C. 20549

STEVEN M.H. WALLMAN,
COMMISSIONER
(202) 942-0800
FAX: (202) 942-3683

February 17, 1995

Thomasina Rogers
Chairperson
Administrative Conference of the United States
2120 L Street N.W.
Washington, D.C. 20037-1568

Re: Government in the Sunshine Act

Dear Chairperson Rogers:

The undersigned members and former members of independent Federal regulatory agencies and the undersigned members or officers of various organizations write to discuss several issues related to the Government in the Sunshine Act. We strongly support the dual goals of the Act — enhanced public understanding of agency actions and improved agency decision making — and are ardent supporters of its intent. However, we have concerns regarding whether the Act, as currently structured and interpreted, achieves these goals as well as it might. The purpose of this letter is briefly to describe our concerns, and — in light of the experience gained by agencies and the public over the approximately 20 years since the Act's enactment — to encourage ACUS and others to reevaluate the effectiveness of the Act in achieving its intended goals.

As a preliminary matter, we oppose any dilution in the Act's primary underlying principle of ensuring greater public access to agency decision making. Instead, our hope is that this letter will help stimulate a candid dialogue about the Act and its effect on agency decision making and the public perception of the Federal government. In this context we would be willing to review possible changes to the Act that might better promote its goals. Accordingly, we have not attempted to arrive now at a consensus as to whether the Act is, in fact, in need of significant revision or whether the Act is the optimal framework for ensuring public access to agency decision making. We also have not attempted to agree upon a collective recommendation as to specific alternatives that might improve the Act.1/ At a minimum, however, we believe strongly that any alternatives to the current structure of the Act that might be considered by ACUS must ensure that the public receives at least as much information regarding agency decision making as that currently afforded under the Act.2/

1/ In fact, given the different regulatory focuses of Federal regulatory agencies and varying concerns of different interest groups, we recognize that any specific alternative may be more or less attractive to any particular agency or group, or may be better applied with respect to some matters as opposed to others, and that agencies or groups may wish to defer coming to any conclusion until after ACUS has proceeded with its review.

2/ For example, consideration might be given to proposals that range from broadening the current exemptive provisions of the Act to granting the public the right to make oral statements or presentations in connection with agency decision making — as opposed to the current right of the public under the Act merely to observe agency actions — in exchange for greater agency discretion to allow private deliberations among their members.

Background

As you know, the Act is founded on the principle that the "government should conduct the public's business in public."3/ The stated purpose of the Act is to make available to the public the fullest practicable information regarding the decision making process of the Federal government, while protecting the rights of individuals and the ability of the government to carry out its responsibilities.4/ Congress believed that achievement of this overriding purpose would have several ancillary benefits including: increasing the public's confidence in government by permitting firsthand observation of the responsible manner in which agency members carry out their duties; promoting greater understanding of government decision making; and improving agency decision making.5/

The central provisions of the Act provide that, subject to limited enumerated exceptions,6/ meetings in which a collegial agency7/ conducts business must be open to the public. It is clear that in adopting the Act, Congress was aware of the tension between openness and collegial decision making and nevertheless chose to maximize openness. However, as ACUS has noted, Congress also believed that, after an initial

---

3/   S. Rep. No. 345, 94th Cong., lst. Sess. 1 (1975). The Act may be viewed as an extension of previously enacted legislation — including the Administrative Procedure Act (originally enacted in 1946), the Freedom of Information Act (enacted in 1966) and the Federal Advisory Committee Act (enacted in 1972) — designed to open the government's decision making process to the public.

4/   Pub. Law. No. 94-409, Section 2.

5/   S. Rep. No. 354, 94th Cong., 1st Sess. 4-6 (1975).

6/   The Act sets forth ten grounds on which agency meetings may be closed and information regarding such meetings withheld from the public. The Act also provides specific procedures governing the closing of agency meetings, including a vote of agency members, public announcement that a meeting will be closed, and guidelines with respect to memorializing closed meetings.

7/   The Act does not apply to agencies headed by a single individual.

period of adjustment, the Act would not have a significant inhibiting effect on collegial exchanges.[8] As discussed below, there is some evidence to suggest that this has not been the case, and that the benefits to the public under the Act may be somewhat limited. Therefore, notwithstanding the laudatory intent of Congress in adopting the Act, we believe it appropriate that a reexamination of the Act be undertaken as soon as practical to determine whether it meets its intended objectives, or is counterproductive.

Issues Related to the Effectiveness of the Act

We have a number of concerns regarding the effect of the Act on both the quality of agency decision making and the public's understanding of the agency decision making process.

1. Effect on Agency Decision Making

We have doubts as to whether the Act achieves its goal of enhancing agency decision making. Specifically, as discussed further below, we believe that ACUS should consider whether the restrictions imposed by the Act (1) infringe on the ability of agency members to deliberate, (2) adversely affect the establishment of an agency's agenda, or (3) promote inefficient practices within agencies.

We believe the Act may significantly impede the ability of agency members to confer in private and reduce the willingness and ability of such members to deliberate in a full and appropriate manner. Notwithstanding the overriding goal of openness underlying the Act, we note that private discussions among agency members help promote collegiality which, in turn, improves regulatory decision making. Under the Act, however, discussions among members that do not fall within one of the exemptions under the Act must be held in the public light. This has a chilling effect on the willingness and ability of agency members to engage in an open and creative discussion of issues. As a result, members are often isolated from one another, forced to deliberate, at best, one-on-one or rely heavily on staff to communicate their concerns

---

[8]   See note 20 *infra*, discussing ACUS Interpretation 84-3, 49 FR 29937 (July 25, 1984).

to other members. In almost all cases, agency members operating under the Act come to a conclusion about a matter before an open meeting and, therefore, without the benefit of any collective deliberations.9/ This is directly in conflict with the free exchange of views that we believe is necessary to enable an agency member to fulfill adequately his or her delegated duties, and to be held accountable for his or her actions.

We are also of the view that the Act is at odds with the underlying principles of multi-headed agencies. These agencies were created to provide a number of benefits, including collegial decision making where the collective thought process of a number of tenured, independent appointees would be better than one. Unfortunately, the Act often turns that goal on its head, resulting in greater miscommunication and poorer decision making by precluding, as a matter of fact, the members from engaging in decision making in a collegial way. As a result, the Act inadvertently transforms multi-headed agencies into bodies headed by a number of individually acting members.10/ It seems incongruous and unlikely that Congress, had it known that this would be the effect of the Act, would have decided to create agencies that would benefit from the collective decision making of a multimember body, and then enact a provision such as the Act that has the effect of limiting collegial decision making.11/

9/ See Welborn, The Federal Government in the Sunshine Act and Agency Decision Making, Administration and Society at 475 (February 1989) (noting that, under the Act, most important agency decisions have not emerged from authentic collegial discussions).

10/ This is somewhat ironic given that agencies headed by a single administrator do not fall under the Act — regardless of the extent of discussions that the administrator may have with his or her advisors in reaching a decision with respect to a particular matter.

11/ See Tucker, Sunshine — The Dubious New God, 32 Admin. L. Rev. 537, 541 (noting that the Sunshine Act is inconsistent with the theory underlying the creation and operation of independent agencies).

Another consequence of the Act is that it limits the ability of agency members properly to consider and establish an agency's agenda. Because agency members may be reluctant to meet privately to develop an agency agenda — out of fear that their discussions may evolve to the point where the Act is implicated, as discussed below — agency heads are frequently required to determine an agency's agenda without the benefit of the collective guidance of the members. Similarly, in effectuating an agency's agenda, staff members may experience difficulty in "ascertaining clearly the thinking of members and relating the views of one member to those of others."12/ In our view, this contributes to a decline in quality of coordinated policymaking and, more importantly, a lack of individual member accountability in agency decisions. Especially now, as government has grown in importance and become more pervasive over the last two decades, it is imperative that agency members be held to the highest level of accountability for their agencies' actions.

The restrictions on closed meetings under the Act often encourage agencies to engage in practices and procedures designed to avoid triggering the Act but which also frequently entail significant inefficiencies. These practices and procedures focus on avoiding instances in which agency members could be deemed to have "deliberated" or to have engaged in deliberations that "determine or result in the joint conduct or disposition of official agency business ***" within the meaning of the Act.13/ For example, because of the difficulty in distinguishing between preliminary conversations, which are outside of the Act — and deliberations, which trigger the Act — many agencies prohibit the gathering of a quorum of agency members as a matter of general policy. By adopting this approach, the issue of determining when agency members become engaged in deliberations or have disposed of

---

12/ See Welborn, supra at 476.

13/ The substantive and procedural restrictions of the Act are triggered only where there is a "meeting" within the meaning of the Act. There are essentially four elements of a meeting for purposes of the Act: (1) a quorum of agency members, (2) acting jointly, (3) to conduct deliberations, (4) that result in the disposition of official agency business. 5 § U.S.C. 552b(a)(2)

agency business becomes irrelevant, as the Act is not triggered in the absence of a quorum of agency members. 14/ While such bright-line, prophylactic policies have the obvious benefits of being easy to apply and effective, in a mechanical sense, in preventing inadvertent violations of the Act, they are often over-inclusive. In many instances these policies prohibit discussion of even the most preliminary views among agency members and, in doing so, they leave little room for flexibility in the exchange of member views and often impede the process of agency decision making. 15/

14/   As a practical matter, it is extremely difficult for an agency to make the distinction between actions that dispose of agency business and those that represent preliminary discussions. Congress itself experienced a fair amount of difficulty in making this determination, ultimately substituting the language "deliberations that result in ***" for the previously suggested language in the proposed legislation that referred to "deliberations that concern ***" in an attempt to exclude general discussions that "concerned" agency business, but did not determine or result in the adoption of firm positions. See Berg & Klitzman, An Interpretive Guide to the Government in the Sunshine Act at 7-8 (June 1978). This judgment is particularly troublesome in that it must be made *a priori*. In many instances, discussions initially anticipated to be preliminary in nature evolve into conversations of a more definitive nature that arguably determine (or affect) agency business.

15/   Where there is a general policy of precluding agency members from meeting in groups constituting a quorum, members may be forced to resort to one-on-one conversations on matters of agency interest. These discussions are useful, but limited, in that in order to be most effective, there must be a series of such meetings so that the views of all agency members are known. Yet, such a series of meetings — which one could argue certainly violates the spirit if not the letter of the Act — still permits results that may not be fully reflective of what would have emerged from collective discussion.

Another manner in which agencies try to avoid triggering the Act is by using intermediaries to discuss agency business. For example, the legal counsel of agency members may meet to discuss issues

Because the Act only applies to agency meetings, we also believe that it has resulted in an increased preference of agency members to use written memoranda to express their views to one another. Further, in order to avoid the notice and other procedural requirements of the Act, agencies are now more likely to vote on agency agenda matters by "notation" or "seriatim" rather than in open meetings. While the use of notational voting may nevertheless be more appropriate than a vote at an open meeting in certain instances, this method of conducting agency business is not effective in achieving the Act's goal of enhancing the public's understanding of agency decision making, and precludes the benefits that obtain from agency member collective deliberation.

Finally, we acknowledge the obvious view that many of these problems are supposedly within the control of agency members, who could, if they so chose, schedule open meetings every few days and deliberate fully at these meetings. We agree that if we did this, many of the concerns expressed here would be modified. We observe, however, that while some might be comfortable in speaking in certain instances, recognizing concerns about making substantive statements that may come back to haunt after more information is known, as well as human nature generally, others would not. Moreover, the impracticability of the concept would appear to make this solution unrealistic. In support of this, we note the fact that the problems discussed with respect to the Act are common to many agencies as good evidence both that the Act's goals are not being satisfied generally, and that if this model of exclusive open meeting deliberations worked well and appropriately, agencies would have moved towards it, not away from it.

---

that will require decision making by their principals. Because these meetings do not involve the actual members of an agency — as opposed to their respective representatives — the restrictive provisions of the Act governing open meetings are not implicated. Several conferences among intermediaries frequently are required with respect to even the most minor decisions to be made. This is not an efficient mechanism and frequently results in comprehension and interpretation problems that hinder agency decision making.

2. Effect on Public Understanding of Agency Actions

We also question whether the Act currently enhances the public's understanding of agency decision making.16/ This concern is illustrated most clearly in the context of agency rulemaking proceedings. At both the proposing and adopting stages of most agency rulemaking proceedings, there is typically a meeting open to the public in which agency members discuss the recommendations at issue, frequently make statements on the matters at hand, and ask the staff for its views on various issues of concern. It is important to remember that, under the Act, the role of the public in these meetings is limited to one of observation.17/

We acknowledge that, on some occasions, open meetings involving rulemaking proceedings involve substantive discussions and deliberations that are enlightening to the public. Notwithstanding appearances however, we believe that in general the benefit the public receives from such meetings is limited to observing final statements regarding agency decision making rather than the deliberations with respect to the matter at issue. We note that many may argue that this is, in fact, what the public ought to see and we do not suggest that this current benefit is not a real one or should be diminished. Rather, we believe that to the extent that the Act was meant to allow the public to see the _process_ by which agency decisions are made, a great number of agency meetings currently fall short of the mark.

Meetings are typically short — in many instances lasting less than one hour for multiple matters — with little deliberation occurring. In

---

16/ In comparison to the limited access of the public to agency decision making prior to the adoption of the Act, the Act has clearly been successful in improving public understanding of agency actions.

17/ Public participation in the decision making process of Federal agencies is normally limited to providing comments on proposed agency action pursuant to the notice and comment procedures for informal rulemaking contained in the APA, 5 U.S.C. 553.

addition, because of the formalistic nature of the open meetings, out of mutual respect and in the interest of avoiding surprises, there is often a fair amount of coordination among agency members and staff with respect to open meetings. In many instances the opening statements and questions of agency members are either prepared by or shared with the staff prior to the meeting to allow than to formulate appropriate responses.18/ To put it simply, at open meetings under the Act there is often less than a spontaneous and thorough exchange of views. To the extent an issue is discussed at an open meeting, it is frequently in a cursory manner that is for the record, rather than to further the deliberative process.19/ Again, we are not stating that this is inappropriate, merely that it is different from what some assert occurs.

At a more basic level, and more importantly, we question whether open meetings — with their formal structures, required advance notices, and media coverage — present the time, place or manner for in depth deliberation of the type that would be fully beneficial to the public. Frequently, for example, additional information or additional persons must be contacted or consulted to obtain answers to detailed questions and, in order for deliberations actually to occur at these meetings, matters would have to be carried — with disjointed deliberations — through several meetings over an extended period before decisions could be made. As a result, members are practically

---

18/ Although such coordination ensures that certain factors deemed important to an agency member are appropriately disclosed in a public forum, it also reduces the likelihood of the spontaneous exchange of views that one might generally associate with a deliberative process.

19/ See Welborn, supra at 471; see also ACUS Recommendation 84-3,49 FR 29937 (July 25, 1984) (noting that discussion in open meetings is sometimes inadequate to allow those in attendance to fully understand the proceedings); Tucker, supra at 543 (noting that because "Federal decision making meetings represent merely the end result of what is often a very long process dealing with complex issues, opening such meetings will be generally not only unenlightening, but also boring to even a highly intelligent spectator.").

precluded from engaging in meetings involving collegial decision making. Moreover, because of the impracticality of having an in depth conversation with each member separately on each issue, resolutions are obtained through the use of intermediaries rather than even through exchanges of views among agency members in one-on-one conversations, as is otherwise permitted by the Act.

Conclusion

In summary, we believe that the Act's objectives of inspiring increased public awareness and participation in government as well as enhancing agency decision making are commendable goals for which it is worth striving mightily. As discussed above, there is some question as to whether the Act currently meets these goals as well as it could. Therefore, we believe it appropriate to initiate a review of the Act as soon as practical to ensure that these objectives are well met. Given ACUS' historical interest in this matter, we would like to meet with you and discuss any thoughts or comments you may have.[20]

To the extent that you know of others who may also share the concerns described in this letter, please let us know so that we may gain the benefits of their thoughts as well.

Very truly yours,

Steven M.H. Wallman

---

[20] In Recommendation 84-3, the ACUS noted that one of the clearest and most significant results of the Act has been to diminish the collegial character of the agency decision making process. The recommendation encouraged Congress to consider whether the present restrictions on closing agency meetings are advisable and, if not, how they might be revised without undercutting the basic principle that "the public is entitled to the fullest practicable information regarding the decision making processes of the Federal government." ACUS Recommendation 84-3. 49 FR 29937 (July 25, 1984).

The undersigned members and former members of independent Federal regulatory agencies agree that the matters described in this letter and other issues arising under the Government in Sunshine Act since its adoption in 1976 merit review by the Administrative Conference of the United States.

/s/ Reed E. Hundt
Reed E. Hundt, Chairman
Federal Communications
Commission

/s/ Arthur Levitt
Arthur Levitt, Chairman
Securities and Exchange
Commission

/s/ Sheila Bair
Sheila Bair, Commissioner
Commodity Futures Trading
Commission

/s/ Andrew Barrett
Andrew Barrett, Commissioner
Federal Communications
Commission

/s/ Rachelle Chong
Rachelle Chong, Commissioner
Federal Communications
Commission

/s/ Susan Ness
Susan Ness, Commissioner
Federal Communications
Commission

/s/ James H. Quello
James H. Quello, Commissioner
Federal Communications
Commission

/s/ Richard Y. Roberts
Richard Y. Roberts,
Commissioner
Securities and Exchange
Commission

/s/ Christine Varney
Christine Varney, Commissioner
Federal Trade Commission

/s/ Joseph Grundfest
Joseph Grundfest, Professor
Stanford University
(Commissioner, SEC 1985-1990)

/s/ Al Sommer
Al Sommer, Esquire
Morgan, Lewis & Bockius
(Commissioner, SEC 1973-1976)

The undersigned organizations agree that the matters described in this letter and other issues arising under the Government in the Sunshine Act since its adoption in 1976 merit review by the Administrative Conference of the United States.

/s/ Laurence Gold
Laurence Gold, General Counsel
AFL-CIO

/s/Alan Morrison
Alan Morrison, Esquire
Public Citizen

Appendix I
Administrative Conference of the United States, Report and Recommendation by the Special Committee to Review the Government in the Sunshine Act, as reprinted at 49 Admin. L. Rev. 421 (Spring 1997)

REPORT & RECOMMENDATION
BY THE SPECIAL COMMITTEE TO REVIEW
THE GOVERNMENT IN THE SUNSHINE ACT*

SPECIAL COMMITTEE,
ADMINISTRATIVE CONFERENCE OF THE UNITED STATES

The Government in the Sunshine Act, enacted in 1976, requires federal agencies headed by a collegial body, a majority of whose members are appointed by the President and confirmed by the Senate, to open its meetings. About 50 federal agencies are subject to the Act, including the major independent regulatory commissions such as the Securities and Exchange Commission, Federal Trade Commission, Federal Communications Commission, and the National Labor Relations Board. (Departments, and many agencies headed by a single individual, are not covered by the Act.) The Act's ten enumerated exemptions generally parallel those in the Freedom of Information Act (FOIA), with one important exception. The Sunshine Act has no exemption that parallels the fifth exemption in the FOIA for interagency and intra-agency "pre-decisional" memoranda and letters. The Act also prescribes in detail the procedures that agencies must follow to invoke an exemption and to close a meeting. The Act's primary purposes are to provide the public with information regarding the decisionmaking processes of federal agencies, and to improve those processes, while protecting the rights of individuals and the ability of the government to carry out its responsibilities.

---

* EDITOR'S NOTE: To maintain the integrity of the report, the main text is presented verbatim and largely unedited. The letters and exhibits referred to throughout the report have not been included in this reproduction. Copies are on file with the author.

In a letter dated February, 17, 1995, signed by over one dozen current and former commissioners of multi-member agencies and several private organizations, the Chair of the Administrative Conference of the United States (ACUS) was asked to review the effectiveness of the Government in the Sunshine Act. The letter's signatories stated strong support for the Act's underlying goal of enhancing public understanding of agency decisionmaking, but expressed concern as to whether the Act is, in fact, meeting this goal as well as it might. They also suggested that the Act has adversely affected the decisionmaking at multi-member agencies because of the Act's "chilling effect" on the willingness and ability of agency members to engage in collegial deliberations.

In a letter to the ACUS Chair, dated May 11, 1995, the members of the Federal Trade Commission, referring to the February 17 letter, endorsed an examination of the effectiveness of the Act. The FTC Commissioners stated:

> Notwithstanding the laudable goals of this legislation, having operated under the Act for more than fifteen years, questions may be raised whether it provides for the proper balance between public access and candor in agency deliberations and whether the purposes arguably served by the Act are not adequately addressed by other statutes such as the Administrative Procedure Act.

A copy of the May 11 letter from the FTC is attached to this Report as Exhibit 2.

The Chair established the Special Committee to study issues raised by these letters. The Committee, in a series of open meetings held from May to September, and at a public hearing held on September 12, 1995,[1] heard from numerous agency officials and reviewed articles written for ACUS and others to the effect that public meetings under the Act often lack [a] meaningful substantive exchange of ideas and real collective deliberation on issues being decided. Among the reasons given for the inhibiting effect of public meetings on collective decisionmaking are the following: concern that providing initial deliberative views publicly, without sufficient thought and information, may harm the public interest by irresponsibly introducing

---

1. A copy of the Federal Register notice, dated August 8, 1995 (60 Fed. Reg. 40302), is attached to the Report as Exhibit 3. The hearing transcript is attached as Exhibit 4.

uncertainty or confusion to industry or the general public; a desire on the part of members to speak with a uniform voice on matters of particular importance or to develop negotiating strategies which might be thwarted if debated publicly; reluctance of an agency member to embarrass another agency member, or to embarrass himself, through inadvertent, argumentative, or exaggerated statements; concern that an agency member's statements may be used against the agency in subsequent litigation, or misinterpreted or misunderstood by the public or the press, as, for example, when the agency member is testing a position by "playing devil's advocate" or merely "thinking out loud"; and concerns that a member's statements may affect financial markets.

In addition, the Committee has received extensive and credible testimony that the restrictions imposed by the Act have had the effect of not only diminishing discussions on the merits of issues before agencies, but also preventing debate concerning agency priorities and the establishment of agency agendas, even though such discussions of a preliminary nature may not technically constitute a "meeting" otherwise required to be held in public under the Act.[2] While it may be permissible pursuant to a literal interpretation of "meeting"[3] for a quorum of agency members to conduct preliminary discussions on an issue, as a practical matter it is extremely difficult for an agency member to make the distinction between actions that actually dispose of agency business and those that merely constitute preliminary discussions. Agency members, and agency general counsel who advise them, are understandably—and appropriately—concerned about engaging in discussions with a quorum of agency members that could be perceived, even arguably, as crossing the line, even though the discussions may, in fact, not dispose of official agency business. And, of course, it is difficult, *a priori*, to know whether a conversation that is anticipated to be preliminary will turn into a conversation that takes on a more definitive cast.

Although there obviously are exceptions, and open meetings held under the current Act are valuable in that they allow an agency to explain publicly the results of its prior decisionmaking, the Committee believes that,

---

2. A "meeting" means the "deliberations of at least the number of individual agency members required to take action on behalf of the agency where such deliberations determine or result in the joint conduct or disposition of official agency business. . . ." 5 U.S.C. § 552b(a)(2) (1994).

3. *See* FCC v. ITT World Communications, Inc., 466 U.S. 463 (1984).

generally, true collective decisionmaking does not occur at agency public meetings. Further, the Committee believes the Act also promotes ineffective practices within agencies which themselves contribute to the erosion of legal decisionmaking and, correspondingly, to a decline in the quality of agency decisions that the public receives. For example, in order to avoid having a meeting of a quorum, the Act has the effect of encouraging agencies to use one-on-one "rotating" meetings in order to reach a consensus among the agency's members. This is obviously an inefficient way for a multi-member body to conduct business, just in terms of the additional time spent by agency members in conducting such meetings, compared to a group meeting at which all members could deliberate together. More importantly, serial meetings of this type are no substitute for collective decisionmmaking; the outcomes of such meetings may significantly vary from those that might have resulted from a free exchange of views among all the members of a multi-member agency. Another consequence of the Act has been that it encourages the deliberative process to be conducted by and through the staff of the agency members, enhancing the power of the intermediary staff members *vis a vis* the agency members and, perhaps, reducing the accountability of appointed agency members.

The Committee is also aware of and is concerned about the tendency for agencies subject to the Sunshine Act to rely increasingly on notation voting (i.e., voting on an item by circulation based on a memorandum without discussion in a public meeting) when taking action on important substantive matters. The Sunshine Act does not prohibit notation voting, and notation voting was used to some extent prior to enactment of the Sunshine Act to deal with routine or emergency matters. Nevertheless, the routine use of this mode of decisionmaking, at least with regard to important substantive matters, does not further the Act's goal of openness and improved public access to agency decisionmaking. Thus, to the extent that the Sunshine Act has increased this use of notation voting, it has diminished whatever opportunity for collective decisionmaking would have existed at a meeting attended by the agency members.

In light of the above, the Committee is concerned that the public is neither receiving the enhanced access to the governmental decisionmaking process that the Act envisioned, nor as discussed below, is it receiving the benefit of better agency decisions through collegial decisionmaking. It should be noted that the Committee also heard from representatives of several major press-related organizations who, while not disputing the view that agency members are generally reluctant to have substantive discussions in public meetings, expressed the view that such public officials should change their behavior and admonished them to do so. These representatives tended to believe that the Act itself was not the problem. The Committee was nevertheless persuaded that the Act does need to be adjusted, and it offers the following recommendations for changes in the Act (and in agency behavior) in the belief that these adjustments will increase collegial decisionmaking among members of multi-member agencies, and at the same time improve, or least not diminish, the public's access to the agency's actual deliberative process.

The Committee notes that concerns with respect to the effectiveness of the Act and its impact on the collegiality of agency decisionmaking have been the subject of debate for some time.[4] Moreover, it must be remembered that the principal reason that Congress has established multi-member agencies in the first place is because Congress has made the judgment that, for the matters subject to the agency's jurisdiction, there is a benefit from a collegial decisionmaking process that brings to bear on the ultimate decisions the diverse viewpoints of agency members who have differing philosophies, experiences, and expertise. If the Act has had the effect, as a matter of fact, of diminishing, or in some cases negating, the collegial decisionmaking process that is the *raison d'etre* for a multi-member agency, without enhancing public understanding of the agency decisionmaking process, it is appropriate to consider alternative models that are consistent with achievement of the objectives of the Act.

Therefore, the Committee recommends that Congress establish a time-limited pilot program that would allow agencies more leeway to have private meetings, subject to appropriate memorialization, if they opt to make commitments to avoid undue use of notation voting and to hold regular meetings. The Committee recommends five to seven years as the time period—enough time to allow an assessment of the pilot to see whether the approach encompassed in it achieves the twin purposes of increasing the availability of information to the public and increasing collegial decisionmaking in the agencies. If Congress finds that the pilot worked well, it could amend the Act accordingly; if the assessment shows

---

4. *See* Improvements in the Administration of the Government in the Sunshine Act Administrative Conference of the United States, Recommendation 84-3, 1 C.F.R. 305.84-3, 49 Fed. Reg. 29,942 (July 25; 1984).

problems or bad faith on the part of agency decisionmakers in carrying it out, it could be terminated at that point.

More specifically, the pilot program should authorize an agency subject to the Government in the Sunshine Act to allow its members to meet in private, without advance notice, provided that the agency requires such meetings to be memorialized by "a detailed summary" of the meeting, made public no later than five working days after the meeting, that would indicate the date, time, participants, subject matters discussed, and a review of the nature of the discussion. Before such a pilot program may go into effect, the participating agency also would have to agree (1) to conduct votes and other official actions on important substantive matters (not covered by the Act's exemptions) in open public meetings and to refrain, to the extent practicable, from using notation voting procedures for such matters, and (2) to hold open public meetings, to the extent practicable, at regular intervals, which it would be in order for members to address issues discussed in private sessions or items disposed of by notation. This opportunity for discussion is not intended to imply that finality of matters previously voted on notation would be affected by such discussions except to the extent that the agency acts consistently with its own procedures for reconsideration. The results of such a pilot program should be examined carefully by Congress and other appropriate entities before it is extended or made permanent.

The Committee recommends, in addition to the institution of the pilot program, that the Act be amended to require agencies to develop and publish rules or policy statements outlining their procedure for notation voting and the types of issues for which it will normally be used. The Committee also recommends that agencies hold regularly scheduled meetings at which it would be in order for members to discuss, among other things, items disposed of by notation.

The Committee was also convinced that there is a special problem caused by the Act with regard to agencies operating in an adjudicative capacity. The Act currently contains an exemption that permits closure of meetings involving the "initiation, conduct, or disposition by the agency of a particular case of formal adjudication pursuant to the procedures in section 554 of [the APA] or otherwise involving a determination on the record after opportunity for a hearing." Agencies such as the Federal Trade Commission and the Occupational Safety and Health Review Commission (OSHRC) frequently and properly close meetings to discuss the disposition of such cases. The problem occurs when, after such a meeting, the commissioners begin writing the opinions necessary in such cases. Should they wish to discuss the wording of an opinion, as would an appellate court, the members have to notice, and vote to close, another "meeting" under the Act. Obviously, this inefficiency is heightened in the case of a three-member commission such as the OSHRC where no two members can ever discuss agency business in private because they would constitute a quorum. Therefore the Committee recommends that the Act be amended to make clear that, when an agency properly closes a meeting under exemption 10, any subsequent meeting to discuss the same specific adjudicatory matter need not be subject to the notice and closure procedures under the Act. The Committee recognizes that this proposal should perhaps be extended to follow-up discussions to meetings closed under other exemptions as well, but it did not have enough time to study that question.

The Committee also heard testimony about special problems caused by the above quoted wording of exemption 10 at the United States International Trade Commission (ITC). The ITC has several types of adjudicative proceedings, some of which are governed by section 554 of the APA, and therefore clearly fall within the terms of exemption 10, and others of which would appear to fit the definition by "otherwise involving a determination on the record after an opportunity for a hearing." The ITC, perhaps due to an abundance of caution, has declined to invoke this exemption for any of its adjudications. The Administrative Conference has already urged the ITC to revisit this issue and seek a statutory clarification if necessary.[5]

---

5. In Recommendation, 91-10, *Administrative Procedures Used in Antidumping and Countervailing Duty Cases*, Part D, ACUS made the following recommendation to the ITC:

> To encourage collegial decision making, the ITC should exchange drafts, views and other information before entering into formal deliberations. The Commission should decide whether informal meetings to discuss the disposition of AD/CVD cases constitute meetings exempt from the Sunshine Act under exemption 10. If the Commission determines that such meetings are subject to the Sunshine Act, then Congress should consider amending the Tariff Act to provide that the Sunshine Act does not apply to informal meetings held to discuss the disposition of the AD/CVD cases.

Finally, the Committee believes that agencies could and should consider steps to make the open meetings more useful and to increase the flow of information to the public. The Committee reiterates the suggestions made by ACUS in 1984[6] and adds a few more.

In addition to the recommendations set forth below, the Committee considered several other ideas. The Committee rejected some of them, such as repealing the Act (which was not supported by any of the participants in Committee meetings or public hearing), amending it to permit each agency to develop its own openness regulations, or amending it to cover only meetings of the full board or commission. Other proposals, beyond those recommended below, and including some of those contained in the August 8 Federal Register[7] notice, may be worthy of further consideration, in lieu of or even in conjunction with, the recommendations contained herein.

Recommendations

(1) Congress should establish a pilot program, to last for five to seven years, that would authorize an agency subject to the Government in the Sunshine Act to allow its members to meet in private, without notice, provided that (a) the agency requires such meetings to be memorialized by "a detailed summary" of the meeting, made public no later than five working days after the meeting, that would indicate the date, time, participants, subject matters discussed, and a review of the nature of the

---

6. The Committee subscribes to the earlier ACUS recommendation made to agencies in this regard in Recommendation 84-3(1):

> Agencies should continually strive to reflect fully in their activities the basic purpose of the Government in the Sunshine Act, which is to enlarge public access to and information about the operations of government. Agencies are strongly encouraged to review periodically their sunshine policies and practices in light of experience and the spirit of the law for the purpose of making adjustments that would enlarge public access to meaningful information, such as (a) invoking the exemptions of the Act only where there is substantial reason to do so; and (b) making open meetings more useful through comprehensible discussion of agenda items and provision of background material and documentation pertaining to the issues under consideration.

7. *See, e.g.,* the various proposals outlined in the Federal Register notice, *supra* note 1.

discussion; and (b) that before such pilot program may go into effect, the participating agency also (i) agrees to conduct votes and take other official actions on important substantive matters (not covered by the Act's exemptions) in open public meetings and to refrain, to the extent practicable, from using notation voting procedures for such matters; and (ii) agrees to hold open public meetings, to the extent practicable, at regular intervals, at which it would be in order for members to address issues discussed in private sessions or items disposed of by notation. This opportunity for discussion is not intended to imply that finality of matters previously voted on by notation would be affected by such discussions except to the extent that the agency acts consistently with its own procedures for reconsideration. The results of such a pilot program should be examined carefully by Congress and other appropriate entities before it is extended or made permanent.

(2) Congress should also amend the Sunshine Act in several particulars:

(a) to require agencies subject to the Act to develop and publish rules or policy statements outlining their procedure for notation voting and the types of issues for which it will normally be used.

(b) to make clear that when an agency properly closes a meeting under exemption 10, any subsequent meeting to discuss the same matter need not be subject to the notice and closure procedures under the Act.

(3) Agencies subject to the Sunshine Act should develop regulations (or policies) that maximize the amount of information made available to the public before, during and after agency meetings. For example, agencies should strive to publish meeting notices further in advance of the date for meetings where feasible; to provide more complete summaries of upcoming agenda items; to make available relevant non-privileged documents before or during meetings; offer closed circuit television coverage of meetings where there is enough interest; and to release minutes, summaries, and decisional opinions as soon as feasible after meetings.

(4) The United States International Trade Commission should follow ACUS Recommendation 91-10[8] and revisit the issue of whether its adjudications are covered by exemption 10 of the Act.

---

8. *See supra* note 5.

Appendix J
Memorandum for J. Virgil Mattingly, Jr., General Counsel for the Board of Governors of the Federal Reserve System
Re: Permissibility of Federal Reserve Board Efforts to Control Access to Buildings and Open Meetings, from M. Edward Whelan III, Principal Deputy Assistant Attorney General, July 9, 2002

U.S. Department of Justice
Office of Legal Counsel

Office of the Principal Deputy Assistant Attorney General   Washington, D.C. 20530

July 9, 2002

MEMORANDUM FOR J. VIRGIL MATTINGLY, JR. GENERAL COUNSEL FOR THE BOARD OF GOVERNORS OF THE FEDERAL RESERVE SYSTEM

Re: Permissibility of Federal Reserve Board Efforts to Control Access to Buildings and Open Meetings

This memorandum responds to your request for our opinion regarding the permissibility, under the Government in the Sunshine Act ("Sunshine Act") and the Privacy Act, of certain actions that might be taken by the Board of Governors of the Federal Reserve System ("Board").[1] You have asked two questions: First, may the Board place all members of the public who wish to observe an open meeting of the

---

[1] See Letter for Paul Colborn, Special Counsel, Office of Legal Counsel, from J. Virgil Mattingly, Jr., General Counsel, Board of Governors of the Federal Reserve System (Apr. 10, 2002) ("Board Letter").

Board in a room that is physically separate from the meeting room, where they can observe and listen to the meeting by closed-circuit television? Second, may the Board screen all members of the public seeking entrance to a Board building to observe an open meeting of the Board, by obtaining personal information and conducting a security check, and refuse admission to those who either refuse to give the information or fail the security check? We conclude that it would be permissible under both the Sunshine Act and the Privacy Act for the Board to engage in these actions.

I.

"Because of its status as the world's most important central bank, the prominence of its Chairman, and the hugely adverse consequences to the United States and world economies that could result from an attack on the Federal Reserve, the Board ... has significant security needs." Board Letter at 2-3. These needs have led the Board to consider adopting the measures outlined above.

As part of its duties, the Board conducts open meetings to discuss the country's economic health and to determine what actions, if any, must be taken to address inflation, unemployment, or other economic concerns. The Board is considering adopting a policy of placing all members of the public who enter the Board's buildings to attend an open meeting of the Board in a room that is physically separate from the meeting room. In this room they can watch and listen to the meeting by closed-circuit television.

In addition, the Board is also considering screening all potential entrants to its buildings. The screening would require obtaining certain information from potential entrants and checking information with established law enforcement sources to evaluate possible security risks. The Board's security staff would solicit information such as name, date of birth, and social security number. The information would be solicited to the greatest extent possible under a pre-screening procedure, but also at the building's entrance. Consistent with current practice, potential entrants would be required to produce a photo ID at the door. Under the proposed plan, the Board would bar from the building any person who fails to provide the requested information or fails the security check.[2]

The first question we address is whether placing members of the public in a separate room to observe a Board meeting would be permissible under the Sunshine Act. We then turn to the permissibility of requiring members of the public to provide personal information and satisfy a security check before they may enter a Board building to observe a meeting. That question entails issues under both the Sunshine Act and the Privacy Act.

II.

The Sunshine Act, 5 U.S.C. § 552b (2000), applies to agencies that are headed by a collegial body of two or more members. *Id.* § 552b(a)(1). The Act requires that covered agencies hold their deliberations on agency action in open meetings: "Members shall not jointly conduct or dispose of agency business other than in accordance with this section. Except as provided in subsection (c) [providing for exceptions not relevant to the question presented here], every portion of every meeting of an agency shall be *open to public observation*." *Id.* § 552b(b) (emphasis added). The contemplated Board action of providing for observation of the meeting in a separate room would be inconsistent with this open-meeting requirement only if the italicized language requires the Board to allow members of the public to enter the actual meeting room and observe the meeting there. We do not believe that the statute imposes such a requirement.

Under a straightforward reading of the "open to public observation" language of subsection (b), the Board may satisfy its statutory requirement by providing a separate room for members of the public to observe Board meetings by closed-circuit television. The Sunshine Act does not authorize members of the public to participate in meetings, nor does it permit them to disrupt meetings. *See* Barbara Allen Babcock, *Department of Justice Letter to Covered Agencies*, April 19, 1977 ("DOJ Letter"), in Richard K. Berg & Stephen H. Klitzman, *Interpretive Guide to the Government in the Sunshine Act* 121 (1978). Since the public is not authorized to participate in the meeting, there is nothing inherent in the

---

[2] The Board notes that the White House and the Treasury Department have similar clearance procedures to control access to their buildings. Board Letter at 2.

concept of "open to public observation" that would obligate the Board to place members of the public in the same room as the Board. As long as the public can adequately see, hear, and understand what takes place in the meeting, the requirement will have been met because the meeting would be "open to public observation."

The legislative history of the Sunshine Act is consistent with our view that "open to public observation" does not contain an implied requirement that members of the public be present in the actual meeting room in order to observe a meeting. The Sunshine Act "is founded on the proposition that the government should conduct the public's business in public. [The Act] requires...all Federal agencies subject to the legislation to conduct their meetings in the open, rather than behind closed doors." S. Rep. No. 94-354, at 1 (1975). In other words, the critical purpose of the Act is to ensure that the decisionmaking meetings of covered agencies be open, not closed. Thus, so long as the Board's meetings are conducted "in the open" and the public can observe the meetings, this purpose would be satisfied.

The phrase "open to public observation" was adopted by the House of Representatives, and accepted by the conference committee, as a substitute for the "open to the public" formulation adopted by the Senate. The House committee gave the following rationale for the change: "The phrase 'open to public observation,' while not affording the public any additional right to participate in a meeting, is intended to guarantee that *ample space, sufficient visibility*, and *adequate acoustics* will be provided." H.R. Rep. No. 94-880, pt. 1, at 8 (1976), *reprinted in* 1976 U.S.C.C.A.N. 2183, 2190 (emphasis added); *see also* H.R. Conf. Rep. No. 94-1441, at 11 (1976), *reprinted in* 1976 U.S.C.C.A.N. 2183, 2247 ("The phrase 'open to public observation' is intended to guarantee that ample space, sufficient visibility, and adequate acoustics will be provided."). Placing members of the public in a large enough separate room with adequate closed-circuit television capability would satisfy that purpose.

III.

Whether the Board may deny individuals access to Board buildings to observe an open meeting turns on whether the Sunshine Act provides each individual member of the public with a right to observe an open meeting of a covered agency. Resolution of that question also determines the Privacy Act question that you have raised.

A.

The open meeting requirement of subsection (b) of the Sunshine Act — that meetings be "open to public observation" — is not stated in terms of granting a right to individuals to attend agency meetings, but rather is articulated in more general language obligating an agency to provide the public as a whole with the opportunity to observe meetings. Thus, we believe that the requirement is satisfied if members of the general public have the opportunity to attend the meeting. The language does not constitute a requirement that all members of the public, or any particular individuals, who wish to observe a meeting be allowed to do so.[3]

The Sunshine Act's Declaration of Policy states that "[i]t is the purpose of this Act to provide the public with . . . information [about government decisionmaking] while protecting . . . the ability of the Government to carry out its responsibilities." 5 U.S.C. § 552b note. Pursuant to other statutory authority, the Board has sole control of its buildings. *See* 12 U.S.C. § 243 (2000) ("The Board may maintain, enlarge, or remodel any building or buildings so acquired or constructed and shall have sole control of such building or buildings and space therein."). Sole control of its buildings implies that the Board should be able to deny access to its buildings for reasonable reasons, such as the significant security concerns expressed by the Board, *see* Board Letter at 1 (citing a desire to implement stronger security measures in controlling access to the buildings "in order to address increased concerns about attacks on its buildings"). Thus, reading the Board's statutory control over its buildings together with the Sunshine Act's open meeting requirement further reinforces our conclusion that

---

[3] Even the Sixth Amendment, which establishes for defendants a constitutional right to a "public trial," does not give an individual member of the public the right to attend a trial. Rather, a trial open to the public in general satisfies the constitutional requirement. *See* Estes v. Texas, 381 U.S. 532, 588-89 (1965) (Harlan, J., concurring) ("Obviously, the public-trial guarantee is not violated if an individual member of the public cannot gain admittance to a courtroom because there are no available seats. The guarantee will already have been met, for the 'public' will be present in the form of those persons who did gain admission.").

although the public as a whole is entitled to observe Board meetings, particular individuals can be turned away.

The legislative history of the Sunshine Act comports with our reading. As discussed above, *supra* at 3, the Sunshine Act's legislative history indicates that Congress's purpose in enacting the open meeting requirement was to ensure that decisionmaking meetings be held in the open and not behind closed doors. That history does not reveal any congressional intent to create a right for every individual to attend the meetings. In addition, Congress used the phrase "open to public observation" to address logistical concerns: it wanted *adequate* space to accommodate meeting observers. The legislative history indicates that an agency is not required under the Act to guarantee that every person who seeks to attend a meeting may do so, so long as accommodation for a reasonable number of people is provided. *See* S. Rep. No. 94-354, at 19 (emphasis added) ("When a meeting must be open, the agency should make arrangements for a room large enough to accommodate a reasonable number of persons interested in attending. Holding a meeting in a small room, thereby denying access to most of the public, would violate this section and be contrary to its clear intent.").[4]

---

[4] We disagree with a portion of the 1977 DOJ Letter that bears on this question. The DOJ Letter states that "[o]f course, any person may attend a meeting without indicating his identity and/or the person, if any, whom he represents and no requirement of prior notification of intent to observe a meeting may be required." *Interpretive Guide* at 121. We find nothing in the text of the Sunshine Act that precludes imposing such requirements, nor do we see anything in the legislative history that suggests such an effect. We note further that the DOJ Letter was signed by the head of the Civil Division, which is a litigation division of the Department of Justice, and not by the Office of Legal Counsel, which is the component of the Department responsible for providing legal advice. The broad interpretation of statutory terms throughout the DOJ Letter apparently reflects a desire to improve the government's litigating position under the Sunshine Act. For example, the DOJ Letter recommends that agencies allow sound recordings, notes, and photography "in order to avoid needless litigation over issues which do not go to the heart of the Act." *Id. See also id.* ("I suggest that you insure that the term 'meeting' is broadly defined in practice so that the statute of limitations can come into play and so that the potential for litigation can be reduced.") Although we understand the practical interest in defining terms broadly to minimize litigation risk, we believe that the correct reading of "open to public observation" is that it is addressed only to the agencies as a requirement that the meeting be open to the public at large.

B.

As discussed above, we believe that the open meeting requirement of the Sunshine Act does not provide all individuals with the right to observe a covered agency's meetings, but rather only imposes on the agency the obligation to hold open meetings - that is, meetings open to the public at large. We therefore concluded that it would be permissible under the Sunshine Act for the Board to require that individuals seeking to observe Board meetings must provide personal information and satisfy a security check. It necessarily follows from that conclusion that such a practice by the Board would not violate section 7 of the Privacy Act, which makes it unlawful for an agency "to deny to any individual any right, benefit, or privilege provided by law because of such individual's refusal to disclose his social security account number." Pub. L. No. 93-579, § 7, 88 Stat. 1896, 1909 (1974). This is so because the Sunshine Act's open meeting requirement does not create an individual "right, benefit, or privilege" within the meaning of section 7 of the Privacy Act.

The legislative history regarding this provision of the Privacy Act supports the view that the provision's reference to "right, benefit, or privilege" refers to individual rights granted by the Constitution or statutes. The Senate debates provide an example of what the provision was intended to cover: "[I]t will be unlawful to commence operation of a State or local government procedure that requires individuals to disclose their social security account number in order to register a motor vehicle, obtain a driver's license or other permit, or exercise the right to vote in an election." 120 Cong. Rec. 40,407 (1974) (statement of Sen. Ervin). Attending a meeting open to the public under the Sunshine Act is qualitatively different from receiving a driver's license or exercising the right to vote. Any individual who meets the necessary requirements may drive a car or vote in an election because the law gives each individual that right. Voting involves a core individual right. Driving a car is a daily activity engaged in by many individuals. Nothing in the Sunshine Act, however, provides any particular member of the public with a right to observe an agency meeting. All the Act does is require the agency to open its deliberative meetings to public observation. The denial of access to an individual who fails to provide a social security number or pass the security check may prevent that particular person from observing the meeting, but it does not foreclose the public observation of the meeting by other members of the public who provide their social security numbers and pass the security check.

IV.

We conclude that the Board may, consistent with its obligations under the Sunshine Act, place observers of an open meeting of the Board in a separate room to watch the meeting on closed-circuit television. We also conclude that it is permissible under both the Sunshine Act and the Privacy Act for the Board to require disclosure of personal information and satisfaction of a security check as a condition of entering the Board's buildings for access to the separate room to observe the open meeting.

M. Edward Whelan III
Principal Deputy Assistant Attorney General

Appendix K
Letter from J. Virgil Mattingly, Jr., General Counsel for the Board of Governors of the Federal Reserve System, to Paul Colborn, Esq., Special Counsel, Department of Justice, Office of Legal Counsel, April 10, 2002

BOARD OF GOVERNORS
OF THE
FEDERAL RESERVE SYSTEM
WASHINGTON, D.C. 20551

J. VIRGIL MATTINGLY, JR.
GENERAL COUNSEL

April 10, 2002

Paul Colborn, Esq.
Special Counsel
Department of Justice
Office of Legal Counsel
Washington, D.C. 20530

Dear Mr. Colborn:

I am writing to request the opinion of the Office of Legal Counsel on two questions that arise out of the need to reconcile the Board of Governors' security concerns with its obligations under the Government in the Sunshine Act and the Privacy Act. The Board is prepared to accept the Office of Legal Counsel's views following your review.

You have discussed these questions and related issues generally with Mr. Stephen Siciliano of my staff on two occasions earlier this year. For your convenient reference, I am enclosing copies of our previous notes that prompted those discussions, and a copy of the April 19, 1977, letter by Assistant Attorney General Barbara Allen Babcock containing interpretations of the Sunshine Act that, in the current security conscious environment, cause us concern.

These questions relate to the more stringent security measures the Board is planning to implement in order to control access to the Board's buildings by the public generally. First, in order to address increased concerns about attacks on its buildings, the Board's professional security staff strongly believe that it is necessary to screen on a consistent basis all potential entrants to the buildings, including those who seek entry in order to attend a public meeting of the Board, by obtaining certain information from such persons and using such information to consult with established law enforcement information sources regarding possible security risks posed by those potential entrants. The information that would be solicited would include name, date of birth, and social security number. The information would be solicited to the greatest extent possible under a prescreening procedure, and also at the door. In addition, potential entrants would be required to produce a photo ID at the door consistent with current practice. Security staff believe it is necessary to exclude from the building any person who fails to provide the requested information.

The Sunshine Act provides that, unless an exemption applies, "every part of every meeting of an agency shall be open to public observation." 5 U.S.C. 552b(B). The April 1977 opinion letter from the Assistant Attorney General providing guidance on the Sunshine Act states that "any person may attend a meeting without indicating his identity . . . and no requirement of prior notification of intent to observe a meeting may be required." Additionally, section 7 of the Privacy Act makes it unlawful for an agency "to deny to any individual any right, benefit, or privilege provided by law because of such individual's refusal to disclose his social security account number." Pub. L. No. 93-579, § 7, 88 Stat. 1897 (1974).

We believe that in the current environment neither the Sunshine Act nor the Privacy Act prohibits the denial of access to a person seeking entry to the Board's buildings, including those seeking to observe a public meeting of the Board pursuant to the Sunshine Act, who fail or refuse to provide the designated information, including social security number. Nothing in the text of the Sunshine Act provides any particular member of the public with a right to observe an agency meeting. Moreover, the Board clearly has the authority to impose reasonable requirements on those with access to its buildings to protect the safety of employees, visitors and the buildings. The reasonable exercise of this authority is fully consistent with the public observation requirement of the Sunshine Act. The denial of access to an individual who fails to meet reasonable security requirements may prevent that particular person from attending the agency meeting, but does not foreclose the public observation of the meeting by other members of the public who meet the security restrictions.

This view is also consistent with the legislative history of the Sunshine Act, which suggests that an agency is not required under the Act to guarantee that every person who seeks to attend a meeting may do so, so long as accommodation for a reasonable number of people is provided. S. Rep. No. 94-354, 94th Cong., 1st Sess. 19 (1975); *see also* Berg & Klitzman, *Interpretative Guide to the Government in the Sunshine Act* 14 (1978). Thus, although the public has a right to attend a meeting, individual persons may be excluded for reasons consistent with the agency's mission, including lack of space, if there has been a reasonable effort by the agency to provide adequate space. If an agency may deny admittance to a meeting room for lack of space, clearly the mandate of the Sunshine Act may not be viewed as granting an absolute right of any individual to attend a meeting.

In addition, as the 1977 guidance letter from the Assistant Attorney General recognized, "the right to observe does not include any right to disrupt the meeting." This guidance confirms the conclusion that the rights provided by the Sunshine Act are not absolute as to any individual and are subject to reasonable security restrictions. It follows, we believe, that the enforcement of a reasonable security protocol applicable to all who seek entry that might exclude some, but not all, members of the public is consistent with the purposes of the Sunshine Act.

Furthermore, in our view, the procedures we are planning to implement are reasonable and as minimally burdensome as possible in light of the current perceived threats to the security of the Board and its buildings. These same procedures are used by some other government agencies, such as the White House and the Treasury Department, which have significant security needs. Although these two entities are not subject to the Sunshine Act, their use of a pre-notification procedure relying on social security numbers for all entrants supports the view that this level of restriction is reasonable in light of current threat assessments. Because of its status as the world's most important central bank, the prominence of its Chairman, and the hugely adverse consequences to the United States and world economies that could result from an attack on the Federal Reserve, the Board also has significant security needs.

We do not believe that the guidance provided by the Assistant Attorney General's 1977 letter with respect to requiring identification or prior notification, which does not appear to be based on any specific provision of the statutory text, contradicts this view. When this letter was issued, government agencies typically had minimal security measures restricting entry to their buildings, if any at all. In this context, imposing an identification or prior notification requirement only on those members of the public who sought to observe an agency meeting imposed a greater burden on those individuals than on other members of the public who sought to enter the agency's building for other purposes. Thus, such restrictions could be viewed as unreasonably interfering with the implementation of the statute's public observation requirement. As we have explained, here the screening procedures the Board is planning would be applied to any person seeking access to the Board's buildings, not just those seeking to attend a Board meeting. Likewise, the procedures are very similar to the restrictions that are now being imposed by other government entities to meet security concerns. Those seeking to attend a public Board meeting would not be singled out for unusual or especially burdensome treatment. Accordingly, we believe the proposed approach is fully consistent with the intent of the guidance contained in the Assistant Attorney General's letter.

For the same reasons, we believe that the planned use of social security numbers as a condition for access to the Board's buildings is consistent with the Privacy Act provision that protects disclosure of individual social security numbers. If agencies for good and sufficient reasons may exclude a particular individual who wishes to attend their meetings, it follows that no particular individual has a "right, benefit, or privilege" under the Sunshine Act to attend agency meetings. Thus, denial of access to the Board's buildings to someone who refuses to provide his or her social security number would not deprive that person of any right, benefit, or privilege protected by section 7 of the Privacy Act.

The second question we are raising is whether, to address security concerns, the Board may place all members of the public who enter the Board's buildings to attend an open meeting in a room physically separate from the room in which the meeting is held, but which is connected to the meeting room by closed circuit television, including audio. We believe that this procedure would not violate the terms or purposes of the public observation requirement of the Sunshine Act. It is well established that members of the public have no right to participate in agency meetings, but are entitled only to observe the meetings. Because all members of the public attending an open Board meeting in a separate room would see and hear the proceedings at the meeting in their entirety, all rights to observation of open meetings would be provided. This proposed procedure is consistent with the Board's past practice when the number of individuals attending a particular Board meeting exceeded the seating capacity in the Board's meeting room. In those cases a separate room with visual and audio connection to the meeting room has been provided for the overflow attendees.

It is not appropriate or feasible to include in this letter details of the security concerns that cause us to urge your prompt attention to this matter. Should the Department seek more information, however, I would be happy to arrange a meeting to address your informational needs, subject to appropriate safeguards for truly sensitive information.

Please call Mr. Stephen Siciliano of my staff if you have questions or need additional information in connection with your consideration of the questions we have posed.

Sincerely,

J. Virgil Mattingly

Appendix L
Federal Reserve Board
"A Guide to the Meetings of the Board of Governors of the Federal Reserve System," 2004

The Federal Reserve Board

Government in the Sunshine

A Guide to Meetings of the Board of Governors of the Federal Reserve System

Skip to content

Open meetings
Closed meetings
Other procedures for handling official business
Sunshine exemptions

Meetings of the Board of Governors, typically held twice a month, cover the regulatory, monetary policy, and other responsibilities of the central bank. The Board conducts its meetings in compliance with title 5, section 552b, of the U.S. Code, known as the Government in the Sunshine Act. The public is welcome to attend all meetings except those that the Board determines should be closed under legal exemptions defined in the Sunshine Act.

This guide describes the procedures that the Board follows for open and closed meetings. Specific exemptions in the Sunshine Act that allow closed meetings are listed at the end of this document. Additional information is available from the Board's Public Affairs Office and Freedom of Information Office.

Open Meetings
Agendas of open Board meetings are released to the public in advance. Routine matters are listed on a "Summary Agenda"; more substantive items are listed on a "Discussion Agenda."

Notice of Open Meetings
The Board submits a notice of an open meeting to the Federal Register seven days in advance of the meeting. At the time of submission, the notice is also available from the Board's Freedom of Information and Public Affairs offices, the Treasury Department Press Room, and the Board Meetings page of the Board's web site. In addition, the Board maintains a "Sunshine" mailing list to announce meetings to interested members of the public. For a 24-hour tape-recorded announcement about open meetings, please call (202) 452-3206. For additional information about agenda items, you may call the Public Affairs Office at (202) 452-2955 between 9:00 a.m. and 5:00 p.m., Monday through Friday.

The Summary Agenda
The items on the Summary Agenda, the first to be considered during an open meeting, typically are recommendations that have the consensus of the staff and are in accord with established policy. The Board generally acts on all of the summary items at once with a single vote, but if a Board member wishes to discuss a proposal, it is moved to the Discussion Agenda.

The Discussion Agenda
The items on the Discussion (or Regular) Agenda are presented by staff members or by Board members with oversight responsibility for the matter. After the discussion of each item, the Board members vote in order of seniority, with the Chairman (or, in the Chairman's absence, the presiding officer) ordinarily casting the last vote.

Open meetings generally begin at 10:00 a.m. at the Federal Reserve Board, Marriner S. Eccles Building (map, 32 KB PDF). Persons attending an open meeting receive an agenda summarizing the matters to be considered and supporting memoranda for each item if available. Nameplates on the Board table identify the Board members.

If you plan to attend an open meeting, please notify us several days before the meeting date and provide your name, date of birth, and social security number or passport number. You may provide this information by calling (202) 452-2474 or you may register on line. You may pre-register until close of business the day before the meeting.

Attendees should use the visitors entrance to the Eccles building, which is on 20th Street between Constitution Avenue and C Street, N. W. Before admittance, you will be asked to provide identifying information, including a photo ID. The Public Affairs Office must approve the use of cameras; please call 202-452-2955 for further information.

Privacy Act Notice: Providing the information requested is voluntary; however, failure to provide your name, date of birth, and social security number or passport number may result in denial of entry to the Federal Reserve Board. This information is solicited pursuant to Sections 10 and 11 of the Federal Reserve Act and will be used to facilitate a search of law enforcement databases to confirm that no threat is posed to Board employees or property. It may be disclosed to other persons to evaluate a potential threat. The information also may be provided to law enforcement agencies, courts and others, but only to the extent necessary to investigate or prosecute a violation of law.

Information Available during and after Open Meetings

The Board releases most of the staff memorandums considered at open meetings, providing them at the meeting and through its Freedom of Information Office and web site.

The Freedom of Information Office also has cassette audio tapes of meetings held in the past two years; the tapes are available for use in the Freedom of Information Office and may be purchased at $6 per copy.

Closed Meetings

Closed meetings are announced to the public on a schedule determined by the nature of the items to be discussed. Items considered in closed session include primarily

- Bank and bank holding company supervisory matters, discussions of which generally disclose information from bank examination reports or commercial and financial information obtained in confidence by the Board
- Monetary policy and other matters whose premature release could be used in financial speculation
- Personnel matters.

Items in these categories fall into one of two types: "recorded" (that is, tape recorded) and "expedited."

A meeting to consider only recorded items generally requires an advance public notice of one week; a meeting to consider only expedited items requires a notice at the earliest practicable time, usually two business days before the meeting. A meeting to consider a combination of recorded and expedited items requires both types of notices.

Recorded Items

Recorded items are those whose discussion is closed to the public under exemptions 1, 2, 3, 4, 5, 6, 7, and 9(B) of the Sunshine Act (see the list of exemptions below). Items closed solely under exemption 4 are recorded, but in all other respects they are treated as expedited items.

Advance notice of recorded items. The Federal Register carries the Board's notices of meetings to consider recorded items. Copies of the notices are generally also available a week before the meeting from the Board's Freedom of Information and Public Affairs offices, the Treasury Department Press Room, and the Board's web site.

The notices give the subject matter of the recorded items, the time and place of the meeting, and the name and telephone number of the official designated to handle inquiries about the meeting.

An additional notice in the Board's Freedom of Information Office cites the applicable exemptions and reasons for closing an item; gives the names of those expected to attend the discussion of that item; and lists the vote of each Board member regarding the decision to close the discussion.

Subsequent notices also indicate, as necessary, any change in the time of a meeting, any deletion or addition of an item, and any change in the open/closed status of an item.

Availability of recordings. After a meeting that includes recorded items, the Board's Freedom of Information Office makes available a full audio cassette recording of the discussion except the portions, if any, that the Board has determined are exempted from release. Audio material initially withheld may be released at a later date when its exempted status no longer applies.

The audio recordings, which give the names of speakers as they speak, are available for use in the Board's Freedom of Information Office and may be purchased at $6 per copy.

Other information available after a meeting. Besides the recording, other information is available in the Board's Freedom of Information Office after a meeting that includes recorded items:

- The certificate of the General Counsel stating that closing the meeting was permissible and citing the applicable exemptions
- The statement of the meeting's presiding officer giving the time and place the meeting was held and the persons present
- If applicable, a statement of the vote by Board members to withhold information from the copy of the recording or transcript released to the public and the exemptions cited.

Expedited Items

Expedited items include matters regarding the oversight of a specific financial institution and matters of monetary policy; their discussion is closed to the public under exemptions 4, 8, 9(A), or 10 of the Sunshine Act. As already noted, items closed solely under exemption 4 are recorded, but otherwise they are treated as expedited items.

Advance notice of expedited items. An advance notice of a meeting on expedited items, issued usually two business days ahead, shows the date and place of the meeting, the name and telephone number of the official designated to handle inquiries about the meeting, and the items expected to be considered.

The notices are available from the Board's Freedom of Information and Public Affairs offices, the Treasury Department Press Room, and the Board's web site.

Bank and bank holding company applications included on these notices are listed on a 24-hour tape-recorded announcement at (202) 452-3206.

Information available after meetings that include expedited items. A final notice, issued at the end of the meeting, gives the time the meeting started, the exemptions applicable to the closing of each item, the vote by the Board members to close the meeting, and the name and telephone number of the official designated to handle requests for information about the meeting.

Except for items closed under exemption 4, the Board keeps minutes of expedited items rather than recordings. The minutes describe all matters discussed and any views expressed on them, summarize any actions taken and the reasons for them, and note the results of any vote. Minutes or portions of minutes initially withheld may be released when their exempted status no longer applies.

The minutes, other than portions exempted from release under the Sunshine Act, are available for inspection in the Board's Freedom of Information Office and may be copied there for ten cents per page. Besides minutes, other information is available in the Board's Freedom of Information Office after a meeting on expedited items:

- The certificate of the General Counsel stating that closing the meeting was permissible and citing the applicable exemptions
- The statement of the meeting's presiding officer giving the time and place the meeting was held and the persons present.

Other Procedures for Handling Official Business
Besides meetings, the Board uses two other procedures for handling official business: notation voting and delegation of authority.

Notation Voting
The Board conducts some routine business by notation vote, in which material circulates among the Board members for written vote and comment. Upon request by a Board member, however, any such item may be placed on the Board's Regular Agenda for discussion, at which time it becomes subject to the Sunshine Act.

Delegation of Authority
The Board may delegate its authority to act on specific items to individual members of the Board, to its staff, or to a Reserve Bank's staff. A copy of the Board's Rules Regarding Delegation of Authority is available from the Board's Publications Office at (202) 452-3244.

Sunshine Exemptions
Here is a summary of the ten conditions under which a meeting is exempt from the open-meeting requirements of the Government in the Sunshine Act. Under the act, meetings may be closed to the public if they are likely to

1. Disclose matters authorized under Executive Order to be kept secret in the interests of national defense or foreign policy
2. Relate solely to internal personnel rules and practices of an agency
3. Disclose matters specifically exempted from disclosure by statute
4. Disclose trade secrets and commercial or financial information obtained from a person that are privileged or confidential
5. Involve accusing any person of a crime or censuring any person
6. Involve personal information whose disclosure would constitute an invasion of personal privacy
7. Disclose certain investigatory records compiled for law enforcement purposes

8. Disclose information contained in, or related to, examination, operating, or condition reports prepared for or used by an agency responsible for regulation or supervision of financial institutions
9. Involve information the premature disclosure of which would
   A. be likely to
      i. lead to significant financial speculation in currencies, securities, or commodities or
      ii. significantly endanger the stability of any financial institution or
   B. be likely to significantly frustrate implementation of a proposed agency action
10. Specifically concern the agency's issuance of a subpoena or participation in a civil action or proceeding.

For additional information about these exemptions, please consult the Government in the Sunshine Act (5 U.S.C. section 552b) and the Board's Rules Regarding Public Observation of Meetings, 12 C.F.R. part 261b.

Appendix M
Sample Agency Meeting Notices

The Federal Reserve Board

Government in the Sunshine Meeting Notice

Agency: Board of Governors of the Federal Reserve System
Time, date: 11:30 a.m., Monday, January 3, 2005
Place: Marriner S. Eccles Federal Reserve Board Building, 20th and C Streets, N.W., Washington, D.C. 20551
Status: Closed

Matters to be Considered:	
1.	Personnel actions (appointments, promotions, assignments, reassignments, and salary actions) involving individual Federal Reserve System employees.
2.	Any items carried forward from a previously announced meeting.

For more information please contact: Michelle Smith, Director, Office of Board Members at 202-452-2955.

Supplementary Information: You may call 202-452-3206 beginning at approximately5 p.m. two business days before the meeting for a **recorded announcement** of bank and bank holding company applications scheduled for the meeting; or you may contact the Board's Web site at http://www.federalreserve.gov for an **electronic announcement** that not only lists applications, but also indicates procedural and other information about the meeting.

Dated: December 23, 2004

(signed) Jennifer J. Johnson

Jennifer J. Johnson,
Secretary of the Board

The Federal Reserve Board

Government in the Sunshine Meeting Notice

Advance Notice of a Portion of a Meeting under Expedited Procedures

It is anticipated that a portion of the closed meeting of the Board of Governors of the Federal Reserve System at **12:00 p.m. on Monday, December 13, 2004**, will be held under expedited procedures, as set forth in section 261b.7 of the Board's Rules Regarding Public Observation of Meetings, at the Board's offices at 20th Street and C Streets, N.W., Washington, D.C. The following items of official Board business are tentatively scheduled to be considered at that meeting.

Meeting date: December 13, 2004

Matters to be Considered:
1. Review and determination by the Board of Governors of the advance and discount rates to be charged by Federal Reserve Banks.

A final announcement of matters considered under expedited procedures will be available in the Board's Freedom of Information and Public Affairs Offices and on the Board's Web site following the closed meeting.

For more information please contact: Michelle Smith, Director, Office of Board Members at 202-452-2955.

Supplementary Information: You may call 202-452-3206 beginning at approximately 5 p.m. two business days before this meeting for a **recorded announcement** of any bank and bank holding company applications scheduled for the meeting; or you may contact the Board's Web site at http://www.federalreserve.gov for an **electronic announcement** about applications and other expedited items, as well as procedural and other information about the meeting.

Dated: December 9, 2004

The Federal Reserve Board

Government in the Sunshine Meeting Notice

Notice of a Meeting under Expedited Procedures

On **Monday, December 13, 2004, at 12:00 p.m.**, a meeting of the Board of Governors of the Federal Reserve System was held under expedited procedures, as set forth in section 261b.7 of the Board's Rules Regarding Public Observation of Meetings, at the Board's offices at 20th and C Streets, N.W., Washington, D.C., to consider the following matters of official Board business.

Meeting date: December 13, 2004

Matters Considered:	Exemption(s)
1. Review and determination by the Board of Governors of the advance and discount rates to be charged by Federal Reserve Banks.	9(A)(i)

Effective **December 13, 2004**, the meeting was closed to public observation by Order of the Board of Governors[1] because the matters fall under exemption(s) **9(A)(i)** of the Government in the Sunshine Act (5 U.S.C. Section 552b(c)), and it was determined that the public interest did not require opening this portion.

For more information please contact: Michelle Smith, Director, Office of Board Members at 202-452-2955.

Supplementary Information: This meeting notice, which is available in the Board's Freedom of Information and Public Affairs Offices, is also available electronically at http://www.federalreserve.gov on the Board's Web site. (The Web site also includes procedural and other information about the closed meeting.)

Dated: December 13, 2004

Footnotes
1. Voting for this action: Chairman Greenspan, Vice Chairman Ferguson, Governors Gramlich, Bies, Olson, Bernanke and Kohn.

U.S. Securities and Exchange Commission

SEC Open Meeting Agenda
Wednesday, December 22, 2004

Agenda as of December 21, 2004. Note that Open Meeting agendas are subject to last-minute changes.

Item 1: Certain Broker-Dealers Deemed Not To Be Investment Advisers

Office: Division of Investment Management

Staff: Paul F. Roye, Robert E. Plaze, Jamey Basham, Nancy M. Morris, and Robert L. Tuleya

1. The Commission will consider a staff recommendation regarding the application of the Investment Advisers Act of 1940 to certain broker-dealers. (*See* Proposing Release, *Certain Broker-Dealers Deemed Not to be Investment Advisers*, Investment Advisers Act Release No. 1845 (Nov. 4, 1999) [64 FR 61226 (Nov. 10, 1999)], and Release Reopening Comment Period, Investment Advisers Act Release No. 2278 (Aug. 19, 2004) [69 FR 51620 (Aug. 20, 2004)]).

For further information, please contact Robert Tuleya, Senior Counsel, Division of Investment Management, at (202) 942-0719.

http://www.sec.gov/news/openmeetings/agenda122204.htm

61016 Federal Register / Vol. 69, No. 198 / Thursday, October 14, 2004 / Notices

[FR Doc. 04-22976 Filed 10-13-4; 8:45 am]
BILLING CODE 6690-01-C

FEDERAL COMMUNICATIONS COMMISSION

Sunshine Act Meeting

October 7, 2004.

The Federal Communications Commission will hold an Open Meeting on the subjects listed below on Thursday, October 14, 2004, which is scheduled to commence at 9:30 a.m. in Room TW-C305, at 445 12th Street, SW., Washington, DC.

Item No.	Bureau	Subject
1	Office of Engineering and Technology	Title: Amendment of Part 15 regarding new requirements and measurement guidelines for Access Broadband over Power Line Systems (ET Docket No. 04-37) and Carrier Current Systems, including Broadband over Power Line Systems (ET Docket No. 03-104). Summary. The Commission will consider a Report and Order regarding changes to the rules applicable to Access Broadband over Power Line systems.
2	Office of Engineering and Technology	Title: Amendment of Part 2 of the Commission's Rules to Allocate Spectrum Below 3 GHz for Mobile and Fixed Services to Support the Introduction of New Advanced Wireless Services, Including Third Generation Wireless Systems (ET Docket No. 00-258) and Amendments to Parts 1, 2, 27 and 90 of the Commission's Rules to License Services in i the 216-220 MHz, 1390-1395 MHz, 1427-1429 MHz, 1432-1435 MHz, 1670-1675 MHz, and 2385-2390 MHz Government Transfer Bands (WT Docket No. 02-8). Summary. The Commission will consider a Seventh Report and Order concerning the relocation of existing Federal Government users from the band 1710-1755 MHz in order to make that band available for Advanced Wireless Services.
3	International	Title: The Effect of Foreign Mobile Termination Rates on U.S. Customers (18 Docket No. 02-324 and 96-261). Summary. The Commission will consider a Notice of Inquiry concerning the possible effects of foreign mobile termination rates on U.S. customers and competition in the U.S. telecommunications services market.
4	Wireline Competition	Title: Review of the Section 251 Unbundling Obligations of Incumbent Local Exchange Carriers (CC Docket No. 01-338); Implementation of the Local Competition Provisions of the Telecommunications Act of 1996 (CC Docket No. 9&-98); and Deployment of Wireline Services Offering Advanced Telecommunications Capability (CC Docket No. 98-147). Summary. The Commission will consider an Order on Reconsideration concerning requests from BellSouth and SureWest to reconsider and/or clarify various broadband unbundling obligations.
5	Wireline Competition	Title: The Pay Telephone Reclassification and Compensation Provisions of the Telecommunications Act of 1996 (CC Docket No. 96-128). Summary. The Commission will consider an Order on Reconsideration concerning its payphone compensation rules.
6	Wireline Competition	Title: Petition of Mid-Rivers Telephone Cooperative, Inc. for Order Declaring it to be an Incumbent Local Exchange Carrier in Terry, Montana, Pursuant to Section 251(h)(2) (WC Docket No. 02-78). Summary: The Commission will consider a Notice of Proposed Rulemaking concerning section 251(h)(2) of the Communications Act of 1934, as amended.

Additional information concerning this meeting may be obtained from Audrey Spivack or David Fiske, Office of Media Relations, (202) 418-0500; TTY 1 (888) 835-5322. Audio/Video coverage of the meeting will be broadcast live over the Internet from the FCC's AudioNideo Events Web page at www.fCc.govIrealaudio.

For a fee this meeting can be viewed live over George Mason University's Capitol Connection. The Capitol Connection also will carry the meeting live via the Internet. To purchase these services call (703) 993-3100 or go to www.capitolconnection.gmu.edu. Audio and video tapes of this meeting can be purchased from CACI Productions, 14151 Park Meadow Drive, Chantilly, VA 20151, (703) 679-3851.

Copies of materials adopted at this meeting can be purchased from the FCC's duplicating contractor, Best Copy and Printing, Inc. (202) 488-5300; Fax (202) 488-5563; TTY (202) 488-5562. These copies are available in paper format and alternative media, including large print/type; digital disk; and audio tape. Best Copy and Printing, Inc. may be reached by e-mail at FCC@BCPIWEB.com.

Federal Communications Commission.
Marlene H. Dortch,
Secretary.

[FR Doc. 04-23189 Filed 10-12-04; 2:15 pm]
BILLING CODE 6712-01-P

FEDERAL ELECTION COMMISSION

Sunshine Act Notice

* * * * *

DATE AND TIME: Tuesday, October 19, 2004 at 10 a.m.

PLACE: 999 E Street NW., Washington, DC

STATUS: This meeting will be closed to the public.

ITEMS TO BE DISCUSSED:
Compliance matters pursuant to. 2 U.S.C. 437g.
Audits conducted pursuant to 2 U.S.C. 437g, 438(b), and Title 26, U.S.C.
Matters concerning participation in civil actions or proceedings or arbitration.
Internal personnel rules and procedures or matters affecting a particular employee.

* * * * *

DATE AND TIME: Thursday, October 21, 2004 at 10 a.m.

PLACE: 999 E Street NW., Washington, DC (Ninth floor).

Commission Meeting Agenda

A Public Notice of the Federal Communications Commission
News Media Information (202) 418-0500
Fax-On-Demand (202) 418-2830
Internet: http://www.fcc.gov
ftp.fec.gov

Federal Communications Commission
445 12th Street, S.W.
Washington, D.C. 20554

November 1, 2001

FCC TO HOLD A CLOSED COMMISSION MEETING THURSDAY, NOVEMBER 8, 2001

The Federal Communications Commission will hold a Closed Meeting on the subject listed below on Thursday, November 8, 2001, following the Open Meeting, which is scheduled to commence at 9:30 a.m. in Room TW-C305, at 445 12th Street, S. W., Washington, D.C.

ITEM NO.	BUREAU	SUBJECT
1	GENERAL COUNSEL	**TITLE:** Commission Internal Processes **SUMMARY:** The Commission will discuss possible changes to its internal processes

This item is closed to the public because it concerns internal practices. (See 47 C.F.R. Sec. 0.603(b)).

The following persons are expected to attend:

> Commissioners and their Assistants
> The Secretary
> General Counsel and members of her staff

* The summaries listed in this notice are intended for the use of the public attending open Commission meetings. Information not summarized may also be considered at such meetings. Consequently these summaries should not be interpreted to limit the Commission's authority to consider any relevant information.

Action by the Commission November 1, 2001. Commissioners, Powell Chairman; Abernathy, Copps and Martin voting to consider these matters in Closed Session.

Additional information concerning this meeting may be obtained from Maureen Peratino or David Fiske, Office of Media Relations, telephone number (202) 418-0500; TTY 1-888-835-5322.

-FCC-

Federal Communications Commission
445 12th Street, S.W.
Washington, D.C. 20554

October 28, 2005

CHANGE IN DATE OF OPEN COMMISSION MEETING TO MONDAY, OCTOBER 31, 2005

The Federal Communications Commission previously announced on October 21, 2005, its intention to hold an Open Meeting on Friday, October 28, 2005, in Room TW-C305, at 445 12th Street, S. W., Washington, D.C.

That date has been changed to Monday, October 31, 2005, commencing at 11:00 a.m.

The prompt and orderly conduct of business required this change and no earlier announcement was possible.

Addition information concerning this meeting may be obtained from Audrey Spivack or David Fiske of Media Relations, (202) 418-0500; TTY 1-888-835-5322.

-FCC-

* The summaries listed in this notice are intended for the use of the public attending open Commission meetings. Information not summarized may also be considered at such meetings. Consequently these summaries should not be interpreted to limit the Commission's authority to consider any relevant information.

Appendix N
Sample Agency General Counsel Certification Forms

U.S. CONSUMER PRODUCTS SAFETY COMMISSION

WASHINGTON, D.C. 20207

Commission Meeting Room 410, Bethesda Towers
xxxx, 2005 4330 East West Highway
xxxx p.m. Bethesda, Maryland 20814

CERTIFICATION OF CLOSED MEETING

The General Counsel, in accordance with the Government in the Sunshine Act (5 U.S.C. § 552b(f)(1)) and the Commission's rules issued under that Act (16 CFR § 1013.4(c)(3)), certifies that this meeting, at which the staff will brief the Commission on the status of various compliance matters, may properly be closed to the public on the basis of the exemptions at 16 CFR §§ 1013.4(b)(3), (7), (9), and (10).

_____ _____
Date   General Counsel

C.P.S.C Hotline 1-800-638-CPSC (2772) * CPSC's Web Site: http://www.cpsc.gov

Federal Communications Commission **CERTIFICATE TO CLOSE MEETING** (Use revserse side when additional space is needed)	TO BE COMPLETED BY AGENDA BRANCH	
	CLAS NUMBER	MEETING DATE

Part 1 - Certification that Commission Meeting May Be Closed to the Public

TO	OFFICE OF GENERAL COUNSEL	DATE
FROM		AGENDA DESIGNATION

SUBJECT:

BASIS FOR CLOSING MEETING (check appropriate items from 47 CFR 0.603):

(a) Executive Order	(e) Crime/Censure	(i) Premature Disclosure
(b) Internal Personnel Rules	(f) Invasion of Privacy	(j) Adjudication
(c) Exempt by Statute	(g) Investigatory Records	
(d) Privileged/Confidential	(h) Financial Institutions	

Explain additional reason(s) for closing meeting. Explain what information is to be withheld from public and reason(s) for withholding:

Are a series of meetings required pertaining to this subject?   Yes [ ]   No [ ]
If YES, will concluding meeting be held no more than 30
  days after initial meeting?   Yes [ ]   No [ ]

I have verified this current meeting of a series is being held within thirty days of initial Commission approval.

SIGNATURE OF THE SECRETARY	DATE:

PERSONS EXPECTED TO ATTEND AND THEIR AFFILIATION

NAME OF STAFF MEMBER WHO PREPARED AGENDA ITEM

I hereby certify that the above-subject Agenda item may be considered at a closed meeting of the Commission under the provisions and for the reasons stated above.

SIGNATURE OF GENERAL COUNSEL	DATE:

PART 2. Record of Commission Action To:	CLOSE MEETING			WITHHOLD INFORMATION		
	Date	Time	Place	Date	Time	Place
	Approve	Disapprove	Not Participating	Approve	Disapprove	Not Participating
	Initials/ Date	Initials/ Date	Initials/ Date	Initials/ Date	Initials/ Date	Initials/ Date
Chairman Martin.						
Commissioner Abernathy.						
Commissioner Copps . . .						
Commissioner Adelstein. .						
Commissioner (Vacant). .						

PART 3.   Statement of Presiding Officer that Closed Meeting Was Held

MEETING DATE:	MEETING TIME:	MEETING PLACE:

PERSONS PARTICIPATING

I hereby certify that the date, time, place, and persons present during consideration of the above-subject Agenda Item were as stated above.

SIGNATURE OF PRESIDING OFFICER	DATE:

SECURITIES AND EXCHANGE COMMISSION

CERTIFICATION

I,_____, General Counsel of the Securities and Exchange Commission, or my delegate, hereby certify, pursuant to 5 U.S.C. 552b(f)(1), and pursuant to Section 200.406 of the Commission's Regulations Pertaining to Public Observation of Commission Meetings, 17 CFR Part 200, Subpart I, that, in my opinion, Commission deliberations concerning

_____

_____

that is scheduled to occur on _____

(and from time to time thereafter as the Commission may, pursuant to the provision in 17 CFR 200.404(a), find appropriate) may properly be closed to public observation.

The relevant exemptions on which this certification is based are set forth in the following provisions of law:

Subsection 552b(c) of Title 5 of the United States Code	Subsection 200.402(a) of Title 17 of the Code of Federal Regulations

Dated: _____

{INSERT NAME HERE}
General Counsel or Delegate

Appendix O
Letter from Michael K. Powell, Chairman, and Michael J. Copps, Commissioner, Federal Communications Commission, to the Honorable Ted Stevens, Chairman, Senate Committee on Commerce, Science and Transportation, February 2, 2005

Federal Communications Commission
Washington, D.C. 20554

February 2, 2005

The Honorable Ted Stevens
Chairman
Committee on Commerce, Science and Transportation
United States Senate
508 Dirksen Senate Office Building
Washington, D.C. 20510

Dear Chairman Stevens:

As Congress contemplates revision of the nation's telecommunications laws, we write regarding a proposal that enjoys bipartisan support among the Commissioners of the Federal Communications Commission: reform of the open meeting requirement of the Government in Sunshine Act ("Sunshine Act" or "Act"). We fully support the Act's goal of informing the public about the decision making processes of multi-member agencies. However, we believe amendments to the Act could enhance the efficiency and soundness of the process. At the same time, safeguards could be devised that would ensure that the goal of open government is not jeopardized.

The open-meeting provision of the Sunshine Act currently requires every portion of every meeting not falling within an exception to be open to public observation when at least a quorum of Commissioners jointly conducts or disposes of official agency business.[1] Both Republican and Democratic Commissioners are on record in recent testimony before Congress that the Commission's decisional processes are impaired by this requirement, and their conclusions about the detrimental effects of the open meeting requirement are echoed by a substantial body of scholarship.[2]

We note initially that the Act is not necessary to the goal of ensuring that federal agencies explain their actions to the public. Judicial review statutes like the Administrative Procedure Act ("APA") impose "a general 'procedural' requirement of sorts by mandating that an agency take whatever steps it needs to provide an explanation . . . [of its] rationale at the time of decision." Pension Benefit Guar. Corp. v. LTV Corp., 496 U.S. 633, 654 (1990).

Nor has the open-meeting requirement generally achieved its goal of having commissioners help shape each others' views in the course of public deliberations. In fact, this requirement is a barrier to the substantive exchange of ideas among Commissioners, hampering our abilities to obtain the benefit of each others' views, input, or comments, and hampering efforts to maximize consensus on the complex issues before us. Due to the prohibition on private collective deliberations, we rely on

---

[1] See 5 U.S.C. § 552b; 47 C.F.R. §§ 0.601-0.607.
[2] See, e.g., Randolph May, *Reforming the Sunshine Act*, 49 ADMIN. L. REV. 415 (1997) ("there appears to be a fairly widespread consensus that the Sunshine Act is not achieving its principal — and obviously salutary — goal of enhancing public knowledge and understanding of agency decisionmaking"); James H. Cawley, *Sunshine Law Overexposure and the Demise of Independent Agency Collegiality*, 1 WIDENER J. PUB. L. 43 (1992). These conclusions were also echoed by the Administrative Conference of the United States ("ACUS") — a body of experts established to advise Congress on administrative law. See David M. Welborn et al., IMPLEMENTATION AND EFFECTS OF THE FEDERAL GOVERNMENT IN THE SUNSHINE ACT, IN ADMINISTRATIVE CONFERENCE OF THE UNITED STATES: RECOMMENDATION AND REPORTS (1984). The ACUS ceased operations in 1995 because Congress eliminated funding, but many of its proposals have been implemented, and scholars such as those listed here still cite its conclusions about the Sunshine Act.

written communications, staff, or one-on-one meetings with each other. These indirect methods of communicating clearly do not foster frank, open discussion, and they are less efficient than in-person interchange among three or more Commissioners would be. Finally, and perhaps most significantly, Commission decisions are in some cases less well informed and well explained than they would be if we each had the benefit of the others' expertise and perspective.[3]

For these reasons, we urge amending the open meeting provision of the Sunshine Act to permit closed deliberations among Commissioners in appropriate circumstances. Scholars and other agency heads have suggested various modification models,[4] some of which include safeguards that may be desirable. For example, some models include a requirement that brief summaries of topics discussed at meetings between all decision makers be recorded and placed in relevant administrative records.

In closing, we want to stress that we are in complete agreement with the Sunshine Act's goal of providing the public with reliable information about the basis for Commission decisions. We support amendment of the Act because we have learned from 28 years experience that we can satisfy this goal through other means that better serve the public interest by promoting bi-partisan deliberation and more efficient decision-making.

We look forward to working with the Committee Chairman, Ranking, and Members of the Committee to resolve this issue.

Sincerely,

Michael K. Powell
Chairman

Michael J. Copps
Commissioner

---

[3] Scholars and other agencies agree. *See, e.g.,* May, *supra* note 2; *Federal Trade Commission Prepared Statement Before the Special Committee to Review the Government In the Sunshine Act*, Administrative Conference of the United States, 1995 WL 540529 (1995).

[4] *See. e.g., id.;* Cawley, *supra* note 2.

TABLE OF CASES

A.G. Becker Inc. v. Board of Governors of the Federal Reserve System, 502 F. Supp. 378 (D.D.C. 1980) 93 n.80; 99 n.2; 113 n.30; 118; 126 n.6; 184 n.6

American Federation of Gov't Employees v. EEOC, Case No. 1:05CV01035 (D.D.C. May 20, 2005) 126 n.6

Amrep Corp. v. Federal Trade Comm'n, 768 F.2d 1171 (10th Cir. 1985), *cert. denied*, 475 U.S. 1034 (1986) 33; 89 n.65

Ardestani v. INS, 502 U.S. 129 (1991) 90 n.68

Aviation Consumer Action Project v. CAB, 418 F. Supp. 638 (D.D.C. 1976) 157 n. 39

Baltimore Gas & Electric Co. v. ICC, 672 F.2d 146 (D.C. Cir. 1982) 177 n.7

Berliner Zisser Walter & Gallegos v. SEC, 962 F. Supp. 1348 (D. Colo. 1997) 67 n.4; 83 n.52

Blazy v. Tenet, 194 F.3d 90 (D.C. Cir. 1999) 200 n.1

Braniff Airways, Inc. v, CAB, 379 F.2d 453 (D.C. Cir. 1967) 192

Braniff Master Executive Council of the Airline Pilots Ass'n Int'l v. Civil Aeronautics Board, 693 F.2d 220 (D.C. Cir. 1982) 189 n.12

Bristol-Myers Co. v. FTC, 469 F.2d 1116 (2d Cir. 1972) 188

Brown v. Board of Education, 347 U.S. 483 (1954) 225

Buckhannon Board & Care Home, Inc. v. W. Va. Dep't of Health and Human Resources, 532 U.S. 598 (2001) 199 n.1

Califano v. Sanders, 430 U.S. 99 (1977) 185 n.9

Central & Southern Motor Freight Tariff Assoc., Inc. v. Interstate Commerce Comm'n, No. 83-2618, 1983 U.S. Dist. LEXIS 10845 (D.D.C. Dec. 12, 1983)   6 n.9

Checkosky v. S.E.C., 23 F.3d 452 (D. C. Cir. 1994)   198 n.25

Chrysler Corp. v. Brown, 441 U.S. 281 (1979)   186

Clark-Cowlitz Joint Operating Agency v. Fed. Energy Regulatory Comm'n, 798 F.2d 499 (D.C. Cir. 1986)   68 n.10; 69 & n.14; 94 n.82; 95 nn.85, 88; 161 & nn.49-50; 163-64 & nn.62, 66-67

Clark-Cowlitz Joint Operating Agency v. Fed. Energy Regulatory Comm'n, 775 F.2d 359 (D.C. Cir. 1985), *vacated on reh'g en banc*, 798 F.2d 499 (D.C. Cir. 1986)   181 n.2

Clarkson v. Internal Revenue Service, 678 F.2d 1368 (11th Cir. 1982)   199-200 n.1

Claxton Enterprises v Evans County Comm'rs, 249 Ga. App. 870, 549 S.E.2d 830 (2001)   27 n.49

Coalition for Legal Services v. Legal Services Corporation, 597 F. Supp. 198 (D.D.C. 1984)   125-29

Common Cause v. NRC, 674 F.2d 921 (D.C. Cir. 1982)   39 n.23; 67 n.4; 69 n.13; 72 n.22; 74 & nn.26-27; 79 & nn.36-38; 85 nn.57-58; 86 n.60; 87 n.63; 95 n.87; 157 n.40; 205 n.5; 220 n.16

Communications Systems v. FCC, 595 F.2d 797 (D.C. Cir. 1978)   30 n.1; 31 n.2; 32 n.7; 37 n.18; 187 n.10; 218 n.12

Consolidated Aluminum Corp. v. T.V.A., 462 F. Supp. 464 (M.D. Tenn. Civ. No. 78-3210, June 30, 1978)   126 n.6

Consumers Union of the United States v. Board of Governors of the Federal Reserve System (D.D.C. Civ. A. #77-1800, Jan. 28, 1978)   62 & n.94; 204 n.4

Critical Mass Energy Project v. NRC, 875 F.2d 871 (D.C. Cir. 1992)   76

Del Papa v. Bd. of Regents, 114 Nev. 388, 956 P.2d 770 (1998)   27 n.49

Department of Air Force v. Rose, 425 U.S. 352 (1976)   73-74

Deukmejian v. NRC, 751 F. 2d 1287 (D.C.Cir. 1984)   195 n.21

Eastern Air Lines, Inc. v. CAB, 271 F.2d 752 (2d Cir. 1959), *cert. denied*, 362 U.S. 970 (1959)   101

Electric Power Supply Ass'n v. FERC, 391 F.3d 1255 (D.C. Cir. 2004) xxxiv

Elkem Metals Co. et al. v. United States, 126 F. Supp. 2d 5672 (C.I.T. 2000) 33

Energy Research Foundation v. Defense Nuclear Facilities Safety Board, 917 F.2d 581 (D.C. Cir. 1990) 1

Environmental Protection Agency v. Mink, 410 U.S. 73 (1973) 205

Essential Information, Inc. v. U.S. Information Agency, 134 F.3d 1165 (D.C. Cir. 1988) 75 n.28

F.A.A. v. Robertson, 422 U.S. 255 (1975) 75 & n.29

Falcon Trading Group, Ltd. v. SEC, 102 F.3d 579 (D.C. Cir. 1996) 7-8 n.11

Federal Communications Commission v. ITT World Communications, 466 U.S. 463 (1984) 5 & n.8; 17 & n.25; 18-22; 28; 30 n.1; 52-53; 217 nn.10-11; 226

Federal Election Commission v. NRA Political Victory Fund, 6 F.3d 821 (D.C. Cir. 1993), *cert. dismissed*, 513 U.S. 88 (1994) 28 n.52

Feshbach v. SEC, 5 F. Supp. 2d 774 (N.D. Cal. 1997) 67 n.4

Fifteen-Forty Broadcasting Corp., 42 Ad.L. 2d 86 (F.C.C., 77-720, Oct. 21, 1977) 106

Flav-O-Rich, Inc. v. NLRB, 531 F.2d 358 (6th Cir. 1976) 101

Friends of the Earth v. Reilly, 966 F.2d 690 (D.C. Cir. 1992) 89 n.66

FTC v. Flotill Products, 389 U.S. 179 (1967) 7-8

FTC v. Standard Oil Co. of California, 449 U.S. 232 (1980) 188 n.11

Gage v. United States Atomic Energy Commission, 479 F.2d 1214 (D.C. Cir. 1973) 176, 187

Gowan v. U.S. Dep't of the Air Force, 148 F.3d 1182 (10th Cir.), *cert. denied*, 525 U.S. 1042 (1998) 199 n.1

Ho Chang Tsao v. INS, 538 F.2d 667 (5th Cir. 1976) 8

Hoke Co., Inc. v. Tenn. Valley Auth., 661 F. Supp. 740 (W.D. Ky. 1987) 191 n.12

Hunt v. CFTC, 484 F. Supp. 47 (D.D.C. 1993) 76 n.31

Hunt v. Nuclear Regulatory Comm'n, 611 F.2d 332 (10th Cir. 1979), cert. denied, 445 U.S. 906 (1980)   6 n.9; 180 n.1; 218 n.12

Investment Company Institute v. Bd. of Governors, Federal Reserve System, 551 F.2d 1270 (D.C. Cir. 1977)   176

Investment Co. Institute v. Federal Deposit Insurance Corp., 728 F.2d 518 (D.C. Cir. 1984)   183; 191 n.12

ITT World Communications, Inc. v. Fed. Communications Comm'n, 699 F.2d 1219 (D.C. Cir. 1983)   17 n.25; 217 n.10; 226 n.26

James v. Baer, Civ. A. No. 89-2841-LFO, 1990 U.S. Dist. LEXIS 5702 (D.D.C. 1990)   92 n.76

Johnston v. Nuclear Regulatory Comm'n, 766 F.2d 1182 (7th Cir. 1985)   175 n.4; 177 n.9; 180 n.1; 187 n.10

Jordan v. U.S. Department of Justice, 591 F.2d 753 (D.C. Cir. 1978)   67

Judicial Watch, Inc. v. Rossotti, 326 F.3d 1309 (D.C. Cir. 2003)   229 n.38

Kansas State Network v. FCC, 720 F.2d 185 (D.C. Cir. 1983)   195; 197; 198 n.25

Kennedy v. Mendoza-Martinez, 372 U.S. 144 (1963)   53

Kennedy v. Upper Milford Twp. Zoning Board, 834 A.2d 1104 (Pa. 2003)   223 n.23

KFC National Management Corp. v. NLRB, 497 F.2d 298 (2d Cir. 1974). cert. denied, 423 U.S. 1087 (1976)   101

LO Shippers Action Committee (LOSAC) v. Interstate Commerce Commission, 857 F.2d 802 (D.C. Cir. 1988)   197

Lujan v. Defenders of Wildlife, 504 U.S. 555 (1992)   175 n.5

McClellan Ecological Seepage Situation v. Carlucci, 835 F.2d 1282 (9th Cir. 1987)   229 n.38

MCI v. FCC, 515 F.2d 385 (D.C. Cir. 1974)   195 & n.19

Mermelstein v. SEC, 629 F. Supp. 672 (D.D.C. 1988)   83 n.52

Metcalf v. Nat'l Petroleum Council, 553 F.2d 176 (D.C. Cir. 1977)   176 n.6

Morgan v. United States, 304 U.S. 1 (1938)   192

Nader v. Dunlop, 370 F. Supp. 177 (D.D.C. 1973)   66 n.3

Nat'l Ornamental and El. Light Xmas Assn. v. CPSC, 526 F.2d 1368 (2d Cir. 1975)   14 n.19

National Ass'n of Broadcasters v. Copyright Royalty Tribunal, 675 F.2d 367 (D.C. Cir. 1982)   33

Natural Resources Defense Council, Inc. v. Nuclear Regulatory Commission, 216 F.3d 1180 (D.C. Cir. 2000)   21 n.35; 24 & nn.41-42; 69 nn.11, 14

Natural Resources Defense Council, Inc. v. Defense Nuclear Facilities Safety Board, 969 F.2d 1248 (D.C. Cir. 1992), *reh'g denied*, 969 F.2d 1248 (1992), *cert. denied*, 508 U.S. 906 (1993)   75 n.30; 164 & n.68; 165 & nn.69-70

New York Times Co. v. NASA, 920 F.2d 1002 (D.C. Cir. 1990)   78 n.35

Nichols v. Reno, 931 F. Supp. 748 (D. Colo. 1996), *aff'd* 124 F.3d 1376 (10th Cir. 1997)   3 n.4

NLRB v. Wyman-Gordon Co., 394 U.S. 759 (1969)   191 n.14

Norwegian Nitrogen Products Co. v. United States, 288 U.S. 294 (1933) xxi

O'Kane v. U.S. Customs Service, 169 F.3d 1308 (11th Cir. 1999)   78; 81 n.46

Oil, Chemical and Atomic Workers v. U.S. Dep't of Energy, 141 F. Supp. 2d 1 (D.D.C. 2001), *rev'd on other grounds*, 288 F.3d 452 (D.C. Cir. 2002)   199 n.1; 200 n.2

Open America v. Watergate Special Prosecution Force, 547 F.2d 605 (D.C. Cir. 1976)   184-85 n.7

Pacific Legal Foundation v. Council on Environmental Quality, 636 F.2d 1259 (D.C. Cir. 1980)   2; 32-33; 37 n.18; 69 n.12

Pan American World Airways, Inc. v. Civil Aeronautics Board, 684 F.2d 31 (D.C. Cir. 1982)   39 n.23; 69 n.13; 189 n.12; 190-91; 195-98

Parravano v. Babbitt, 837 F. Supp. 1034 (N.D. Cal. 1993)   3 n.4

PBW Stock Exchange v. SEC, 485 F.2d 718 (3d Cir. 1973), *cert. denied*, 416 U.S. 989 (1974)   176

Pennzoil Co. v. FPC, 534 F.2d 627 (5th Cir. 1976)   103

Philadelphia Newspapers, Inc. v. Nuclear Regulatory Commission, 727 F.2d 1195 (D.C. Cir. 1984)   68; 69 n.13; 71 n.21; 90 nn.70-71; 91 & nn.72-73; 93 n.78; 94 nn.80, 83

PJM Interconnection, L.L.C. et al., 97 F.E.R.C. P61,319 (Dec. 20, 2001)   164 n.64; 165 n.71

Planning Research Corp. v. Federal Power Comm'n, 555 F.2d 970 (D.C. Cir. 1977)   185-86

Portland Audubon Society v. Oregon Lands Coalition, 984 F.2d 1534 (9th Cir. 1993)   197

Proffitt v. Davis, 707 F. Supp. 182 (E.D. Pa. 1989)   211 n.1

Prometheus Radio Project et al. v. FCC, 373 F.3d 372 (3d Cir. 2004)   47 n.52

Public Citizen v. Barshefsky, 939 F. Supp. 31 (D.D.C. 1996)   3 n.4

Public Citizen Health Research Corp. v. FDA, 185 F.3d 898 (D.C. Cir. 1999)   67 n.4; 76 n.32

Public Citizen v. National Economic Commission, 703 F. Supp. 113 (D.D.C. 1989)   39 n.23; 67 n.5; 85; 87 n.64; 220 n.16

Public Utility District No. 1 of Snohomish County, Washington v. Federal Energy Regulatory Commission, 270 F. Supp. 2d 1 (D.D.C. 2003)   198 n.25

R.J. Reynolds Tobacco Co. v. F.T.C., 1999 WL 816699 (D.D.C. 1999)   125 n.6

R.J. Reynolds Tobacco Co. v. Federal Trade Commission, 14 F. Supp. 2d 757 (M.D. N.C. 1998)   188 n.11

Railroad Comm'n of Texas v. United States, 765 F.2d 221 (D.C. Cir. 1985)   33; 89 n.66; 190 n.12; 218 nn.12-13

Railroad Yardmasters of America v. Harris, 721 F. 2d 1332 (D.C. Cir. 1983)   8 n.11

Renegotiation Board v. Bannercraft Clothing Co., 415 U.S. 1 (1974)   188

Republic Airlines v. Civil Aeronautics Board, 756 F.2d 1304 (8th Cir. 1985)   26 n.47; 33

Rockford Newspapers, Inc. v. Nuclear Regulatory Comm'n, No. 83C 20074; 83 C 3625, 1984 U.S. Dist. LEXIS 19244 (N.D. Ill. Feb. 22, 1984)   6 n.9

Rushforth v. Council of Economic Advisers, 762 F.2d 1038 (D.C. Cir. 1985)   3; 175 n.5

San Luis Obispo Mothers for Peace v. U.S. Nuclear Regulatory Commission, 789 F.2d 26 (D.C. Cir. 1986) (en banc), *cert. denied*, 479 U.S. 923 (1986)   196-97

Shurberg Broadcasting of Hartford, Inc. v. FCC, 617 F. Supp. 825 (D.D.C. 1985)   95 n.85

Soucie v. David, 448 F.2d 1087 (D.C. Cir. 1971)   1

State ex rel. Delph v. Barr, 44 Ohio St. 3d 77, 541 N.E.2d 59 (1989)   190 n.12

Symons v. Chrysler Loan Guarantee Board, 670 F.2d 238 (D.C. Cir. 1981)   4; 218 n.12

Tax Reform Research Group v. IRS, 419 F. Supp. 415 (D.D.C. 1976)   206

Time, Inc., et al. v. United States Postal Service, 667 F.2d 329 (2d Cir. 1981)   90 n.70; 91 & n.72; 164; 191 n.14

TransWorld Airlines v. National Mediation Board, 1982 WL 2077 (D.D.C. 1982)   37 n.18

U.S. Dep't of Defense v. Federal Labor Relations Authority, 510 U.S. 487, 496-97 n.6 (1994)   80 nn.40, 46

U.S. Dep't of Justice v. Reporters Comm. for Freedom of the Press, 489 U.S. 749 (1989)   79; 80 & nn.40-45; 81 & n.47; 82 n.51

U.S. Dep't of State v. Washington Post Co., 456 U.S. 595 (1982)   78 n.35

United States v. Fla. East Coast Railway, 410 U.S. 224, 234 (1973)   89 n.66

United States v. Giordano, 416 U.S. 503 (1974)   148 n.10

United States v. Morgan, 313 U.S. 409 (1941)   196 n.23

United States v. Rankin, 616 F.2d 1168 (10th Cir. 1980)   56 n.76

United States v. Storer Broadcasting Co., 351 U.S. 192 (1956)   176

United States v. Students Challenging Regulatory Agency Procedures, 412 U.S. 669 (1973)   175

Washington Ass'n for Television & Children v. FCC, 665 F.2d 1264 (D.C. Cir. 1981)   25 n.44; 187 n.10

WATCH v. FCC, 665 F.2d 1264 (D.C. Cir. 1981)   130 n.18

We the People, Inc. of the United States v. Nuclear Regulatory Commission, 746 F. Supp. 213 (D.D.C. 1990) 47 n.52;   55-56

Wilkinson v. Legal Services Corp., 865 F. Supp. 891 (D.D.C. 1994), *rev'd on other grounds*, 80 F.3d 595 (D.C. Cir.), *cert. denied*, 519 U.S. 927 (1996)   69 n.13; 74; 79 n.37; 84 n.56; 86 n.60; 93 n.80

Wu v. Nat'l Endowment for Humanities, 460 F. 2d 1030 (5th Cir. 1972), *cert. denied*, 410 U.S. 926 (1973)   79 n.39

INDEX

A

Abzug, Bella Rep. 193
Administrative Conference of the United States 34–35, 57, 59, 70, 147, 149–50, 173–74, 214–15, 227–28
Administrative Orders Review Act 176
Administrative Procedure Act 89–90
AFL-CIO 35
agency 1–4
    definition 1–4
    subdivision 4–6
American Bar Association 22–23, 25, 227–28
announcing meetings, procedures for 119–42
    addition, deletion or carry over of agenda items 134–38
    advance notice, contents and timing of 120–33
    cancellation 133–34
    changing decision to open or close 134–38
    changing subject matter 134–38
    changing time or place 133
    notice to *Federal Register* 138–42
    providing no or limited notice 130–33
    providing shorter notice 124–30
    public announcements, circulation of 140–42
        withholding notice information 123–24
annual reporting requirement 230–31
    elimination of 230–31
assessment of costs 199–201
    attorney fees 199–201
    "reverse Sunshine" cases 201

C

Central Intelligence Agency 215
certification
    general counsel certification 144–50
    retention of 150–52
Chiles, Lawton Senator 159, 165
Civil Aeronautics Board 194–95
Civiletti, Benjamin 99
closed meetings 97-118
    presiding officer's statement 150–52
        standard for deletion 157–61
        subsequent review of transcript material 163–66
    transcript, recording or minutes
        administrative appeals of determinations to withhold 167–68
        agency retention of 153
        agency's duty to edit record 157–61
        description of minutes 152–53
        fees for furnishing copies 168–71
        Freedom of Information Act 206–09
        generally 150–53
        maintenance and use of verbatim copies 171–72
        maintenance of 152

obligation of agency to make promptly available 153–57
procedural requirements and delegation 161–62
public access to 153–61
use in judicial review 192–98
closed meetings, general counsel certification of 144–51
certification and public interest determination 150
contents of the certification 150
delegation 147–48
effect of refusal to certify 144–47
retention of certification 150–52
timing 149–50
closing meetings, grounds for 65–95
accusation of crime or formal censure 76
Commodity Credit Corp. 71
Commodity Futures Trading Commission 75, 105–06
CRS Report 70
Defense Nuclear Facilities Safety Board 75
Federal Advisory Committee Act 66
Federal Mine Safety and Health Review Commission 94
financial institution reports 82–83
financial speculation and stability 83–87
"foreseeability standard" 71–72, 157–58
Freedom of Information Act Exemption (5) 66–67
formal agency adjudication 88–95
frustration of proposed agency action 83–87
internal personnel rules and practices 72–74
invasion of privacy 68, 76–81
investigatory records 68, 81–82
issuance of subpoena 88
matters required by statute to be withheld 68
national defense 68
national defense and foreign policy 72–74
Nuclear Regulatory Commission 68
overview 65–72
participation in civil action or proceeding 88–95
proprietary information 76
statutory exemption 74–76
closing meetings, procedures for 97–118
expedited closing procedures 111–18
computing the majority 115–17
documentary justification 117–18
full written explanation of closing 107–08
information "proposed to be withheld" 98–101
list of all expected attendees 108–10
majority of members required 98
open meetings, requests to 105–06
portion of meeting, defined 99
procedures under subsection (d)(2) 103–04
request to close meetings 101–03
requests to close on other grounds 103
required majority vote on 98–101
availability of vote 107
notation procedure 98–99
recorded vote and no proxies 100–01
series of meetings procedure 100

Coalition for Legal Services 127
Communications Act of 1934 176
conduct of business 29-63
   joint conduct or disposition of agency business 30–39
   notation procedure 30–39
Congressional Research Service 34, 70
congressional review of Sunshine Act
   definition of meeting 226–28
   lack of collegiality 219–25
   need for 219–31
Consumer Product Safety Commission 57, 61, 108, 171
Continuity of Operations Plans 49–52
Council of Economic Advisers 3
Council on Environmental Quality 3

D

Davis, Kenneth Culp 215–17
Defense Nuclear Facilities Safety Board 3, 75
definitions 1–28
   agency 1–4
      advisory bodies 2
   meeting 7–25
      1978 Sunshine Guide 14–17
      American Bar Association Recommendation 22–23
      deliberations 9–10, 14–16, 22–25
      electronic communications 26–28
      legislative history 10–13
      official agency business 16
      teleconferencing 9, 20, 26, 53–55
      threshold for 10
   member 28
   subdivision 4–6

E

electronic communications 26–28
Equal Employment Opportunity Commission 48

F

Farm Credit Administration 46
Federal Advisory Committee Act 66, 170
Federal Communications Commission 5, 17, 31–32, 47–48, 52, 106, 123–24, 129, 151, 155–56, 166, 171, 194–95, 226
Federal Deposit Insurance Corporation 48, 82, 84, 130
Federal Election Commission 28, 151
Federal Energy Regulatory Commission 46, 48, 50, 137, 154, 163, 171
Federal Home Loan Bank Board 82–83
Federal Mine Safety and Health Review Commission 94, 103
Federal Open Market Committee 2
Federal Power Commission 137
Federal Register 120–22, 125–28, 130–33, 138–41
Federal Reserve Board 46–47, 59, 62, 82, 84, 112, 118, 154
Federal Reserve System 41, 45, 48
Federal Trade Commission 60, 95, 99, 103, 105, 108–09, 131, 140–46, 151
fees and fee waivers 168–71, 228–30
Flowers, Walter 32
"foreseeability standard" 71–72, 95, 157–58
Freedom of Information Act 1, 3, 58, 63, 66–68, 73, 75, 78–81, 83, 88, 169–71

Electronic Freedom of Information Act 170
  implementation of 215
  Reform Act of 1986 169
  Sunshine Act, relationship to 203–09, 215–17
    applicability to requests for access to transcripts 206–09
    confidentiality of internal memoranda 204–06
    records disposal 209

G

general counsel certification 144–51
  delegation 147–48
  effect of refusal to certify 144–47
  public interest determination 150
  timing 149–50

I

Interstate Commerce Commission 142, 197–98

J

Javits, Jacob Senator 159–60
"joint conduct or disposition" of agency business" 30–39
judicial review of agency rules 173-77
judicial review of particular agency actions 179–98
  independent enforcement suits, jurisdiction, remedies 181–84
  "reverse Sunshine" cases 185–86, 201
    suits to obtain access to transcripts 184–85
  judicial review proceedings 186–98
    relief under 5 U.S.C. Section 552b(h)(2) 188–91
    use of transcript for review 192–98

L

Legal Services Corporation 125–29
Longstreth, Bevis 58–59
Lyons, William 34

M

meeting
  defined 7–25
  deliberations 9–10, 14–16, 22–25
  electronic exchanges 26–28
  quorum requirement 17–18
member 28
minutes 152–53

N

National Council of Senior Citizens 127
National Credit Union Administration 140, 155
National Labor Relations Board 112
National Museum Services Board 166
National Science Foundation 155, 171
National Transportation Safety Board 46, 60
Natural Resources Defense Council 24
Neighborhood Reinvestment Corporation 2
notation voting procedures 31–39, 98–99
notice of meetings 119–42
  changes in notice 133–38
  contents and timing 120–33
  no or limited notice 130–33
  shorter notice 124–30
Nuclear Regulatory Commission 22–24, 48, 50, 55–56, 68, 104

O

Occupational Safety and Health Review Commission 131
Office of Management and Budget 229
Overseas Private Investment Corporation 49

P

Parker, Barrington 127
presiding officer's statement 150–52
presumption of openness 39–41
proxy voting 100–01
Public Citizen, Inc. 35
public observation of meetings 39–58
   access to staff memoranda 61–63
   Department of Justice memo to Federal Reserve Board 41–45
   Farm Credit Administration 46
   Federal Energy Regulatory Commission 46, 48
   Federal Reserve practices 45–46
   meaningfulness of 61–63
   National Transportation Safety Board 46
   post–September 11 Washington, D.C. 49–53
      Continuity of Operations Plans 49–52
   public participation 55–58
   public understanding 58–61
      Welborn Report 59
   right to record, photograph, or televise open meetings 48–49
   teleconferencing 9, 20, 26, 53–55
   "virtual meetings" 26–28, 53–55

Q

quorum requirement 7–8, 17–18

R

"reverse Sunshine" cases 185–86, 201
Rogers, Thomasina 35
reporting requirements, annual 230–31

S

Securities and Exchange Commission 35, 57, 60, 77, 84, 109–10, 112, 136, 141, 154
subdivision 4–6
Sunshine Act
   general considerations 211–19
   need for congressional review 219–31
   perceptions, problems, and proposals 211–31
   Special Committee to Review 227–28
Surface Transportation Board 103

T

Thomas, Larry 34
transcripts, minutes, or recordings, fees for 228–30. *See also* closed meetings

U

U.S. Commission on Civil Rights 2
U.S. Department of Energy 4
U.S. Department of Homeland Security 49
U.S. Department of Justice 30, 41–45, 77, 200, 229
U.S. Environmental Protection Agency 215
U.S. Merit Systems Protection Board 36
U.S. Parole Commission 48, 136

U.S. Postal Rate Commission 48, 141
U.S. Postal Service 48, 57
United States International Trade
    Commission 120–21

V

"virtual meetings" 26–28, 53–55

W

Wallman, Steven M.H. 35, 57
Welborn, David 34
Welborn Report 34, 38, 59, 70, 147